THE TRANSFORMATION OF AMERICAN LAW
1870–1960

THE

TRANSFORMATION

OF

AMERICAN LAW

1870–1960

The Crisis of Legal Orthodoxy

MORTON J. HORWITZ

New York   Oxford

OXFORD UNIVERSITY PRESS
1992

Oxford University Press

Oxford   New York   Toronto
Delhi   Bombay   Calcutta   Madras   Karachi
Kuala Lumpur   Singapore   Hong Kong   Tokyo
Nairobi   Dar es Salaam   Cape Town
Melbourne   Auckland

and associated companies in
Berlin   Ibadan

Copyright © 1992 by Oxford University Press, Inc.

Published by Oxford University Press, Inc.,
200 Madison Avenue, New York, New York 10016

Oxford is a registered trademark of Oxford University Press

Library of Congress Cataloging-in-Publication Data
Horwitz, Morton J., 1938–
The transformation of American law, 1870–1960:
the crisis of legal orthodoxy / Morton J. Horwitz.
p. cm.   Includes bibliographical references and index.
ISBN 0-19-507024-0
1. Law—United States—Philosophy—History.
2. Law—United States—Interpretation and construction—History.
3. Sociological jurisprudence—History
I. Title.   KF380.H67   1992
349.73—dc20   [347.3]
91-30273

2 4 6 8 9 7 5 3

Printed in the United States of America
on acid-free paper

For Pnina

PREFACE

In terms of its chronology, this book can be regarded as taking up the story of the history of American law as I left it in *The Transformation of American Law, 1780–1860* (1977). But it is a very different book.

The reader will notice that I have begun this book in 1870, not 1860. Though I make many references to the influence of the Civil War, I believe that only a separate book can do justice to the profound significance of the Civil War in American legal history. I hope to write that book someday.

As compared to *Transformation* this book gives cultural factors somewhat more explanatory weight, although I continue to insist that the development of law cannot be understood independently of social context. Questions of power are obviously an important part of that context. The source of the change in emphasis derives from the massive challenge to traditional ideas of historical explanation that have invaded both the worlds of theory and historical practice since *Transformation* was written.

This is not the place to say a great deal about these changes. Briefly, they involve the disintegration of the nineteenth-century conception of explanation in the natural as well as the social and historical sciences. Nineteenth-century social theory sought to find general laws of society modeled on the natural sciences, just as historical thinkers as varied as Hegel and Marx, or Whig historians like McCauley, or conservatives like Sir Henry Maine, sought to find the general laws of history, change, and social progress.

In social thought, belief in the explanatory possibility of very general "covering laws" capable of making "if-then" predictive statements has plummeted (except as economics deploys ever more elaborate tautologies to conceal this fact). The result has been a dramatic turn toward highly specific "thick description" in which narratives and stories purport to substitute for traditional general theories. Today there are scholars in all fields of social thought who view orthodox claims to objectivity as contests over the appropriate generality of discourse. I have acknowledged this problem by offering perspectives at different levels of generality.

At the same time, several of the most important assumptions underlying nineteenth-century social thinkers' and historians' confidence in the objectivity of their explanations have been severely challenged.* Not only has the separation between fact and value as the basis for value-free social science or history been drawn into question, but self-consciousness of the contingency of categories, theories, and frames of reference has been accelerating as the message of the sociology of knowledge has been absorbed into interpretative and deconstructive intellectual movements. Also, intense skepticism about the nineteenth-century working assumption that causation was objective—notwithstanding Hume, Kant, and Mill—has, in the twentieth century, begun dramatically to undermine the claimed objectivity of explanation. A complex, multi-factored interdependent world has lost confidence in single-factor "chains of causation" that were embedded in most nineteenth-century explanatory theories. But how does one *explain* anything objectively in a world of complex multiple causation?

The practicing historian needs to be conscious of these theoretical debates without either solving the problems or being paralyzed by them. Yet these debates have influenced me in taking many more factors into account than before. There remains the serious question of whether the new cult of complexity does not simply avoid through fiat the admirable generalizing and simplifying goals of nineteenth-century modes of explanation.

One of the prominent casualties of multi-factored explanation is the disintegration of those philosophical dualisms that have stereotyped all forms of theoretical debate over the last two (or is it four?) centuries. Just as recent neo-pragmatism has rejected the "on-off" choice between deontological and utilitarian moral theory, so too has it followed John Dewey in refusing to accept a deep chasm between "principled" and "result-oriented" ethics or jurisprudence. Whether it is the "fact-value" or "mind-body" or "theory-practice" or "subjective-objective" or "idealism-materialism" or "freedom-coercion" dualities, almost all these efforts at mutually exclusive categorical formulations have come to seem less and less satisfying.

My acceptance of multi-factored complexity has produced a certain tendency in this book toward multiple (and perhaps sometimes contradictory) explanations. As one sees both theories and causes as more contingent, one's belief in one's own objectivity is also drawn into question. Is it just my story, with all the connotations of skepticism and subjectivity that the word "story" implies? No; I still aspire to give the best possible explanation, but without the wish to suppress all difficulties by intoning pieties about what a terrible place the world would be without an objective account.

* See the brilliant book by Peter Novick, *That Noble Dream: The "Objectivity Question" and The American Historical Profession* (Cambridge University Press, 1988).

As a result, the book constantly wavers between, on the one hand, conventional efforts at historical explanation that continue to derive from nineteenth-century models of objectivity, and, on the other hand, the recognition that modernism has challenged the objectivity of these forms in many different ways.

A portion of chapter 2 has previously appeared in *The Politics of Law* (Pantheon, 1982) as "The Doctrine of Objective Causation." Chapter 3 has been somewhat revised from a version that appeared in the *The West Virginia Law Review* and was reprinted in Warren J. Samuels and Arthur S. Miller, eds. *Corporations and Society* (Greenwood Press, 1987). Chapter 4 was originally presented as the Julius Rosenthal Lectures at Northwestern University Law School.

During the time I have been working on this book, I have been the beneficiary of an extraordinarily dedicated and talented group of research assistants, all of them Harvard Law School students. I wish to thank Greg Bibler, Thomas Brown, Stephanie Farrior, Anthony Herman, Carl Landauer, Mark Linder, Judson Lobdell, and, especially, Marta Wagner. Stephen Wagner was very helpful in preparing the manuscript for publication. Kenneth Halpern prepared an outstanding index. At Oxford University Press, Valerie Aubrey was the very ideal of a supportive but critical editor.

I also wish to express my gratitude to my colleagues Todd Rakoff, who commented on chapter 8, and Duncan Kennedy, with whom I have been discussing the ideas in this book over the course of a decade. Robert Gordon, Stanley N. Katz and G. Edward White offered valuable comments on the manuscript. In addition to providing significant suggestions for improving chapters 6 and 9, Pnina Lahav has been a source of love and inspiration throughout.

I have received extensive research support during the period of writing this book. The National Endowment for the Humanities and the Guggenheim and Rockefeller Foundations were generous sources of research grants. The legal history program at the University of Wisconsin during the summer of 1982 not only provided stimulating discussion of the legal history of organizations but also supported my research into the history of corporate theory. The generous research support program of Harvard Law School was indispensable.

Cambridge, Massachusetts   M. J. H.
February 1992

CONTENTS

THE TRANSFORMATION OF AMERICAN LAW
1870–1960

Introduction

The recent political crises over the appointments of judges Robert Bork and Clarence Thomas to the U. S. Supreme Court have once again raised to consciousness the question of whether and in what sense law is political. The appointments triggered political crises because they were widely understood to represent the culmination of a constitutional revolution initiated by the Reagan Administration.

Like scientific revolutions, constitutional revolutions have been rare events in American history. The New Deal constitutional revolution of 1937 represented a fundamental shift in the constitutional relationship of the states to the federal government as well as of government to the economy. The constitutional legitimation of an interventionist and redistributionist federal government did not only reflect the political triumph of the New Deal. It also constituted the successful culmination of a generation of intellectual struggle against the legal foundations of the old order. The New Deal constitutional revolution thus represented a genuine paradigm shift, a fundamental overthrow of a system of legal consciousness that reached the apex of its development a century and a half after the ratification of the Constitution. Whether the Warren and Rehnquist courts will also come to be regarded as having produced constitutional revolutions will become clearer as time passes.

A constitutional revolution can take place only when the intellectual ground has first been prepared. The New Deal revolution can only be understood in light of the success of the previous generation of legal thinkers in undermining the existing system of legal orthodoxy.

This book traces the struggle between late nineteenth-century legal orthodoxy, often called "Classical Legal Thought,"[1] and "Progressive Legal Thought," which began to crystallize in reaction to the decision of the U.S. Supreme Court in *Lochner v. New York* (1905). That struggle, which drew into question the funda-

3

mentals of the legal order, expressed a deep crisis the stress lines of which could be traced directly to the ideological foundations of American society. The most basic conflict was over whether law could be characterized as neutral and non-political.

The Progressive attack on Classical Legal Thought developed, above all, into a challenge to the world view that endowed nineteenth century orthodoxy with legitimacy. In law, it came to represent no less than a fundamental reexamination of the core of ideas that constituted the "rule of law"—the conviction that there existed a structure of impartial and self-executing norms suggested by the phrase "a government of laws, not of men."

Classical Legal Thought was rooted in what I call an "old conservative" world view, one that presumed that the existence of decentralized political and economic institutions was the primary reason why America had managed to preserve its freedom. A self-regulating, competitive market economy presided over by a neutral, impartial, and decentralized "night-watchman" state embodied the old conservative vision of why America had uniquely been able to avoid falling victim to tyranny.

The Progressive critique of Classical Legal Thought emerged out of a crisis of legitimacy generated by the fantastic social and economic changes during the generation before World War I. The rapid centralization of economic power resulting from the cartelization and concentration of the American economy during the last years of the nineteenth century shook the authority of those who had proclaimed the naturalness and necessity of decentralized institutions. Moreover, the dislocating forces of urbanization, massive immigration, and industrialization triggered unprecedented levels of social struggle. This, in turn, placed enormous stress on the traditional legitimating ideal of equality of opportunity as practiced within a market system that was thought to distribute rewards more or less fairly according to the value of one's economic contribution. In particular, an increase in social and economic inequality drew into question the dominant old conservative commitment to the ideal of a neutral, non-redistributive state. The assault on Classical Legal Thought cannot be understood independently of struggles over the meaning of social justice and challenges to the moral foundations of individualism that had emerged by the turn of the century.

As in any authentic legitimacy crisis, Classical Legal Thought was forced to confront both external and internal attacks on its very foundations. Externally, it suffered from its close connection to a world of decentralized institutions that was rapidly fading away. In particular, much of the system of private law rules—contract, tort, property, and commercial law—had been infused with the individualistic premises of a self-executing market economy composed of small, competitive units. As these common law rules were themselves transformed to accommodate an increasingly interdependent and organizational society, they frequently contradicted established legal principles that had been derived from an earlier vision of American society. Often, however, these increasingly anachronistic principles stood unyielding against the winds of change, adding fuel to the ever more prominent accusation that American law had grown fundamentally out of touch with society.

If private law was forced to come to terms with the emergence of organizational society and the decline of decentralized markets, American public law, both constitutional and regulatory, was made to confront the meaning of its longstanding commitment to the ideal of neutrality. Amidst increasing pressure to bring law into closer touch with society, what could remain of the post-revolutionary ideal of a government of laws whose judges saw their role as impartially discovering and declaring pre-existing law? What was to be the fate of the still-broader nineteenth-century liberal ideal of a neutral, non-redistributive state standing astride an American society becoming ever more unequal in wealth and power?

In this book, I seek to provide a picture of the structure of Classical Legal Thought and of the crisis of legitimacy it encountered. That crisis was manifested both inside the structure of thought, where increasingly numerous and serious stress points emerged from attempts to accommodate changing reality, and outside of that structure, as represented by the pervasive challenge of Progressive Legal Thought itself. That challenge took the form of narrowly focused and technically powerful internal assaults on one or another postulate of Classicism, as well as of large and expansive jurisprudential critiques of the political and philosophical legitimacy of the old order.

The culmination of the Progressive challenge to legal orthodoxy was the emergence of "Legal Realism" during the 1920s and 1930s. In this book, I make the case for regarding realism as essentially a continuation of the reform agenda of pre–World War I Progressivism. In particular, I wish to dispute the view put forth by its most important spokesman, Karl Llewellyn, that Realism was simply a methodology or "technology" unrelated either to substantive intellectual disputes or to social or political struggle. I seek to show instead that Llewellyn's positivism—his wish to sharply separate law and morals, as well as facts and values— was hardly typical of Realism. Moreover, the intellectually fertile alliance between reformist social science and Realism should not be confused with the austere positivism that Llewellyn advocated.

Yet it is true that one branch of Realism did succumb to the most barren forms of value-free social science, and that Llewellyn's commanding position in the movement has persuaded historians to see this as both the essence and the fatal flaw of Realism. While I too see important connections between this positivistic strand of Realism and the increasingly conservative and apologetic turn of some Realist thinkers after World War II, the important point is that many Realists remained consistently hostile to any sharp separation between law and morals or facts and values. Moreover, while the supposed "value relativism" of Legal Realism has been emphasized, its "cognitive relativism" expresses what is most lasting and significant about its contribution to legal thought.

Beginning with their challenge to the constitutionalization of "freedom of contract" in *Lochner v. New York* (1905), which struck down a maximum-hours law for bakers, Progressive legal thinkers sought to undermine the claim of Classical

Legal Thought that law was a "science" that could be separate from politics and that legal reasoning could be sharply distinguished from moral or political reasoning.

This attack on the autonomy of law was combined with an increasing insistence that law had lost touch with society. Explaining why the "law in books" was out of touch with the "law in action" produced a powerful and intellectually self-conscious body of writing about law that continues, even after a half century, to radiate critical power. In their challenge to the self-executing and non-discretionary character of legal reasoning, Progressives and Legal Realists were among the earliest American thinkers to see the implications of cognitive relativism and cultural modernism for legal justification and explanation. As they mounted their assault on Classical Legal Thought, it began to dawn on them that they faced a broad interlocking structure of thought, a complex system of categorization and classification that could be thought of as a form of legal architecture. The point of the Realist critique was to emphasize that the architecture of Classical Legal Thought was neither neutral, natural, nor necessary, but was instead a historically contingent and socially created system of thought. The Realistis were thereby led to connect with many of the intellectual movements of the 1920s and 1930s that today we would identify as creating an interpretativist or hermeneutic understanding of the relationship between thought and reality. The discovery of "frames of reference" in the sociology of knowledge or in the newly emerging field of anthropology marched hand in hand with an insistence that all schemes of categorization and classification embody debatable political and moral premises.

The Progressive critique of legal orthodoxy as oblivious to questions of social change and social justice developed side by side with its modernist recognition of the plastic and malleable character of law and legal categories. It sought to combine a pre-modern sense of moral outrage with both the social reformers' instrumental commitment to the social sciences and the modernists' critique of positivist social science. It thus nurtured both objectivists and those who believed that the objectivity of the social sciences, like the supposed objectivity of legal doctrine within Classical Legal Thought, was a delusion. In the process, Progressive legal thought attained a level of critical brilliance and self-consciousness that makes it speak to us across almost an entire century.

The first seven chapters of this book present a detailed story of the battle of Progressive and Realist thinkers against the orthodoxy of the old order. They include a focused study of the history of corporate theory in chapter 3 as well as a close examination of the significance of the legal thought of Justice Oliver Wendell Holmes, Jr., in chapter 4. Every discussion of specialized areas of the law, such as torts and contracts or taxation and regulation, has been designed to illustrate my conviction that there has always been a close connection in legal history between practical and theoretical discourse, between social struggle and jurisprudential controversy. I hope that the readers will bear this in mind as they find themselves in the midst of one or another difficult or unfamiliar legal discussion.

Chapter 8 demonstrates the close connection between the Legal Realist critique and the emergence during the New Deal of administrative law in the regulatory welfare state. Neither the intimate relationship between Realists and New Dealers nor the influence of the New Deal in blunting the critical edge of Realism has been fully appreciated. Finally, chapter 9 assesses the fate of Realism after World War II. I offer an overview—not a complete account—of the state of postwar legal culture, focusing on the effects of totalitarianism, McCarthyism, and the astonishingly hostile academic reactions to the monumental decision of the U.S. Supreme Court in *Brown v. Board of Education*.

What became of Legal Realism after World War II? Here I differ from previous accounts that treat Realism not only as having expired in the postwar period but, in fact, as having self-destructed due to its alliance with value-free social science. I suggest that Realism—at least its critical dimension—continued to be an intellectual force in the postwar period. Where it did retreat, it did so primarily because its heirs had lost all connection to the Progressive politics that originally gave it meaning and inspiration.

One of my most fundamental goals in this book is to challenge what continues to be the dominant form of legal historiography of the Gilded Age. Although in every other field of American history, Progressive historiography, premised on a conflict between the "people" and the "interests," has been overthrown as simplistic, in the constitutional history of the *Lochner* era it has continued to be the standard mode of explanation. This, I have suggested elsewhere, has as much to do with the legitimating needs of the New Deal as with the realities of Classical Legal Thought. The New Deal's constitutional revolution of 1937 was justified not as a powerful break with the old order but as a conservative restoration of neutral constitutional principles that had supposedly been thrown overboard by the *Lochner* Court. The result has been to buttress historical intepretations that, for example, continue to treat the late-nineteenth-century judiciary as having capitulated to big business. In fact, it is quite clear, as I hope to show, that the *Lochner* Court was strongly representative of the old conservative view that big business was unnatural and illegitimate. Indeed, by seeking to stigmatize the *Lochner* era, Progressive historians lost sight of the basic continuity in American constitutional history before the New Deal. The constitutional revolution of 1937 was itself the culmination of a generational revolt against a structure of legal thought that had crystallized over more than a century since the American Revolution.

ONE

The Structure of Classical Legal Thought, 1870–1905

The separation between law and politics has always been a central aspiration of American legal thinkers. Operating uncomfortably within a democratic political culture that has been obsessed with the threat of "tyranny of the majority," American jurists since the Revolution have striven to embody "a government of laws and not of men" in a conception of an autonomous system of law untainted by politics.

The conflict between law and politics has taken many different forms in American history. Its most prominent expression during the antebellum period was in the debate over codification of the law.[1] The underlying argument between Jacksonian proponents of codification and the orthodox defenders of the common law system turned on whether judges "make" or "declare" law.[2] The question of whether law is "political"—and, hence, to be appropriately determined by democratic legislators enacting codes—or, instead, is "scientific," and thus capable of being expounded by judges, was at the heart of the codification controversy.

The law-politics controversy was itself an expression of the fear of tyranny of the majority that has been a persistent theme in American legal and political thought. Throughout the revolutionary period and for a time thereafter, the problem of tyranny of the majority expressed as much the fear of religious as of cultural, political, or economic domination. Yet already in *The Federalist*, its central future meaning had been propounded: It stood for the paramount dangers of redistribution of wealth and of leveling. As Madison declared, "the most common and durable source of factions has been the various and unequal distribution of property."[3] The fundamental issue of American political thought was how this most politically democratic country in the world could avoid the threat of coerced economic equality.

Law carried an unusual burden in this conception. It was hoped that it could provide a non-political cushion or buffer between state and society. Unless law could be rendered non-political, how could it avoid becoming simply an instrument of democratic politics?

At precisely the moment that the codification movement of the 1820s and 1830s produced the first sustained challenge to the democratic legitimacy of the common law, there arose a countervailing movement to defend the non-political character of judge-made law. Beginning with the first volume of James Kent's Commentaries,[4] published in 1826, the treatise tradition continued for the next century to propound the orthodox view that law is a science and that legal reasoning is inherently different from political reasoning.[5] Replicating similar debates that had resonated throughout modern English constitutional history— symbolized by the early-seventeenth-century confrontation between James I and Sir Edward Coke over whether law depended on "natural" or "artificial" reason[6]— the treatise writers sought, above all, to establish a non-political oasis through law.

After the trauma of the American Civil War, amid heightening social conflict produced by immigration, urbanization, and industrialization, orthodox legal thinkers and judges sought ever more fervently to create an autonomous legal culture as part of their "search for order."[7] Through a process of systemization, integration, and abstraction of legal doctrine, they refined and tightened up what had previously been a loosely arranged, ad hoc system of legal classification. To understand late-nineteenth-century Classical Legal Thought, one must first appreciate the significance of that process of systemization.

Legal Architecture

Every complex legal system presents a structure of classification and categorization that reveals many of its dominant concerns and points of tension and contradiction. For example, Eugene Genovese has focused on the structure of the law of slavery to understand how Southern society sought to resolve the contradiction between the wish to conceive of slaves as property and the reality of slaves exercising will.[8] He has emphasized how the universal problem of generality versus particularity of legal classification was especially evident in the contradictory efforts of Southern judges to assimilate slaves to property while recognizing the impossibility of applying inanimate property concepts generally to human beings with will. Mark Tushnet also shows how slave law was structured according to the contradictory principles of interest and humanity.[9]

Similarly, the effort of late-nineteenth-century legal thinkers to create a system of legal thought free from politics produced a structure of classification that sought to depoliticize law by mediating a series of basic contradictions in antebellum legal thought. It is to that structure of classification that we now turn.

The Distinction between Public and Private Law

One of the most powerful tendencies in late-nineteenth-century law was the move to create a sharp distinction between what was thought to be a coercive public law—mainly criminal and regulatory law—and a non-coercive private law of tort, contract, property, and commercial law, designed to be resistant to the dangers of political interference.

The distinction between public and private law was in part a culmination of more long-standing efforts of conservative legal thinkers to separate the public and private realms in American political and legal thought.[10] One of the earliest efforts to create an oasis of private rights free from state interference was the distinction between public and private corporations first elaborated in the *Dartmouth College Case* (1819).[11] It was soon to be incorporated into a more general antebellum constitutional doctrine of "vested rights,"[12] whose function was to posit the existence of a private realm immune from political coercion.

Beginning in the 1840s, the public-private distinction was further developed in state constitutional cases that created a sharp distinction between legitimate public and illegitimate private purposes for state exercise of its power of eminent domain.[13] In the eminent domain cases, the public purpose doctrine was explicitly designed to prevent state redistribution of wealth. By the 1870s, this idea was extended to the taxing power.[14] Cases dealing with the constitutionality of municipal sales of bonds to support railroad development invoked the public-private distinction to invalidate taxation for mere private purposes.[15]

Standing behind the widening public-private distinction in law were developments in nineteenth-century political, social, and economic thought that posited basic dichotomies between state and society, between the market and the family, and between politics and the market.[16] All of these conceptualizations sought to establish a separate, "natural" realm of non-coercive and non-political transactions free from the dangers of state interference and redistribution.[17]

The more formal and systematic distinction between public and private law that began to be articulated in the 1870s was in one sense a logical outgrowth of these earlier developments. The private law of tort, contract, and property, legal writers regularly maintained, was concerned only with *meum* and *tuum*, with private transactions between private individuals vindicating their pre-political natural rights.[18] In these matters, it was insisted, the state had no independent interest beyond ensuring that the legal order was impartial and non-political. An independent realm of private law was thus conceived of as the perfect analogue to an increasingly dominant conception of a self-regulating market, whose "invisible hand" reflected natural and impartial economic laws that needed to remain uncorrupted by political interference.

The Creation of Increasingly Abstract and General Classifications

While the creation of a public law-private law distinction owes much to developments outside of the law, it should also be understood in terms of important internal changes in the structure of legal ideas. At the beginning of the nineteenth century, American law was still dominated by the system of common law writs or forms of action.[19] The common lawyers' practical understanding of the writ system as remedies provided by the state stood in sharp contrast to the efforts of liberal social contract theorists after Locke to establish the pre-political origins of individual rights. Despite Blackstone's attempt to integrate the lawyers' history of the forms of action with the liberal theorists' ideas of natural rights,[20] it was only with the demise of the writ system between 1825 and 1850[21] that any fundamental restructuring of the architecture of the legal system became possible. Perhaps the best place to see this change is in the common law treatise literature itself.

In virtually every field of law, late-nineteenth-century legal literature became more integrated, systematic, general, and abstract. At the beginning of the century, a handful of published American law texts were supplemented by widely circulated handwritten manuscript "precedent books," as well as English law books. The systematic and "scientific" *Commentaries* of Blackstone remained very much the exception compared to the still more widely used eighteenth-century English "abridgements." Joseph Story's 1805 book of pleadings[22] and Nathan Dane's *Abridgement*,[23] begun in 1823, were the typical source books for practicing American lawyers. The dominant purpose of these texts was to offer a useful catalogue of the appropriate forms of pleadings for bringing and defending different kinds of common law actions.

As the old forms of action disintegrated, successive legal writers began to attack the "fragmentary and disconnected"[24] structure of legal classification. In his treatise on *The Law of Torts* (1859)—the first effort at writing a systematic treatise on the subject—Francis Hilliard wrote that under the traditional forms of action, "the natural order of things" was "reverse[d]," presenting "a false view of the law, as a system of forms rather than principles."[25]

Hilliard criticized the typical legal treatise of the day for arranging its subject matter with "no scientific basis" and for failure "to present a connected, systematic, or complete view of any one of the somewhat heterogeneous topics of which they promiscuously treat." "I have never been able to understand upon what principle, in treatises of this description, some subjects are selected, and others wholly omitted," he concluded.[26]

When Hilliard published his treatise on *Torts*, negligence still played a modest role in his scheme of classification. Shearman and Redfield also noted in 1869 that although it had been part of the "original plan" of their treatise on torts to make negligence the organizing concept, they had been forced to yield to "the present chaotic state of legal literature."[27] "This plan was modified, however, for the sake of the convenience and advantage of the profession, by adding chapters upon the law of negligence with reference to Attorneys, Bankers, Passenger Carriers, Physicians and Telegraphs. . . ."[28]

By the middle of the century, a burgeoning number of American law books had begun to be similarly organized according to functional categories useful to practicing lawyers. A typical treatise on contracts, for example, contained separate chapters on the law of sales, insurance, negotiable instruments, agents, railroads, and so forth. This new organizational structure was itself symptomatic of the demise of the forms of action as the dominant mode of legal classification.

Yet further generalization continued to be hindered not only by conservative attachment to an already disintegrating system of common law forms of action but, more important, by professional resistance to any move away from organizing the law according to particular statuses and functional relationships—for example, attorneys, bankers, passengers, doctors, and telegraphs. Practicing lawyers feared that such a move would not yield sufficiently usable general principles, and might therefore only encourage the development of abstract and integrated fields of law that sacrificed professional utility.

By the 1870s, nevertheless, legal thinkers began to call for a more "philosophical" or "scientific" arrangement of the law while heaping scorn on the practical and functional classifications still in vogue.[29] In contract law, the effort centered on attempts to subsume all rules and doctrines under the heading of "will."[30] In tort law, there were various attempts to unite all sub-categories under the heading of duty.[31] But the most prominent efforts at generalization focused on making "negligence" and "fault" the organizing concepts of the law of torts.[32] Consequently, between 1870 and 1900, the architecture of law was once more rearranged, this time around general concepts that submerged the concrete particularity of the previous organizing schemes. For example, legal writers sought to subsume the different branches of contract law under general and abstract headings such as "offer and acceptance" and "consideration." The modern categorization of intentional, negligent, and strict liability torts also appeared for the first time, providing a new organizational structure based on general principles.

In 1873 Oliver Wendell Holmes, Jr., wrote "The Theory of Torts,"[33] which represented one of his most influential early efforts to establish a general theory. He accomplished this by ignoring traditional status or functional relationships while searching for more abstract and transcendent principles of liability. For the next twenty years, Holmes and other writers sought to make the negligence principle the normal and ordinary rule of tort liability. In the process, it was necessary to attack contradictory and competing legal principles as "anomalous."

Everywhere after 1870, negligence was proclaimed to be the general rule of the common law. In case law, the most powerful recognition of the triumph of the negligence principle can be seen in two leading cases decided in 1872–1873 rejecting strict liability principles laid down in the English case of *Rylands v. Fletcher* (1868). Under strict liability, enterprises, especially railroads, would be held liable for all injuries regardless of fault. Many jurists, including Holmes, devoted themselves to marginalizing this feared authority for redistribution in torts.[34]

Two other areas of tort law stood out as most resistant to recasting according to principles of negligence, and each became a famous battleground in the legal literature. The first was the rule that shippers and other common carriers were strictly liable to their customers. "If there is a sound rule of public policy which ought to impose a special responsibility upon common carriers . . . and upon no others," Holmes declared in *The Common Law*, "it has never been stated." He proceeded to trace the history of strict liability of common carriers for the purpose of showing that it was a latecomer to the common law—a "public policy invented by Chief Justice Holt" early in the eighteenth century and "part of a protective system which has passed away." Any attempt generally to apply Holt's paternalistic and regulatory premises "at the present day," Holmes wrote, "would be thought monstrous." So, Holmes concluded, strict liability of common carriers was an anomaly—"a merely empirical exception from general doctrine"—for which there was "no common rule of policy." Hence, "courts may well hesitate to extend the significance" of any supposed principle of strict liability derived from this area. Indeed, Holmes endorsed the recent strong tendency of American courts to allow common carriers—especially railroads—to "contract out" of strict liability, since "notions of public policy which would not leave parties free to make their own bargains are somewhat discredited in most departments of the law."[35]

Just as strict common carrier liability stood as a disquieting exception to the attempt of legal thinkers to organize an abstract and integrated system of tort law around the negligence principle, so too did the rule that masters were liable for most of the torts of their servants. By imposing "vicarious liability" on employers, the common law seemed to make them liable regardless of their own fault.

In two articles on agency published in 1891 but written eight years earlier, Holmes described the strict liability underlying the rule of *respondiat superior* as a "series of anomalies" that were contrary to "common sense." "I assume," he wrote, "that common-sense is opposed to making one man pay for another man's wrong, unless he actually has brought the wrong to pass. . . ." The history of the development of vicarious liability of the master could, therefore, be explained only as "the resultant of a conflict at every point between logic and good sense." "The survival from ancient times of doctrines . . . based on substantial grounds which have disappeared long since" could have occurred only because they were "generalized into a fiction" and subsequently took on a life of their own.[36]

Between 1870 and 1900, one sees everywhere this tendency to generalize and systematize fields of law that had previously been conceived of as a series of special cases and particular rules. This reorganization of legal architecture can be understood as an effort to create a systematic and autonomous system of private law derived from concepts such as will, fault (that is, the impairment of will), and property. It strove to erect an abstract set of legal categories that would subordinate particular legal relationships to a general system of classification. As we have witnessed the disintegration of these late-nineteenth-century imperial categories during the past seventy-five years—as the law of contract, for example, has been disaggregated into specialized areas of sales, labor, consumer, and landlord-tenant law—we see once again the historically contingent character of legal architecture.

We have seen how the late-nineteenth-century process of abstraction was accompanied by a strong effort to purify legal categories through identification and isolation of various anomalies that contradicted the basic structure. One early example is the law of insurance. In 1800, American lawyers regarded insurance law as one of the three or four most prominent sub-categories of a still loosely defined law of contract. By 1850, the law of insurance had been relegated to an independent and separate area of legal categorization. The explanation for this re-classification seems to be that as contract law was becoming increasingly general-ized around the law of sales—with its developing doctrine of *caveat emptor*—long-standing insurance doctrines requiring the insured to "disclose fully all material risks" (*caveat venditor*) became ever more subversive of the general system. As it stood in the way of further generalization of the law of contract, it needed to be expelled.[37]

This identification of anomalies was a central part of the task of legal integra-tion after 1870. We have seen how Holmes consistently labeled various strict liability doctrines as anomalies whose appearance in the law could be explained only by historical peculiarities. We have also seen that he sought to discredit strict master-servant and common carrier liability, both of which contradicted his proj-ect of integration. In a simliar spirit, we shall soon see, William Keener published a book on *Quasi-Contract* in 1893 for the purpose of isolating a paternalistic, non-will-based set of doctrines from a pure and supposedly voluntaristic system of contract law.[38]

The process of generalization and abstraction in late-nineteenth-century law was identified with the goal of rendering private law more scientific and less po-litical. It also had the effect of freeing legal rules from the reality testing that regular encounters with the concrete particularities of social life might entail. For example, generalization permitted judges to apply the same set of rules that were applicable between sophisticated businessmen of relatively equal information and bargaining power to labor and consumer contracts between vastly unequal parties. Indeed, such indifference to context was regarded as an important safeguard that would ensure that law would remain neutral and non-political.

While the task of integration and abstraction was undertaken to create a pow-erful system of private law insulated from politics, it ultimately sowed the seeds of its own destruction. Although its very general and abstract character led eventually to the charge that it was out of touch with reality, in fact it had also already rendered itself internally vulnerable. First, the process of integration gradually eliminated a series of built-in "mediation" devices that had allowed various con-tradictory principles and doctrines to coexist without totally consuming each other. As we will see in a number of areas of law, systematization simply exposed con-tradictions that earlier compartmentalized structures had been able successfully to suppress. For example, as the concept of property was made more abstract, judges and jurists turned away from an earlier, more restricted, "physicalist" conception of property that limited "takings" to physical expropriations of land.[39] As the def-inition of property was expanded to include not only various *uses* of land, but also stable market values as well as expectations of future income from property, vir-tually every governmental activity was rendered capable of being regarded as a taking. Earlier mediation devices for preventing such a *reductio ad absurdum*, to be discussed later, were swept away by this process of abstraction, thus rendering the entire system more vulnerable to attack.

What follows is an effort to capture initially the essential structure of Classical Legal Thought by focusing in some depth upon several major areas of legal doctrine that help to express its characteristic tensions and contradictions. First, we look at the well-known income tax case of 1895, *Pollock v. Farmers' Loan & Trust Co.*,[40] in order to highlight perhaps the most central tenet of late-nineteenth-century legal orthodoxy—its commitment to a neutral, non-redistributive state. Next, we turn to the famous Supreme Court decision in *Lochner v. New York* (1905)[41] to identify the moment at which many of the suppressed contradictions within the classical ideal of a neutral state came to the surface and produced a powerful political and intellectual reaction. In particular, we study the development of limits on police power, which were used in *Lochner* to deny the authority of the state to regulate maximum hour laws.

As we seek to capture the texture of Classical legal consciousness by focusing on these specific areas, we also need to see the particular ways in which orthodoxy made itself more vulnerable to attack, often by eliminating earlier legal distinctions that existed precisely in order to mediate or deny some political, social, or moral contradiction.

The Structure of Legal Reasoning

The late-nineteenth-century effort to integrate legal doctrine was accompanied by an equally important attempt to create a self-contained system of legal reasoning that would be immune to the charge that it was simply political. As a first approximation, it is accurate to describe this mode of reasoning as "formalistic" or "conceptualistic." It aspired to import into the processes of legal reasoning the qualities of certainty and logical inexorability. Deduction from general principles and analogies among cases and doctrines were often undertaken with a self-confidence that later generations, long since out of touch with the inarticulate premises of the system, could only mistakenly regard as willful and duplicitous. However difficult it is for us to recapture this aspect of the late-nineteenth-century mindset, it stood as among the most important elements that supported the conviction of legal thinkers that it was possible to distinguish the legal from the political.

Late-nineteenth-century legal formalism represented the crystallization of a "legalistic" mindset[42] that had emerged in seventeenth- and eighteenth-century English constitutional thought and was further elaborated in liberal political theory and post-revolutionary American legal thought. It was marked by a series of basic dichotomies: between means and ends, procedure and substance, processes and consequences. In a world of conflicting ends, it aspired to create a system of processes and principles that could be shared even in the absence of agreed-upon ends. Law played a crucial role in this system of thought. If legal concepts could be neutral, they could then be used to decide disputes without resort to the substantive merits of a case. Thus, well before the late nineteenth century, the ideal of the rule of law had emerged to oppose "result-oriented" or consequentialist modes of legal thought.

Perhaps the best example of the triumph of these ideas is the position of equity in the Anglo-American system of legal ideas. During the late Middle Ages, the English chancellors had succeeded in erecting a system of equitable jurisdiction that often stood in conflict with the common law courts. While many of the disputes between "law" and "equity" dealt simply with questions of power or with technical issues of jurisdiction, one major ideological issue came to be increasingly prominent during the eighteenth century. Common lawyers frequently charged that the chancellors, still often acting out of a medieval or paternalistic conception of their role as "a court of conscience," were deciding questions of substantive justice in ways completely at odds with the rule of law. The charge that chancery cases were decided according "to the length of the chancellor's foot" was contrasted unfavorably with "fixed and settled principles of law."

By the beginning of the nineteenth century, the system of equity had been almost completely subordinated to the common law, as even the chancellors began to maintain that the substantive doctrines of law and equity were the same; only their remedies were different.[43] The merger of law and equity in the New York Field Code of 1848 symbolizes the end of a separate, equitable system of substantive justice. Equity thus had finally submitted to the long-standing criticism that judicial enforcement of substantive conceptions of justice was contrary to the rule of law.

The Categorical Mind

Nothing captures the essential difference between the typical legal minds of nineteenth- and twentieth-century America quite as well as their attitude toward categories. Nineteenth-century legal thought was overwhelmingly dominated by categorical thinking—by clear, distinct, bright-line classifications of legal phenomena. Late-nineteenth-century legal reasoning brought categorical modes of thought to their highest fulfillment.

By contrast, in the twentieth century, the dominant conception of the arrangement of legal phenomena has been that of a continuum between contradictory policies or doctrines. Contemporary thinkers typically have been engaged in balancing conflicting policies and "drawing lines" somewhere between them. Nineteenth-century categorizing typically sought to demonstrate "differences of kind" among legal classifications; twentieth-century balancing tests deal only with "differences of degree."

There were a number of familiar categories that late-nineteenth-century judges invoked to decide cases: "direct-indirect" tests in a number of legal areas, especially under the commerce clause;[44] "business affected with the public interest";[45] "intervening" and "supervening" causes in the law of causation;[46] a "literalist" interpretation of the Sherman Act that purported to distinguish clearly between contracts in restraint of trade and those not in restraint of trade;[47] legislation that interfered with contract "rights" versus contract "remedies";[48] distinctions between "taxation" and "takings"[49] and between exercises of police power (or regulation) and confiscation;[50] and the exercise of eminent domain or taxing powers that served a public purpose and those that did not.[51] One could extend the list indefinitely.

Nineteenth-century legal classification expressed a mindset that also sharply distinguished legal from legislative reasoning by separating the legislative functions of trading and balancing among competing policies or interests from the supposedly judicial task of simply identifying the existing legal categories to which a dispute belonged. It was an extension of modes of legal reasoning that had long existed under the forms of action, where the lawyer's basic task was to identify the appropriate writ or form of pleading that would cover a particular case.

While judges and lawyers of the nineteenth century clearly believed that there were identifiable bright-line boundaries that judges could apply to a case without the exercise of will or discretion, it is all too easy to caricature their position. Most legal thinkers believed that legal categories contained what we might call a "core" and a "periphery." There was a class of cases that clearly belonged to the core; there were others, more difficult, that were part of the periphery. If the state should assign the title of A's property to B without compensation, that was clearly a core case of taking. But there were many cases of "indirect" or "consequential" injury to property that were at the more problematic periphery of the category. While the task of applying these categories frequently required difficult exercises of judgment in particular cases, the intellectual goal was the same: to decide whether a dispute fell within one or another mutually exclusive category.

This distinction between core and periphery led nineteenth-century judges to intone a formula that is all but incomprehensible to twentieth-century jurists. While the application of a constitutional provision varies with changing circumstances, these judges often declared, its meaning is nevertheless fixed and unchanging. For late-nineteenth-century jurists, the difference between the meaning and the application of a legal rule or doctrine was the difference between the core and the periphery of that doctrine. The task of the judge in hard cases was to decide whether they looked more like the core cases in one class rather than another.

Early-twentieth-century legal thought was devoted to attacking these modes of categorical thinking by portraying them as formalistic and artificial. The emergence of balancing tests in numerous areas of the law is a prominent measure of the success of Progressive legal thinkers in undermining categorical thought. One sees the appearance of balancing tests in many different areas of the law after 1910: in the "rule of reason" in anti-trust law;[52] in the law of nuisance;[53] in the "reasonableness" (Hand) standard in negligence;[54] in the test of when a regulation becomes a taking;[55] and in the clear and present danger test for free speech.[56] In 1921 the most important Progressive legal thinker, Roscoe Pound, declared that a new jurisprudence should encourage a "weighing of social interests."[57]

In the realm of academic thought, it was Holmes who had prepared legal thinkers for the attack on categorical modes of thought. His emphasis on line drawing and his insistence that legal reasoning was all a matter of degree were designed to subvert the dominant mode of thought. Yet ultimately one feels that it was the old order itself that had prepared the seeds of its own destruction. For one can identify the moments at which categorical thought began to break down within legal orthodoxy itself. As proponents of the old system of thought began the process of abstraction and integration, they extended its categories too far. The compartmentalizing mechanisms within orthodoxy for regulating or denying the limits of categorical thought were stretched to the breaking point. And the old order itself reached in desperation for a balancing test.

The Neutral State and Classical Legal Thought

In progressive constitutional historiography, the decision of the U.S. Supreme Court in *Pollock v. Farmers' Loan & Trust Co.* (1895)[58] has always stood for the essence of judicial usurpation. In that case the Court held, seemingly contrary to the existing precedents, that an income tax was a direct tax requiring apportionment among the states. And since state-by-state apportionment of a tax on individual income was practically impossible to implement, the decision delayed for eighteen years—until the passage of the Sixteenth Amendment—any federal tax on incomes.

I will show that, far from marking a sharp break with the past, the decision in *Pollock* instead exemplified the crystallization and culmination of ideas that had been gathering strength in American constitutional thought for over fifty years. *Pollock* simply represented one of the most dramatic applications of a recent convergence of constitutional doctrines that would restrict the power of the state to redistribute wealth.

The "night watchman" state that was first outlined for Americans in Madison's Tenth *Federalist* embodied what would become a pervasive nineteenth-century liberal vision of a neutral state, a state that could avoid taking sides in conflicts between religions, social classes, or interest groups. While the hope of achieving such neutrality was articulated from the beginning of the Republic—with law being assigned a special cultural role as neutral arbiter—there were other, perhaps more dominant political or legal ideas that first needed to be defeated or marginalized. In some states, religious disestablishment did not take place until 1833.[59] The vision of law embodied in the English and American constitutional systems did not really gel until the 1820s. For example, judicial review at the state level was not entirely legitimated until the 1840s and, at the federal level, until after the Civil War.[60] While one strand of the antebellum codification movement challenged the neutrality of the common law, its considerable practical success can only be appreciated once we realize that by 1840 a majority of the states, which had once appointed judges, now elected them.[61] There were, in short, many institutional and ideological impediments to reaching the ideal of a government of laws and not of men.

What has variously been called a Republican or Whig or Commonwealth conception of the state stood opposed to the liberal idea of neutrality.[62] In political economy as well, the triumph of laissez-faire liberalism can be dated from the second half of the century.

It was perhaps the trauma of the Civil War that crystallized these separate antebellum tendencies in favor of a state that could stand above all factions and interests. Or perhaps each of the separate strands in law, politics, and economics grew stronger and finally converged around the ideal of a neutral state. Or perhaps the triumph of the neutral state in late-nineteenth-century thought should be seen in relationship to the clear increase in social conflict and inequality that was emerging at the same time. In this version, the ideal of neutrality represents a form of denial: As the level of social conflict produced ever more anxiety, the yearning to believe in an idealized oasis of neutrality became correspondingly greater.

Whatever the explanation, the ideal of the neutral state came to represent a central form of legitimation during the late nineteenth century. At just this moment, Classical Legal Thought emerged as perhaps the dominant expression of the idea of neutrality.

Taxation and the Idea of Neutrality

The power of taxation presented the most formidable difficulties for nineteenth-century jurists intent upon establishing a neutral state by limiting the redistributive capacities of government. The English constitutional tradition provided virtually no legal limitations on redistributive legislative designs. The great constitutional struggles of the seventeenth century were waged entirely over the legitimate constitutional powers of king and Parliament, not over whether there were general limitations on the government's power to tax.

When Michigan's Chief Justice Thomas Cooley came to write his *Treatise on the Law of Taxation* in 1876, he had to concede in his opening pages that the constitutional tradition provided few legitimate grounds for judicial restrictions:

> The power of taxation is an incident of sovereignty, and is coextensive with that of which it is an incident. All subjects, therefore, over which the sovereign power of the state extends are, in its discretion, legitimate subjects of taxation; and this may be carried to any extent to which the government may choose to carry it. In its very nature it acknowledges no limits, and the only security against abuse must be found in the responsibility of the legislature which imposes the tax to the constituency who are to pay it. The judiciary can afford no redress against oppressive taxation, so long as the legislature, in imposing it, shall keep within the limits of legislative authority.[63]

By importing his conception of "fixed principles of justice" into his definition of "legislative authority," however, Cooley was eventually able to establish anti-redistributive tax principles.[64] Yet he was never able entirely to constitutionalize limits on a taxing power that had been derived from a long tradition of wide legislative discretion.

Cooley's most important contribution to the constitutional law of taxation was to formalize the norm of "equal and uniform" taxation as a guiding principle of American constitutional law. In this sense, his treatise represented the culmination of a generation of efforts in the states to amend their constitutions in order to add equal and uniform tax provisions.

A vast expansion of state taxation had begun during the 1840s in reaction, after the Panic of 1837, to the elimination of extensive state revenues derived from canal tolls. Urbanization after the Civil War also produced a massive increase in local property taxes devoted to public works; and by 1875, systems of special assessments, primarily for road building, had "of late years become very frequent and extensive."[65]

Between 1840 and 1870, a movement to add strict constitutional provisions requiring equal and uniform taxation prevailed in the vast majority of states. Whereas in 1792 the state constitutions of ten of the thirteen former colonies contained no such restrictions, and even the remaining three (Maryland, Massachusetts, and New Hampshire) had promulgated only vague constitutional provisions, "there was a sharp turn in practice" in 1818–1820, and after that time almost all newly admitted states included some type of uniformity clause in their constitutions.[66] But it was only after a flurry of activity during the period 1845–1851 that equal and uniform taxation became the constitutional norm in the states.[67]

Cooley wrote his treatise for the purpose of codifying these new developments in the constitutional law of taxation. The reader, he acknowledged, might think "that on some points, too much importance has been attached to those fundamental principles which restrict the power to tax" until "one considers how vast is this power, how readily it yields to passion, excitement, prejudice or private schemes, and to what incompetent hands its extention is usually committed."[68]

The *Treatise on Taxation* is duly modest about the "serious and often insurmountable difficulties in the way of equal taxation. . . ."[69] "Perfect equality" in the assessment of taxes, Cooley constantly reiterated, is practically unattainable.[70] Yet, despite cautious pragmatism about the difficulties of institutionalizing the principle of equality, Cooley had no doubt whatsoever concerning the correctness of the principle.

> [A]re there not cases which on their face are manifestly so unequal and unjust as to furnish conclusive evidence that equality has not been sought for but avoided; that oppression, not justice was desired, and confiscation, not taxation intended?[71]

The central purpose of the *Treatise on Taxation*, then, was precisely to distinguish between "taxation" and "confiscation" by establishing the norm of equality as a "fixed principle of justice,"[72] a "fundamental principle which [would] restrict the power to tax."[73] For if the principle of inequality were "once admitted there is no reason but its own discretion why the legislature should stop short of imposing the whole burden of government on the few who exhibit most energy, enterprise and thrift."[74] Thus, under the inspiration of recent state constitutional changes, Cooley sought to shift the law of taxation away from its historic association with unfettered legislative sovereignty and to articulate clear constitutional barriers against the use of taxation for redistributive ends. Compared to other constitutional restrictions on the redistributive impulse, the movement to constitutionalize the taxing power was a relative latecomer in American law, reflecting the fact that until the 1840s taxation played only a minor role in state financing.

There were substantial difficulties confronting anyone who wished to constitutionalize the law of taxation. Treating equality as a fundamental principle of justice, Cooley sought to make this norm applicable regardless of whether a state had specifically incorporated it into its constitution. For this purpose, he enthusiastically cited a Kentucky case that derived constitutional limitations on taxation from "the declared ends and principles of the fundamental laws. Among these political ends and principles, *equality*, as far as practicable, and security of property against irresponsible power, are eminently conspicuous in our state constitution."[75]

Cooley's argumentative strategy is a prominent example of what Edward Corwin has called the "doctrine of implied limitations."[76] Since separation of powers is a basic doctrine of American constitutional law, the argument went, the legislative branch is confined to acts of legislation. Taxation is within the definition of the legislative power only when it is used to raise revenue. It follows that an unequal tax, being clearly for redistributive purposes, is not within the legislative power. Unequal taxation was thus defined to be in fundamental conflict with the theory underlying separation of powers and was unconstitutional even without a specific provision requiring equal and uniform taxation.

Another version of the effort to create implied limitations on the taxing power was to derive such limitations from constitutional provisions requiring just compensation for a taking of property. "[W]henever the property of a citizen shall be taken from him by the sovereign will, and appropriated without his consent to the benefit of the public, the exaction should not be considered as a tax unless similar contributions be made by the public. . . ."[77] In Pennsylvania, which did not have a constitutional provision requiring equal and uniform taxation, the judges in 1871 held a local special assessment unconstitutional. Anticipating the spirit of Cooley's treatise, they declared that unless taxation is "reasonably just and equal in its distribution," it "is confiscation, not taxation, extortion not assessment."[78] Any other conclusion would result "in the overthrow of the right of private property."[79]

The Uses of the State Taxation Decisions

The Supreme Court justices who struck down the federal income tax in 1895 came to legal maturity when the central constitutional question of taxation focused on the power of municipalities to issue bonds in order to encourage the building of railroads. After the Civil War, Midwestern towns outdid each other with promises of financial subsidies in order to encourage railroads to build lines through the towns. Eventually, especially after the Panic of 1873, many towns defaulted on these bonds, and courts in Iowa, Michigan, and other states were besieged by the lawsuits of disappointed municipal bondholders.

Judge Thomas Cooley of Michigan and U.S. Supreme Court Justice Samuel F. Miller of Iowa were among many Midwestern jurists whose legal views on taxation were deeply affected by the bond cases.[80] Both Cooley and Miller wrote judicial opinions that deprived bondholders of relief on the ground that municipalities did not have the power to spend and hence to tax for "non-public" purposes.[81]

The "public purpose" doctrine in taxation was an extension of constitutional principles that had been forged in many state courts during the antebellum period to limit the power of the state to take property for non-public purposes.[82] Its extension to taxation after the Civil War was an important development in the movement toward legal integration during the late nineteenth century. The powers of eminent domain and taxation, formerly treated under widely divergent legal conceptions, began to be subordinated to a common set of anti-redistributive principles after the Civil War.

The views of Cooley and Miller on the bond cases were expressions of long-standing Jacksonian fears that the state would be used to favor special interests at the expense of the public interest. Earlier Jacksonian attacks on corporate monopolies and on the use of the eminent domain power to subsidize transportation companies were eventually generalized into an ideal of a neutral state free from the corruption of "class legislation." "To lay with one hand the power of the government on the property of the citizen," Justice Miller wrote in *Loan Association v. Topeka* (1874), "and with the other to bestow it upon favored individuals to aid private enterprises and build up private fortunes, is none the less a robbery because it is done under the forms of law and is called taxation."[83]

Traditional conservative fears that the state might be used to protect debtors or to take property in order to equalize wealth were thus matched by neo-Jacksonian anxieties that the state would be taken over by corporate interests. It is important to recognize that these twin fears of state power combined to produce laissez-faire ideology after 1850.[84]

If the public purpose doctrine brought the eminent domain and taxing powers into the same sphere of legal discourse, it was only a matter of time before the question of what constituted a taking under eminent domain law would be extended to the taxing power as well. If it was clear, as antebellum judges had frequently reiterated, that the state could not take the property of A and give it to B, could the taxing power be used to accomplish the same illegitimate objective? How, in short, could one distinguish between a tax and a taking?

By degrees, then, judges and jurists, aided by state constitutional provisions, worked their way to the principle that only equal taxation could avoid the charge that the use of the taxing power was simply a disguised form of confiscation.

The Federalization of Taxation Doctrine

In 1873, Justice Miller wrote his famous opinion in *The Slaughterhouse Cases*,[85] holding that the recently ratified Fourteenth Amendment, and in particular its privileges and immunities clause, had introduced only minor limitations on state power. The facts of the case seemed to present an extreme version of the Jacksonian nightmare of the use of state power to favor special interests.

Miller's majority opinion resisting the constitutional challenge to a New Orleans slaughterhouse monopoly was dominated by his effort to prevent the Fourteenth Amendment from becoming a centralized charter of federal regulation that would overthrow the federal system. The dissents of Justices Stephen Field and Joseph Bradley were classical Jacksonian polemics on the evils of monopoly, polemics that on other occasions Miller himself endorsed with enthusiasm.

Progressive historiography, written from the perspective of the subsequent development of "substantive due process" and its culmination in *Lochner v. New York*,[86] has tended to overlook the considerable substantive agreement in the social visions of Justices Miller, Field, Bradley, and, later, even John Marshall Harlan. In the 1870s and 1880s, the real source of division in the Supreme Court, except perhaps over questions of race, turned on different views of the dangers of federal power and of governmental centralization, not on substantive conceptions of social justice.

A Miller opinion written one year after the *Slaughterhouse* decision underlines this interpretation. *Loan Association v. Topeka* (1874) was a diversity case[87] in which Miller held that a city had no power to issue municipal bonds to subsidize private enterprise. In a diversity case, Miller felt free to decide the question under state constitutional law, so that the reach of the Fourteenth Amendment did not need to be addressed. Deciding as if he were a state court judge, he held that even in the absence of any express constitutional provision, a tax not for a public purpose was in reality a taking. The power of taxation, Miller wrote, "can as readily be employed against one class of individuals and in favor of another, so as to ruin the one class and give unlimited wealth and prosperity to the other, if there is no implied limitation of the uses for which the power may be exercised."[88] Three years later, he made it clear that, out of respect for the federal system, he was unwilling to extend these views to the Fourteenth Amendment.[89]

By contrast, Justice Field sought to force just such an expansive view of the Fourteenth Amendment on the Supreme Court. In two circuit court tax cases in 1882 and 1883, he held that a California statute providing different tax rates for individual and corporate property was a violation of the equal protection clause of the Fourteenth Amendment.[90] "Unequal exactions in every form, or under any pretense, are absolutely forbidden," Field wrote, "and of course unequal taxation, for it is in that form that oppressive burdens are usually laid."[91] "What is called for under a [state] constitutional provision requiring equality and uniformity in the taxation of property must be equally called for by the fourteenth amendment," Field concluded.[92]

Field's circuit court decisions were affirmed by the Supreme Court but on very limited grounds.[93] Before its decision in *Pollock v. Farmers' Loan & Trust Co.* (1895),[94] in fact, the Supreme Court managed to avoid the question Field had already decided. By the time of this decision, however, the distinction between a legitimate tax and a tax that was really an illegitimate taking had been turned into a deeply ingrained part of American constitutional doctrine. It was buttressed by the simultaneous de-physicalization of the takings doctrine during the preceding generation, a development that eliminated earlier conceptual blocks to regarding taxes and takings as in the same sphere of legal discourse.[95]

Progressive constitutional historiography has regarded *Pollock* as one of the prime examples of judicial usurpation during the 1890s.[96] It is true that the formal holding of the Supreme Court, that a federal income tax was a direct tax requiring apportionment among the states according to population, was contrary to a small number of earlier Supreme Court precedents that consistently limited the category of what constituted a direct tax.[97] Yet, if we regard the direct-indirect tax provision as the most acceptable available federal constitutional vehicle for expressing more fundamental ideas about taxation that had crystallized in state courts during the preceding half century, the result reached should have come as no surprise.

As *Pollock* was being heard by the U.S. Supreme Court, one of the most influential American jurists, former Judge John F. Dillon, delivered a rousing defense of private property before the New York State Bar Association. "[I]n our own day," Dillon declared, ". . . great primordial rights, including the right of private property," were being "drawn in question by combined attacks upon them and upon the social fabric that has been builded upon them. This assault upon society as now organized is made by bodies of men who call themselves . . . communists, socialists, anarchists, or by like designations."[98] While Dillon's speech addressed the full range of suggested restrictions on the power of property holding, we should pause over the section entitled "Attacks Upon Private Property Through the Exercise of Power of Taxation."[99]

"Socialistic organizations," Dillon began, had mounted various "attacks" on private property; "[t]he most insidious, specious and therefore, dangerous" were "those that are threatened" concerning "the State's power of taxation."[100]

> Forasmuch as the power to tax is supposed to involve the power to destroy, it is boldly avowed by many socialistic reformers, and it is implied in the schemes of others, that the power of taxation is an available and rightful means to be used for the express purpose of correcting the unequal distribution of wealth, and that this may be done without a violation of the essential or constitutional rights of property.[101]

"[R]easonable and proportional" taxation "imposed as a *bona fide* means of raising revenue" was entirely legitimate. But when taxes are imposed "for the real purpose of reaching the accumulated fruits of industry, and are not equal and reasonable, but designed as a forced contribution from the rich for the benefit of the poor, and as a means of distributing the rich man's property among the rest of the community—this is class legislation of the most pronounced and vicious type; is, in [a] word, confiscation and not taxation." "Such schemes of pillage" are "violative of the constitutional rights of the property owner, subversive of the existing social polity, and essentially revolutionary."[102]

Dillon proceeded to invoke the idea of a neutral state that "knows or ought to know no classes."[103]

> The one thing to be feared in our democratic republic, and therefore to be guarded against with sleepless vigilance, is class power and class legislation. Discriminating legislation for the benefit of the rich against the poor, or in favor of the poor against the rich, is equally wrong and dangerous. Class legislation of all and every kind is anti-republican and must be repressed.[104]

One is struck with the overwhelming attention paid in the arguments before the Supreme Court in *Pollock* to the income tax's progressive rate structure. Joseph Choate's argument for its unconstitutionality is well known. The income tax, he declared, "is communistic in its purposes and tendencies, and is defended here under principles as communistic, socialistic—what shall I call them—populistic as ever have been addressed to any political assembly in the world."[105] Indeed, the more forthright argument that the progressive features of the income tax violated the constitutional requirement of uniformity of taxation was perhaps the most prominent point before the Court. Attorney General Richard Olney, in his argument in defense of the tax, regarded the absence of uniformity as "*the* constitutional objection which, notwithstanding all that has been so earnestly and forcibly said on the direct tax part of this controversy, is, I am satisfied, the plaintiffs' main reliance."[106]

Justice Field's concurring opinion rested almost entirely on the view that the income tax was a violation of the uniformity clause of the Constitution. He relied on Cooley's *Treatise on Taxation*, on state cases distinguishing between a tax and a taking, and, of course, on his own earlier circuit court opinions under the equal protection clause.[107]

By the time the *Income Tax Case* was decided, then, the anti-redistribution principle had come to be thought of as part of the very essence of the constitutional law of a neutral state. More generally, the impermissibility of redistribution embodied one of the central tenets of the nineteenth-century idea of the liberal state.[108] As this idea was slowly absorbed into the defining structure of legitimacy, it also came to be gradually woven into the fabric of everyday legal assumptions. Not only did the constitutional framework come to express these premises; they were also woven into a complex system of legal doctrine. The emergence of a distinction between public and private law is one important example of the effort to create a private realm immune to the dangers of redistribution.

We turn next to other areas of Classical Legal Thought to see how its creators sought to advance the anti-redistributive principle and how the early-twentieth-century Progressive challenge sought to undermine this anti-redistributive structure of Classical Legal Thought.

Police Power Doctrine: Categorical Thought and Neutrality

The history of constitutional doctrines about the police power presents an excellent illustration of my assertion that, until very late in the nineteenth century, categorical modes of thought made it possible for jurists to believe that there could be a form of neutral legal reasoning that was fundamentally different from political reasoning. It also illustrates the ways in which the processes of integration, generalization, and abstraction of legal categories eventually strained the distinction between the legal and the political to the breaking point.

The idea that the police power was one of the headings of legislative power—along with, for example, taxation and eminent domain—began to emerge during the 1850s and became a standard description of legal architecture by the 1870s. Before Massachusetts Chief Justice Lemuel Shaw's derivation of the police power from sovereignty in *Commonwealth v. Alger* (1851),[109] jurists did not generally derive the regulatory powers of the state over health, safety, and morals from notions of inherent state power. Instead, the dominant mode of earlier post-revolutionary legal analysis was to treat state power in essentially private law contractual terms: regulatory power was derived from "reservations" in the state's grants to landowners or corporations. Shaw's shift to sovereignty as the source of regulatory power is an important measure of the declining vitality of the grant theory as social reality moved away from land grants and as free incorporation laws eviscerated the "grant" or "concession" theory of the corporation.[110]

By the 1870s, police power had become the standard legal category for talking about the state's regulatory power over the health, safety, and morals of its citizens. At this point, the question that most concerns us emerged: How did jurists analyze what, for twentieth-century thinkers, would come to be perceived as an irreconcilable contradiction between regulation and takings? How did they believe themselves able to deploy categorical thinking to avoid the necessity of political modes of analysis by way of line drawing and balancing tests?

In virtually all legal fields, the aspiration of late-nineteenth-century legal thinkers was to depoliticize public law categories by deriving them from those of private law. In the police power area, for example, they sought to develop doctrines that were congruent with the common law of nuisance. Wherever it was legitimate for the state to invoke its power to abate a public nuisance (which, for Blackstone, was only a delegation of the individual's private right to abate that nuisance),[111] it was also legitimate for the state to act under the police power. During the 1870s and 1880s, police power analysis was regarded as largely derivable from categories developed in the common law of nuisance.

How did nineteenth-century nuisance law manage to avoid the balancing test that dominates its twentieth-century counterpart? First, in most fields covered by nuisance law, common law judges managed to invoke the maxim *sic utere* ("use you own so as not to injure another's") to avoid balancing.[112] They did this in a number of ways. First, they developed a long list of per se nuisances, which could be abated without hearing any justification of the defendant. Houses of prostitution, bars, and stills were at the top of the list, but such places as gunpowder storage facilities, cemeteries, and slaughterhouses were also frequently included. The *content* of the class of per se nuisance was derived from customary—and, as the nineteenth century wore on, increasingly Victorian—norms.[113] Second, most nineteenth-century nuisance cases reflected a clear preference for inactivity over active uses of land, and courts frequently chose natural over artificial uses.[114] In general, except over the question of injunctions, where a balancing test did emerge in the late nineteenth century,[115] courts simply held that most substantial interferences with the "quiet enjoyment" of land were nuisances. The abundance of land in America enabled them to postpone the issue of conflicting land uses that by the 1860s had already become a pressing question in the overpopulated and polluted English industrial cities.

For judges deciding police power cases in the 1870s, the law of nuisance provided the categories for determining when it was legitimate for the state to regulate on behalf of the health, safety, and morals of its citizens. When Chief Justice Morrison Waite invoked the category "business affected with a public interest" to uphold the regulation of grain elevator rates in *Munn v. Illinois* (1876),[116] he was attempting to infuse the newly emerging public purpose doctrine with the content of common law nuisance categories.

Let us see how differently courts approached four major categories of cases that shaped state and federal police power decisions between 1850 and 1905. Two dealt with issues of public health: restrictions or prohibitions on the sale of liquor that derived from the re-emergence of the temperance movement during the 1850s,[117] and restrictions or prohibitions on the sale of oleomargarine that reflected legislative motivations ranging from protection of dairy interests to protection of consumers against deception.[118] Two other categories were regulation of rates charged by railroads and grain elevator operators, and regulation of working conditions, dealing with minimum wages, maximum hours, and working hours of women and children.

The U.S. Supreme Court decision in *Mugler v. Kansas* (1887),[119] unanimously upholding a Kansas prohibition statute, illustrates how both state and federal courts had little conceptual difficulty in dealing with anti-liquor legislation. Since it was within the well-recognized category of protection of "the public health, safety, and morals," courts did not need to inquire further about the confiscatory consequences of such a statute. If a state could abate a public nuisance without compensation, it could similarly prohibit such a nuisance by statute.[120]

Judicial treatment of anti-margarine legislation presented somewhat more complicated issues. Was such legislation really aimed at protecting consumers' health or guarding against consumer deception, or was it an effort to protect the dairy industry? Since regulation of the sale and ingredients of food was tradition-ally within the police power, courts also, as in the liquor cases, strongly tended to avoid close scrutiny of these acts.

But the margarine cases[121] raised more general questions that increasingly came to dominate adjudication under the police power. Here, as in the *Slaughterhouse Cases*,[122] courts revealed increasing sensitivity to the power of legislatures to con-fer monopolies under the guise of protecting the public health. Some judges were simply unwilling to go behind the legislative declaration that they were acting under the police power. Others—an increasing number by the end of the cen-tury—began to quote from Thomas Cooley's influential *Constitutional Limita-tions* (1868)[123] on the limits of the police power:

> The limit . . . in these cases must be this: [T]he regulations must have reference to the comfort, safety, or welfare of society; . . . they must not, under pretence of regulation, take from the corporation any of the essential rights and privileges which the charter confers. In short, they must be police regulations in fact, and not amendments of the charter in curtailment of the corporate franchise.[124]

Until the 1890s, virtually all of the police power cases that struck down legislative regulations did so on the view that they were "under pretence of regulation" and not "real" exercises of the police power. Courts did not have to confront formally the conflict between regulation and takings because the question was answered at a prior categorical state: Was this a real exercise of the police power?

Just as this mode of analysis avoided structuring the legal question in terms of a real conflict between the police power and property rights, so too, for a time, did analysis of the regulation of working conditions avoid presenting the question as a choice between two conflicting positions. The question continued to be ana-lyzed in terms of whether a particular regulation was within the traditional scope of the police power or was a mere disguise for interference with the market.

Lochner v. New York (1905)[125] was argued in terms of whether a law limiting bakers to a sixty-hour work week fell within the legitimate province of the legis-lature to protect the health of workers. Despite clear evidence that the health of bakers was especially susceptible after long hours of work, the U.S. Supreme Court insisted that "any law . . . might find shelter under such assumptions, and con-duct, properly so called . . . would come under the restrictive sway of the legis-lature."[126] "It is impossible for us to shut our eyes to the fact that many of the laws of this character, while passed under what is classed to be the police power for the purpose of protecting the public health or welfare are, in reality, passed from other motives." The "other motives" regarded as illegitimate by the Court were those behind regulations that invoked the police power in order to justify interference with contractual freedom for the purpose of redistributing economic power.

If a court suspected the redistributive motives of the legislature, how could it distinguish between what, on the one hand, Cooley had called "police regulations, in fact," and, on the other, redistribution "under pretence of regulation"? To do so meant that it was necessary to suppose that there was an inherent category of things that affected health. "In looking through statistics regarding all trades and occupations," the court in *Lochner* concluded, "it may be true" that the trade of baker is more unhealthy than many other occupations. Still, "[we] think that there can be no fair doubt that the trade of baker, in and of itself, is not an unhealthy one to that degree" that would justify regulation.[127] In short, every time a legislature offered statistics to argue that there was a continuum of unhealthy occupations, a court, suspecting its redistributive motives, needed to inquire whether the particular occupation in question was "in and of itself" unhealthy. When it was argued that only the legislature could legitimately draw the appropriate line involving questions of degree, the court was forced to support its suspicion of legislative motives by asserting that unless the question was really one of kind, involving an inherent category of things affecting health, there could be no real constitutional check on the legislature. Here was the intellectual process by which the categories of Classical Legal Thought became ever more essentialist at precisely the moment when the judges were confronting the claim that in a changing world only the legislature could decide what in fact affected the health of a citizen.

The emergence of industrial society thus meant not only that redistributive motives would inevitably be activated by the reality of an increasingly unequal society. It also meant that the relatively fixed common law categories on which police power doctrines had been erected would fall apart, as any categorical distinction between the health of a worker and the conditions of industrial life became ever more difficult to maintain. As these traditional categories of police power doctrine dissolved, every exercise of the police power could suddenly be seen as disguising redistributive motives, for, indeed, every exercise of the police power had always been capable of being characterized as confiscation or redistribution. Only the common law foundations of police power doctrine had obscured this conclusion. By representing the intellectual inquiry as one of deciding whether the challenged regulation was really within the police power and then limiting that category to standard common nuisances, judges traditionally had been able to avoid the charge that they were engaged in the political task of choosing which regulations to approve. But once the problems generated by industrial society undermined the ability of courts to continue to offer traditional definitions of the category of health, safety and morals, the inherently redistributive potential of the police power emerged with a vengeance.

In chapter 2, we turn from public law to private law to see the ways in which the constitutionalization of "freedom of contract" in *Lochner* produced a widespread and sophisticated attack on the underlying premises of contractual freedom. This also serves to introduce Progressive Legal Thought, which, in reaction to the *Lochner* decision, developed an increasingly all-encompassing critique of Classical Legal Thought. Next, we examine the law of agency to illustrate two separate but related themes in Classical Legal Thought. Agency law serves as a litmus test for the characteristic tensions that arose out of the emergence of organizational society in the late nineteenth century. Defining the relation between principal and agent not only became an important expression of the growing problem of controlling an increasing number of employees within large and impersonal corporations; it also represented an important collision between the premises of individualism and those of organizational society. The attempt to absorb agency law into the law of contract became the catalyst for the most important challenges to freedom of contract. Finally, we turn to the Progressive assault on the idea of objective causation in order to highlight one of the areas in which the scientific claims of Classical Legal Thought were overthrown.

TWO

The Progressive Attack on
Freedom of Contract and
Objective Causation

The decision of the U.S. Supreme Court in *Lochner v. New York* (1905)[1] brought Progressive Legal Thought into being. *Lochner*, which struck down a maximum hours law for bakers as an unconstitutional interference with freedom of contract, galvanized Progressive opinion and eventually led to a fundamental assault on the legal thought of the old order.

Freedom of Contract

It was appropriate that the elevation of freedom of contract to the level of a sacred constitutional principle should have become the focal point of controversy, for it represented the convergence of some of the most basic themes in Classical Legal Thought. It expressed, above all, the post–Civil War triumph of laissez-faire principles in political economy and of the view that "that government is best which governs least." Closely connected to the laissez-faire position was a view of the market as a self-executing system that justly distributed rewards through voluntary agreement among individuals. The institution of contract thus represented the legal expression of free market principles, and every interference with the contract system—such as regulation of the terms and conditions of a labor contract—was treated as an attack on the very idea of the market as a natural and neutral institution for distributing rewards.[2]

Ironically, the constitutionalization of freedom of contract in *Lochner* came after two decades of astonishing change in the structure of the American economy that had resulted in the creation of giant corporations capable of exercising enormously disproportionate market power. Monopolization of the economy now would provide a catalyst for Progressive critiques of the traditional assumption of relatively equal bargaining power that had formed the foundation of legitimacy for the freedom of contract doctrine within Classical Legal Thought.

The Progressive attack on freedom of contract gradually developed not only into a critique of the voluntariness of the existing system of contract but, more basically, into a challenge to the fairness and justice of the entire structure of market relations.

Roscoe Pound's powerful article on "Liberty of Contract" (1909)[3] represented the most important early reaction of legal Progressivism to the *Lochner* decision and its progeny.[4] The freedom of contract doctrine, Pound argued, was of recent growth in the courts and represented a conception of "equal rights" between employers and employees that could only be called a "fallacy to everyone acquainted at first hand with actual industrial conditions." Pound asked, "Why then do courts persist in the fallacy? Why do so many of them force upon legislation an academic theory of equality in the face of practical conditions of inequality?"[5]

The explanation was not that "individual judges project their personal, social and economic views into the law" or that the politics of judges had dictated these decisions.[6] Since it had become so deeply embedded in the law, "[s]urely the sources of such a doctrine must lie deeper," in a more pervasive system of legal consciousness.[7] Pound then proceeded to offer a series of explanations of why so great a chasm existed between "academic theory" and "practical conditions"— between what he would soon call the "law in books" and the "law in action"— that would amount to the critical explanatory framework of Progressivism. There was "an individualist conception of justice, which exaggerates the importance of property and of contract [and] exaggerates private right at the expense of public right. . . ."[8] While these views had come to dominate not only law, but also economics and politics, they were out of touch with "the social conception of the present."[9] These ideas had been perpetuated by the training of judges and lawyers in an eighteenth-century natural law philosophy at the same time as they had "pretended contempt" for all forms of legal philosophy. "As a result . . . we exaggerate the importance of property and of contract . . . [and] exaggerate private right at the expense of public interest."[10]

It is important to realize precisely how the assault on freedom of contract emerged. For every sweeping article like Pound's great piece on "Liberty of Contract," there were twenty others that offered a more technical challenge to one or another specific aspect of contract doctrine. It was this internal critique of late-nineteenth-century contract doctrine that initially undermined the foundations of Classical Legal Thought.

The Development of the Progressive Critique of Classical Contract Theory

Private law provided the intellectual source of most legal theory within Classical Legal Thought. And, as we will see in many other areas as well, the Progressive critique of freedom of contract as a constitutional doctrine began with an elaborate assault on the intellectual premises of the private law of contract. After the *Lochner* decision, most technical internal disputes within the law of contract were often displaced struggles over whether contract law could be justly characterized as a neutral and voluntary system in which the judge simply carried out the will of the contracting parties. It was this "will theory" that Progressive legal thinkers began to criticize immediately after *Lochner*.

Objectivism and the Law of Contract

The most striking feature of the attack on the will theory of contract is that it developed directly out of objectivism, which had arisen in the second half of the nineteenth century for the purpose of strengthening and consolidating the will theory. Under the will theory, the basis for enforcing a contract was a "meeting of minds" or convergence of the wills of the contracting parties. If, for example, two parties contracted for the sale of one thousand bushels of Grade A wheat, courts held that the meaning of "Grade A wheat" would not be allowed to depend on an unusual or eccentric understanding held by one of the parties. Judges thus rejected any search for the "subjective" or real intent of the parties and satisfied themselves with the customary meaning held by an average, ordinary person. This shift from a subjective to an objective theory after the Civil War was part of a broader tendency to create formal, general theories that would provide uniformity, certainty, and predictability of legal arrangements.[11] Since subjective theories necessarily gave juries extensive powers to determine the actual will of the parties, the shift to an objective theory was part of a self-conscious effort of judges and jurists to establish uniformity by subordinating the fluctuating decisions of juries to judicially created formal rules.

In the process of formalizing and generalizing the system of contract law, the legal rules came to bear a more and more tenuous relationship to the actual intent of the parties. What once could be defended and justified as simply a more efficacious way of carrying out the parties' intentions came eventually to be perceived as a system that subordinated and overruled the parties' will.

An objective theory of contract was not even the best practical approximation of the actual will of the parties, it was argued, for the law often does not even "create that relation which the parties would have intended had they foreseen." "The fact is," wrote Arthur L. Corbin, ". . . that the decision will depend upon the notions of the court as to policy, welfare, justice, right and wrong, such notions often being inarticulate and subconscious."[12] When the attack on the premises of freedom of contract began in earnest early in the twentieth century, it became immediately clear that an objective theory of contract had already sown the seeds of its own destruction. The established principles of contract, the critics maintained, could no longer be defended as simple reflections of the will of the parties or of a "meeting of minds." Objectivism could not be reconciled with individual autonomy or voluntary agreement. In fact, it demonstrated that the existing law of contract had regularly subordinated individual freedom to collective determinations based on policy or justice.

As in many other areas of the law, late-nineteenth-century contract jurisprudence had actually shifted away from post-revolutionary natural rights theories. Its increasingly utilitarian efforts to use law to promote economic growth often sacrificed an individualized sense of justice. The claims of individualism and localism were thus frequently subordinated to the perceived need for standardization in national markets and a national economy. Subjectivism was also associated with utopian natural rights philosophy which was widely regarded as subversive of the "search for order" in a society experiencing ever increasing levels of social and economic conflict. [13]

Objectivism, in short, had prepared the way for those who wished to argue that the goals of intervention and regulation were already deeply embedded in the existing law and that the individualistic world of autonomous wills had long since passed from the scene.

The attack on objectivism in contract law was well advanced before it was extended to tort. [14] Though there were many prior anticipations, the challenge basically crystallized as a series of reactions to the constitutionalization of freedom of contract in *Lochner v. New York* (1905). From that time on, Progressive legal thinkers gradually elaborated the argument that since the institution of contract did not actually express the wills of private individuals, when the state either enforced or refused to enforce agreements it was only because of considerations of public policy.

An attack on the will theory of contract had been building for some time even prior to 1905. It focused first on the doctrine of "implied contracts." When courts implied the existence of a contract or a term in a contract, the critics asked, were they enforcing or overruling the parties' intentions? In his first article, written in 1870, Oliver Wendell Holmes, Jr., identified the category of implied contract as including "both contracts which are truly express, and cases which are not contracts at all." [15] But it was still too early for him to conclude anything other than that a "legal fiction" had clouded thought on the subject. Yet, recognition of both express and implied contracts had seemed to suggest that there were many contracts that could be enforced regardless of whether there was any meeting of minds or convergence of the parties' wills. Following Holmes's lead, Professor William Keener of the Harvard Law School published his treatise on *Quasi-Contract* in 1893. [16]

For the purpose of clarifying this dilemma, Keener took the willed contract as the paradigm for the "true" or "pure" contract. Among implied contracts, he distinguished between those that were "implied in fact," which were also true contracts because actual intention could be proven on evidence of the parties' behavior, and "implied in law" or quasi-contracts, which had nothing to do with the actual will or intention of the parties. The effect of Keener's classification was to insulate the pure contract from the accusation that it was simply an obligation imposed by the state. By candidly identifying quasi-contract with non-contractual principles, Keener believed he had preserved the realm of contract as the expression of individual autonomy.[17]

But the identification of a separate realm of quasi-contract did not always help to sustain the general idea that contract, correctly understood, did in fact express the parties' wills. Many legal writers after Keener actually pointed to quasi-contract as proof that the general category of contract concededly contained non-volitional doctrines. Though this was apparently far from Keener's intention, it did nevertheless underline a deeper truth.

The publication of *Quasi-Contract* can be understood as representing the beginning of the gradual disintegration of the imperial ideal of contract as it had unfolded from early in the nineteenth century. Until the publication of Keener's treatise, the dominant impulse was toward ever-increasing levels of generality and inclusiveness of contract doctrine. *Quasi-Contract* moves in the opposite direction—toward a disaggegration of concepts. The abstract ideas of the will of the parties and the meeting of minds can no longer hope to explain a series of doctrines in which courts clearly imposed their own ideas of justice on the contracting parties. Earlier in the century, legal writers had actually sought to root out all non-voluntaristic elements in contract law.[18] But they failed, and courts had never completely abandoned intervention in pursuit of uniformity or of justice. So that by the time Keener wrote, he was presented with a clear choice between conceding the existence of non-voluntaristic doctrines in contract law or else excluding these elements from the definition of contract itself. In taking the latter course, he was forced both to cast doubt upon the generalizing tendencies of contract doctrine and to underline the frequency of non-consensual obligation in the law.

The next step in the challenge was undertaken by those who argued that volition was often ignored even in supposedly pure contracts. It was Holmes's objective theory of contract put forth in *The Common Law* that ultimately provided the foundation for this move.[19] As we have seen, from the middle of the nineteenth century, judges and jurists had begun to retreat from the subjective theory on the ground that it undermined certainty and predictability as well as uniformity and consistency of legal results. In an increasingly national corporate economy, the goal of standardization of commercial transactions began to overwhelm the desire to conceive of contract law as expressing the subjective desires of individuals.

For a long while, however, objectivism was still primarily regarded not as in conflict with a will theory of contract but as necessarily supplementing it. For example,the function of judicial "interpretation and construction" of contracts, Holmes originally wrote, "is to work out, from what is expressly said and done, what would have been said with regard to events not definitely before the minds of the parties, if those events had been considered."[20] In this view, while the role of judicial interference and discretion was greatly expanded compared with a model of complete deduction from the parties' intentions, the principal source of guidance remained the actual intention of the parties.

This had led Mark DeWolfe Howe to ask whether Holmes did not actually follow the orthodox view and "allow subjectivism, in the end, to control his theory of contract?" "I take it that he did not," Howe concluded, and I agree.[21] And he proceeds to argue that Holmes "was urging a revolutionary change in legal thought."[22] "[T]he last of the contract lectures made it quite clear that Holmes saw the objective standard as no less controlling in the law of contract than it was in the law of torts and of crime," Howe declared.[23] His goal was an increased "concentration of analytic attention upon the formal and objective aspects of obligation and a reduced concern for the subjectivities of assent."[24]

Yet it is true that objectivism in contract law could be ambiguously understood as not necessarily in conflict with a theory based on a meeting of minds of the parties. And that is why, for a long time after Holmes wrote *The Common Law*, objectivism was not understood as a frontal assault upon the will theory itself.

It was Holmes who took the argument one step further. In three sentences in "The Path of the Law" (1897), which were as influential as any he wrote, he simply assumed that the very process of implying a contract or a term in a contract was an act of judicial legislation for reasons of policy. "You always can imply a condition in a contract," he wrote. "But why do you imply it?"

> It is because of some belief as to the practice of the community or of a class, or because of some opinion as to policy, or in short, because of some attitude of yours upon a matter not capable of exact quantitative measurement, and therefore not capable of founding exact logical conclusions.[25]

Here, for the first time, Holmes could not be understood ultimately to base contractual liability on the intentions of the parties. It is the revolutionary moment at which objectivism is finally recognized to be incompatible with a will theory of contracts.[26] In terms of the much discussed question of how a "paradigm shift" occurs, it is striking that Holmes did not even try to refute the dominant paradigm from an internal perspective but instead simply asserted that it was untrue. It was still possible, after all, to account for the process by which courts imply a contractual condition in terms of the more orthodox theory of contract interpretation he used in *The Common Law*.

Now, however, Holmes simply declared that when courts interpret or construe a contract, they impose some policy on the parties regardless of any supposed intention. The bright-line distinction between contract and quasi-contract that Keener had formulated just four years earlier was denied. There was no distinction between the interpretation of real contracts and those implied in law.

The influence of Holmes's assertion was overwhelming and became a standard point of departure in the unfolding attack on freedom of contract. In two articles in 1903 and 1904, Clarence Ashley directly challenged the "fetish of this favorite theory of mutual assent."[27] Where courts imply conditions in a contract, they "vigorously disclaim any idea of changing the contract of the parties and argue that by interpretation they find the intent of the parties," Ashley wrote, "but this is simply a convenient fiction, and the fact remains, that absence of intent is the basis on which these rules of court rest."[28] "As a matter of fact . . . in all these cases the courts have in reality made a new contract for the parties."[29] What objectivism actually means is that "there does not seem to be any difference . . . between the obligation of Tort and Contract. . . ."[30]

In 1907 George Costigan carried the implications of objectivism one step further. Teachers of contract law, he wrote, "are . . . obliged to tell our students that the 'meeting of minds' talked of in the contract cases is often a misnomer. . . ."[31] Objectivism in contract law means that "a meeting of the expressions of the parties . . . is enough to make a mutual assent contract despite the fact that in an accurate sense of the words the minds of the parties never meet at one and the same moment of time."[32]

In many articles attacking freedom of contract such as Ashley's, Keener's distinction between contract and quasi-contract seems to have been ignored for polemical purposes. Thus, Ashley continued to write as if contracts implied in law were indistinguishable from real contracts. Since in those cases courts could easily be shown to have "in reality made a new contract for the parties," he simply asserted that this was true for contracts in general. But perhaps Holmes took advantage of precisely the same ambiguity in his famous passage in "The Path of the Law."[33]

The first practical area of the law to bear the brunt of the attack on the will theory of contract was the law of agency, which had only recently grown in legal significance as the corporate form of business became dominant. The effort of late-nineteenth-century legal thinkers to unify most areas of agency law around will and meeting of minds had never completely succeeded, due perhaps to resistance of the judges to extending the will theory to the corporation. The law of agency thus became one of the major battlegrounds in the campaign to challenge the individualistic framework on which the constitutionalization of freedom of contract had been erected. In order to see this, we need first to see the relationship between agency law and the growth of large organizations.

The Law of Agency and the Growth of Organizational Society

The history of the law of agency is important for several reasons, both institutional and ideological. First, it is one of the best expressions of the emergence of organizational society and, in particular, of the growth of large corporations in the late nineteenth century. Until the rise of the corporation, the law governing the authority of agents for acts done to advance the interests of their principals was not a major area of the law. Economic specialization and organizational complexity moved agency law to center stage in the creation of Classical Legal Thought.

Several of the most important tensions involved in the emergence of organizational society converged around the law of agency. Within the corporation, agency law defined the extent to which superiors in the corporate hierarchy could exercise control over their subordinates. There was a trade-off between, on the one hand, corporate control of the behavior of employees and, on the other, the level of confidence that third parties would have in the legitimate authority of these employees. To the extent that courts restricted the authority of agents only to the most specific and express commands of their superiors, there could be tight control from above but also correspondingly little authority to deal with the outside world. If the requirement of evidence of actual authority became more stringent, therefore, the ability of the rest of the world to rely on the agent's authority would inevitably be reduced.

Agency law thus embodied a host of contradictory tendencies throughout the nineteenth century. Perhaps the most fundamental was that it sought to bring under one heading both the law of master and servant and the law of principal and agent. The first, *respondeat superior*, continued to represent a status-based liability derived from traditional notions of the identity of master and servant; the second, while it had always contained some consensual elements, tended during the late nineteenth century to push toward the outer limits of contractualism.

The starting point for the nineteenth-century law of agency is the publication of Joseph Story's famous treatise in 1839.[34] Its most striking feature is its failure to make the modern distinction between the bases of liability of the principal and of the master.[35] The liability of a principal for the contracts of her agent rested on grounds similar to the liability of the master for the torts of his servant.[36]

For late-nineteenth-century legal thinkers, who feared the extension of the strict liability tendencies of master-servant liability, it became necessary either to discredit the entire doctrine of *respondeat superior*, as Holmes sought to do,[37] or, at least, to create a substantial gulf between the two theories of liability. The law of principal and agent, they hoped, could be grounded largely in terms of consensual categories, and not be contaminated by the status-based or regulatory character of the master's tort liability.

Though one can find many points of tension in Story's treatise that foreshadow the future bifurcation of the field, the really important observation is that he was largely unconcerned with the issue. Only later in the century, when great increases in railroad and industrial injuries made the strict liability of the employer a central—and costly—concern, was there any strong inducement to radically separate the two fields.

The central legal issue for Story, as it continued to be for all later legal thinkers, was what constituted the authority conferred on the agent. As if to underline the still close relationship between master and servant and between principal and agent, Story wrote of the agent's authority as a kind of status. His basic division was between "general" and "special" authority. In the case of general authority, the principal was bound by the acts of his agent, "although he violates by those acts his private instructions and directions, which are given to him by the principal, limiting, qualifying, suspending, or prohibiting the exercise of such authority under particular circumstances."[38] For the agent with special authority, by contrast, the principal was not bound by acts exceeding that limited authority.

In the commercial world of Story's day, the embodiment of the general agent could be "familiarly seen in the common case of factors." [39] The factor, employed by a merchant to sell goods on consignment, was one of the earliest examples of the shift to commercial specialization in nineteenth-century America. "In the 1790's the general merchant . . . was still the grand distributor. . . . He was an exporter, wholesaler, importer, retailer, shipowner, banker, and insurer." [40] During the next fifty years, the all-encompassing functions of the general merchant began, one by one, to be subdivided into specialized commercial activities.

By 1815, the stupendous rise in the cotton trade expanded the importance of the factor. "The spread of commercial agricultural in the south encouraged commercial specialization in the east. The unprecedented volume of the cotton trade helped to make New York the nation's leading city and initiated the swift decline of the all-purpose general merchant." [41]

For Story, the factor was the model of the agent with general authority. "A third person has a right to assume," Story wrote, that a factor or a broker "has also an unqualified authority to act for his principal in all matters, which come within the scope of that employment." [42] The agent could bind the principal even in situations that exceeded his express or implied authority. The agent's power, Story wrote,

> extends farther, and binds the principal in all cases, where the agent is acting within the scope of his usual employment, or is held out to the public, or to the other party, as having competent authority, although in fact he has, in the particular instance, exceeded or violated his instructions, and acted without authority. For, in all such cases, where one of two innocent persons is to suffer, he ought to suffer, who misled the other into the contract, by holding out the agent, as competent to act, and as enjoying his confidence. [43]

We see, in this passage, the ambiguity that was to become central in late-nineteenth-century agency law. On the one hand, Story conceived of a general agency as a relatively fixed, well-known category defined by commercial practice. He did not hesitate to use "scope of employment" language later associated with a more extensive master-servant liability to define the authority of the agent. All those who dealt with the factor could legitimately assume that he possessed general authority, and could bind the principal even if "in the particular instance" he "exceeded or violated his instructions, and acted without authority." On the other hand, Story traced the justice of this rule to a kind of negligence in the principal, who "misled" the third party "by holding out the agent, as competent to act. . . . [44] Story also employed precisely the same "holding out" language to justify the liability of the master for the torts of his servant. Above all, the overwhelming concern of his treatise was with protecting the third party's stable expectations rather than with the individual culpability of the principal—"for otherwise, such secret instructions and orders would operate as a fraud upon the unsuspecting confidence and conduct of the other party." [45]

Story wrote his treatise just as a radical increase in business specialization was undermining the coherence of his simple distinction between general and special agents. "Little institutional innovation occurred in American business before the 1840s," Chandler has written.[46] Thereafter, "the much larger flows of a greater variety of goods" produced dramatic increases in specialization and impersonality in business arrangements.[47] Moreover, the small business partnership began to be replaced by the chartered, stock-issuing corporation and the self-employed worker by the wage-earning employee. Almost from the moment Story's treatise was published, judges and jurists struggled to free themselves from its categories.

If specialization undermined Story's categories, changes in the theory of tort liability of employers produced the far more threatening prospect of strict liability. When Story wrote, the dominant theory of *respondeat superior* still contained consensual elements. The "command theory" held the master liable for his servant's torts only if he had authorized the servant's acts.[48] The litmus test of this doctrine was that the master was not liable for the willful torts of the servant, since they were clearly outside of the master's control. But as the corporate employer replaced the personalized employment relation, courts began to resort to an objective "scope of employment" test, so that by the last quarter of the nineteenth century it had become largely irrelevant whether the master had commanded or authorized an employee to perform a particular act.[49] At this point, a status-based master-servant liability, largely exorcised of earlier consensual elements, had come to represent the anomaly of strict liability that Holmes protested against.[50] The uncritical ease with which Story had moved between the liability of masters and of principals was no longer possible.

If strict liability triggered the fear of arbitrary redistribution of wealth, the institution of contract expressed the individualistic ideal of completely private and voluntary transactions. Hence, the aspiration of late-nineteenth-century thinkers was to place the law of principal and agent on unmistakably contractual foundations. Their first step was to replace Story's "general" and "special" agents with the categories of "actual" and "apparent" authority.

Story's treatise went through nine editions by 1882 under the supervision of different editors. Until Francis Wharton published his own treatise in 1876,[51] no other general text on agency had appeared in America, though the subject of principal and agent had been treated in most contracts texts. By the time Wharton's work appeared, not only had a great gulf developed between the two subdivisions of Story's treatise but the decisions of courts had greatly undermined its structure.

By mid-century, the spread of specialization began to produce judicial resistance to the status-based framework that Story had erected for the law of agency. Judges started to insist that Story's distinction between general and special agents was "highly unsatisfactory, and will be found quite insufficient to solve a great variety of cases."[52] By 1866, in the fifth edition of his treatise on contract, Theophilus Parsons inserted, for the first time, a criticism of Story's classification and attacked its strong tendency to impose liability on principals.

> Of late years, courts seem more disposed to regard this distinction [between general and special agents] . . . as altogether subordinate to that principle which may be called the foundation of the law of agency; namely, that a principal is responsible,

either, when he has given to an agent sufficient authority, or, when he justifies a party dealing with his agent in believing that he has given to this agent this authority.[53]

Parsons thus sounded the major theme of all late-nineteenth-century efforts to reconceptualize agency law: that, in the words of an English judge, "No one can become the agent of another person except by the will of that other person."[54] Unless a principal either had actually authorized an agent to act or had negligently misled a third party into believing he had given such authority, he could not be bound.

The culmination of the effort to overthrow Story's categories and to root the law of agency directly in the will of the principal was Francis Wharton's *Commentary on the Law of Agency and Agents* (1876). Wharton was the first writer to acknowledge a clear bifurcation of the field between principal-agent and master-servant. This permitted him to confine the doctrine of *respondeat superior* so as to prevent its strict liability underpinnings from devouring the law of agency,

Even within tort law, Wharton sought to reduce the scope of strict master-servant liability. He posited a novel distinction between "agency" and "service" in which "the former relates to business transactions, in which there is more or less discretion allowed to the employee, while the latter relates to manual services, which the employee is, as a rule, obliged to perform under specific orders."[55] At the very moment at which the tort law, dominated by railroad accidents, was beginning to impose more extensive liability on employers for the torts of their employees, Wharton sought to restore an anachronistic "command" justification by grounding master-servant liability in the requirement of "specific orders." This move permitted him not only to reinterpret the employer's vicarious liability in terms of the will of the master but, even more important, it enabled him to shrink strict master-servant liability to cover only the very special case in which courts could plausibly merge the identities of master and servant.

The bifurcation of agency law permitted late-nineteenth-century jurists to divide the field along tort-contract lines. Whereas in the first half of the century agency had been treated as a separate and autonomous branch of law, by the end of the century it had become common to subsume the field within tort or contract treatises. Sir William Anson, one of the leading English contract writers of the late nineteenth century, defended this approach by insisting that the liability of a principal arises "not in virtue of any occult theory of representation" but through contract.[56]

Just as Wharton sought to separate sharply and to isolate the strict liability standard in master-servant law from the negligence standard in principal-agent law, he also completed the attack, begun by Parsons, on Story's classification of general and special agents. Story's framework, he wrote, "cannot be accepted without some modification." He approvingly quoted an English legal writer:

No principal can be held, by merely appointing one his agent, to guarantee the world against any undue assumption of powers on his part, or fraudulent abuse of the opportunities his agency may give him for deceiving others; and if, without [the principal's negligence], damage has accrued to a third party by the agent's assumption of authority or abuse of his position, the loss must fall on the party dealing with him.[57]

Thus, Wharton sought to reverse Story's virtually conclusive presumption that a general agent was "held out" to the world as authorized to bind the principal.

This effort to reverse Story's presumption, we have seen, arose in the midst of fundamental changes in the structure of business enterprise. In Story's day, there had usually existed a personal relationship between principal and agent, which the explosion of the business corporation did much to reverse. Especially in the railroad and banking fields, there were now large numbers of employees, serving in specialized roles and spread across large geographical areas, who had the power to misrepresent the scope of their authority.

This structural shift in business was highlighted in an important series of New York cases between 1856 and 1865, in which a sharply divided Court of Appeals argued over the authority to be imputed to agents who misappropriated various forms of negotiable paper—bank drafts, checks, bills of lading—that subsequently passed into the hands of innocent third parties. Typical cases were ones in which a bank teller erroneously certified that a drawee had deposited enough funds to pay his draft or in which a railroad employee issued a bill of lading for non-existent grain.[58] "In each of these cases," the New York Court of Appeals observed, "the extrinsic fact which constituted the condition of the authority was peculiarly within the agent's knowledge, and was necessarily represented to exist by the execution of the agent's powers."[59]

The division within the court turned on the realization that if a principal could be liable for the act of an agent who misrepresented his own authority, it was easy for an agent to defraud his principal. On the other hand, as one judge put it, as between an innocent third party and a principal who held out his agent as authorized to act, "who is to bear the consequences of this false and fraudulent representation of the agent?"[60]

Those who wished to bring the law of agency more closely into line with the will of the principal sought to distinguish the holding out situation from the agent's own enlargement of his authority. The "fundamental proposition," declared New York Justice George F. Comstock in 1856, ". . . is that one man can be bound only by the authorized acts of another. He cannot be charged because another holds a commission from him and falsely asserts that his acts are within it."[61] "The appearance of the power is one thing," he argued, "and for that the principal is responsible. The appearance of the act is another, and for that, if false, I think the remedy is against the agent only."[62] Comstock's formula for limiting the liability of principals was adopted by Theophilus Parsons in the 1857 edition of his contracts treatise and was repeated even after it had been rejected in New York.[63]

The distinction between a general "power" and a particular "act" was, however, difficult to apply to the most typical cases in which the agent fraudulently misrepresented some fact, such as whether there was actual property standing behind a bill of lading or actual deposits supporting a certified draft. "In truth," the New York court observed, "the power conferred in these cases, is of such a nature, that the agent cannot do an act, appearing to be within its scope of authority, without, as a part of the act itself, representing . . . that the condition exists upon which he has the right to act. Of necessity, the principal knows this fact, when he confers the power."[64] In fact, these cases permitted the New York courts to refuse to distinguish between master-servant and principal-agent liability. "The liability of principals for the negligence and for the frauds of their agents rests upon the same grounds," the New York court declared in 1862.[65] The principal was liable for the fraudulent misrepresentation of the agent for the same reason that the master was liable for the negligence of his servant.

The result of these decisions was that there was a substantial gap between the thrust of the case law and that of the treatise literature. After the Civil War, the case law moved decisively in the direction of holding an organization liable for an agent's contracts if a third party could reasonably have believed that the agent had authority, whether or not he actually did. The case law, in short, tended to hold that apparent, not actual, authority was sufficient to charge a principal. These decisions weakened internal control within the corporation but strengthened the ability of strangers to rely on the representation of its agents.

By contrast, the central effort of the treatise literature was to subordinate the law of agency to the law of contract and to emphasize that only actual authority could justify liability. In its emphasis on will, the legal literature sought, above all, to proclaim that contractual freedom was the foundation of the law of agency, and that the necessities of organizational life could not justifiably restrict individual autonomy.

How does one account for these differences? The first thing to note is that an objective standard—apparent authority—triumphed earlier in the law of agency than in any other field, leading one to suppose that there is a strong correlation between the rise of the corporation and the emergency of objective standards. Once it is realized that the individualistic underpinnings of the will theory were difficult to apply to large organizations—indeed, that the emergence of large organizations threatened to render the will theory impractical, if not virtually incoherent—it is no surprise that courts turned to an objective "reasonableness" standard. In general, there appears to be a strong correlation between the rise of the corporation and the emergence of an anti-individualistic objective theory in all fields of law.

But how does one explain the contrary thrust of the treatise literature? Perhaps this is a clue to one of the primary functions of the classical legal treatise, which sought not simply to report on the state of the law but to advance a highly abstract and integrated version that was grounded in a picture of a decentralized, individualistic economic and political order. Its most fundamental expression can be found in the set of ideas that constituted the doctrine of freedom of contract. It was here that the Progressive attack on Classical Legal Thought began.

Objectivism and the Law of Agency

One of the most surprising examples of the power of the contractual paradigm is the first law review article written by Arthur Corbin in 1906.[66] Soon to become a major influence on the development of Legal Realism and the preeminent figure in the subversion of the will theory in contract law, Corbin, in his first effort, argued for a completely orthodox subordination of the law of agency to contract doctrine.

As in contract law, after 1905, the supposed anomalies in the law of agency were used to discredit the will theory itself. The most widely accepted doctrine that did not fit into the will theory was the rule that an undisclosed principal was liable for his agent's contract. How could the principal be held liable, the defenders of orthodoxy asked, for a contract between his agent and a third party? Since the third party had entered into the contract with no knowledge that anyone but the agent was involved, there was no meeting of minds between the principal and the third party.

Courts had nevertheless widely enforced the liability of an undisclosed principal on the ground that it was unjust for him to receive a benefit without undertaking a corresponding burden. And in perhaps the last effort to justify agency doctrines exclusively in terms of the contractual assent of the parties, James Barr Ames, dean of the Harvard Law School, declared in 1909 that the liability of the undisclosed principal was an anomaly that "ignores . . . fundamental legal principles. . . ."[67] In his view, the law of agency was simply a subcategory of the law of contracts in which the will theory governed.

Perhaps the most practically significant area of controversy in agency law was the doctrine of "apparent authority." Under this doctrine, a principal could be liable if his agent held himself out as authorized to enter into a contract even if he had been conferred no actual authority. It was thus possible for a principal to be liable for acts of his agent that were actually contrary to his express will. How could such a doctrine be reconciled with the prevailing will theory of contract?

As we have seen, the doctrine of apparent authority had grown by leaps and bounds during the last two decades of the nineteenth century in response to the growing prominence of the corporate form in business relations. It reflected an increasing unwillingness of courts to allow corporations to disavow the actions of their employees on grounds of absence of actual authority.

The defenders of orthodoxy denied that there was any independent doctrine of apparent authority. Whether an actor has been authorized to do an act, Harvard Professor Joseph Beale wrote, "is purely a question of fact, depending solely upon evidence. The authorizing of an act by an agent is not the creation of a right; it depends solely upon the will of the party, not the law."[68] In other words, apparent authority differed from express authority only in terms of the kind of evidence used to prove the principal's state of mind. Both were in fact actual delegations of authority.

Beale's argument was simply a repetition of a debate about implied contracts that had been going on for a half century in America.[69] The publication of Keener's *Quasi-Contracts* (1893) is the ultimate evidence of orthodox acceptance of the view that implied contracts were not necessarily voluntary. Yet Beale sought to ground the parallel doctrine of apparent authority in a will theory that nobody any longer believed could unify the entire body of contract doctrine. It was only a matter of time before the argument was put forth that, just as implied contracts were not necessarily actual contracts, so too apparent authority was not necessarily based on actual authority.

It was one of the founders of Legal Realism, Walter Wheeler Cook, who first saw in 1905 that these judicial developments in the law of agency drew into question the much broader issue of the meaning of the existing contractual paradigm. Like Beale, Cook also argued that the doctrine of apparent authority was based on "a true contractual liability, as well where the authority of the agent is only apparent as where it is real; in other words, that the principal is bound because according to all sound principles he has entered into a contract with the third party."[70] Thus, Cook did not simply attempt to show that apparent authority was inconsistent with a theory of contract based on a meeting of minds. Rather, he proposed the more audacious view that since even "true contractual liability" was not based on actual assent, there was no reason why a contract-based agency law required such assent. Cook did not challenge Beale's assertion that agency principles were direct derivations from contract principles. Rather, he pushed much further and attacked the orthodox theory of contractual obligation itself.[71]

Cook thus drew into question once more the paramount issue of the voluntariness of the institution of contract. The dominant orthodox reaction to the criticism that many areas of contract were not based on a meeting of minds was represented by Keener's effort to redefine the contractual relationship simply to exclude all non-voluntary relations from its definition. But Cook returned to the Holmesian effort to objectivize contract law and carried the implications of that move one step further.

Contract law itself, Cook declared, was based on objectivism—"the principle of manifested intention."[72] As a result of this, contracts often "arise where there has been no mutual assent, no meeting of the minds of the parties, in fact."[73] Thus, in cases of apparent authority, the principal is liable only because he manifested an intention to be bound regardless of his actual intention.

Two years after Cook wrote, George Costigan challenged his conclusions. In the spirit of Keener, Costigan coined the term "constructive" to distinguish those contracts from "consensual" or "actual" contracts in which there was a real meeting of minds. And he declared that Cook was "in error" for confounding the two categories.[74]

Did this battle over terminology make any difference? Costigan, like Keener before him, seems, above all, to have wished to prove that there remained an oasis of voluntarism despite mounting instances of the non-voluntaristic interpretation of contract. Cook, by contrast, was inspired by the more revolutionary implications of objectivism, which, he believed, meant that most agreements bore little necessary relationship to a supposed actual intent of the parties. For Cook, there was no necessary realm of contract law based on a meeting of minds; for Costigan, there was.

For the next thirty years, these two perspectives confused the strategies of those attacking the will theory of contract. For some, the effort was to show that most areas of contract in fact were based on regulatory tort principles. For others, like Cook, the ultimate goal was to show that the institution of contract law itself did not need to be based on any actual will of the parties. Ultimately, these two positions merged when the outer limits of objectivism were seen to leave no basis for any clear distinction between contract and tort.[75]

The issue ultimately turned on whether tort principles could be said to be distinguishable from contract. In 1909, William Draper Lewis directly challenged Ames's assertion that the liability of the undisclosed principal was an anomaly that "ignores . . . fundamental legal principles."[76] The basis of liability in contracts, Lewis argued, following Holmes, was "not the promise of the defendant, but the fact that one man has caused another to do or not to do an act for a stipulated benefit."[77] Since the basis of contract was not will but benefit, there was no anomaly in holding an undisclosed principal liable for a beneficial relationship, regardless of whether he promised anything. Socially imposed duties in tort had begun to consume contract.

Agency thus became the first area of the law to feel the full force of the attack on the will theory of contract. And it was not an accident that the attack should have begun here. The corporate form had become dominant precisely at the moment when legal theorists began their efforts to unify and integrate legal theory around the ideas of contract and will. On the one hand, the corporation made agency law more significant than ever, since the corporation necessarily pursued business through agents. On the other hand, the corporation subverted the fundamentally individualistic assumptions behind the law of agency. Who was the principal whose will determined the scope of authority of a corporate agent? How could the will of a corporation be determined? In their efforts to apply the law of agency to corporations, pragmatically inclined judges turned to the doctrine of apparent authority to express a presumption that the agent acted in pursuance of the corporate will.

The corporate form thus forced judges to objectivize legal concepts, to look for the reliance of a "reasonable person" rather than the actual subjective (or particular) command of a principal. Indeed, the influence of the corporate form on the law of agency ran parallel to its tendency in the law of contract to promote an objective standard. Both trends ultimately expressed the same set of perceptions about legal and economic relationships. An increasingly organized, well-structured, and concentrated economy placed a premium on order, predictability, and standardization of transactions. Objectivism was the legal expression of this quest for uniformity. It shifted legal inquiry away from a focus on actual intent or will toward a concern with reasonable, average, or customary practices. Protecting

the eccentric individual will—for, ultimately, that is the principal difference between subjective and objective legal standards—came to be overshadowed by the
desire to ensure that the rest of the world could rely upon uniform and predictable
legal consequences.

In agency law, as in contract theory generally, the move toward objectivism
was first defended on the ground that it was simply the closest practical expression
of the subjective will of the parties. But, by degrees, objectivism came to be
understood as in fundamental conflict with the premises of individualism. Legal
writers began to see that there was little difference between, on the one hand, an
objective theory of contract and, on the other, tort duties imposed by the state.
So when Holmes declared in 1897 that courts imply contractual conditions "because of some belief as to the practice of the community or of a class, or because
of some opinion as to policy,"[78] he was expressing the revolutionary conclusion
that the institution of contract itself was subordinate to social and political goals.
Duties deriving from contract and tort could not be distinguished in terms of the
source of obligation. In both cases, collective social objectives might legitimately
overrule the individual will.

In both contract and agency law, the attacks on the will theory crystallized
into a new legal theory during the second decade of the twentieth century. The
central figure in contract law was Arthur Corbin of Yale Law School, who, like
many transplanted Westerners of this period, brought an earthy, pragmatic skepticism to his intellectual work.[79] Their experience seemed to confirm their suspicion of large, abstract, and integrated theories that they associated with Eastern
elegance and conceptualism. In law, in fact, there was a strong correlation between Eastern anglophilism and the effort to synthesize and formalize legal doctrine in the late nineteenth century.[80]

Corbin's writing in contract is perhaps the ultimate legal expression of the
pragmatic temperament at work, though if he had even heard of William James
or John Dewey, I doubt that Corbin would have cared much for their high-toned
philosophizing. Indeed, Corbin never even bothered formally to argue against the
will theory. Rather it appears that he simply felt that it no longer made much
sense as a way of organizing legal ideas. As John Dewey observed, "[I]ntellectual
progress usually occurs through sheer abandonment of questions together with
both of the alternatives they assume—an abandonment that results from their
decreasing vitality and a change of urgent interest. We do not solve them: [W]e
get over them."[81]

In a series of monumentally influential articles on particular aspects of contract law between 1912 and 1918, which ultimately formed the foundation of his
famous treatise, Corbin worked out the implications of Holmes's critiques of orthodox contract theory. He began by asserting that "an obligation to pay damages
for breach of contract is created by the law and not by the agreement."[82] Like
Walter Wheeler Cook, his colleague at Yale, Corbin refused to accept Keener's
effort to preserve a realm of pure contract. "A quasi-contract cannot be distinguished from a contract or tort on the ground that the obligation is created by the

law. All enforcible obligations are created by the law."[83] "[T]he law itself, independently of the expressed will of the parties," often imposes conditions on the enforcement of contracts. "In such cases," Corbin wrote, "the legal requirement is based upon principles of justice, policy, and right, and not on the expressed will of the parties."[84]

An objective theory of contract could not be regarded as simply the best practical approximation of the actual will of the parties, for the law often does not even "create that relation which the parties would have intended had they foreseen. The fact is . . . that the decision will depend upon the notions of the court as to policy, welfare, justice, right and wrong, such notions often being inarticulate and subconscious."[85]

As "policy, welfare, justice, right and wrong" were substituted as the foundation of contract law, the orthodox effort of the previous generation to distinguish sharply between contract and tort principles began to disintegrate. It was no longer possible to preserve such bright-line categories in order to maintain a pure realm of individual autonomy and unfettered control over one's destiny.

The cutting edge of all efforts to continue to insist upon a sharp distinction between contract and tort was the doctrine of privity of contract. Since judicial decision making had never managed completely to accommodate itself to the will theory, perhaps the most threatening contract law anomaly was the doctrine that a third party could sue on a contract made for his or her benefit even though this person had not participated in the agreement. Since there was no privity and hence no meeting of minds between the promisor and the third party, will theorists reasoned that it violated the underlying rationale of contract.

For Corbin, however, policy, welfare, justice, right and wrong supplied the missing ingredient to justify the suit of the third-party beneficiary. "To many students and practitioners of the common law," he declared, *"privity of contract became a fetish. As such, it operated to deprive many a claimant of a remedy in cases where according to the mores of the time the claim was just."*[86]

The result of Corbin's writing was not only to deny that there was any coherent boundary between tort and contract but, ultimately, to bring into question whether there was any meaningful distinction between public and private law. If for orthodox social theorists of the late nineteenth century the institution of contract was the purest legal expression of a regime of private self-determination free from the dangers of collectivism and regulation, Corbin's Progressive legal theory denied that even contract law embodied a pure realm of individual autonomy. In this sense, all law was a reflection of collective determination, and thus inherently regulatory and coercive.

Corbin was not an original thinker. He took the large ideas and insights of others and worked them into concrete legal rules with care and precision. His ability to abide contradiction and his large dose of Western pragmatism and good sense made him the perfect vehicle for shaping the Progressive legal critique into a practical system that was easily accessible to unspeculative judges and practioners. Corbin's success lay in his appeal to their undogmatic common sense. Yet, since "common sense" is itself an historically changing category, Corbin's unrivaled influence is perhaps the best measure we have of the extent to which ordinary lawyers could no longer find in their own experiences of the world a clear distinction between public and private realms.

What Corbin did for contract law, Warren Seavey of Harvard Law School did for agency law. In an influential article, "The Rationale of Agency" (1920), Seavey brought together the twin strands of the Progressive critique of contract and agency law.[87] He explained both the doctrine of apparent authority and the liability of an undisclosed principal as "powers created by law irrespective of the intent of the parties."[88] Defending these doctrines against the charge of Ames and Pollock that they were anomalies, he saw the liability of undisclosed principals as resting on "an obligation created by law . . . based upon the justice of the situation. . . ."[89] Analogizing it to the third-party beneficiary doctrine that Corbin had defended in contract law, Seavey saw the undisclosed principal rule as expressing a "sort of common law equity."[90]

For Seavey, the doctrine of apparent authority illustrated the "power of an agent to subject his principal to a contractual duty when acting contrary to his instructions."[91] Thus, the law of agency, like the law of contract, was based not on private law but on social conceptions of "justice." "In all the cases where an agent exceeds his authority, one of two persons, both innocent, must suffer. Between these two classes of persons, we must select the class which, in the long run, should suffer."[92]

The most significant feature of Seavey's mode of justification of the liability of the principal was that it was close to various theories of "enterprise liability" that were simultaneously being put forth in tort.[93] Indeed, Seavey brought together categories that had previously occupied entirely different realms. Beginning with Holmes's attack on the liability of the master for the torts of the servant, there had been various attempts to justify the doctrine of *respondeat superior* on the ground that corporate enterprise could best bear the risk of loss.[94] That Seavey should have seen no problem in advancing an argument developed in tort to justify a supposedly contractually based liability is a striking measure of the extent to which Progressive legal thought had brought the distinction between contract and tort to the verge of collapse.

The Doctrine of Objective Causation

At the conceptual center of all late-nineteenth-century efforts to construct a system of private law free from the dangers of redistribution was the idea of objective causation. In tort law especially, where the dangers of social engineering had long been feared, the idea of objective causation played a central role in preventing the infusion of politics into law.

If tort law was to be private law, legal thinkers reasoned, its central legitimating function had to be corrective justice, the restoration of the status quo that existed before any infringement of a person's right. The plaintiff in a tort action should recover only because of an unlawful interference with his or her right, not because of any more general public goals of the state.

The idea of vindication of individual rights was intimately connected with the notion of objective causation. Only if it was possible to say objectively that A caused B's injury would courts be able to take money from A and give damages to B without being charged with redistribution. Without objective causation, a court might be free to choose among a variety of possible defendants in order to vindicate the plaintiff's claim. If the question of which of several acts caused the plaintiff's injury was open to judicial discretion, how could private law stay clear of the dangers of the political uses of law for purposes of redistribution?

There were two basic metaphors used by legal thinkers to express the idea of objective causation. The first was the notion of a distinction between "proximate" cause and "remote" cause. This idea had worked its way into the common law from Lord Bacon's *Maxims of the Law*, the first of which was: *In jure non remota causa, sed proxima spectatur* ("In law, look to proximate, not remote, causes").[95] The second, related notion, taken over from the natural sciences, was that there were objective "chains of causation" from which judges could determine scientifically which acts in a complicated series of events actually caused the plaintiff's injury. A number of related legal doctrines also sought to classify situations in which separate acts constituted "intervening" or "supervening" causes sufficient to break the "chain" and hold another defendant liable. But, above all, it was necessary to find a single scientific cause and thus a single responsible defendant, for any acknowledgement of multiple causation would open the floodgates of judicial discretion.

The earliest attacks on this system of causation can be traced back to the 1870s and to efforts of young American philosphers to counter a growing movement in America toward philosophical idealism.

Along with his fellow members of the informal Metaphysical Club, Oliver Wendell Holmes, Jr., "had come very early to share their deep distrust and antagonism to the *a priori* categories of Kant and the conceptual dialectic of Hegel. A philosophy of law, an analysis of legal history, which was built on Kantian or Hegelian foundations must be repudiated and cast aside."[96] Together with future Harvard philosophers William James, Charles Peirce, and Chauncey Wright, Holmes shared membership in the Metaphysical Club with a young instructor at Harvard Law School named Nicholas St. John Green.

In the midst of his Metaphysical Club speculations in 1870, Green published an article in the recently established *American Law Review* on "Proximate and Remote Cause," which, so far as I know, was by far the earliest direct challenge to orthodox legal notions of objective causation and was not to be repeated for fifty years. Green disputed the fundamental Baconian maxim that the law could objectively distinguish between proximate and remote causes in order to assign legal liability in a nondiscretionary manner. "The phrase 'chain of causation,' . . . embodies a dangerous metaphor," wrote Green.

It raises in the mind an idea of one determinate cause, followed by another determinate cause, created by the first, and that followed by a third created by the second, and so on, one succeeding another till the effect is reached. The causes are pictured as following one upon the other in time, as the links of a chain follow one upon the other in space. There is nothing in nature which corresponds to this. Such an idea is a pure fabrication of the mind.[97]

There is no single, objective, proximate cause, Green argued. "To every event there are certain antecedents. . . . It is not any one of this set of antecedents taken by itself which is the cause. No one by itself would produce the effect. The true cause is the whole set of antecedents taken together."[98]

In a passage typical of those that have led historians to see the roots of pragmatism and skepticism in these early speculations of the Metaphysical Club,[99] Green declared: "When the law has to do with abstract theological belief, it will be time to speculate as to what abstract mystery there may be in causation; but as long as its concern is confined to practical matters it is useless to inquire for mysteries which exist in no other sense than the sense in which every thing is a mystery."[100] "When [courts say that] this damage is remote, it does not flow naturally, it is not proximate," he wrote four years later, "all they mean, and all they can mean, is, that under all the circumstances they think the plaintiff should not recover. They did not arrive at that conclusion themselves by reasoning with those phrases, and by making use of them in their decision they do not render that decision clearer to others."[101]

It is important to note nevertheless that Green did not dispute the possibilities of objective causation in the physical sciences, where "there is a search for what may with some propriety, perhaps, be called the proximate cause." In the sciences, he conceded, it was possible to use causation as "not an absolute but a relative term," signifying "the nearest known cause considered in relation to the effect, and in contrast to some more distant cause."[102]

Green surveyed the uses of causation in various fields of law to demonstrate how courts manipulated the terms "proximate" and "remote" to accomplish other purposes. In contract cases, courts employed these terms to determine what damages might "reasonably be supposed to have been contemplated by the parties." In negligence cases, "misconduct is called the proximate cause of those results which a prudent foresight might have avoided." But above all, there is "no settled rule" in tort because the determination of causation "often var[ies] in proportion to the misconduct, recklessness, or wantonness of the defendant."[103] In law, moral conceptions constantly intruded upon scientific ones.

Green thus not only anticipated Holmes's famous "prediction theory" of law.[104] He also previewed what a half-century later would be the most powerful argument of the Legal Realists against the continued insistence of legal orthodoxy upon the objective character of causation in law: that because judges and jurists inevitably imported moral ideas into their determinations of legal causation, they were making discretionary policy determinations under the guise of doing science.

There are many reasons why the later Legal Realists' critique of causation doctrine largely succeeded while Green's challenge seems to have been ignored. In the realm of ideas, however, one important difference between the two periods stands out. While Green was prepared to concede that the notion of objective causation "may with some propriety" be used in the physical sciences, his Legal Realist successors were to witness an internal challenge to causation in the natural sciences themselves. Without pretensions to scientific foundations, legal conceptions of objective causation became increasingly vulnerable.

Though we may pay tribute to Green's prescience and originality, his direct influence on legal doctrine seems to have been non-existent. If we are to find Green's influence, we must trace it through a more indirect process by which a number of his perceptions were taken up by others and gradually accumulated into a critical whole. Prescient and original as Green was, if he is to be allowed any measure of immortality, it must be either specifically through his effect on Holmes or, more generally, because of his contributions to the development of pragmatism.

Causation and Ideology

The underlying ideological issues in the controversy over legal causation were directly confronted in 1874, four years after Green wrote, by the orthodox treatise writer Francis Wharton. The recent appearance of John Stuart Mill's *Autobiography*, Wharton wrote, had "revived" "the controversy on Causation originally stirred up by the publication of Mill's *System of Logic* (1843).[105] "The doctrine advocated by . . . Mill, that the cause of an event is the sum of all its antecedents," Wharton argued, was "irreconcilable with the principles of Roman and of Anglo-American law." Besides, he maintained, the inevitable result of a doctrine of multiple causation was "communism."[106]

Wharton's major argument was that the theory of causation was different in law than it was in the natural sciences. "[P]hysicists who treat all antecedents as causes, and who can only judge of material forces, can afford no aid to jurisprudence when it undertakes to distinguish those conditions which are material, and therefore merely consecutive, from those which are moral and causal."[107] Given the fact that the scientific definition of causation "has not, with rare exceptions, been considered, by Anglo-American courts, to call even for discussion, this shows that so far as concerns practical life, the materialistic view of causation has no ground on which to stand."[108]

Thus far, it should be noticed, Wharton's main strategy was simply to dissociate legal causation from scientific causation. There was not yet an attempt to argue that the claims of legal science can or should be grounded on those of the natural sciences. For Wharton, the distinctively legal emphasis on moral causation was connected with the search for a free agency among the multiple antecedent causes. By the "levelling of all antecedents to the same parity," but not only failing to "distinguish between physical and moral forces" by also neglecting to "requir[e] that physical forces be directed in conformity with moral law," Mill was "denying man's moral primacy over and responsibility for nature. . . ."[109]

The result was "the practical communism which this theory of the causal character of all antecedents promotes."[110]

> "Here is a capitalist among these antecedents; he shall be forced to pay." The capitalist, therefore, becomes liable for all disasters of which he is in any sense the condition, and the fact that he thus is held liable, multiplies these disasters. Men become prudent and diligent by the consciousness that they will be made to suffer if they are not prudent and diligent. If they know that they will not be made to suffer for their neglects; if they know that though the true cause of a disaster, they will be passed over in order to reach the capitalist who is a remoter condition, then they will cease to be prudent. . . . No factory would be built. . . . Making the capitalist liable for everything, therefore, would end in making the capitalist, as well as the non-capitalist, liable for nothing; for there would be soon no capitalist to be found to be sued.[111]

This seemingly sudden leap that Wharton makes from the technical question of legal causation to his warning of the destruction of capitalism is startling only if one fails to understand the systemic character of legal thought in the late nineteenth century.

Mill himself had attacked the existing doctrine of objective causation because it was associated with German idealist metaphysics, which he later noted was

> in these times, the great intellectual support for false doctrines and bad institutions. . . . There never was such an instrument devised for consecrating all deepseated prejudices. It is the main doctrinal pillar of all the areas which impede human improvement. And the chief strength of this false philosophy in the departments of morals and religion lies in the appeal which it is accustomed to make to the evidence of mathematics and of the cognate branches of physical science.[112]

Wharton's defense of objective causation and his insistence on a single responsible legal cause were repeated by all late-nineteenth-century treatise writers. For Wharton's generation, the ideas of moral causation and of free agency were still regarded as intelligible and objective a priori categories. That Nicholas St. John Green alone could argue that the confusion of scientific and moral notions was precisely what made legal doctrines about causation unintelligible is evidence of his premature skepticism. In the 1870s few were prepared to agree that the infusion of moralism into law made it political. Indeed, it was the amoral that Wharton identified with communism. By the end of the nineteenth century, however, orthodox legal thinkers would begin to downplay the moral element in causation while emphasizing the scientific basis of objective causation in law. As they thereby implicitly conceded their own growing skepticism about the objectivity of moral categories, they also laid themselves open for the final assault on causation by the Legal Realist heirs of Nicholas Green, who could now show not only the illicit moralism of legal causation but the collapse of causation in the natural sciences as well.

There were few occasions before the twentieth century when the ideological problems underlying the question of objective causation burst forth with the clarity of a Green or a Wharton. By and large, orthodox judges and jurists continued to invoke the metaphors of "chains of causation" and "natural and probable consequences" as if these were concepts capable of objective determination.

But the skepticism of Green found another channel: the prediction theory of law articulated by Oliver Wendell Holmes, Jr. There are two separate elements in Holmes's theory. The first, expressed by his famous aphorism from "The Path of the Law" (1897), is that "[t]he prophecies of what the courts will do in fact, and nothing more pretentious, are what I mean by the law."[113] Indeed, as early as in his Harvard University lectures of 1871–1872, Holmes first expressed a similar idea virtually contemporaneously with Green's, which does suggest a reciprocal influence between Green and Holmes. Above all, Holmes's emphasis on the probabilistic nature of prediction was an effort to deny the claims of the legal system to logical or "mathematical" certainty.[114]

But there was another similar but far more practically significant shift to a prediction theory in Holmes's thought: his emphasis on foresight in the law of torts. Not only is Green's influence quite clear here but, as we shall see, the function of foresight in both Green and Holmes was to avoid the problems inherent in any claims to objectivity in legal cause.

A shift to foresight as a substitute for natural sequence had begun to appear in the case law of the 1860s. By the early 1870s, there were already "two views," Wharton noted, concerning liability for negligence:

> The first view is that a person is liable for all the consequences which flow in ordinary natural sequences from his negligence; the second, that he is liable for all the consequences that could be foreseen as likely to occur.[115]

Wharton opposed the foreseeability view and insisted on "ordinary natural sequence" as the basis for determining causation and hence liability. "If the consequence flows from any particular negligence according to ordinary natural sequence, without the intervention of any independent human agency, then such consequence, whether foreseen as probable or unforeseen, is imputable to the negligence."[116]

More than any other writer, Wharton was responsible for clearly formulating the orthodox view of objective causation that would continue to dominate late-nineteenth-century legal thought. Only a half century later would legal critics derisively refer to this formula as "negligence in the air."[117]

By that time, the idea of negligence as a relational concept had completely triumphed, and the notion of objective causation had begun to disintegrate. While he himself was something of a transitional figure with respect to the moralistic foundations of negligence, Wharton basically continued to draw on the earlier notion that it was simply just to hold immoral actors liable for the proximate consequences of their acts.

For the late nineteenth century, one judicial decision stood out as a radical rejection of the idea of objective causation; and every treatise writer, including Wharton, was forced to take a stand on its merits. In *Ryan v. New York Central Railroad* (1866),[118] the New York Court of Appeals had held that a railroad that negligently caused a fire was liable only to the owner of an immediately adjacent house and not to more distant owners whose houses were destroyed by the spreading fire.

The court had employed traditional language in rejecting the claim of the second-house owner. Only the destruction of the first house was the proximate result of the railroad's negligence; all of the remaining injuries were remote, the court declared. Yet, even the use of traditional language offered little comfort to believers in the nondiscretionary and self-executing character of the orthodox categories. The result, limiting liability to the first house, seemed contrary to any commonsense understanding of the difference between proximate and remote consequences. And even more important, the court spent far more time explaining why any other result "would . . . create a liability which would be the destruction of all civilized society."[119]

The New York court, Judge Thomas Cooley contemptuously noted, was "apparently . . . more influenced in their decision by the fact that the opposite doctrine 'would subject to a liability against which no prudence could guard, and to meet which no private fortune would be adequate,' than by a strict regard to the logic of cause and effect."[120]

The decision in *Ryan* is one of many in the period after 1840 limiting the liability of the agents of economic growth, especially the railroad. Yet, the typical judicial strategies for extending entrepreneurial immunity had rarely dealt so cynically with the idea of causation. Even though virtually all judges and jurists of the nineteenth century had also promoted doctrines limiting entrepreneurial liability, the *Ryan* decision remained an outcast throughout the entire period.[121]

The explanation gives us some insight into the relative autonomy of legal ideas. The conception of objective causation was too central to the legitimation of the entire system of private law for it to be abandoned even in the interest of erecting another barrier to entrepreneurial liability. Many judges, to be sure, manipulated the proximate-remote distinction in other cases to limit entrepreneurial liability, but few did so as brazenly as in *Ryan*, threatening to bring the entire intellectual system into disrepute.

Wharton seems to have come closer than any treatise writer to defending the *Ryan* decision. While never explicitly endorsing it, he did cite it as illustrative of the slightly different orthodox principle that the intervention of an "independent responsible human agency" relieves a negligent defendant from liability.[122] "If a house is properly built, if it is properly watched, if a proper fire apparatus is in operation, it can be prevented, when a fire approaches from a neighboring detached house, from catching the fire."[123] From this Wharton seems to have concluded that the owner of the second house was, in effect, contributorily negligent and thus produced a break in the chain of causation. But unlike the court in *Ryan*, even Wharton recognized a Michigan court's assertion that without an intervening cause, "the principle of justice, or sound logic . . . is very obscure, which can exempt the party through whose negligence the first building was burned from equal liability for the burning of the second." [124]

Wharton thus sought to absorb the *Ryan* case into his own orthodox paradigm of objective causation. Indeed, he devoted considerable energy to demonstrating the terrible consequences of failing to relieve entrepreneurs of liability when an intervening cause broke the negligent chain of causation.

"Whether a railroad company is to be liable for all fires of which its locomotives are the occasion," he wrote, "is a question . . . important to the industrial interests of the land. . . ." [125] Unless abutting landowners are "held to be personally responsible for the consequences of placing combustible materials by the side of a railroad," the "noncapitalists" will be "skipped over" and "the rich corporation" will be "attacked." [126]

> Capital, by this process is either destroyed, or is compelled to shrink from entering into those large operations by which the trade of a nation is built up. We are accustomed to look with apathy at the ruin of great corporations, and to say, "well enough, they have no souls, they can bear it without pain, for they have nothing in them by which pain can be felt." But no corporation can be ruined without bringing ruin to some of the noblest and most meritorious classes of the land. Those who first give the start to such corporations are men of bold and enterprising qualities, kindled, no doubt, in part by self-interest, but in part also by the delight which men of such type feel in generous schemes for the development of public resources, and the extension to new fields of the wealth and industry of the community. Those who come in, in the second place, to lend their means to such enterprises after these enterprises appear to be reliable objects of investment, are the "bloated bond-holders," consisting of professional men of small incomes, and widows and orphans whose support is dependent on the income they draw from the modest means left to them by their friends. Nor is it these alone who are impoverished by the destruction of the corporations of which I here speak. The corporation may itself be soulless, and those investing in it may deserve little sympathy, but those whom it employs are the bone and sinew of the land. There is no railroad, no manufacturing company that does not spend three-fourths of its income in the employment of labor. When the corporation's income ceases, then the labor is dismissed. We hear sometimes of the cruelty of the eviction of laborers from their cottages at a landlord's caprice. But there are no evictions which approach in vastness and bitterness to those which are caused by the stoppage of railway improvements or of manufacturing corporations; in few cases is there such misery to the laboring classes worked, as when one of these great institutions is closed. I think I may, therefore, safely say that the question before us relates eminently to the industrial interests. [127]

It was the doctrine of independent, intervening causes on which Wharton staked his entire hopes for limiting entrepreneurial liability within the orthodox paradigm of objective causation. And it was here that the emerging doctrine of foreseeability seemed to him to pose the greatest danger. "The consequence" of any foreseeability test, Wharton wrote, "would be that the capitalist would be obliged to bear the burden, not merely of his own want of caution, but of the

want of caution of all who should be concerned in whatever he should produce."
If courts could argue that even intervening causes of an injury were foreseeable,
the result "would be traced back until a capitalist is reached. . . . If this law be
good, no man of means could safely build a steam engine, or even a house."[128]
But whether or not the choice between natural sequence and foreseeability tests
had, in fact, any real effect on aggregate levels of liability, it is clear that any
formulation of causation in terms of foresight presented major dangers.

We have already seen that Wharton regarded the natural sequence idea as a
major intellectual barrier against multiple causation, which he identified as leading to communism. But Wharton also saw an entirely different threat emanating
from any reliance on a foreseeability test: the potential of redistribution through a
theory of strict liability. There existed

> certain necessary though dangerous trades, of which we can say statistically that in
> them will be sacrificed prematurely the lives not merely of those who voluntarily
> engage in them, but of third persons not so assenting. Yet in such cases (e.g. gas
> factories and railroads), we do not hold that liability for such injuries attaches to
> those who start the enterprise foreseeing these consequences.[129]

In a statistical world, Wharton saw, any foreseeability test would lead to the
conclusion that all risks were predictable in the aggregate. Indeed, though he was
not alarmed at the prospect, Green saw similar results from a shift to a prediction
theory and noted that "[w]ith events of this kind, underwriters deal."[130]

In a world of randomness, where there is no necessary connection between
particular causes and effects, all we can hope to do is statistically to correlate acts
and consequences in the aggregate. Wharton's individualistic notions of moral
causation and free agency had begun to yield to a world of probabilities and statistical correlations.[131]

When, in 1897, Holmes declared that in law "the man of the future is the
man of statistics and the master of economics,"[132] he already clearly understood
the implication that flowed from the radical change in the conception of responsibility that a prediction theory entailed. Earlier, in *The Common Law* (1881),
Holmes had opposed turning the state into "a mutual insurance company against
accidents" that would "distribute the burden of its citizens' mishaps among all its
members." Not only was "state interference . . . an evil, where it cannot be
shown to be a good"; more important, "the undertaking to redistribute losses simply on the ground that they resulted from the defendant's act" would "offend the
sense of justice," since it was based on "the coarse and impolitic principle that a
man acts always at his peril."[133]

Now, however, he recognized both the pressure of organized labor for worker's
compensation laws and "the inclination of a very large part of the community
. . . to make certain classes of persons insure the safety of those with whom they
deal." Most injuries

> with which our courts are kept busy today are mainly incidents of certain well-
> known businesses. They are injuries to person or property by railroads, factories,
> and the like. The liability for them is estimated, and sooner or later goes into the

price paid by the public. The public really pays the damages, and the question of liability, if pressed far enough, is really the question [of] how far it is desirable that the public should insure the safety of those whose work it uses.[134]

Without objective causation, the problem of assigning liability had become simply a question of the fairness of the distribution of risks, "a concealed half conscious battle on the question of legislative policy." Liability for injury had become just another cost of doing business, which could be estimated, insured against, and ultimately included in "the price paid by the public." The individualistic world of Wharton's moral causation and free agency had begun to be transformed into a world of liability insurance in which the legislative question of who should pay would ultimately undermine the self-contained, individualistic categories of private law.

With the movement for workers' compensation after 1910,[135] the shift to a statistical or actuarial conception of risk came to be allied with a new vision of causation as probabilistic. Beginning in the 1920s, Legal Realists began the final assault on the citadel of objective causation.

The lightning rod for criticism of the old order in this area, as in many others, was Harvard Law School Professor Joseph Beale, who in 1920 offered a formalistic defense of orthodox doctrine.[136] "The rules . . . formulated by Beale," Hart and Honoré have written, "were presented in a terminology of mechanical 'forces.' " "[I]t is impossible not to sympathize with the wish to cut loose from the tradition which gave such rules birth." The "appearance of defining proximate cause in factual, policy-neutral terms was little more than a sham."[137]

In the midst of widespread attacks on courts in worker injury cases, Progressives not only sought to take these cases out of the judicial system entirely; they also wished to undermine and subvert legal doctrines that enabled judges confidently to withdraw cases from juries. Just as an entire literature developed attacking the defenses of contributory negligence and assumption of risk[138]—two other major doctrines that permitted judges to rule in favor of defendants as "a matter of law"—so too did causation become a target of those who wished to deprive the judge of any naive confidence that causation could be invoked on a neutral, objective, or scientific basis. The result was that by the time the Realist revolution had run its course, causal doctrines were substantially deprived of their power to take cases from ordinarily pro-plaintiff juries.[139]

The challenge to the objectivity of causation by the Legal Realists highlighted several important themes. The notion that there were objective chains of causation with intervening and supervening causes—Beale's "mechanistic" theory—usually had operated within the legal system to favor corporate defendants over plaintiffs. Like many other questions involving jury control, traditional causation doctrine gave judges a scientific and objective basis for refusing to submit a case to a normally pro-plaintiff jury. "Courts know very well that juries are inclined to be sympathetic to plaintiffs and less so to defendants. . . . When . . . it submits the case to the jury, [the court knows] full well that its verdict may be impelled . . . by entirely extra-legal and prejudicial items."[140] To the extent that a court was able to refuse to submit a case to the jury on the grounds that there was no causation, therefore, it could deprive the plaintiff of a victory. By contrast, "if the court has decided to submit a case to the jury, it has already decided in the plaintiff's favor the only real issue of proximate cause. . . ."[141]

The article that launched the Legal Realist attack on the orthodox theory of causation was written by Henry Edgerton, professor of law at George Washington University and soon to become a major New Deal figure on the U.S. Court of Appeals for the District of Columbia.[142] He was followed by Leon Green, who, starting with his *Rationale of Proximate Cause* (1927), soon came to dominate the Legal Realist approach to the issue.[143] Green combined persistent attacks on the "legal theology" of objective causation with an insistence that the question of proximate cause needed to be determined not by judges but by juries.

The Legal Realist challenge to orthodox conceptions of causation came to a head in one of the most famous cases ever decided, *Palsgraf v. Long Island Railroad* (1928).[144] In an opinion by Judge Benjamin N. Cardozo, the New York Court of Appeals reversed a lower court judgment in favor of a plaintiff who had been injured after a bizarre series of events. The question was whether the plaintiff could recover after an explosion at one end of a Long Island Railroad station overturned a scale that fell on the plaintiff, who was standing at the other end of the platform. The explosion occurred when a railroad guard pushed a passenger into a crowded train and accidentally knocked a package of fireworks he was carrying onto the tracks.

Judge William S. Andrews's dissenting opinion, in favor of the plaintiff, was as clear a statement of the Legal Realist position on causation as any ever uttered by a judge. The explosion was clearly the actual or "but for" cause of the injury, Andrews explained. "A boy throws a stone into a pond. The ripples spread. The water level rises. The history of that pond is altered to all eternity."[145] The real issue, however, is how to limit responsibility for these infinite consequences through some idea of proximate cause:

> What we . . . mean by the word "proximate" is, that because of convenience, of public policy, of a rough sense of justice, the law arbitrarily declines to trace a series of events beyond a certain point. This is not logic. It is practical politics. . . . It is all a question of expediency. There are no fixed rules to govern our judgment. . . . There is in truth little to guide us other than common sense.[146]

How did Judge Cardozo's majority opinion stand in relation to this emerging Realist challenge to causation? Surprisingly, he insisted that the case was not one about causation at all. "The law of causation, remote or proximate, is . . . foreign to the case before us," he declared. Rather, the question was really about the "anterior" issue of whether the defendant owed any duty at all to the plaintiff.[147] "The conduct of the [railroad] guard, if a wrong in its relation to the holder of the package, was not a wrong in its relation to the plaintiff, standing far away. Relative to her it was not negligence at all. . . . 'Proof of negligence in the air, so to speak, will not do.' "[148]

Cardozo's effort to shift the issue from the question of causation to the one of duty was closely related to many complex issues in the history of tort theory. It seems to indicate that Cardozo had accepted the Legal Realist critique of the objectivity of causation, and thus instead sought to find a solution in the area of duty. Did framing the analysis in terms of duty really make any difference?

From our post-Realist perspective, it might be thought that the same policy considerations that would enter into determinations of proximate causation would also determine the question of duty. Yet, it appears that Cardozo, a transitional figure with respect to Realism, still thought of the duty question as capable of mediating between a purely political conception of causation and a strictly formalist conception of legal obligation.

Duty was also the central issue in Cardozo's even more famous earlier opinion in *MacPherson v. Buick* (1916).[149] In that case, the question was whether, in the absence of privity between an automobile manufacturer and a consumer (who *was* in privity with the intermediate dealer who sold him the car), the manufacturer owed any duty to the consumer not to be negligent. Cautiously embracing one of the most radical and controversial opinions of a late-nineteenth-century English judge, who suggested that everybody owed a duty to the entire world not to be negligent,[150] Cardozo directly attacked the citadel of privity. The dramatic point of *MacPherson*, then, was to overthrow the traditional private law conception of duty in which one generally owed an obligation only to someone who was not a stranger. Before *MacPherson*, unless there was a legal interaction between the defendant and the plaintiff, there was no duty.

In sharp contrast to the generalized "duties owed to the world" approach of *MacPherson* is the disaggregated and particularized private law conception of duty in Cardozo's *Palsgraf* opinion. In *Palsgraf*, we have seen, Cardozo distinguished between the duty that the railroad owed to the passenger and the duty owed to Mrs. Palsgraf. The negligence of the railroad guard, as previously stated, "was not a wrong in its relation to the plaintiff, standing far away," Cardozo concluded.[151] This would be the equivalent of saying in *MacPherson* that the negligence of the automobile manufacturer was a wrong in its relation to the intermediate dealer, but not in relation to the consumer with whom there was no contractual relationship. As we have seen, that is precisely the traditional view that *MacPherson* had overthrown.

It appears, therefore, that between the time of *MacPherson* and *Palsgraf*, Cardozo had begun to have second thoughts about the potential for unlimited liability that his view of duty in *MacPherson* seemed to entail. He thus retreated to a more individualized private law conception of duty to restore traditional limitations on the scope of liability. Indeed, it was only after the scope of duty expanded around the turn of the century that causation prominently emerged as a separate limiting device. Before that time, limitations on the scope of duty served the same liability-limiting function that causation came to perform. So why did Cardozo not also turn to causation to limit the reach of duty?

By the time *Palsgraf* was decided, objective causation had begun to be discredited in most fields, especially in the natural sciences. The collapse of causation in the natural sciences was actually occurring at virtually the same time that *Palsgraf* was decided. When the Viennese philosopher Friedrich Waissman lectured at Oxford University on "The Decline and Fall of Causality," he pinpointed 1927, the year that Heisenberg enunciated the "uncertainty principle," as the year that "saw the obsequies" of causality in contemporary science.[152]

Moving beyond the natural sciences, Thomas Haskell points to a general decline of causal analysis in American social thought beginning around the turn of the century.[153] The attack on formalism, Haskell argues, was at bottom an attack on causation by a new generation of thinkers who "from their concrete social experience in an urbanizing, industrializing society" understood the world as radically more interdependent. "Where all is *inter*dependent," Haskell writes, "there can be no '*in*dependent variables. . . . To insist on the interconnectedness of social phenomena in time and in social space is to insist on the improbability of autonomous action."[154] Haskell continues:

> Things near at hand that had once seemed autonomous and therefore suitable for causal attribution were now seen as reflexes of more remote causes. Those factors in one's immediate environment that had always been regarded as self-acting, spontaneous entities—causes: things in which explanations can be rooted—now began to be seen as merely the final links in long chains of causation that stretched off into a murky distance. One's familiar milieu and its institutions were drained of causal potency and made to appear merely secondary and proximate in their influence on one's life.[155]

During the 1920s and 1930s, Legal Realists created the distinction between actual or "but for" causation, on the one hand, and legal or proximate causation, on the other, in recognition of the collapse of objective causation. Thereafter, the question of proximate cause would be addressed, as Judge Andrews had argued, as an issue of "convenience [and] public policy."

THREE

Santa Clara Revisited: The Development of Corporate Theory

The gradual acceptance of the reality of multiple causation was one measure of recognition that a more complex and interdependent society had emerged by the turn of the century. During the quarter century after 1873, Americans had been forced to come to terms with an accelerating sense of loss of control over their destinies, as those familiar "island communities" that had structured an earlier way of life were seen to be rapidly fading away. It was a period marked by three deep economic downturns. As the Panic of 1873 was followed by depressions in 1885 and 1893–1897, Americans discovered the seemingly harsh inexorability of the business cycle. If the Paris Commune of 1871 introduced fear of socialism into American culture, the Great Railroad Strike of 1877 triggered a pervasive fear that, by succumbing to the disease of European class struggle, America had finally been drawn into the bitter cycles of European history.

After the rapid growth of the Knights of Labor during the Depression of 1885, social tensions were brought to a boil in the Haymarket riot of 1886, which reinforced the view that America would no longer be immune from the laws of history and economic development. As in Europe, industrialization was producing greater inequality and more intense forms of social conflict. The inexorability of the business cycle meant that America could not even hope to find special favor in escaping from the universal laws of economics.

During the 1890s, the sense of crisis spread as the long depression of 1893–1897 and a series of major strikes from Homestead (1892) to Pullman (1894) moved the country to levels of internal strife that revived memories, perhaps exaggerated, of the Civil War. As social conflict finally erupted into national poli-

A version of this chapter was delivered at the West Virginia University College of Law as an annual Edward G. Donley Memorial Lecture and published in 88 W. Va. L. Rev. 173 (1985). © 1986 by the author.

tics, the strong showing of the Populists in the elections of 1892 set the stage for the colossal struggle between Bryan and McKinley in the presidential election of 1896.

The widening sense of crisis may have served as a catalyst for orthodox legal thinkers, as they defensively strove to systematize and tighten up the structure of Classical Legal Thought. At the same time, it induced other Americans to re-examine the fundamental premises of social thought. During the late nineteenth century, Dorothy Ross has shown, American social thinkers experienced a "crisis of exceptionalism" that brought into question the very foundations of a long-standing American faith that, through the guidance of Providence, the nation could manage to escape from the torments of Europe.[1]

The conviction that only a decentralized political and economic system could increase wealth while maintaining freedom and avoiding the tyranny of European statism was a central tenet of American exceptionalism. If increasing inequality challenged the premise that an impersonal and self-executing market system could produce, "as if by an invisible hand," a just distribution of wealth, the emergence of large, concentrated economic enterprises drew into question the very naturalness and necessity of decentralized economic institutions. The project of re-defining the market system to recognize a legitimate role for the new corporate giants represented a central theme in American social thought at the turn of the century. It expressed no less than a crisis of legitimacy, testing the intimate relationship between classical economic and social theories, on the one hand, and decentralized political and economic institutions, on the other. An old conservatism, rooted in an increasingly nostalgic vision of the naturalness and necessity of a decentralized, competitive market system, struggled with a new conservatism that proclaimed the inevitability and efficiency of large organizations that derived from economies of scale.

The struggle between old and new conservatism was one of the most important background conditions for the challenge to Classical Legal Thought. Rooted in an old conservative picture of the world, Classical Legal Thought was constantly criticized for its insistence on an anachronistic vision of social relations, a vision that expressed outmoded individualistic ideals that had been nurtured by decentralized institutions.

The *Santa Clara* Case and Corporate Theory

The 1886 decision of the U.S. Supreme Court in *Santa Clara v. Southern Pacific Railroad*[2] has always been puzzling and controversial. From the time Progressive constitutional historians began to mount their attack on the Supreme Court after the *Lochner* decision in 1905,[3] the *Santa Clara* case became one of the prominent symbols of the subservience of the Supreme Court during the Gilded Age to the interests of big business.[4]

The *Santa Clara* case held that a corporation was a person under the Fourteenth Amendment and thus was entitled to its protection. For such a momentous decision, the opinion in the *Santa Clara* case is disquietingly brief—just one short paragraph—and totally without reasons or precedent. Indeed, it was made without argument of counsel. It declared:

> The court does not wish to hear argument on the question whether the provision in the Fourteenth Amendment to the Constitution, which forbids a State to deny to any person within its jurisdiction the equal protection of the laws, applies to these corporations. We are all of opinion that it does.[5]

Can it be that so casual a declaration as this did in fact represent a major controversial step in American constitutional history? Did the decision actually represent a significant departure from American constitutional jurisprudence? I think not. The *Santa Clara* decision was not thought of as an innovation but instead was regarded as following a line of cases going back almost seventy years to the *Dartmouth College Case*.[6]

My interest in the *Santa Clara* case extends far beyond the question of whether it was consistent with previous constitutional decisions. Whatever the Supreme Court justices had in mind, the case is usually thought to express a new theory of the corporation or, as it soon became fashionable to call it, of "corporate personality." The *Santa Clara* case is thus asserted to be a dramatic example of judicial personification of the corporation, which, it is argued, radically enhanced the position of the business corporation in American law.[7]

But the question remains whether the *Santa Clara* case did in fact proceed from a theory that the corporate entity was no different from the individual in its constitutional entitlements. To answer this question, I provide a long excursion into the history of the theories of the corporation that were prevalent when the *Santa Clara* case was decided. I hope to show, first, that a "natural entity" or "real entity" theory of the corporation that the *Santa Clara* case is supposed to have adopted was nowhere to be found in American legal thought when the case was decided; second, that those who argued for the corporation as well as Supreme Court Justice Stephen Field, who decided in favor of the corporation in two elaborate circuit court opinions presented below,[8] clearly had no conception of a natural entity theory of the corporation; and, third, that when the natural entity theory emerged about a decade later, it was only then gradually absorbed into the *Santa Clara* precedent to establish dramatically new constitutional protections for corporations.

So initially, I show not only that the real meaning of the *Santa Clara* decision has not been understood, but also that it did not express the pro–big-business theory of the corporation that came to fruition shortly before the First World War.

This focus on the *Santa Clara* case and on the history of corporate theory is designed to explore a still more difficult question about the role of legal theory in legal decision. For almost forty years after 1890, American jurists, like their German, French, and English counterparts, were preoccupied with the theory of corporate personality. Then the issue suddenly vanished from controversy. The

last great analysis of the question, which is sometimes thought to have permanently put it to rest, appeared in a 1926 *Yale Law Journal* article[9] by the philosopher John Dewey. Writing in sympathy with the powerful contemporaneous Legal Realist attack on "conceptualism,"[10] Dewey sought to show that theories of
corporate personality were infinitely manipulable, and that at different times the
same theories had been used both to expand and to limit not only corporate but
also trade union powers. "Each theory" of group personality, he maintained, "has
been used to serve . . . opposing ends."

> [I]t has been employed both to make the state the supreme and culminating per-
> sonality in a hierarchy, to make it but primus inter pares, and to reduce it to
> merely one among many. . . . Corporate groups less than the state have had real
> personality ascribed to them, both in order to make them more amenable to lia-
> bility, as in the case of trade-unions, and to exalt their dignity and vital power,
> against external control. . . . The group personality theory has been asserted both
> as a check upon what was regarded as anarchic and dissolving individualism, to set
> up something more abiding and worthful than a single human being, and to in-
> crease the power and dignity of the single being as over against the state.[11]

There are very few discussions of corporate personality after Dewey. The Legal
Realists, in general, succeeded in persuading legal thinkers that highly abstract
and general legal conceptions were simply part of what Felix Cohen, quoting Von
Jehring, derisively called "the heaven of legal concepts."[12] Only more concrete
statements of functional relations, Cohen argued, were useful in deciding legal
questions.

I wish to dispute Dewey's conclusion that particular conceptions of corporate
personality were used just as easily to limit as to enhance corporate power. I hope
to show that, for example, the rise of a natural entity theory of the corporation
was a major factor in legitimating big business and that none of the other theoretical alternatives could provide as much sustenance to newly organized, concentrated enterprise.

The central thrust of the Realist legacy ultimately derives from Holmes's famous statement, "General propositions do not decide concrete cases."[13] Holmes,
as well as John Dewey and Felix Cohen after him,[14] was attacking the formalist
claim that one could reason deductively and without discretion from a general
concept to a particular application. As a matter of legal logic, their attack on
formalism continues to be as powerful today as it was fifty years ago. But their
attempt to discredit the then orthodox claim to a non-political, non-discretionary
mode of legal reasoning led them to ignore the obvious fact that when abstract
conceptions are used in specific historical contexts, they do acquire more limited
meanings and more specific argumentative functions. In particular contexts, the
choice of one theory over another may not be random or accidental because
history and usage have limited their deepest meanings and applications.

The *Santa Clara* Case in Context: The Real Meaning of the *Santa Clara* Decision

The *Santa Clara* case, along with several companion cases, came to the U.S. Supreme Court from California.[15] They presented the question whether the equal protection clause of the Fourteenth Amendment barred California from taxing corporate property—in this case, railroad property—differently from individual property.

These California tax cases were clearly regarded as important and momentous events in giving meaning to the newly enacted Fourteenth Amendment. Above all, they represented another effort mounted by business interests after their narrow failure to get the Supreme Court to construe the Fourteenth Amendment broadly in the *Slaughterhouse Cases*.[16] In that decision, Justice Samuel Miller, speaking for a five-man majority, not only offered an extremely narrow construction of the privileges and immunities clause but also construed the equal protection clause as limited to protecting the status of recently freed slaves. In dissent, Justice Stephen Field, who argued for a much more expansive definition of each of the provisions of the Fourteenth Amendment, sought, in effect, to create a general federal charter of constitutional rights.[17]

The central issue in the *Slaughterhouse Cases* was whether the Fourteenth Amendment had radically altered the constitutional relationship between the states and the federal government. Justice Miller's "race theory" interpretation of the Fourteenth Amendment, drawing upon traditional fears of centralized power, was meant to produce as little change in the federal balance of power as possible. By contrast, Justice Field interpreted the Fourteenth Amendment as ratifying a dramatic alteration in the federal system as a consequence of the Civil War.[18]

So when the California tax cases came before Justice Field, sitting on circuit, the most basic and controversial question before him was whether it was possible, after the *Slaughterhouse* decision, to construe the equal protection clause as extending to questions not related to race. The central thrust of his decision was to continue his battle, which was eventually successful, to expand the meaning of the amendment beyond the boundaries of race relations. Indeed, the real significance of the Supreme Court's decision in *Santa Clara* may be precisely that it did go beyond Justice Miller's *Slaughterhouse* effort to confine the scope of the equal protection clause.

How did Justice Field justify applying the equal protection clause to corporations when the language of the amendment was written to protect persons?

Let us turn to the major argument in the brief on behalf of the corporation before the U.S. Supreme Court. Written by the eminent California lawyer John Norton Pomeroy, the central argument was that the Fourteenth Amendment protects the property rights not of some abstract corporate entity but rather of the individual shareholders. As Pomeroy declared in his brief, provisions of state and federal constitutions "apply . . . to private corporations, not alone because such corporations are 'persons' within the meaning of that word, but because *statutes violating their prohibitions in dealing with corporations must necessarily infringe upon the rights of natural persons.* In applying and enforcing these constitutional guaranties [sic] *corporations cannot be separated from the natural persons who compose them."* [19] Pomeroy argued:

> That this conclusion must be true, appears from the following principle: Whatever be the legal nature of a corporation as an artificial, metaphysical being, separate and distinct from the individual members, and whatever distinctions the common law makes, in carrying out the technical legal conception, between property of the corporation and that of the individual members, still in applying the fundamental guaranties of the constitution, and in thus protecting rights of property, *these metaphysical and technical notions must give way to the reality.* The truth cannot be evaded that, *for the purpose of protecting rights, the property of all business and trading corporations* IS *the property of the individual corporators.* A State act depriving a business corporation of its property without due process of law, does in fact *deprive the individual corporators of their property.* In this sense, and within the scope of these grand safeguards of private rights, there is no real distinction between artificial persons or corporations, and natural persons. [20]

Justice Field made exactly the same point in his circuit court opinion in the companion *San Mateo* case:

> Private corporations are, it is true, artificial persons, but . . . they consist of aggregations of individuals united for some legitimate business. . . . It would be a most singular result if a constitutional provision intended for the protection of every person against partial and discriminating legislation by the states, should cease to exert such protection the moment the person becomes a member of a corporation. . . . On the contrary, we think that it is well established by numerous adjudications of the supreme court of the United States . . . that whenever a provision of the constitution, or of a law, guaranties to persons the enjoyment of property . . . the benefits of the provision extend to corporations, and that the courts will always look beyond the name of the artificial being to the individuals whom it represents. [21]

The arguments of Pomeroy and Field are very different from a real entity or natural entity theory of corporate personality that is often ascribed to the *Santa Clara* case but that in fact emerged some time after *Santa Clara* was decided. Only this later theory can truly be said to personify the corporation and treat it just like individuals.

Corporate Theory in the Late Nineteenth and Early Twentieth Centuries

The theory of corporate personality attributed to the *Santa Clara* case—the natural entity theory—was not available at the time the case was decided. This becomes clear after reviewing the American legal struggle to re-conceptualize the corporation and the philosophical debates that arose in the late nineteenth and early twentieth centuries on the nature of corporate personality.

THE PHILOSOPHICAL DEBATES. There was a flood of writing on the subject of corporate personality in Germany, France, England, and America near the turn of the century. Why should so metaphysical a subject, even if it attracted the speculative instincts of German and French jurists, have appealed to the practical, earth-bound sensibilities of English and American legal thinkers?

The intellectual history of the subject is quite clear. It was introduced into Western thought by the publication in 1881 of the third volume of the German legal theorist Otto Gierke's great work on the history of associations in German legal theory.[22] By 1900, dozens of books had been published in French and German on "group personality," "corporate personality," or, as the French liked to call it, "moral personality."[23] It became accessible to English and American thinkers after 1900 when Frederic Maitland, the great English legal historian, published a portion of Gierke's work under the title *Political Theories of the Middle Age*,[24] to which Maitland contributed an introduction. Between 1900 and 1904 Maitland published four other articles on the early history of corporations, culminating in his paper "Moral Personality and Legal Personality,"[25] which sought to advance Gierke's idea that corporations were "real" or "natural" entities that possessed legal personalities deserving of recognition. In America, Gierke's work was first noticed by the German-trained University of Chicago Professor Ernst Freund, who in 1897 published *The Legal Nature of Corporations*.[26]

If the intellectual history of the subject is relatively clear, the question remains of why so abstruse an inquiry should have engaged the attention of Anglo-American lawyers. Maitland—wrongly, it turns out—lamented the fact that the English could not have cared less. He wondered "[w]hy we English people are not interested in a problem that is being seriously discussed in many other lands,"[27] and his article "Trust and Corporation"[28] sought to explain how the trust "enabled us to construct bodies which were not technically corporations and which yet would be sufficiently protected from the assaults of individualistic theory."[29]

Americans, in fact, were especially receptive to questions involving group theory. Even before Gierke was known or Maitland's writings had crossed the Atlantic, American legal thinkers had begun to wrestle with the problem of conceptualizing group personality and, in particular, the corporation. Beginning in the 1890s, they too sought to develop a picture of the corporation as a real or natural entity, as well as to explain or justify the inscrutable holding of the U.S. Supreme Court in the *Santa Clara* case.

What united all of these inquiries, whether German, French, English, or American, was the spectacular rise to prominence during the late nineteenth century of the business corporation as the dominant form of economic enterprise. In 1890, Justice Stephen Field estimated that three-quarters of the wealth of the United States was controlled by corporations.[30] This growth in the corporate form of economic enterprise presented essentially two fundamental challenges to traditional Western legal theory. First, in all of these countries, the corporation was treated as a legal fiction or an artificial entity created by the state. Gierke and his successors devoted themselves to showing that the corporation—indeed, group activity generally—was real and natural, not artificial or fictional. The proponents of Realism ranged all the way from overt apologists for big business, whose primary objective was to free the corporation from a theory that justified special state regulation, to those who for a variety of reasons wished to attack nineteenth-century liberal individualism.

The challenge to individualism produced a second fundamental set of questions. On the Continent, individualism was under attack, first, by romantic conservatives, who loathed the atomistic features of modern industrial life and yearned for a return to a pre-commercial, organic society composed of medieval statuses and hierarchies.[31] They were joined in their attacks by socialists who wished to transcend the anti-collectivist categories of liberal social and legal thought.[32] While the attack focused on the rise of corporations, it also sought to take account of the recent prominence of labor unions and of trade and professional associations.[33] And even Maitland, whose legal history was devoted to affirming the liberal vision of individual property holding against the collectivist historians' search for pre-modern forms of communal property,[34] promoted the real entity theory and sympathetically regarded the trust as a fictional device covertly designed to evade "the assaults of individualistic theory."[35]

The corporation, in short, was the most powerful and prominent example of the emergence of non-individualistic or, if you will, collectivist legal institutions. The artificial entity theory of the corporation, by contrast, sought to retain the premises of what has been called "methodological individualism," that is, the view that the only real starting point for political or legal theory is the individual. Groups, in this view, were simply artificial aggregations of individuals. On the other hand, it was the goal of the Realists to show that groups, in fact, had an organic unity, that the group was greater than the mere sum of its parts. In all the Western countries, therefore, the sudden focus on theories of corporate personality was associated with a crisis of legitimacy in liberal individualism arising from the recent emergence of powerful collective institutions.

THE AMERICAN LEGAL STRUGGLE TO RE-CONCEPTUALIZE THE CORPORATION. By the late nineteenth century in America, fundamental changes had already taken place in the legal treatment of the corporation. The first, and by far the most important, was the erosion of the "grant" or "concession" theory of the corporation, which treated the act of incorporation as a special privilege conferred by the state for the pursuit of public purposes.[36] Under the grant theory, the business corporation was regarded as an artificial being created by the state, with powers strictly limited by its charter of incorporation. As we shall see, a number of more specific legal doctrines were also derived from the grant theory in order to enforce the state's interest in limiting and confining corporate power.

The political mechanism used to enforce the grant theory was the special charter of incorporation, passed by the state legislature after negotiation between private interests and the state. During the Jacksonian period, special charters were denounced for their encouragement of legislative bribery, political favoritism, and, above all, monopoly. As a result, the movement for "free incorporation" laws that would break the connection between the act of incorporation and political favoritism and corruption triumphed between 1850 and 1870.[37] Gradually, by making the corporate form universally available, free incorporation undermined the grant theory. Incorporation eventually came to be regarded not as a special state-conferred privilege but as a normal and regular mode of doing business.

The problem faced by legal thinkers during the late nineteenth century was how to re-conceptualize the corporation after the demise of the grant theory. On the one hand, free incorporation provided the opportunity to treat the corporation under ordinary contractual categories familiar to partnership law. On the other hand, many of the special attributes[38] of the corporation could not be explained or defended by partnership analogies. As a result, during the last quarter of the nineteenth century, the legal literature was filled with discussions of the nature of the corporation—whether, like a partnership, it is a mere aggregate of individuals or whether, instead, it is an entity, separate from the individuals who compose it.

Up to the 1880s, there was a strong tendency to analyze corporation law not very differently from the law of partnership.[39] Indeed, many of the rules involving the internal governance of the corporation were borrowed from partnership law, the most important of which was the requirement of shareholder unanimity for "fundamental" changes in corporate purpose.[40] Moreover, the erosion of the grant theory seemed to leave no choice but to create a conception of the corporation with powers flowing form the bottom up—from shareholders to directors to officers. This basic model of the corporation, emphasizing the property rights of shareholders, is the one put forth in *Santa Clara* by John Norton Pomeroy and Justice Field.

Later, shortly before the First World War, the partnership conception could not equally accomplish the task of legitimation when the court turned to less material, less property-centered claims of corporate constitutional rights against unreasonable search and seizure and self-incrimination. Here it was difficult to reduce the constitutional claim of the corporation to the constitutional rights of the shareholders. In constitutional law, therefore, the first Supreme Court natural entity opinion was the 1905 decision in *Hale v. Henkel*[41] extending Fourth Amendment protections to the corporation. But the Court's continuing reluctance to entirely personify the corporation is underlined by its decision in the same case refusing to extend Fifth Amendment protection against self-incrimination to corporations.

Despite the Supreme Court's continued hesitance, by 1900 the entity theory had largely triumphed and corporation and partnership law had moved in radically different directions. The success of legal thinkers in reconceptualizing the corporation seems to have had important consequences for the legitimacy of the corporate entity.

The triumph of the entity theory parallels another development in late-nineteenth-century corporate law—the tendency to shift power away from shareholders, first to directors and later to professional managers.[42] By contrast, in 1875, by analogy to the partnership, American law had tended to conceive of directors as agents of shareholders. After 1900, however, directors were more frequently treated as equivalent to the corporation itself.[43] This realignment of legal powers within the corporation thus made the entity theory ever more plausible. In turn, the entity theory produced court decisions that promoted oligarchical tendencies within the business corporation.

The collapse of the grant theory eventually produced the best of all possible worlds for the expansion of corporate power. By rendering the corporate form normal and regular, late-nineteenth-century corporate theory shifted the presumption of corporate regulation against the state. Since corporations could no longer be treated as special creatures of the state, they were entitled to the same privileges as all other individuals and groups. While the state thus lost any special claims arising out of the original theory of corporate creation to regulate corporations, the once powerful grant theory did make it easier to continue to conceive of the corporation as a supra-individualistic entity. As a result, late-nineteenth-century entity theorists drew on the early history of the corporation to justify their assertion of its organic and collective nature at the same time as they disavowed the completely subordinate position that that theory had created for the corporation.

Thus, one can clearly see that the natural entity theory of the corporation ascribed to the *Santa Clara* case was just beginning to be formulated at the turn of the century. In 1886 corporate theory was in a state of flux both legally and intellectually, and the natural entity theory was not yet available to justify the holding in the *Santa Clara* case. It was only afterward that theorists began to recognize the reality of corporate growth.

The Concept of Corporate Personality and Its Determinate Legal Significance

Corporate Personality

The corporation occupied an anomalous position in American law throughout the nineteenth century. In a legal system whose categories were built around individual activity, it was not at all easy to assimilate the behavior of groups. Inherently individualistic legal conceptions like "fault" and "will" were difficult to apply to corporations. Ernst Freund asked in 1897: How is it possible,

upon any other basis [than the individual person], to deal with notions that are constantly applied to the holding of rights, and which explain their most important incidents: intention, notice, good and bad faith, responsibility? How can we establish, unless we have to deal with individuals, the internal connection between act and liability?[44]

Any conception of corporate rights, Freund emphasized, would involve "a departure from well-settled principles":

> If the individual, private, and beneficial right is to measure and govern all rules relating to rights of whatsoever nature, then the corporate right will continue to be abnormal and illogical. If, on the other hand, we emancipate ourselves from the absolute recognition of one form of right as orthodox, . . . we may well arrive at the conclusion, that in dealing with associations of persons we must modify the ideas which we have derived from the right of property in individuals, and what has first seemed to be an anomaly will appear simply as another but equally legitimate form of development.[45]

The corporation also stood in clear contradiction to a legal culture dominated by Lockean ideas of pre-political natural rights. In post-revolutionary America, there was no better example of the social creation of property than the chartered business corporation. As natural rights theories grew in power and scope after the Civil War,[46] the corporation thus seemed to constitute a standing contradiction to any claims to the pre-political character of property rights.

Three conceptions of the legal organization of the corporation competed for dominance after 1880. The traditional conception, derived from the antebellum grant theory, as well as older English corporation law, characterized the corporation as "an artificial entity created by positive law."[47] But as the movement for free incorporation eroded the force of the grant theory, two other conceptions of the corporation began to emerge, with radically different implications for the development of corporation law. In substantially different ways, these two newer theories sought to convey the idea that incorporation was a normal and natural mode of business organization, not a special privilege bestowed by the state.

In reaction to the grant theory, some legal writers during the 1880s began to put forth a polar opposite conception of the corporation as a creature of free contract among individual shareholders, no different, in effect, from a partnership. In this conception, the corporation was not a creature of the state but of individual initiative and enterprise. It was private, not public.

A third theory, which emerged during the 1890s, also sought to represent the corporation as private, yet neither as artificial, as fictional, or as a creature of the state. This natural entity theory soon began to be projected onto the ambiguous opinion of the Supreme Court in the *Santa Clara* case.

The term "corporate personality" is itself an important clue to the intellectual crisis. The aggregate or contractual view of the corporation seemed capable of restricting corporate privileges and, in particular, the rule of limited liability. That there was a close relationship between the justification for limited liability and a conception of the corporation as a separate (though artificial) entity distinct from its shareholders was clear to Chief Justice Roger Taney as early as 1839. If the entity were disregarded, Taney wrote,

> and . . . the members of a corporation were to be regarded as individuals carrying on business in their corporate name, and therefore entitled to the privileges of citizens in matters of contract, it is very clear that they must at the same time take upon themselves the liabilities of citizens and be bound by their contracts in like manner. The result of this would be to make a corporation a mere partnership in business, in which each stockholder would be liable to the whole extent of his property for the debts of the corporation; and he might be sued for them in any state in which he might happen to be found.[48]

Not only did Taney believe that there was a logical connection between an entity theory and limited liability; he also maintained, in perfectly straightforward Jacksonian fashion, that every effort of corporations to claim that they were constitutionally "entitled to the privileges of citizens" would erode the entity theory by forcing courts to turn to the rights of shareholders. There was a trade-off, he supposed, between the grant of corporate privileges and the claim of shareholder constitutional rights. He could not yet even imagine that the fictional entity itself could plausibly claim constitutional privileges. The effort to protect corporate property in *Santa Clara* through a conception of shareholder rights thus raised precisely the danger that Chief Justice Taney had identified—it might undermine the justification for limited liability.

The effort of some legal thinkers beginning in the 1880s to treat the corporation as no different from a partnership was reinforced in a series of anti-consolidation cases in which courts looked behind the corporate entity to treat the shareholders as the real legal actors in the corporation. The most famous of these cases was the attack on the Standard Oil Trust by the state of Ohio.[49] Ohio brought proceedings to dissolve the Standard Oil Company, maintaining that it had acted beyond its corporate powers in joining the trust. Since a majority of the individual shareholders had voted to transfer their stock to the trust, the corporation maintained that only the shareholders, not the corporation, had acted. In piercing the corporate veil, Ohio Supreme Court Justice Minshall treated the idea "that a corporation is a legal entity apart from the natural persons who compose it" as "a mere fiction."

It appears that the intense efforts of most judges and legal writers during the 1880s and 1890s to equate the corporation with its stockholders were motivated by a delegitimating strategy deriving from anti-corporate and anti-consolidation sentiment. Of course, the defenders of corporate property in *Santa Clara* also made use of this theory, which seemed to them at the time more favorable to the corporation than the traditional artificial entity theory. Yet, given the structure of American legal ideas, it may have seemed the only way to turn once the implications of the demise of the grant theory rendered the entity conception of the corporation more problematic.

Ultra Vires

[U]nfortunately, there is now in this country a newer growth of corporation lawyers and authors, fostered and fashioned in the same school, who would confuse the subject by regarding the rights, duties and powers of a corporation as identical with the rights, duties and powers of the individuals composing it. To recognize such an anomalous position would clearly nullify, in great measure, the whole doctrine of *ultra vires*.

> Reuben A. Reese, *The True Doctrine of Ultra Vires in the Law of Corporations* (1897)[50]

The doctrine that a corporation cannot act beyond its legal competence is perhaps the best reflection of the traditional legal conception of the nature of the corporation. At one pole, to the extent that the corporation is thought of as an artificial entity created by the state, we would expect courts strictly to construe powers granted in the corporate charter and to refuse effect to corporate activity regarded as beyond the powers conferred. At the opposite pole, to the extent that the corporation is regarded simply as a convenient device for conducting business activity, not as a privilege or concession derived from the state, we would expect the death of the ultra vires doctrine.

Before the Civil War, in fact, the ultra vires doctrine was strictly applied by American courts, thereby voiding most transactions held to be outside the grant of a corporation's powers.[51] By 1930, the ultra vires doctrine was, if not dead, substantially eroded in practice,[52] reflecting the triumphant view that corporate organization was a normal and natural form of business activity.

During the half century after 1880, we can trace the tension between those doctrines that reflected the old vision of corporate power as a state-conferred privilege and the emergence of newer theories representing the corporation as a natural form of business organization. The changing scope of ultra vires also represents one of many technical expressions of the conflict over political economy between small entrepreneurs and emergent big business over the legitimacy of large-scale enterprise. In this setting, the doctrine of ultra vires provides us with one measure of conflict.

At first glance, the doctrine of ultra vires was still a powerful judicial tool as late as 1900, despite the seemingly contrary message of state general incorporation laws, which had become the norm between 1850 and 1870. Yet there was still a long ideological distance to travel between the first general incorporation laws, which continued to impose many restrictions on corporate financing and structure, and the New Jersey incorporation law, first enacted in 1889, whose major premise was that a corporation could do virtually anything it wanted.[53] Even within the context of early general incorporation, therefore, the state did not entirely renounce its role as creator and regulator.

While judicial decisions during the last decades of the nineteenth century thus continued to invoke the ultra vires doctrine and its underlying conception of the corporation as an artificial entity, many important changes in corporation law had strengthened the view that the ultra vires doctrine was an anachronism "now honored more in the breach than in the observance."[54] Even in jurisdictions that still dealt harshly with ultra vires acts, the definition of legitimate corporate powers had long been expanding. William W. Cook, in his 1894 treatise on corporation law, wrote:

> The courts are becoming more liberal, and many acts which fifty years ago would have been held to be ultra vires would now be held to be intra vires. The courts have gradually enlarged the implied powers of ordinary corporations until now such corporations may do almost anything that an individual may do, provided the stockholders and creditors do not object.[55]

Even concededly ultra vires activity had begun to receive recognition by the courts. Since corporations had already been made liable in tort as well as prosecuted criminally for ultra vires acts, the doctrine had increasingly reflected considerable internal contradiction. The exceptions, many commentators noted, were beginning to eat up the rule. Even within the last remaining bastion of the ultra vires rule, the law of contracts, courts after the Civil War had begun a retreat. While they continued to refuse to enforce "executory" contracts (those where neither party had performed), they now refused to intervene to upset property rights acquired under "executed" ultra vires contracts. By the 1880s, the majority of state courts had gone one step further to enforce even contracts that, despite lack of corporate power, had been performed by one party to the agreement.[56] Yet the U.S. Supreme Court, after a short flirtation with a liberalized ultra vires rule during the 1870s, became the most ardent defender of traditional doctrine, consistently rejecting the majority view that partially performed contracts could be enforced.[57] Until at least 1930, the Supreme Court continued to resist the trend of state decisions,[58] as well as the appeals of legal scholars to relax ultra vires limitations.[59]

The contradictions and inconsistencies in ultra vires doctrine were becoming unmanageable. In 1898, William W. Cook wrote:

> The doctrine of ultra vires is disappearing. The old theory that a corporate act beyond the express and implied corporate powers was illegal and not enforceable, no matter whether any actual injury had been done or not, has given way to the practical view that the parties to a contract which has been partially or wholly executed will not be allowed to say it was ultra vires of the corporation.[60]

While judges thus continued to sound like antebellum grant theorists when they were deciding executory contract cases, the vitality and coherence of the grant theory and the regulatory premises that underlay it had long been eroded.

Foreign Corporations

Despite the advent of general incorporation laws by the 1870s, we have seen that the Supreme Court continued into the twentieth century to treat the corporation as an artificial entity subject to ultra vires constraints.[61] It was only a series of state corporation statutes, buttressed by Legal Realist attacks, that finally destroyed most ultra vires limitations during the 1920s.

A second set of doctrines provides another measure of the gradual shift in the conception of the corporation from an artificial to a real or natural entity. They deal with the power of a state to prevent "foreign" corporations—that is, corporations chartered in another state—from doing business within its boundaries.

The "original fountain head of the law of foreign corporations"[62] was Chief Justice Taney's decision in *Bank of Augusta v. Earle* (1839),[63] which represents as clear a statement of the artificial entity theory as any in American law. The corporation "exists only in contemplation of law, and by force of the law," wrote Taney. Since it is "a mere artificial being" of the state of its creation, "where that law ceases to operate, and is no longer obligatory, the corporation can have no existence."[64] Thus, a state was not constitutionally obliged to allow foreign corporations to do business within its boundaries.

The doctrine of *Bank of Augusta v. Earle* was vigorously reaffirmed after the Civil War[65] and continued to find favor in the U.S. Supreme Court throughout the nineteenth century, even in the face of the Court's assumption that the corporation was a person under the Fourteenth Amendment. By the end of the nineteenth century, however, there were signs of increasing strain not only between an expanding Supreme Court protection of interstate commerce and the foreign incorporation doctrine but also between the latter and the natural entity conception that was emerging in legal thought. And yet it was only in a group of cases in 1910 that the Supreme Court finally put to rest the doctrine of *Bank of Augusta v. Earle*.[66] From that time on, expanding Fourteenth Amendment protections of the corporation swept aside Taney's vision of the business corporation as an artificial creature of the state.

As with the history of ultra vires, we see that it was not the Supreme Court of the Gilded Age that renounced the artificial entity theory of the corporation, but rather the judges and legal writers of the early twentieth century who came to understand the corporation as a normal and natural mode of doing business. And, as we shall see, it was a group of Legal Realist thinkers who developed and articulated this new conception of the corporation.

From the era of general incorporation on, legal writers had commented on the disparity between the reality of free incorporation and those artificial and unrealistic restrictions on corporate power that continued to derive from the antebellum grant theory. Yet, in the Supreme Court, an old conservative majority perpetuated the Jacksonian tradition of competitive capitalism and suspicion of corporate power,[67] not only by continuing to invoke legal doctrines derived from the artificial entity theory but also by giving a strict literalist reading to the Sherman Anti-Trust Act.[68] By 1911, the new conservatives finally overthrew the strict construction of the Sherman Act in the *Standard Oil* case;[69] they also reversed those doctrines in corporation law based on a conception of the corporation as a creature of the state. They were creating the distinction ultimately articulated in 1912 by Theodore Roosevelt between "good" and "bad" trusts.[70]

The "Inevitability" of Concentration

Are the large combinations of capitalists and corporations known as "trusts" a local and therefore proper development of the present economic system, or are they abnormal excrescences that can and should be eradicated by legislation?

Question to Professor William W. Folwell of the University of Minnesota by a Committee of the Minneapolis Socialist Labor Party (1888)[71]

The efforts by legal thinkers to legitimate the business corporation during the 1890s were buttressed by a stunning reversal in American economic thought—a movement to defend and justify as inevitable the emergence of large-scale corporate concentration.

Until the late 1880s, prevailing American economic thought refused to accept either the inevitability or the naturalness of large-scale concentrations of capital. Most discussion of the "monopoly problem" during the 1870s and early 1880s focused on the railroad, which was treated as something of a special case.[72] Whether defenders and opponents of railroad consolidation emphasized the "overproduction" of lines after the Civil War or argued about a "natural monopoly" analysis of the railroad, they tended to regard the problem as unique. Before the late 1880s, few saw in the railroad problem a more general pattern of industrial concentration.

Popular attention began to be drawn to the question of industrial concentration with the publication of Henry Demarest Lloyd's muckraking articles on monopoly. His first magazine article, "The Story of a Great Monopoly,"[73] in 1881, was an attack on the Standard Oil Company. "As early as 1884 he asserted that combinations were dominating most, if not all, industries in the country, from coffin-making to iron pipe foundries."[74] Above all, the attention paid to the formation of the notorious trusts during the 1880s raised more general questions concerning the causes of industrial concentration.

In 1882 the first great trust, Standard Oil, was born after "the sharp mind of Standard's legal counsel, S. C. T. Dodd, conceived of the new trust form of organization."[75] The trust was designed to bring about corporate consolidation while avoiding the prohibition under state corporation laws of one corporation holding the stock of another. Since the individual shareholders of the consolidating corporations tendered their stock to trustees in exchange for trust certificates, the resulting trust was not incorporated and hence was thought to be immune from the limitations of corporation law.

Five other successful nationwide trusts were organized during the 1880s: the American Cotton Oil Trust (1884), the National Linseed Oil Trust (1885), the National Lead Trust (1887), and the Whiskey and Sugar trusts (1889). The "trust problem" therefore became a central issue of public policy only a few years before the Sherman Act was enacted in 1890. The act itself reflected the still widely shared orthodox laissez-faire position that industrial concentration was an unnatural interference with the laws of free competition and could be achieved only through conspiracy or illicit financial manipulation.[76] Except for the relatively rare case of natural monopoly, it was thought that the "laws" of the market— especially the "law of diminishing returns"—would continue to prevail.

Some orthodox theorists traced the causes of monopoly to illegitimate governmental interference in the economy—through tariffs and other intrusions on free competition, governmental grants to railroads, grants of corporate privileges, and the operation of the patent laws. But most were complacently confident that monopoly was inherently impermanent. " 'Trusts', as a rule, are not dangerous," the dean of the Columbia Law School, Theodore W. Dwight, wrote in 1888. "They cannot overcome the law of demand and supply nor the resistless power of unlimited competition."[77] Indeed, the intellectual paralysis of laissez-faire theorists in the face of combination was captured best in 1891 by Judge Seymour Thompson of St. Louis, a vocal opponent of the trust.

> The problem . . . of restraining corporate and individual combinations and monopolies, is the problem of restraining a species of communism; it is communism against communism, and the question is, how far communism ought to go in restraining communism. The general rule is that it ought not to go at all. The general rule is that commerce should be free. . . .[78]

Beginning in the late 1880s, however, several writers began to ponder the question of whether large-scale enterprise was inevitable. Perhaps the earliest was Arthur T. Hadley, whose book, *Railroad Transportation* (1885), was the first to generalize from railroad consolidation to the inevitability of industrial concentration. Seeing the "present age" as "an age of industrial monopoly," Hadley argued that the American economy was moving away from free competition. Yet the existing system of thought blinded men to the changes that were occurring.

> All our education and habit of mind make us believe in competition. We have been taught to regard it as a natural if not necessary condition of a healthful business life. We look with satisfaction on whatever favors it, and with distrust on whatever hinders it. We accept almost without reserve the theory of Ricardo, that, under open competition in a free market, the value of different goods will tend to be proportional to their cost of production.[79]

But, ultimately, Hadley's analysis was limited by his effort to generalize from the railroad problem. He sought to explain the particular forms of cutthroat competition that enabled railroads to cut prices below marginal costs, but he did not propose any general analysis of how industrial concentration could be explained in terms of economic theory. That task fell to another writer, Henry C. Adams, the chief statistician for the newly formed Interstate Commerce Commission.

Adams's path-breaking and influential tract, "The Relation of the State to Industrial Action," was the best expression of the new anti-laissez-faire sentiment behind the recently formed American Economic Association.[80] It sought to define the conditions under which governmental regulation would be legitimate. Seeking to explain industrial concentration, Adams invoked John Stuart Mill's tripartite distinction among industries that displayed "constant," "diminishing," or "increasing" returns to scale. While the railroad was "a good illustration of this third class of industries,"[81] there were also "many other lines of business which conform to the principle of increasing returns, and for that reason come under the rule of centralized control."[82]

> Such businesses are by nature monopolies. We certainly deceive ourselves in believing that competition can secure for the public fair treatment in such cases, or that laws compelling competition can ever be enforced. If it is for the interest of men to combine no law can make them compete. For all industries, therefore, which conform to the principle of increasing returns, the only question at issue is, whether society shall support an irresponsible, extra-legal monopoly, or a monopoly established by law and managed in the interest of the public."[83]

Though it was thereafter expressed in many different ways, the argument of the inevitability of industrial concentration always represented some variation on Adams's original insight about increasing returns to scale.

Among the earliest to proclaim the inevitability of industrial concentration were social thinkers who were influenced by European socialism and Marx's prediction of the inevitability of monopoly capitalism. In 1889, President E. Benjamin Andrews of Brown University declared that the competitive system was fast disappearing and giving way to trusts and combinations.[84] Although competition had "hitherto been assumed as the certain postulate of all economic analysis and generalization," in fact "in a great variety of industries, perhaps a majority of all, permanent monopolies may be maintained, apart from any legislative or special aids. . . . No economic laws prevent the permanent existence of monopolies. . . ."[85]

In the same year, the Christian Socialist Edward Bellamy pronounced with satisfaction the "doom" of the competitive system. Competition was at odds with the fundamental principles of Christianity. "[T]he competitive system tends to develop what is worst in the character of all, whether rich or poor. The qualities which it discourages are the noblest and most generous that men have, and the qualities which it rewards are those selfish and sordid instincts which humanity can only hope to rise above by outgrowing."[86]

Moving from the "moral inequities of competition,"[87] Bellamy turned to an analysis of the causes of consolidation. "It is a result of the increase in the efficiency of capital in great masses, consequent upon the inventions of the last and present generations. . . . The economies in management resulting from consolidation, as well as the control over the market resulting from the monopoly of a staple, are also solid business reasons for the advent of the Trust."[88]

> The few economists who still seriously defend the competitive system are heroically sacrificing their reputations in the effort to mask the evacuation of a position which, as nobody knows better than our hard-headed captains of industry, has become untenable. . . . While the economists have been wisely debating whether we could

dispense with the principle of individual initiative in business, that principle has passed away, and now belongs to history.[89]

Except for his conclusion, Bellamy's vision of the inevitability of economic concentration was echoed by the new titans of industry. In 1888, the president of the American Cotton Oil Trust, John H. Flagler, defended the development of trusts as a reflection of "a steady, logical and wise evolution, or improvement in the method of conducting industrial affairs." There was an historical evolution in the conduct of business that passed through "successive stages of development" from individual to partnership to corporation and, now, to the trust. "This progressive development in the machinery for the conduct of business was impelled by the growing and ever-increasing demand for larger facilities, greater capital, greater energy, combination of activities, skill and intelligences."[90]

The courts did not yet agree. Beginning in the late 1880s, six different states brought suits to revoke the charters of corporations that had become constituents of one of the great trusts.[91] The most famous lawsuits involved the successful Ohio and New York attacks on, respectively, the Standard Oil and Sugar trusts.[92] In both cases, the courts dealt a setback to any entity theory of the corporation, holding that the act of the individual shareholders in joining the trust was really the act of the corporation.

As the attacks on the trust form mounted, corporation lawyers realized that the earlier strategy of simply evading the restrictions of corporation law would no longer work. "It was considered wise to yield in the matter of form. The trusts were transformed into companies."[93] In the words of the biographer of one of these lawyers, William Nelson Cromwell, "[t]he vulnerability of the trust arrangement to the combination and conspiracy concept of the Sherman Act and to the legal analysis of the Ohio and New York decisions led to the finding of new legal techniques. The need was met by an amendment to the corporation law of New Jersey."[94] Several corporation lawyers connected with Cromwell's firm, "were among those active in the drafting of this amendment."[95] And, as Alfred D. Chandler has written, "The New Jersey legislature quickly obliged."[96]

The New Jersey Law of 1889,[97] which permitted incorporation "for any lawful business or purpose whatever," was among the first to allow one corporation to own the stock of another, thus legalizing the holding company and making the trust device unnecessary. Cromwell himself seems to have been the first lawyer to use the New Jersey provisions. As counsel to the Cotton Oil Trust, he appears to have conceived of the need for the New Jersey law after a lower court in Louisiana in 1889 sustained the state's effort to dissolve several of the trust's constituent corporations.

Pending the appeal of an adverse decision, Cromwell called special meetings of all of the constituent corporations, obtained the necessary proxies and quietly dissolved the Louisiana corporations and transferred all their assets to a Rhode Island corporation set up for that purpose, whose stock was held by the trustees. When the appeal came on, he announced to the consternation of the Attorney General of

Louisiana that the relief requested was no longer necessary for the Corporations were no longer in existence.[98]

In the same year, the American Cotton Oil Trust was reorganized once more as a New Jersey holding company, perhaps the first major enterprise to take advantage of the change in New Jersey law. The successful New York attack on the Sugar Trust also led it to reorganize as a New Jersey corporation. It soon received the additional benefit of immunity from the Sherman Anti-Trust Act when the U.S. Supreme Court held in the *E. C. Knight Case*[99] that the act could not constitutionally reach "manufacturing."

After the passage of the New Jersey Act, the entire expenses of the state of New Jersey were paid out of corporation fees. "[S]o many Trusts and big corporations were paying tribute to the State of New Jersey," noted New York corporation lawyer Charles F. Bostwick, "that the authorities had become greatly perplexed as to what should be done with [its] surplus revenue. . . ."[100] "[T]he relation of the state toward the corporations resembles that between a feudal baron and the burghers of old, who paid for protection," observed William H. Cook.[101] Lincoln Steffens simply called New Jersey the "traitor state."[102]

The passage of the New Jersey Corporation Law followed by the rapid capitulation of many other states, marked the end of all serious efforts to use corporation law to regulate consolidation. Urging repeal of many New York restrictions on corporations, New York lawyer Charles F. Bostwick noted "the sudden exodus of hundreds upon hundreds of millions of dollars, controlled by corporate interests and financiers from New York into the State of New Jersey"[103] during the decade after the passage of the New Jersey law. "New York, although disclaiming any intention of entering into legislative competition for the securing of corporate capital within its jurisdiction, is, in fact, one of the most ardent bidders," Bostwick wrote.[104] For example, only three years after the passage of the New Jersey law, "the State of New York could no longer withstand the temptation, and the incorporation laws of this State were radically amended" to match the single most attractive New Jersey provision allowing holding companies. "[B]ut this came too late to get back any fugitive capital and still it continued to go elsewhere."[105]

The lesson, for Bostwick, was to remove most restraints on corporations. "The laissez faire doctrine is good in government, and a similar doctrine applied in politico-economic life is equally good," he concluded.[106] The infamous "race to the bottom" had begun. As state legislatures during the 1890s outbid each other in passing ever more "liberal" corporation laws that removed many of the remaining legal barriers to consolidation, the focus of those who hoped to preserve competition shifted to the Sherman Act.

But the New Jersey law confirmed the views of those who saw consolidation as inevitable, and during the 1890s, in both legal and economic writings, there is a marked shift toward the inevitability thesis.[107] By 1891, William W. Cook could declare that concentration was the result of "an established principle of economics." "It is a law of nature," he proclaimed. "These great concerns arise because by doing business on a large scale they can do it more cheaply."[108] "[M]ost of the younger economists of the country who have studied the question thoroughly," Von Halle reported in 1896, were "in favour of combinations." "Under the influence of historical thought, they feel convinced that the movement is an unavoidable step in an organic development, and that it finds its justification in the tendencies of modern capitalism. . . ."[109]

For the first time, the full implications of general incorporation laws began to be developed, and the view that legal forms cannot interfere with the natural evolution of the economy gained ascendancy. Commenting on the failure of legislation to check consolidation, Cook began the fifth edition of his celebrated treatise on corporation law with the aphorism "The laws of trade are stronger than the laws of men."[110]

In these writings on corporations, we find the earliest articulation of the contempt for legal form that eventually came to characterize Legal Realism. "Whether true or false, the maxim 'combination is the life of trade,' is an economic and in no sense a legal proposition," wrote Arthur J. Eddy, the author of a well-known legal treatise on combination in 1901. "If sound, economic forces will protect it; if unsound, neither legislative enactments nor judicial utterance can give it life . . . the courts might as well try to conserve Gresham's law, the Malthusian theory, Ricardo's doctrine of rent, or any other economic, scientific or philosophic notion."[111]

Legal structures merely reflect the underlying economic substructure. "[T]he corporate form of cooperation has been like all other industrial, commercial, social and political forms a matter of development," Eddy explained. "[I]n some sort it existed prior to its recognition by law . . . the law simply sanctioned a form of organization which the commercial and industrial world found useful and indispensable." Even if there were no laws creating corporations, "men would necessarily act together . . . in joint associations. . . ." "Since the law is simply the application of common sense and reason to existing conditions . . . the law would follow the economic tendency, [and] the collective bodies would be recognized . . . there would inevitably spring up in a progressive community organizations in form similar to the modern corporation."[112] The large industrial corporation was, in short, a natural reflection of the rational economic tendency toward combination. "Consolidation," concluded William W. Cook, "is the spirit of the age, moving on resistlessly, regardless of human laws and hostile public sentiment."[113] Those who "disapprove of trusts and combinations [for] general anti-centralistic and individualistic reasons," wrote the economist Ernst von Halle in 1895, "play into the hands of socialism."[114]

Consolidation and Majority Rule

If the private law of corporations—that is, the law regulating relations within the corporation as well as with private parties—had not changed after 1880, it is difficult to imagine how the enormous corporate consolidation of the next thirty years could have taken place. For until the First World War—by which time the centralization of the American economy was largely accomplished—state corporation law was deeply involved in the question of corporate consolidation.

After 1880, ultra vires doctrines continued to limit the power of corporations to consolidate. While courts still refused to enforce ultra vires executory contracts, they generally were not willing to unravel contracts that had already been performed. Most judicial decisions that stood in the way of corporate consolidation did so on the grounds that a corporation had no power to lease its property to another corporation or to transfer its stock to a holding company. The single area that dominated Supreme Court ultra vires decisions between 1880 and 1900 involved railroad consolidations. In a series of opinions during the last two decades of the nineteenth century, the Court consistently struck down as beyond corporate power arrangements by which one railroad leased all of its facilities to another line. The terms of these leases almost always exceeded the productive life of the assets transferred under them. Indeed, the Court occasionally gave its approval to the truly Draconian rule that the lessor under a void ultra vires agreement could not sue to recover the leased property or its value.[115]

While these "loose" forms of consolidation confronted various legal impediments, an outright sale of corporate assets to produce a merger rarely ran afoul of ultra vires limitations, since by the time the transactions were challenged in court they had already become executed contracts.

Some state courts were even noticeably unreceptive to the Supreme Court's views on leases used for consolidation. In 1886, the New Jersey Supreme Court treated such a lease as a fully executed contract that could not be interfered with.[116] And following a series of decisions generally hostile to the ultra vires doctrine, the New York Court of Appeals in 1896 enforced the terms of a public utility lease, denouncing "the rank injustice" produced by the Supreme Court's ultra vires rule.[117] William W. Cook, the treatise writer on corporation law, cheered the New York decision as "breaking away entirely from the decisions of the Supreme Court of the United States and of the English courts on this subject. . . ." "The court," he wrote, "will not declare a contract void merely to satisfy a superannuated principle of law."[118] The lease cases caused even Judge Seymour Thompson of St. Louis, in his 1899 treatise on corporation law, to denounce "the abominable doctrine of ultra vires."[119]

It is quite clear that the Supreme Court's strict attitude toward the ultra vires doctrine during the late nineteenth century was substantially related to hostility to corporate consolidation. An old conservative majority, favoring small competitive units of production and fearing large-scale enterprise, never really abandoned the traditional view of the corporation as an artificial creature of state power. It thus consistently deployed the ultra vires doctrine for the purpose of preventing further concentration.

There were essentially three stages in the efforts of corporations to achieve consolidation. The first stage, the "pool," represented a loose form of agreement employed by railroads, beginning in the 1870s, to fix rates and regulate traffic.

Through a combination of ultra vires and antitrust attacks, this form of carteli-zation was eventually defeated, though it had already proved to be largely unstable and impossible to enforce.[120]

A second effort, the "trust" or holding company, was fiercely and successfully attacked by state dissolution proceedings brought against the constituent compa-nies. The New Jersey Corporation law of 1889 was drafted to save the trusts, since it was among the first statutes to allow corporations to own shares in other cor-porations.[121] But even before federal power was successfully deployed against holding companies in the *Northern Securities* case (1904),[122] the trust form had lost favor and was replaced by direct merger.

The merger movement of 1898–1903 seems to have been based on the legal conclusion that courts might not deploy the Sherman Act to attack consolidation if it took the form of outright purchase of other businesses. Arthur Eddy wrote in 1901:

> The courts having condemned simple combinations [for example, pools or price-fixing agreements] and the trust form of combination as contrary to public policy, the corporate form naturally suggested itself as a possible escape from the force and effect of the many decisions adverse to the other forms. It was argued that while the courts might deny the right of individuals, firms or corporations to meet to-gether and form associations, pools or agreements with the intent to control prices and outputs, no court would deny the right of an individual, or of a partnership, or of a corporation to purchase outright the assets, business and good-will of any individual, firm or corporation engaged in the same line of trade or manufacture. . . . So long as the state sanctions the creation of corporations without limitations as to power and capital, then it would seem to follow that within their chartered rights corporations have the same power to acquire property as has an individual.[123]

It was the task of legal theory to show that there was no difference between the rights of individuals and corporations to acquire property.

With the merger movement beginning in 1898, corporate strategists thus turned to outright consolidation. This strategy was undoubtedly encouraged by the un-willingness of both state and federal courts to use the ultra vires doctrine to un-ravel already consummated transactions.[124] While the Supreme Court throughout the 1890s had regularly supported attacks on loose forms of consolidation by re-fusing to enforce arrangements for long-term lease of corporate assets, the merger movement rendered ultra vires constraints practically irrelevant.

The new legal pressure point in attacks on corporate consolidation shifted to the common law rule, required by nearly all courts during the 1880s, that unan-imous shareholder consent was necessary for the sale of corporate assets—or, in-deed, for any fundamental change in corporate purposes.[125] The rule of unani-mous consent, it should be noted, is a dramatic example of the extent to which partnership-contract categories governed important aspects of corporation law in the period immediately after the Civil War.[126] Any fundamental corporate change was regarded as a breach of the individual shareholder's contract, as well as, in effect, an unconsented taking of his property.[127]

The obstacle that unanimous shareholder consent presented for consolidation was seen as early as 1887 by New York lawyer William W. Cook, whose successive treatises on corporation law proclaimed the inevitability of economic concentration. With respect to the legal rule permitting any shareholder to object to a sale of assets, Cook accurately predicted in 1887 that "large interests will require and in some way will obtain a removal of the legal right of stockholders to object to the changes toward which the times are rapidly approaching."[128]

By the time the merger movement began, nearly all the states had passed general consolidation statutes applicable to railroad corporations.[129] These statutes permitted consolidation of lines with less than unanimous shareholder consent. In addition, by 1901, fourteen states, including Delaware (1899), New York (1890), and New Jersey (1896), had authorized any corporation "carrying on any kind of business of the same or similar nature" to merge with less than unanimous shareholder agreement.[130] The earliest consolidation statutes, therefore, permitted "horizontal" integration within industries while still denying corporations the power to engage in "vertical" mergers among different lines of business.

Vertical integration, therefore, came about not through statutorily authorized consolidations but through sale of assets. It still had to confront the general common law rule that any sale of corporate assets to achieve consolidation required unanimous agreement of the shareholders.

There was one small exception to the unanimity rule that was first exploited by consolidating corporations to avoid the consequences of the rule. Where a corporation was insolvent and had no prospects of profit, courts had permitted a simple majority of shareholders to wind up the business and sell all of its assets. In the wake of the merger movement, courts began simply to rubber-stamp the claims of the majority that the business was a failing one.[131] As a leading proponent of corporate consolidation put it in his 1902 treatise on consolidation:

> It has been urged that this power of a majority to wind up a corporation, and to dispose of its assets for such purpose, exists only in the case of failing concerns. The distinction is not well drawn. . . . The very best time to wind up the affairs of a corporation may be in view of future uncertainties when it is most prosperous and has accumulated a large surplus. The determination of the question when this action should be taken, must rest in the discretion of the majority.[132]

This position was soon adopted by the courts. Since it was clear that a majority could dissolve an insolvent corporation, "must [they] wait until the stockholders' investment is all lost before taking action?" the New Hampshire Supreme Court asked in 1912. "If the majority may sell to prevent greater losses, why may they not also sell to make greater gains?"[133] As a student of the subject has concluded: "In many [cases], it was . . . clear that the losing business was not being abandoned but was instead being continued by the new corporate owner of the assets. . . . By steps, then, these asset sales became de facto consolidations."[134]

At the same time as the judiciary was "sliding ineluctably toward majoritarianism in major corporation decisions involving shareholders,"[135] state legislatures began to take the lead in passing statutes allowing a majority to sell corporate assets. One of the earliest was a New York statute of 1893, which overruled the leading New York case expounding the unanimity rule.[136] In addition, Delaware in 1899 and New Jersey in 1902 passed legislation providing for appraisal and "buy out" of the shares of dissenting minority stockholders.[137] By 1926, there was "hardly a state where the dominant common law rule . . . ha[d] not been abrogated by statute or decision."[138]

The shift to majority rule in fact made the merger movement legally possible. It not only made consolidations much easier to effect; it also dealt the final blow to any efforts to conceptualize the corporation as a collection of contracting individual shareholders.

When the rule of unanimous shareholder consent began to be widely articulated by courts around the time of the Civil War, the leading treatise on corporations still regarded business corporations as "little more than limited partnerships, every member exercising through his vote an immediate control over the interests of the body."[139] As late as 1890, the leading decision of the U.S. Supreme Court did "not see that the rights of the parties in regard to [the sale of] the assets of [a] corporation differ from those of a partnership on its dissolution."[140] It referred to a treatise on partnership before reaffirming the rule of unanimity.

In his penetrating study *The Legal Nature of Corporations* (1897), Ernst Freund understood that the emergence of majority rule within a corporation could be justified only by some entity theory of the corporation that moved beyond contractualism and conceptions of individual property rights. How could the "corporate will" be identified with a simple majority of shareholders?, Freund asked.

> The true corporate will would be expressed by unanimous action resulting from common deliberation and mutual compromise and submission; but for purposes of convenience the law stops the process of reaching the conclusion halfway, and is satisfied with the concurrence of the greater portion of those acting. The justification of this legal expedient lies in the fact that the will of the majority may be presumed to express correctly what would be the result of forced unanimity; a presumption not always agreeable to fact, but convenient and more practicable than any other. . . . In so far as the presumption fails to be correct, it cannot be denied that a will which is not identical with the corporate will is imputed to the corporation, just as we impute the will of the agent to the principal without insisting that it should in all cases accord with the principal's will. The same view must be taken of the acts of other corporate organs; they may likewise be presumed to voice correctly the corporate will, but their will is not the corporate will strictly speaking.[141]

While Freund was tempted to derive majority rule from unanimous shareholder consent, he was forced to admit that it was a fiction "not always agreeable to fact." He turned instead to a theory of a separate corporate entity, "imput[ing]" to the corporation the "will" of the shareholders. Above all, majority rule was another example of Freund's conclusion "that in dealing with associations of persons we must modify the ideas which we have derived from the right of property in individuals, and what has first seemed to be an anomaly will appear simply as another but equally legitimate form of development."[142]

Attack on the Entity Theory

The first sustained effort to reconceptualize the corporation in the light of the triumph of general incorporation laws began during the 1880s.

In 1882, Victor Morawetz first published *A Treatise on the Law of Private Corporations*, which proposed a radical reinterpretation of the legal status of the corporation. The corporation, Morawetz wrote in the second edition, "is really an association formed by the agreement of its shareholders, and . . . the existence of a corporation as an entity, independently of its members, is a fiction."[143]

Morawetz treated corporations as virtually indistinguishable from partnerships. "[T]here is no reason of immediate justice to others, why a number of individuals should not be permitted to form a corporation of their own free will, and without first obtaining permission from the legislature, just as they may form a partnership or enter into ordinary contracts with each other."[144]

General incorporation laws "to a great extent . . . leave the right of forming a corporation and of acting in a corporate capacity free to all, subject to such limitations and safeguards as are required for the protection of the public." The only argument for restricting corporate powers, he claimed, was that notice of the limited liability of shareholders needed to be communicated to potential creditors. "And this seems to be the chief office of the general incorporation laws which are now in force nearly everywhere."[145]

The source of corporate power was, for Morawetz, the shareholders. The principle of majority rule was derived, as in a partnership, from *unanimous* shareholder consent. So the majority could not go beyond the purpose specified in its charter without the unanimity of the shareholders. Thus, the doctrine of ultra vires, originally derived from the grant theory of the corporation, should be replaced by the requirement of unanimous shareholder agreement, as in a partnership. Regulation of corporate activity would come not from the state but from the shareholders.

Morawetz's effort to disaggregate the corporation into freely contracting individuals must have seemed at the time the only entirely logical conclusion to draw in light of the triumph of general incorporation law. It not only dispensed with an increasingly fictional conception of the corporation as a creature of the state, it also made it possible to fit corporation law into the now dominant individualistic mode of private contract law.

The tendency to reconceptualize the corporation along partnership-contractualist lines continued during the 1880s. In 1884, two years after Morawetz's treatise, Henry O. Taylor, another New York lawyer, wrote *A Treatise on the Law of Private Corporations Having Capital Stock*, which was aimed, he said, at "dismissing this fiction" of the "legal personality" of the corporation so that "a

clearer view" of individual rights and interests could be determined "without unnecessary mystification."[146]

Taylor was supported by John Norton Pomeroy, the California lawyer who
was simultaneously putting forth this argument on behalf of the corporation in
the *Santa Clara* case. Pomeroy emphasized the significance of general incorporation laws in rendering older conceptions of incorporation anachronistic. "The
common-law conception of the 'legal personality' of the metaphysical entity constituting the corporation, entirely distinct from its individual [members], arose at
a time when corporations were all created by special charters," Pomeroy wrote.
This situation had changed under general incorporation laws in which "persons
complying with a few formal requisites can organize themselves into a company
for almost any business purpose . . . these associations differ very little in their
essential attributes from partnerships."[147]

It is not entirely clear to what extent the legal thinkers who advocated a
partnership-contractualist conception of the corporation during the 1880s were
motivated by any particular political vision or attitude toward corporations. Overtly,
they seemed only to wish to bring corporation law into line with the new reality
of free incorporation. Pomeroy and Justice Field clearly believed that the partnership theory offered the greatest chance of success in protecting the corporation
under the Fourteenth Amendment. Yet their individualistic language harkened
back to earlier Jacksonian criticisms of corporations as special privileges and monopolies. And despite the fact that the clear tendency of attacks upon the traditional theory that corporations were creatures of the state was to undermine any
claims to special state control of corporations, the partnership theory was soon
treated as supporting an anti-corporate position.

Perhaps that was a correct understanding of its ultimate tendency. For example, Henry O. Taylor, the New York lawyer and corporate law treatise writer,
appears to have been aware that his effort to dismiss the "fiction" of corporate
personality for producing "unnecessary mystification" might also call into question
the legitimacy of limited shareholder liability. Like Chief Justice Taney,[148] Taylor
observed that limited liability was "the logical outcome of the notion of a corporation as a person, as a subject of rights and liabilities distinct from its members,"[149] a notion he was doing his best to undermine.

There were many suggestions during the 1890s that a contractual theory might
subvert corporate privileges. Writing in 1892, Dwight A. Jones focused on the de-
legitimating tendency of the partnership theory.

> The main value of a corporate charter arises from the fact that powers and privi-
> leges are thereby acquired which individuals do not possess. It is this that makes
> the difference between a business corporation and a partnership. In the former
> there is no individual liability. . . . There is no death. . . . It is not policy there-
> fore for a corporation to break down its own independent existence by burying its
> original character in the common place privileges of the individual. . . . *Any
> mingling of corporate existence with the existence of the shareholders will weaken
> corporate rights.*[150]

Indeed, opponents of corporate consolidation during the 1890s often advocated elimination of the corporate form and return to the partnership. One of the most influential American economists, Henry C. Adams, saw in the extension of the corporate form the root cause of the growth of economic concentration that was destroying competitive society. "[T]hese corporations," he wrote in 1894, "assert for themselves most of the rights conferred on individuals by the law of private property, and apply to themselves a social philosophy true only of a society composed of individuals who are industrial competitors." [151] Adams's solution was to limit the benefits of the corporate form to those "natural monopolies" that could actually demonstrate economies of scale. [152]

Was there not good reason, then, to suspect that any contractualist theory of the corporation was only the first step toward attacking the corporate form itself? In 1900 Christopher G. Tiedeman published his *Treatise on State and Federal Control of Persons and Property in the United States*, [153] a greatly expanded and retitled version of his influential *Treatise on the Limitations of Police Power* (1886). The later book is filled with the anguish of the old conservative witnessing the rise of industrial concentration. Tiedeman wrote:

> It does not take a very keen observer to note that, for the past fifteen or twenty years, the tendency to the establishment of all-powerful and all-controlling combinations of capital . . . has been increasing year by year in this country. . . .
> The rapid accumulation of vast fortunes has inspired some of their possessors with the desire for the acquisition of power through the control of industries of such great extension and scope, that they may earn the appellation of kings instead of princes of industry. If this economic tendency were left unchecked, either by economic conditions or law, the full fruition of it would be a menace to the liberty of the individual, and to the stability of the American States as popular governments. . . . [154]

Finally, Tiedeman brought the power of incorporation itself into focus:

> [A]ll attempts to suppress and prevent combinations in restraint of trade must necessarily prove futile, as long as the statutes of the State permit the creation of private corporations. . . . The grant of charters of incorporation . . . only serves to intensify the natural power which the capitalist in his individual capacity possesses over the noncapitalist, by the mere possession of the capital. I advocate, as a return to a uniform recognition of the constitutional guaranty of equality before the law, the repeal of the statutes which provide for the creation of private corporations. [155]

The contractualist view of the corporation as essentially no different from a partnership began to come under attack from the moment it was presented. Its most forceful claim was that any entity theory of the corporation was fictional and an anachronistic carryover from a bygone era of special corporate charters. Yet the picture of the corporation as a contract among individual shareholders was itself becoming a nostalgic fantasy at the very moment the partnership view was most forcefully put forth.

Some of the contractualists seemed to have had in the backs of their minds an ideal of what in a later age would be called "shareholder democracy." But during the 1880s it was beginning to become clear that the managers, not the shareholders, were the real decision makers in large, publicly owned enterprises.[156] Ironically, Morawetz published his contractualist theory in the same year that Standard Oil was organized into the first of the great trusts. Soon the oligarchic tendency of the trusts became a point of standard observation.

During the 1880s, the judicially imposed requirement of shareholder unanimity for fundamental corporate changes continued to provide the doctrinal foundation for a partnership theory of the corporation. But during the 1890s, several states, including the commercially significant jurisdictions of Delaware, New York, and New Jersey, passed statutes that overthrew the unanimity rule for corporate consolidations. Many of these statutes also substantially enhanced the power of the board of directors to initiate such action.[157]

By the time of the First World War, it was common for legal writers to observe that "the modern stockholder is a negligible factor in the management of a corporation."[158] "It cannot be too strongly emphasized," another wrote, "that stockholders today are primarily investors and not proprietors."[159]

The Demise of the Trust Fund Doctrine: The New Relationship of the Shareholder to the Corporation

One of the best measures of the shift in the conception of shareholders from "members" to "investors" in the corporation is the demise of the "trust fund doctrine" beginning in the 1890s. The demise of the doctrine was paralleled by the growth of corporations, the diversification of corporate ownership, and the subsequent expansion of the stock market.

The rise of the natural entity theory at the same time presented a picture of the corporation that legitimated the doctrine's demise.

The origin of the doctrine is found in Justice Story's celebrated opinion in *Wood v. Dummer* (1824),[160] declaring that the capital stock of a corporation was a trust fund for the benefit of corporate creditors. Its central purpose was to make the stockholders of an insolvent corporation liable for their failure to pay the full or par value of any stock to which they subscribed from a corporation.[161] This question of the extent of shareholder liability for "watered stock"—stock issued for less than par value—represented one of the two or three most important issues in corporate law during the late nineteenth century and generated hundreds of cases and thousands of pages of legal writing.

Accusations of widespread corporate fraud and financial manipulation focused on the watered-stock question. And amid the wreckage of the 1893 depression, judges and legal writers faced the fact that enforcement of the trust fund doctrine had "punished the innocent and unsettled hundreds of millions of dollars of investments."[162]

In one case prior to the depression, the U.S. Supreme Court held stockholders liable for watered stock more than twenty-five years after the company failed.[163] In observing the changes that the depression had produced, William W. Cook wrote: "Corporation ruin has created corporation law."[164]

HISTORY OF LIMITED SHAREHOLDER LIABILITY. It is not usually appreciated that truly limited shareholder liability was far from the norm in America even as late as 1900.[165] Though by the time of the Civil War the common law had evolved to the point of presuming limited shareholder liability in the absence of any legislative rule, in fact most states had enacted constitutional or statutory provisions holding shareholders of an insolvent corporation liable for more than the value of their shares. The most typical provision, which first appeared in an 1848 New York statute providing for general incorporation of manufacturing companies,[166] imposed double liability on shareholders. By the end of the nineteenth century, this provision "ha[d] been copied, in its essential features, in almost every State in the Union."[167] Many other constitutional or statutory enactments imposed even more extensive potential liability on shareholders.[168] As a result, the distinction between the liability of the members of a corporation and a partnership, so clear to modern eyes, was still regarded as a matter of degree rather than of kind throughout the nineteenth century. And even within the strictest limited liability jurisdictions, the trust fund doctrine promulgated by the courts made innocent shareholders potentially liable for the difference between the par value and the purchase price of their shares.

When the doctrine came under attack during the 1890s, its defenders emphasized that its main function was to protect creditors who had a right to suppose that the stated capital stock of a corporation reflected its real value. For a corporation to sell shares at discount was, they argued, a fraud on subsequent creditors. But unlike its original partnership rationale, this argument for the trust fund doctrine already conceded that corporations were separate entities and that the stockholders were only investors, not owners, managers, or members of a corporation. If the trust fund doctrine was simply designed to give notice to protect creditors, the doctrine's opponents replied, it could only apply to subsequent creditors, since existing creditors could not have relied on a subsequent issue of watered stock.

By degrees, courts beginning in the 1890s gradually eroded the trust fund doctrine. One of the most important immediate influences in producing the change was the rise of a national stock market, which definitively converted shareholders into impersonal investors. Yet, this was only the culmination of a long-term transformation by which shareholders, once regarded as members of a corporation, not fundamentally different from partners, came to be treated as completely separate from the corporate entity itself.

THE STRUCTURAL TRANSFORMATION OF THE CORPORATION. In order to comprehend the changes in legal doctrine during the 1890s, we should first understand the dramatic changes in the structure of the business corporation, as well as the market for stock that developed during the 1880–1900 period.

The major changes were in the size and scale of industrial companies. Before 1890, only railroads constituted "large, well-established, widely known enterprises with securities traded on organized stock exchanges, while industrials, though numerous, were small, scattered, closely owned, and commonly regarded as unstable."[169] Most of the manufacturing enterprises of the 1880s have been described as "small" companies, with a net worth under $2 million. For the sake of comparison, there were extremely few "very large" companies worth more than $10 million, and even enterprises classified as "large" (worth between $5 million and $10 million) were also "fairly rare."[170] By contrast, "each of the country's ten largest railroads had more than $100 million of net worth and the largest of them all, the Pennsylvania Railroad, had over $200 million."[171]

In manufacturing, "the partnership form of organization predominated. . . . Where enterprises were incorporated, and, therefore, had outstanding securities, these were generally held by a small group of persons and were infrequently offered for sale to the public."[172]

Most of the leading manufacturing companies were family-owned. Even two of the "very large" companies, Singer Manufacturing and McCormick Harvesting Machine, were controlled by and had a majority of their stock owned by the family. And Andrew Carnegie's combined steel interests, which constituted among the very largest of manufacturing enterprises, were organized as closely owned partnerships until they converted to the corporate form in 1892.[173]

Nearly all of the distributive enterprises—wholesalers like Marshall Field in Chicago, and retailers like R. H. Macy's in New York and John Wanamaker in Philadelphia—were organized as partnerships, as were companies in gold mining and oil drilling. And while the processing branch of industry—oil refining, sugar refining, lead smelting—was the first category in which large-scale, publicly owned enterprises (besides railroads) developed during the 1880s, the meat processing giants, Swift and Armour, retained the partnership form well into the 1880s:

> Before 1890 a man with excess capital to invest was likely to put his money into real estate. If he chose to buy securities, he had a relatively narrow range from which to select. The principal type of security investment was in railroading. Industrial securities, except in the coal and textile industries, were almost unknown.[174]

Those industrial securities that did exist were usually exchanged only in "direct person-to-person sales."[175] Between 1890 and 1893, however, industrials began to be listed on the New York Stock Exchange and to be traded by leading brokerage houses. Only after 1897, in the midst of the merger movement, did companies publicly offer shares of stock, replacing the system of private subscriptions that had prevailed throughout the nineteenth century. Between 1896 and 1907, the number of shares traded on the Stock Exchange soared from 57 million to 260 million.[176] It is perhaps at this point that we can clearly identify the beginning of the shift away from "the traditional point of view" of shareholders as "the ultimate owners, the corporate equivalent of partners and proprietors."[177]

THE OVERTHROW. When Seymour Thompson published his six-volume treatise on corporation law in 1895, he lamented the fact that the trust fund doctrine had only recently "been greatly modified" by American courts—"so much so, that it may now be doubted whether the capital of a corporation is a trust fund for its creditors in any different sense than the sense in which the property of a private person is a trust fund for his creditors."[178]

Beginning in 1887, the New York Court of Appeals overthrew the trust fund doctrine.[179] And, in a widely followed opinion, the Minnesota Supreme Court held in 1892 that only fraud could permit a creditor to recover against a holder of watered stock.[180] The most important consequence of this shift to a fraud theory was that in a majority of jurisdictions only subsequent creditors—those who presumably had relied on representations about the capital stock of the corporation—could sue on watered stock.[181]

But the most controversial departures from the trust fund doctrine appeared in a series of cases decided by the U.S. Supreme Court in 1891 through 1893. In the leading case of *Handley v. Stutz* (1891),[182] the Court, while purporting to reaffirm the trust fund doctrine, distinguished between the original subscription to corporate shares, to which traditional trust fund shareholder liability applied, and a subsequent issue of shares at a discount by a "going concern," which created non-liability. Even Seymour Thompson conceded that where an established corporation "finds itself in urgent need" of money, "it would be a hard and perhaps a mischievous rule that would prevent it from reselling the shares at their market value."[183] Yet he protested that, taken together, Supreme Court decisions had "overturn[ed] all former rulings" of the Supreme Court and "totally obliterat[ed]"[184] the trust fund doctrine.

Handley v. Stutz and companion cases provided the opportunity for those who wished to attack the trust fund doctrine. In its different treatment of the original and subsequent stock issues, wrote George Wharton Pepper, the Supreme Court had undertaken "the impossible task of distinguishing on principle between the status of two sets of stockholders."[185] Based on the Court's decisions, he concluded, the trust fund doctrine "is neither a theory nor a doctrine."[186]

The seeming incoherence of the Court's distinction between the liability of different classes of shareholders encouraged advocacy of the more restricted fraud theory of liability.[187] Indeed, between 1891 and 1893, the Supreme Court itself wavered between theological reaffirmation of the trust fund doctrine and statements that went to the verge of overruling it.[188]

The root of the problem was that the relationship of the shareholder to the corporation had begun to change fundamentally during the 1890s. "[T]he liability of the stockholder to pay in full for his stock was an obligation placed upon him because of his relation to the corporation." Under "the traditional point of view," the shareholders were "the ultimate owners, the corporate equivalent of partners and proprietors."[189]

But as the market for shares widened, the relation of the shareholders to the corporation began to be redefined. For example, one of the major limitations on the trust fund doctrine began to take shape even before *Handley v. Stutz* was decided. Was a subsequent bona fide purchaser of watered stock liable to creditors? No, answered the influential jurist John F. Dillon in an 1879 railroad stock case.

> Millions of dollars of stocks are sold in this country every week, and there is no practice on the part of purchasers, and no understanding that the law requires of them that they shall ascertain . . . that certificates of full-paid stock have, in fact, been fully paid. . . . Besides, on what principle is it that a purchaser of the company's shares is to be held to be the guardian of the rights of the company's creditors and bound to protect them?[190]

As the marketing of corporate shares moved away from formal private subscriptions, the meaningfulness of the Supreme Court's distinction between original and subsequent issues of stock began to collapse. So too, as Judge Dillon had suggested, did the difference between bona fide purchasers of original and subsequent shares. William W. Cook wrote in 1898:

> Certificates of stock have become such important factors in trade and credit, and general investment by all classes, that the law is steadily tending towards the complete protection of a bona fide purchaser of them in open market. . . . The constant tendency of the courts to increase the negotiability of certificates of stock will probably establish the rule that the purchaser in good faith of a certificate of stock is not liable on any unpaid subscription price thereof, unless such liability is stated on the face of the certificate itself. Indeed, even now this may be said to be the established rule.[191]

With the development of investment banking after 1900, even the marketing of original shares of corporate stock no longer entailed a formal relationship between the corporation and a subscriber. The original investor who purchased shares in the market for less than par value now was in a position no different from that of the subsequent bona fide purchaser whom courts had already been protecting against creditors.[192]

The establishment of a complete market for stock thus made an anachronism of the trust fund doctrine. Indeed, New York in 1912 and Delaware in 1917 permitted the issue of stock without par value, and by 1924 thirty-four states had followed suit.[193] The Delaware law "in effect though not in form . . . cut off the creditors' remedy of shareholders' liability" when stock was issued for property or services.[194] By 1924, James C. Bonbright noted "that many lawyers with a long and extensive practice in corporation cases have never had a single suit involving a shareholder's liability on watered stock."[195] Little more than a generation earlier, by contrast, such suits had been the stock in trade of legal writing on corporation law.

When the trust fund doctrine first came under attack during the 1890s, George Wharton Pepper noted that "many fundamental questions in regard to the legal status of corporations are still unsettled. . . . [I]t may be doubted whether any six learned judges would to-day give explanations even substantially similar of the difference between corporations and joint stock companies or statutory partnerships."[196] Indeed, as Pepper noted, one of the theories that might make the trust fund doctrine coherent was a partnership theory, "the view that the corporation is identical with the members that compose it."[197] But the tendency of courts to distinguish between prior and subsequent purchasers of watered stock—a shift from the trust fund to the fraud doctrine—had already begun to erode such a conception.

When Pepper introduced Maitland's work on Gierke to an American audience in 1901, he was quick to notice that a natural entity theory of the corporation made the trust fund doctrine "unnecessary."[198] And a year later, a critic of the doctrine charged the Supreme Court with "refus[al] to accept the consequences" of an entity theory of the corporation, which meant, he believed, overthrow of the trust fund doctrine.[199]

The natural entity theory of the corporation thus emerged at virtually the same moment that the trust fund doctrine began to collapse. As we have seen, one of the major organizing premises of the natural entity theory was to posit the existence of a sharp distinction between the corporate entity and the shareholders. It was precisely this distinction that ultimately subverted the coherence of the trust fund doctrine.

The Corporate Entity and the Power of Directors

At some point at the beginning of the twentieth century, American legal opinion began to shift decisively to the view that "the powers of the board of directors . . . are identical with the powers of the corporation.";[200] Earlier, the dominant view, as expressed by the U.S. Supreme Court, was that "when the charter was silent, the ultimate determination of the management of the corporate affairs rests with its stock holders."[201] "The law," said one federal court in 1881, "recognizes the stockholders as the ultimately controlling power in the corporation. . . ."[202] But modern corporate legislation, passed during the first quarter of the twentieth century, ratified a new "absolutism" that courts themselves had already begun to bestow upon corporate directors.[203]

Writing in 1895, Seymour Thompson identified "three radically different views"[204] that were still entertained by courts and legal thinkers concerning the nature and limits of the powers of corporate directors.

> 1. That the directors, being chosen representatives of the corporation, constitute, for all purposes of dealing with others, *the corporation itself*; hence, that within the scope of the objects and purpose of the corporation they have all the powers of the corporation itself. 2. That the directors have all the powers of *general agents* in the management of corporate affairs. 3. That they have only the powers of *special agents*. . . .[205]

In an early Supreme Court case involving the Bank of the United States, the Court, per Justice Story, had clearly rejected, over a dissent by Chief Justice John

Marshall, the first, and most expansive, definition of the powers of directors.[206] "In ordinary business corporations," Thompson concluded, "the powers of the board of directors fall far short of being co-equal with the powers of the corporation."[207] In England, the judges had limited the directors' powers even further by classifying them within the most restrictive category of special agents. "On the whole," Thompson concluded, "judicial theory, at least in America, greatly preponderates in favor of the proposition that the directors of a business corporation are its *general* or managing agents."[208]

The classification of directors as agents itself underwent some important changes. The leading antebellum treatise on corporation law, by Angell and Ames, best reflects the earlier understanding of the limited legal position of the board of directors in the corporation. Whereas Judge Thompson's 1895 treatise devoted almost 500 pages to the legal status of directors, there is not even a separate chapter on the subject in the 1861 edition of the Angell and Ames treatise. Their discussion of directors is scattered throughout a chapter on "Agents of Corporations," which indiscriminately lumps together officers and directors. The authors confidently declared that, in the absence of any contrary legal provisions, "the power to appoint officers and agents rests, of course, like every other power, in the body of the corporators" or shareholders.[209] And, most important, they announced the widely held view that directors have no inherent power "to appoint subagents to contract for the corporation . . . and accordingly contracts made by such subagents will not be binding on the corporation."[210]

In his 1877 treatise on corporation law, George W. Field observed that it was "usual" for corporations to confer the authority for managing the business "upon a limited number of the members usually called directors or managers, who act, in most respects . . . as agents for and in place of the corporation, and of the stockholders." In the absence of any other legal provision, wrote Field, "it is evident, on general principles, that the corporators [stockholders] would possess such power."[211] However, when in 1897 Professor Ernst Freund addressed the question of whether the relation between the board of directors and "the members at large of the corporation" was the same as or different from "that of principal and agent," he concluded that "both views have found judicial support."[212] While Freund saw that the agency analogy broke down to the extent that a majority shareholder resolution could not supersede the managing authority of the board, he did insist that, logically, unanimous shareholder action was the ultimate authority in the corporation. Indeed, Freund seemed to have endorsed "the view that the members at large are the true and ultimate holders of the corporate rights."[213]

The judicial reaction to the idea that corporate directors, being agents, could not delegate their powers to subagents is perhaps the best litmus test for identifying the changing legal status of directors. Only in the early twentieth century did courts widely assert that, because the directors were "the primary possessors of all the powers which the charter confers," the board's powers were therefore "original and undelegated" and hence could be conferred upon agents.[214]

The leading twentieth-century treatise on the power of corporate directors was written to reflect this shift in legal opinion. Howard Holton Spellman wrote in 1931:

> The enlargement of facilities for the purchase and sale of corporate securities, the tendency toward combinations of corporations, and the consequent desirability of diversification of individual investments have joined to create a class of stockholders who regard themselves as investors rather than co-entrepreneurs. . . . Accordingly, modern decisions tend toward an emphasis of the directors' absolutism in the management of the affairs of large corporations; the board of directors has achieved a super-control of corporate management and of the corporation's legal relations. . . .[215]

This shift in the internal constitution of the corporation was among the most important reasons for the demise of the partnership-contract theory of the corporation after 1900. Ernst Freund's "representation" theory of the corporation, for example, was directly dependent on "the view that the members at large are the true and ultimate holders of the corporate rights."[216] In 1897, Freund could still suppose that the realities of internal corporate organization could support such a theory. Yet he already saw that "where the whole sum of corporate powers is vested by law directly in a board of directors . . . such an organization . . . allows us to see in a large railroad, banking or insurance corporation rather an aggregation of capital than an association of persons."[217]

The Natural Entity Theory

For orthodox legal writers of the 1880s, it still seemed sufficient to quote John Marshall's view of the corporation as an artificial entity in order to combat the partnership theory. They could also cite many of Supreme Court ultra vires decisions that continued to treat the corporation as a creature of the state.

Above all, the artificial entity theory stood in the way of corporate consolidation. For those who, like Arthur Eddy, wished to argue that "corporations have the same power to acquire property as has an individual,"[218] it was essential that the artificial entity theory be overthrown. For Eddy, theories such as that of the New York Court of Appeals in the celebrated Sugar Trust case amounted to "a positive restriction of that liberty which is guaranteed by free institutions." The New York court had written:

> It is not a sufficient answer to say that similar results may be lawfully accomplished; that an individual having the necessary wealth might have bought all these refineries, manned them with his own chosen agents, and managed them as a group at his sovereign will; for it is one thing for the State to respect the rights of ownership and protect them out of regard to the business freedom of the citizen, and quite another thing to add to that possibility a further extension of those consequences by creating artificial persons to aid in producing such aggregations. The individuals are few who hold in possession such enormous wealth, and fewer still who peril it

all in a manufacturing enterprise; but if corporations can combine, and mass their forces in a solid trust or partnership, with little added risk to the capital already embarked, without limit to the magnitude of the aggregation, a tempting and easy road is opened to enormous combinations, vastly exceeding in number and in strength and in their power over industry any possibilities of individual ownership; and the State by the creation of the artificial persons constituting the elements of the combination . . . becomes itself the responsible creator, the voluntary cause of an aggregation of capital which it simply endures in the individual as the product of his free agency. What it may bear is one thing, what it should cause and create is quite another.[219]

During the 1890s, one finds a growing attack on this artificial entity theory of the corporation. Perhaps the original appeal of the contracturalists to the underlying meaning of general incorporation laws had begun to sink in. Or, perhaps, the casual declaration by the Supreme Court in 1886 that the business corporation was a person under the Fourteenth Amendment was beginning to have an effect, though the real significance of that doctrine was still in the future. More probably, the phenomenal migration of corporations to New Jersey after 1889 made legal thinkers finally see that, in fact as well as in theory, corporations could do virtually anything they wanted. The literature of the 1890s on the inevitability of concentrated enterprise reflected this new reality by emphasizing for the first time the epiphenomenal nature of legal forms.

Beginning in the 1890s and reaching a high point around 1920, there is a virtual obsession in the legal literature with the question of corporate personality.[220] Over and over again, legal writers attempted to find a vocabulary that would enable them to describe the corporation as a real or natural entity whose existence is prior to and separate from the state. What the contractualists first tried to express, with only the vocabulary and concepts of natural rights individualism then available to them, the entity theorists completed.

Along with the contractualists, they sought to represent the corporation as entirely separate from the state and therefore private. Contrary to the contractualists, they insisted that groups were just as real as individuals and that, in addition, the corporation was separate and distinct from its shareholders.

The earliest group of these natural entity theorists, writing in ignorance of both Gierke and Maitland, simply repeated over and over again that the corporation was not fictional but real, and that it was a fact like any other holder of rights.[221] Corporations were "autonomous, self-sufficient and self-renewing bod[ies]," and "they may determine and enforce their common will." "[N]either the group nor its functions is created by the state."[222]

The most powerful of these early efforts to express the reality of groups was German-trained University of Chicago Professor Ernst Freund's *The Legal Nature of Corporations* (1897). Influenced by the work of Gierke on the nature of the corporation, Freund sought to translate Gierke's Hegelian analysis for a practical-minded and anti-metaphysical American bar.

For Freund, the basic conflict was between the fiction theory, which denied the idea of a distinct legal personality in the corporation, and the organic theory, propounded by many German jurists, "who insist that the distinctiveness of the corporate personality is as real as the individuality of a physical person."[223] The proponents of the fiction theory, by contrast, argued that a corporate entity "is nothing but the sum of its parts,"[224] ultimately reducible to the reality of individual wills.

Running through Freund's argument is the effort to overcome the traditional private law emphasis on the individual character of legal rights. "If the individual, private and beneficial right is to measure and govern all rules relating to rights of whatsoever nature, then the corporate right will continue to be abnormal and illogical."[225] On the other hand, the organic theory was "illusory" in encouraging "the impression that . . . corporate personality possesses an absolute unity and distinctiveness. . . ."[226] Its emphasis on the psychological cohesiveness and organic unity of groups did not really describe the business corporation, whose members were "without any noticeable psychological connection" even though they "may easily exercise common rights."[227] Above all, German organicist theory had lost itself "in metaphysical speculations and refined distinctions of little substantial value."[228]

Between individualism and organicism, Freund presented a theory of "representation," which portrayed the corporation as a representative democracy governed by majority rule. When "we speak of an act or an attribute as corporate, it is not corporate in the psychologically collective sense, but merely representative, and imputed to the corporation for reasons of policy and convenience."[229]

But Freund acknowledged the radical break with individualism he was proposing for corporate theory. He was, after all, attempting to justify the power of the corporate majority to bind the minority:

> That each person should fully answer for all his acts, and should not answer for the acts of others, is indeed a maxim of extraordinary importance, and it seems to be violated in the admission of representative action not resting upon express delegation. Against this it can only be urged that the maxim without modification is unjustifiable, because it antagonizes or prevents the full protection of joint interests, which, as we have seen, demand representation. The foundation of all liability upon principles of moral responsibility is a legal conception which may be carried to excessive lengths; even if fully justified where liability is penal and the moral quality of the act is of the essence of its legal aspect, it may be inadequate where it is simply a question of adjusting conflicting interests in accordance with prevailing ideas of justice and equity.[230]

Yet, as with the earlier contractual theorists, Freund had his greatest difficulty in accounting for the oligarchic tendencies that were already becoming dominant within the large corporation. Many statutes vested corporate powers directly in the board of directors, he noted. At that point, he acknowledged, "corporate capacity would thereby be shifted from the members at large to the governing body. . . . Such an organization reduces the personal cohesion between the [shareholders] to a minimum, and allows us to see in a large railroad, banking or insurance corporation rather an aggregation of capital than an association of persons."[231]

At the very moment, then, at which Freund sought to derive the corporate personality from majority rule of the shareholders, the corporate entity itself was becoming virtually independent of the shareholders. It required a still more abstract justification of corporate personality, divorced entirely from any pretense that, ultimately, the shareholders ruled.

Two years after Freund wrote, Henry Williams attempted that justification. In an article in the *American Law Register* he asserted that shareholders "possess no actual existing legal interest . . . whatever" in a corporation. Even in the case of dissolution, "when their actual legal rights first accrue," shareholders' rights were "entirely subsidiary" to those of creditors. "The stockholders," he concluded, "are in the position of the heirs, or next of kin or residuary legatees of a living person."[232]

In the flood of articles on corporate personality after the turn of the century, legal writers continued to reinforce the notion that a group must be treated as "an organic whole . . . which cannot be analyzed into the mere sum of its parts."[233] The corporation, these writers insisted, was a real entity, a fact, not a fiction.[234] University of Chicago Law Professor Arthur W. Machen summed up these views in an influential 1911 article, emphasizing "the naturalness and indeed inevitableness of the conception of a corporation as an entity":

> In these days it has become fashionable to inveigh against the doctrine that a corporation is an entity, as a mere technicality and a relic of the Middle Ages; but nothing could be further from the truth. A corporation is an entity—not imaginary or fictitious, but real, not artificial but natural.[235]

Following the inevitability theorists, Machen underlined the new view that the corporation existed prior to law. "All that the law can do is to recognize, or refuse to recognize, the existence of this entity. The law can no more create such an entity than it can create a house out of a collection of loose bricks."[236]

What was the political significance of the thousands of pages devoted to the question of corporate personality? The argument between entity and contractual theorists during the 1880s and 1890s was, at bottom, a conflict over whether the individual or the group was the appropriate unit of economic, political, and legal analysis. Some contractualists were openly hostile to big business and offered the partnership model as an alternative to the corporate form, to which they ascribed most of the evils of consolidation and monopoly. But other contractualists were not so much opposed to the corporation as they were to its oligarchic tendencies. Contractualism was, for them, a way of reasserting the primacy of shareholder control.

In one important respect, contractualism prepared the way for the triumph of the natural entity theory. Reasoning from individualist premises so prominent in the decades immediately after the Civil War, the contractualists were the first to see the anomalous character of the artificial entity theory of the corporation, not only because it clashed with the underlying spirit of general incorporation laws but also because of its hostility to any theory of natural rights. Every bit as much as the natural entity theorists, the contractualists worked from a conception of property as existing prior to the state. By contrast, the artificial entity theory represented a standing reminder of the social creation of property rights.

The main effect of the natural entity theory of the business corporation was to legitimate large-scale enterprise and to destroy any special basis for state regulation of the corporation that derived from its creation by the state. Indeed, the demise of the ultra vires doctrine, as well as of constitutional restrictions on foreign corporations, was an expression of the triumph of the natural entity theory. An entity theory was also helpful for advocating even more limited shareholder liability while justifying the growing irrelevance of the shareholders in the modern business corporation. Finally, it obliterated the claim that corporate mergers were different from individual acquisitions of property.

In their emphasis on corporate personality, early natural entity adherents attempted simply to capitalize on the language of natural rights individualism by portraying the corporation as just another right-bearing person. Most later Progressive legal thinkers, however, followed Ernst Freund's more realistic effort, dismissing the idea of corporate personality as merely a metaphor. But the Progressives were at one in seeking to demonstrate the real and natural character of corporations.

If the natural entity theory arose to legitimate emerging large-scale enterprise, it became in the hands of Progressive thinkers a way of being realistic about social and economic trends. Large corporations were here to stay, and, as one of the ablest Progressive legal writers, Gerard Henderson, put it in 1918, the natural entity theory "looks upon a corporation . . . as a normal business unit, and its legal personality as no more than a convenient mechanism of commerce and industry. . . . [T]he material basis is the growing internationalism of business, of trade, of investment."[237]

By the time Henderson wrote, Progressives were struggling to emancipate themselves from legal conceptions rooted in natural rights individualism. If the central goal of earlier natural entity theorists had been to extend the natural rights of individuals to the corporate personality, the Progressives instead sought to show that all rights, both corporate and personal, were entirely the creatures of the state. Henderson wrote:

> When we speak of a corporation being the subject of rights, we mean that it has the capacity to enter into legal relations—to make contracts, own property, bring suits. Rights, in this sense, are pure creatures of the law. . . . There is no reason, except the practical one, why, as some one has suggested, the law should not accord to the last rose of summer a legal right not to be plucked.[238]

Thus, the "corporate device" was "not an expression of any inherent philosophic quality in the group—of any group will, or group organism. It is no more than a convenient technical device . . . to achieve the practical results desired, of unity of action, continuity of policy, [and] limited liability. . . .[239]

Both the fictional and the realist schools had unnecessarily assumed that only persons could be the bearers of legal rights, Henderson argued. "The assumption that a person alone can be the subject of rights is based on the conception of a right as a philosophic entity, springing out of the nature of man, independent of the law and anterior to it."[240] This view "modern jurisprudence has very generally rejected."[241]

Henderson echoed Pound in arguing that there were, in fact, not "rights" but "interests."[242] Thus, the "practical" recognition of the corporate entity in no way implied special privileges or protections for corporations. "The social purposes for which legislation may override private interests are of the broadest sort, and fortunately their scope is constantly growing. . . . All legislation must be tested . . . by the fundamental criterion [of] whether it is reasonably adapted to securing these interests. . . ."[243]

However often the Progressives ridiculed discussions of corporate will and personality as metaphysical inquiries derived from outmoded natural rights conceptions, they were not indifferent to whether the corporation should be treated as a real entity. Here they stood together with earlier entity thinkers in insisting that the recognition and protection of group interests was a practical necessity of modern life. "The commercial world," wrote Henderson, "whose habits of thought so largely influence the development of law, has come to regard the business unit as the typical juristic entity, rather than the human being. . . . New economic phenomena, railroads, industrial combinations, the emergence of hitherto disregarded social classes, determine its growth."[244]

It was the task of Legal Realist thinkers to adjust legal conceptions to these changes. For example, the earlier conception that the stockholders constitute the corporation, Henderson wrote, "is of no value under modern conditions. The modern stockholder is a negligible factor in the management of a corporation."[245] Standing behind the pragmatism of the Progressive view of corporations, then, was an acceptance of the recent triumph of the corporate form as "a normal business unit."[246] No longer was it necessary to resort to metaphysics to establish the legitimacy of the business corporation. It had become a fait accompli.

Conclusion

The *Santa Clara* case did not represent the triumph of a natural entity theory of the corporation. In 1886, when old conservatism still dominated the world view of Supreme Court justices, any such conception of corporate personality would have been received with hostility by an old conservative court still actively suspicious of corporate power and the emergence of concentrated enterprise. The 1905 case of *Hale v. Henkel*[247] underlines how late it was before the Supreme Court ambivalently began the move towards a natural entity theory in corporate constitutional jurisprudence. Its opinion that the search and seizure provisions of the Fourth Amendment apply to the corporation, while the Fifth Amendment's self-incrimination clause does not, still wavers between the past and the future.

In *Santa Clara* a natural entity theory was unnecessary for the immediate task of constitutionalizing corporate property rights. An aggregate or partnership or contractual vision of the corporation—with well-established roots in the *Dartmouth College Case*[248]—was sufficient to focus the conceptual emphasis on the property rights of shareholders. Either a partnership or a natural entity view could equally successfully have subverted the dominant artificial entity view of the corporation as a creature of the state.

If the choice between a natural entity and a partnership theory was a toss-up when *Santa Clara* was decided, other nonconstitutional considerations soon pushed American legal theory toward the entity conception.

First, by 1900 it was no longer easy to conceive of shareholders as constituting the corporation. Changes in the conception of the shareholder from active owner to passive investor weakened the evocative power of partnership theory. Moreover, the entity theory was better able to justify the weakened position of the shareholders in internal corporate governance. Second, the partnership theory represented a threat to the legitimacy of limited liability of shareholders. The entity theory, by contrast, emphasized the distinction between corporations and partnerships. Third, while the partnership theory pushed in the direction of requiring shareholder unanimity for corporate mergers, the entity theory made the justification of majority rule possible. Fourth, the entity theory was superior to the partnership theory in undermining Chief Justice Taney's foreign corporation doctrine, which represented a substantial legal threat to the emergence of national corporations doing business in each of the states. The foreign corporation doctrine's reversal, shortly before World War I, can be associated with the triumph of the entity theory.

While it might be possible, at some high level of abstraction divorced from concrete social understandings, to demonstrate that the partnership theory could have been manipulated to accomplish any of the legitimating tasks for which I have claimed the natural entity theory was superior, in many of the specific historical contexts I have identified, the two conceptions of corporate personality did not have equal evocative or persuasive power. Indeed, they carried with them considerable legal and intellectual baggage that did not permit random deployment or infinite manipulability.

While John Dewey may have been correct in identifying the contradictory or random deployment of these conceptions as applied to labor unions and business corporations, he could not, I believe, have demonstrated successfully that each theory of corporate personality could have equally legitimated the practices of emergent large-scale business enterprise.

An important task of legal theory, then, is to uncover the specific historical possibilities of legal conceptions—to "decode" their true concrete meanings in real historical situations. We have spent far too much intellectual energy in the increasingly sterile task of discussing legal theory in a historical vacuum. That is one of the reasons why Anglo-American jurisprudence constantly seems to get no further than repeated rediscoveries of the wheel. By contrast, in more specific settings, one finds that legal theory does powerfully influence the direction of legal understanding.

FOUR

The Place of Justice Holmes in American Legal Thought

In the first two chapters I sought to capture the basic structure of Classical Legal Thought and to set the stage for the Progressive assault on its premises. In chapter 3, I began to focus on the vast institutional and ideological changes in American society that triggered the crisis of legitimacy at the turn of the century. In this chapter I demonstrate how these changes affected the legal thought of Oliver Wendell Holmes, Jr., the most important and influential legal thinker America has had. Holmes published his first article on legal theory in 1870 when he was twenty-nine.[1] His masterpiece, *The Common Law*,[2] was rushed to publication in 1881, Holmes noted, so that it could appear in advance of his fortieth birthday.[3] Later in the same year, he was appointed to the Supreme Judicial Court of Massachusetts, where he served for twenty years. His last important work in legal theory is his famous Boston University Law School address, "The Path of the Law," published in 1897.[4] Five years later, past his sixtieth birthday, he was appointed to the U.S. Supreme Court, where he served for the next thirty years.

This chapter focuses on Holmes's theoretical writings through "The Path of the Law," which represents his last effort at self-conscious, abstract discussion of legal theory. Though the influence of Holmes's judicial career—especially his years on the U.S. Supreme Court—is undoubtedly of major significance for the history of legal thought, these were not years of jurisprudential innovation. In fact, Holmes seems to have abandoned his efforts at systematic legal thought after "The Path of the Law." He never again tried to do what in his youth he most aspired to do—"to twist the tail of the cosmos."[5]

Almost everything that has been written about Holmes's legal theory has been written from the perspective of "winner's history." Thus, much has been written

This chapter was originally presented as the Julius Rosenthal Lectures at Northwestern University Law School on March 16, 17, and 18, 1981.

about Holmes as the father of the later Legal Realist movement, and his writings are studied for anticipations of pragmatism, anti-formalism, realism, functionalism, instrumentalism, and modernism in law.[6] Because he was noted for his brilliant, often revolutionary, but easily misunderstood aphorisms—"The life of the law has not been logic: it has been experience;"[7] "general propositions do not decide concrete cases"[8]—and because he was something of a cult figure for two generations of liberal thinkers,[9] there has been a strong tendency to stereotype his contributions to American legal thought. And because his great work, *The Common Law*, meets several of the tests for a classic—it is obscure and inaccessible, in addition to being rarely read—Holmes has not often been studied in his own terms. Above all, I believe it has never been argued that in reality there is an early and a late Holmes, and that his own intellectual journey from *The Common Law* in 1881 to "The Path of the Law" in 1897 parallels a major change in American social, economic, and legal thought and in the structures of legitimacy in the two periods.

Subjective versus Objective Standards

If there is a single, overriding, and repetitive theme running through Holmes's writing, it is the necessity and desirability of establishing objective rules of law, that is, general rules that do not take the peculiar mental or moral state of individuals into account. We saw in chapter 2 how the subjective-objective debate dominated the discourse over the nature of contracts. Holmes believed that only through objective legal rules could the law provide the certainty and predictability necessary to regulate an increasingly complex and interdependent society. In articulating this vision, Holmes confronted and dismissed legal arguments deriving from natural right theories, which emphasized that laws based on objective standards were immoral because they failed to take into account the state of mind of individuals when assigning liability.

Societies, he argued, had "frequently punish[ed] those who have been guilty of no moral wrong, and who could not be condemned by any standard that did not avowedly disregard the personal peculiarities of the individuals concerned."[10] Indeed, "[n]o society has ever admitted that it could not sacrifice individual welfare to its own existence."[11] Therefore, "the law does undoubtedly treat the individual as a means to an end, and uses him as a tool to increase the general welfare at his own expense."[12]

Holmes used the example of the doctrine that ignorance of the law is no excuse. "The true explanation of the rule is the same as that which accounts for the law's indifference to a man's particular temperament, faculties and so forth. Public policy sacrifices the individual to the general good."[13]

This theme of the sacrifice of individuals to the general good is overwhelming in Holmes's writing. Rules of law regularly "sacrificed" the innocent individual "as a means to an end."[14] It was romantic and naive to believe that the law could be tailored to individual peculiarities.

Holmes began his attack on subjective standards by challenging natural rights–based theories of criminal law. Here was one area in which punishment had traditionally been defended in terms of the moral failings of the individual with the requirement that the criminal receive his just deserts.

Hegel, Holmes wryly observed, had argued for a "mystic bond between wrong and punishment" in his notion that there must be proportionality between the two.[15] And Kant had denounced a preventive theory of punishment as immoral because, in Holmes's words, "it treats man as a thing, not as a person; as a means, not as an end in himself."[16] In fact, Holmes argued, the "actual personal unworthiness of the criminal"[17] ought not to be determinative in inflicting punishment, as "the purpose of the criminal law is only to induce external conformity to rule."[18] Thus, the law is frequently "ready to sacrifice the individual so far as necessary in order to accomplish" its purpose.[19]

But criminal law was only the first, if the most difficult, step in Holmes's argument. He further sought to demonstrate that "the general principles of criminal and civil liability are the same"[20] and that the same issue of objective versus subjective standards permeated the entire law.

In tort law, for example, there were "two theories of the common-law liability for unintentional harm"[21] that divided legal thinkers along the same lines as the debate over theories of punishment in criminal law:

> The first is that of [the founder of English jurisprudence, John] Austin, which is essentially the theory of a criminalist. According to him, the characteristic feature of law, properly so called, is a sanction or detriment threatened and imposed by the sovereign for disobedience to the sovereign's commands. As the greater part of the law only makes a man civilly answerable for breaking it, Austin is compelled to regard the liability to an action as a sanction, or, in other words, as a penalty for disobedience. It follows from this, according to the prevailing views of penal law, that such liability ought only to be based upon personal fault; and Austin accepts that conclusion, with its corollaries, one of which is that negligence means a state of the party's mind.[22]

Holmes sought to show that Austin's teaching that "personal moral shortcoming"[23] was necessary for establishing liability in tort was also erroneous. Law only "works within the sphere of the senses."[24] It deals only with "the external phenomena, the manifest acts and omissions."[25] "[I]t is wholly indifferent to the internal phenomena of conscience."[26]

Now, the question arises, why was Holmes obsessed with the issue of subjective versus objective legal standards? True, as Mark DeWolfe Howe shows so well, Holmes was bent on attacking German idealism and its philosophy of natural rights.[27] In the realm of jurisprudence, Hegel, Kant, and, in much more limited ways, Austin, were clearly the enemy.

But even when analyzing so creative and cosmopolitan a legal thinker as Holmes, it would be a mistake to overlook the more immediate context of the American intellectual and legal culture in which he existed. It seems to me that it is in the more concrete realm of legal and social experience that we have failed to understand Holmes. By treating his thought almost exclusively as a jurisprudential debate with thinkers of the first rank, we have failed to see it as a response to specific dilemmas confronting American social and legal thought at the end of the nineteenth century.

To understand Holmes's significance in the history of legal thought, one must appreciate the two-front war that orthodox legal thinkers were forced to wage after the Civil War.

The integrity of private law—and of the power of common law judges—rested on the assertion that judges were not policymakers, that their sole function was the vindication of individual natural rights. In contract law, we saw, judges insisted that their only role was to carry out the intention of the parties to an agreement.[28] To impose their own conception of desirable outcomes in a contract dispute would represent the ultimate act of judicial usurpation and political intervention.

But however often they reiterated this basic element of legitimacy, the judicial system had long been drawn into serving more or less overt policymaking functions.[29] By the second half of the nineteenth century, the growth of the corporation and the increasing standardization of market transactions in a national economy put pressure on the legal community to adopt objective standards in contract law. There arose a new insistence on an objective theory of contract that would ensure the "rectitude, consistency and uniformity"[30] of results.

As law became increasingly implicated in the process of promoting economic growth, the earlier natural rights justifications for the judicial function began to be overwhelmed by the overtly instrumental use of private law to advance utilitarian objectives. From the post-revolutionary period on, but reaching a special intensity during the codification movement of the 1820s and 1830s, there were regular challenges to the claims that common law judges neutrally and apolitically vindicated natural rights.[31]

By the time Holmes began to write in the 1870s, natural rights and utilitarian justifications were approaching a head-on collision in the legal system. The process of economic growth had drawn common law judges into openly instrumental uses of private law, thereby undermining their claim to political neutrality.[32] Holmes's attack on subjectivism in law was part of a more general effort of late-nineteenth-century thinkers to resolve the conflict by freeing the law from its post-revolutionary ties to natural rights.[33]

But by insisting on personal fault as a precondition for liability, the natural rights theory had also impeded the use of private law for redistributive purposes. If a utilitarian theory permitted a society to "sacrifice individual welfare to its own existence,"[34] why would it not be equally legitimate in the name of utility to redistribute wealth through the legal system?

Thus Holmes was forced to fight a two-front war. On one front, he challenged orthodox legal theory for its moralism and individualism, qualities that, he maintained, unrealistically ignored the actual regulatory functions of law. On the other front, like his natural rights adversaries, he wished to resist the view that because an objective theory allowed liability without regard to personal blameworthiness, it thereby led inevitably to codification or permitted, on utilitarian grounds, a redistribution of wealth in the interest of the general welfare.[35] It was necessary, Holmes saw, to bring about a "reconciliation of the doctrine that liability is founded on blameworthiness with the existence of liability where the party is not to blame."[36]

Moralism versus Amoralism in Private Law

Holmes wrote just as the question of moral fault had moved to center stage in American law. Beginning in the 1850s, a debate arose about the moral foundations of private law. The issue first surfaced in connection with the question of punitive damages in tort. To the extent that punitive damages were allowable, many legal writers reasoned, the function of tort law was not merely to compensate plaintiffs for injury but to enforce more general policies of the state. If there was a clear line separating public—in this case, criminal—law from private (tort) law, it was based on the notion that only public law could legitimately pursue deterrent and regulatory goals. To the extent that plaintiffs were permitted to recover damages beyond their actual injuries, it was argued, courts were using private law to further social goals. The plaintiff's recovery then became not a matter of personal right but a utilitarian device for private enforcement of essentially public duties. The distinction between public law and private law would be eroded, leaving no theoretical barrier between tort law and the feared redistributive tendencies of regulation.[37]

The debate over punitive damages began in 1842 with the publication of Simon Greenleaf's *Treatise on the Law of Evidence*,[38] which sought to show that punitive damages were both undesirable and unprecedented. When Theodore Sedgwick published his *Treatise on the Measure of Damages*[39] five years later, however, he demonstrated overwhelmingly the long-standing authority behind punitive damages.[40] As late as 1873, the first American treatise writer on torts, Francis Hilliard, had no difficulty in confirming Sedgwick's statement of the traditional view. "Compensation is the measure of redress for the legal wrong; but for the moral wrong, the recklessness of the act, the personal malice with which it is done, the violence and outrage attending it, reasonable exemplary [punitive] damages will be allowed."[41]

During the late 1870s and 1880s, however, the debate revived, and this time the theoretical issue of the true nature of public versus private law overshadowed the question of precedent. Opposition to punitive damages was widespread on the ground that it allowed private law to serve purposes thought proper only to public law. While an award of compensatory damages could be understood as vindicating the individual rights of a party, the addition of punitive damages implied regulatory and confiscatory purposes. "If the plaintiff is entitled to damages as a matter of right, let him receive them in their proper character of indemnity,"[42] one legal writer argued in 1881. "If he is not so entitled, there is no power in any government which can justly deprive another of his property for [the] plaintiff's benefit. Judicial procedure ought not to be made a cover for the confiscation of private property."[43]

"[T]he State inflicts punishment, not individuals,"[44] another legal writer maintained. "[A]s between individuals, courts enforce rights. The law protects everyone in the enjoyment of his property, and it cannot be taken from him, under the pretext of punishment, and given to another."[45]

Only a clear distinction between the punitive functions of public law and the compensatory purposes of private law could dampen the confiscatory impulse of juries. "The injured party ought not to be made the avenger of a public wrong,"[46] another commentator declared in 1878:

> In the gross injustice its application causes in many cases, by allowing a man ten or twenty, or sometimes fifty-fold the amount of damages he has actually sustained, it has been an instrument of mischief, encouraging a multitude of lawsuits of a speculative character. It has, in part, demoralized an honorable profession, by the prices held out to the litigious and unscrupulous, and their advocates in court, expecting to share in the promised confiscation of another man's property. Let the breaker of the public peace and the offender of the laws make his fine to the state, the duty of which it is to protect, and which pays for the administration of justice, but not to the injured person, who, when compensated liberally for his individual loss, has no further claim on his opponent.[47]

When the Supreme Courts of New Hampshire (1873) and Colorado (1884) overthrew the doctrine of punitive damages, it was through a process of deduction from the supposedly different inherent functions of public and private law. "What is a civil remedy but reparation for a wrong inflicted, to the injury of the party seeking redress,—compensation for damage sustained by the plaintiff?"[48] the New Hampshire court asked. "How could the idea of punishment be deliberately and designedly installed as a doctrine of civil remedies? Is not punishment out of place, irregular, anomalous, exceptional, unjust, unscientific, not to say absurd and ridiculous, when classed among civil remedies?"[49]

> The true rule, simple and just, is to keep the civil and the criminal process and practice distinct and separate. Let the criminal law deal with the criminal, and administer punishment for the legitimate purpose and end of punishment,—namely, the reformation of the offender and the safety of the people. Let the individual, whose rights are infringed and who has suffered injury, go to the civil courts and there obtain full and ample reparation and compensation; but let him not thus obtain the "fruits" to which he is not entitled, and which belong to others.[50]

Public and private law, the Colorado Supreme Court announced in 1884, should be kept "separate and distinct."[51] "It is not unlikely," it declared while striking down the institution of punitive damages, "that courts will in the course of time generally condemn the practice of blending the interests of the individual with those of society, and using a purely private action to redress a public wrong." [52]

By 1891, even the editor of *T. Sedgwick, a Treatise on the Measure of Damages* had abandoned Theodore Sedgwick's original moral defense of the doctrine of punitive damages and conceded that it was "an exceptional or anomalous doctrine, at variance with the general rule of compensation; hence that, logically, it is wrong." [53]

Related to the controversy over punitive damages was another problem that consumed thousands of pages of legal writing in the late nineteenth century—the question of whether there were different "degrees of negligence." [54] Purporting to rely on Roman law, British Chief Justice Holt in *Coggs v. Bernard* (1703) [55] had elaborated a three-tier classification of negligence—gross, ordinary, and slight—in order to define the duties of various bailors. Yet it was only 150 years later that there was any widespread challenge to Holt's scheme. Led by Francis Wharton's investigations of Roman law, large numbers of legal writers in the 1870s devoted enormous energy to demonstrating that Holt had misunderstood Roman law and that there was only a single standard—that of the "ordinary and prudent man"—for determining negligence. [56]

In fact, the only operational significance of a category of "gross" negligence was that, by contrast to "ordinary" negligence, it would permit a jury to award punitive damages for extremely bad-hearted or anti-social conduct. Therefore, a finding of gross negligence not only required a moralistic and subjective evaluation of conduct by an unreliable jury, it also permitted an inherently discretionary assessment of punitive damages by that jury.

Just as the category of "gross" negligence signaled questions about the legitimacy of punitive damages, the category of "slight" negligence raised the possibility of strict liability. The basic idea of the three-tier classification of negligence was that different degrees of care were appropriate to different circumstances or relationships. In the context of the 1870s, the most pressing question was whether the railroads and other new forms of technology would be treated as "dangerous instrumentalities" and hence held liable even for "slight negligence" because of failure to use "the highest level of care." [57]

But most important, perhaps, the three-tier conception of negligence and the doctrine of punitive damages cut against the efforts of late-nineteenth-century legal thinkers to develop a clear boundary between an apolitical, anti-redistributive private law and an inherently unstable, political public law. If the functions of tort and criminal or regulatory law were overlapping—if the tort law could legitimately move beyond the realm of corrective justice into that of punishment for immoral behavior—the idea of an apolitical private law whose sole function was to vindicate private rights was threatened.

The treatise writers of the late nineteenth century were virtually unanimous in rejecting as unsound the three-tier system of negligence. [58] Yet they were constantly embarrassed not only by the repeated use of the gross negligence concept by common law courts but also by the frequent moralism of the judges in expounding the negligence standard.

It was in this setting that Oliver Wendell Holmes, Jr., began to write about the common law, especially the law of torts. More audacious than his contemporaries, he was not satisfied simply to banish moralism from the private law; he also sought to show that moralism was unsound even in criminal law. Yet it is clear that all of the central themes in Holmes's writing were prominent in American legal literature of the 1870s, especially his attack on moralism in the common law. His were not simply the abstract and disembodied speculations of the legal philosopher, but rather the effort to come to terms with a number of basic, concrete contradictions in the American legal system of the late nineteenth century.

Holmes's attack on moralism and subjective standards in tort law grew in part from a desire for stability that he shared with much of late-nineteenth-century American culture. Order, uniformity, certainty, and predictability were the main goals of legal as well as non-legal writers of the late nineteenth century.[59] There were numerous attacks on the arbitrary character of juries and on their penchant for favoring the noncorporate plaintiff.[60] Natural rights individualism was seen as too personal, too idiosyncratic, too moralistic—as a threat to order.

For Holmes, subjective standards in law derived from more than one hundred years of natural rights individualism. Like many of his contemporaries, Holmes feared the anarchic and disorderly implications of all appeals to individual conscience and morality. Much of his writing was devoted to rooting out of the law all concepts that could appeal to the "idiosyncrasies" of juries or "would leave all our rights and duties . . . to the necessarily more or less accidental feelings of a jury."[61] All criteria based on conscience or morality, he believed, would inevitably degenerate into personal idiosyncrasies.

As George Fredrickson shows, Holmes was marching to the same drummer as his mentor Ralph Waldo Emerson, who after the Civil War abandoned the "individualism and anarchism" of his youth. Indeed, Holmes's own "search for order" was probably connected with his youthful flirtation and eventual disillusionment with abolitionism.[62] As Saul Touster has pointed out, Holmes enlisted in the Civil War "as a convinced abolitionist" but came later to identify abolitionism with fanaticism. For the later Holmes "the word 'abolition' is associated not with young men of deep sympathies and generous sentiments but with communists, Christian Science, the Catholics on Calvin, Calvin on the Catholics, Trotsky on Stalin, Prohibitionists, Emma Goldman."[63] The lesson Holmes seems to have derived from his own Civil War experiences is that all passionate appeals to conscience and morality invariably resulted in the destruction of a fragile social order.

But natural rights individualism represented only one of the two fronts over which orthodox legal thinkers were battling. At the other extreme was continental positivism and its American offshoot, codification. If law was not the recognition of some pre-political natural right of individuals, was it inevitably the arbitrary command of a legislative sovereign?

Codification

Except for Holmes, there was little, if any, formal or speculative American juris-prudence in the late nineteenth century. Jurisprudence as a distinct field did not come into being in America until the critical spirit of the early-twentieth-century jurists forced them for the first time to call into question the fundamentals of the legal order.

The functional equivalent of late-nineteenth-century American jurisprudence was brought forth by a single question of public policy—codification. And it was the debate over codification of the common law—a debate that produced several hundred books, articles, and pamphlets in the last thirty years of the century—that provides us with the best overview of the general issues that were provoking a challenge to the old order.

Codification was a perennial issue in American legal history. After the Revo-lution, several states codified their criminal laws, throwing off many of the bar-barities of the English criminal system.[64] But it was only after 1820 that a full-scale movement to codify the common law sprang up in many states.[65] Whether the codification movement of the Jacksonian period was really a movement with deep social roots, and whether the "radical codifiers," who wished fundamentally to change the substance of the common law, were really radical have not yet received sufficient study. In any event, by 1848, when the New York legislature adopted the Field Code of Civil Procedure drafted by David Dudley Field, the debate over codification had turned to relatively technical questions of procedure and had become primarily an internal debate within a rapidly growing legal profession.

Field, however, did not rest content with his triumph in the procedural realm. Between 1857 and 1865, as one of the Code commissioners mandated "to reduce into a written and systematic code the whole body of the law of the state of New York,"[66] he and his colleagues prepared a Penal Code (eventually enacted in 1881 after several rejections),[67] a Political Code (which never passed),[68] and finally, and most important, a Civil Code containing 2,034 sections dealing with the whole body of common law.[69]

The Civil Code, on which most of the controversy over codification turned, was enacted into law four times by the New York Assembly and twice by both houses of the legislature, only to be vetoed by two different governors after intense opposition by the legal profession. Several further unsuccessful attempts to secure enactment of the Code in 1875 and 1884–1886 produced a flurry of professional debate over the nature and function of law.

Meanwhile, California in 1851 had adopted its own Civil Practice Act, mod-eled after Field's New York Code and shepherded through the legislature by Field's brother Stephen, soon to be appointed to the U.S. Supreme Court. Finally, in 1872, California enacted a Civil Code, fashioned after the already rejected and much maligned New York Code of David Dudley Field. The Dakota Territory had adopted Field's Civil Code in 1866; Georgia had enacted a code of its own in 1860.

Unlike the codification movement of fifty years earlier, this attack on the common law finally produced the political results that were widely feared by orthodox jurists. No other subject produced such an outpouring of controversy or as much attention from legal thinkers as the struggle over codification.

Without closer study, it is difficult to know which of the hundreds of detailed substantive legal changes produced major controversy. Field and his fellow Code commissioners singled out three areas in which the New York Code made substantial changes in the common law—"the rights of married women, the adoption of children, and the assimilation of the laws of real and personal property."[70] But they also noted that there were 120 other changes "of less importance, which ought not to be overlooked."[71]

The enacted California Code was perhaps more radical. For example, it substantially overhauled the state's corporation law, establishing detailed regulations for railroad, insurance, and telegraph companies, as well as for savings and loan associations. Railroad and telegraph rates were regulated, as were the investments by health and accident insurance companies. Savings and loan companies were barred from making loans without full and adequate security, and their officers were prohibited from borrowing or engaging in personal financial transactions with their associations. There were also major departures from the common law in provisions dealing with women's property and contracts, community property, inheritance and succession, contingent remainders, and the abolition of the common law rights of dower and courtesy. Hundreds of other changes in the common law, too detailed to analyze here, threatened to upset existing social and economic arrangements.[72]

New York became the battleground for halting the threatened tide of codification after the Bar Association of the City of New York in 1883 unanimously passed a resolution opposing passage of a Civil Code. James Coolidge Carter, a member of the New York Establishment Bar, was chosen as its leading spokesman, and he successfully led the opposition to what a committee of the Bar Association called "the greatest misfortune which has ever threatened the State of New York."[73]

The opponents of codification did not, in general, focus upon the particular details of proposed changes. Instead, they directed their energies to a more general and abstract discussion of the nature and function of law. Through his writings on codification, Carter, in particular, articulated the jurisprudence of American legal orthodoxy at the end of the nineteenth century.

The codification debate reopened perennial conflicts in American legal thought. From the time of the Revolution, there had been periodic challenges to the abundant power of common law judges to make law. In one way or another, the defenders of the common law system invariably sought to show that judges did not legislate and that common law reasoning was different from political reasoning. Every defense of the common law system was based on some assertion of the objective, apolitical, and scientific character of common law adjudication.

In this respect, Carter was no different from his orthodox predecessors. "That the judge can not make the law is accepted from the start,"[74] he told the American Bar Association in 1890:

> That there is already existing a rule by which the case must be determined is not doubted. Unquestionably the functions of making and declaring the law are here brought into close proximity; but, nevertheless, the distinction is not for a moment lost sight of. It is agreed that the true rule must be somehow found.[75]

In one form or another, a declaratory theory of the judicial function stood at the center of all orthodox defenses of the common law. For if common law judges did not merely find the law but made it, there was no basis for insisting that this concededly legislative function should be assigned to courts.

At bottom was a long-standing fear of legislative intrusion into the distribution of wealth and privilege. Codification, Carter argued, would produce "[i]ncessant, frequent, sharp and often ill-conceived changes in the law. . . . The habit of changing the law necessarily tends to destroy that sense of the necessity of stability which is now (although unfortunately diminishing) one of the greatest safeguards for property, business, and liberty."[76] Yet there was also a well-established American tradition to which Carter appealed, one that employed the language of popular government for essentially conservative ends. A code system, Carter asserted, was "a characteristic feature in those [countries] which have a despotic origin, or in which despotic power, absolute or qualified, is, or has been, predominant."[77] By contrast, a common law system prevailed in "States of popular origin. . . .[78]

> Nor is this contrast accidental. It arises necessarily from the fundamental difference in the political character of the two classes of States. In free, popular States, the law springs from, and is made by, the people; and as the process of building it up consists in applying, from time to time, to human actions the popular ideal or standard of justice, justice is the only interest consulted in the work. In despotic countries, however, even in those where a legislative body exists, the interests of the reigning dynasty are supreme; and no reigning dynasty could long be maintained in the exercise of anything like absolute power, if the making of the laws and the building up of the jurisprudence were intrusted, in any form, to the popular will. The sovereign must be permitted at every step to say what shall be *the law*. He cannot say this by establishing a *custom*, or by interpreting popular customs. He can say it only by a positive command, and this is statutory law; and when such positive command embraces the whole system of jurisprudence it becomes a *Code*. The fundamental maxim in the jurisprudence of popular States is, that whatever is in consonance with justice as applied to human affairs, should have the force of law.[79]

Thus, Carter shrewdly sought to reconcile opposition to legislation with the democratic spirit. For this purpose, he insisted that the concept of customary law as an alternative to legislation better fulfilled the ideal of popular sovereignty. Custom stood as a cushion between state and society. As the principal discoverers and expositors of custom, judges, not legislators, were the ultimate representatives of the people.

For Carter, the common law "consists of rules springing from the social standard of justice, or from the habits and customs from which that standard itself has been derived."[80] The task of the judges was to "*search* to find a rule" from "the habits, customs, business and manners of the people."[81] Finally, he "tacitly assumed that the sense of justice is the *same* in all those who are thus engaged— that is to say, that they have a *common standard of justice* from which they can argue with, and endeavor to persuade, each other. . . ."[82]

Law, then, or at least the private law "which governs the ordinary private transactions of men with each other . . . ," is identical with custom. "And it is well to keep constantly in mind that this law, being tantamount to the custom enforced by society, is an existing fact, or body of facts, and that courts do not make it, or pretend to make it, but to find and ascertain it, acting upon the true assumption that it already exists."[83]

Carter was even moved to the verge of denying that legislation was lawmaking. While he acknowledged that it was "not worth while to dispute the correctness of the common phraseology which ascribes to the legislature the office of making law," he did argue that "the deeper and more philosophical view" would make legislatures appear to be more like courts, since the proper legislative function was simply that "of affixing the public mark and authentication upon the customs and rules already existing, or struggling into existence, in the habits of the people."[84] "It is important to firmly grasp the truth that the work of declaring or making law, whether committed to the hands of a judge, a legislature or a codifier, is substantially the same,"[85] Carter concluded.

"[L]egislation should never attempt to do for society that which society can do, and is constantly doing, for itself,"[86] Carter wrote. Since the creation of custom "is the unconscious work of society . . . the passage of a law commanding things which have no foundation in existing custom would only endeavor to create custom, and would necessarily be futile."[87]

Thus, law was not the creature of the state but of society. "The law is a department of sociology,"[88] Carter declared. It was

> not a body of commands imposed upon society from without. . . . It exists at all times as one of the elements of society springing directly from habit and custom. It is therefore the unconscious creation of society, or in other words, a growth. For the most part it needs no interpreter or vindicator. The members of society are familiar with its customs and follow them; and in following custom they follow the law.[89]

From this, Carter concluded that courts and legislatures were needed only "for the exceptional instances"[90] where customs were doubtful or in conflict. But ordinary officials simply performed the self-executing function of "declaring what actually is."[91] "It is the unconscious resolve of society that all its members shall act as the great majority act."[92]

Carter's worship of custom was part of a more general system of Social Darwinism that came to exercise sway over American thought in the late nineteenth century. William Graham Sumner, the dominant social thinker of the age, had borrowed Herbert Spencer's evolutionary philosophy and had used social determinism "with great effect in his fight against reformers. . . ."[93] Sumner, Richard Hofstader observed, insisted that "society, the product of centuries of gradual evolution, cannot be quickly refashioned by legislation."[94] As Sumner wrote:

> The great stream of time and earthly things will sweep on just the same in spite of us. . . . Every one of us is a child of his age and cannot get out of it. He is in the stream and is swept along with it. All his science and philosophy come to him out of it. Therefore the tide will not be changed by us. It will swallow up both us and our experiments. . . . That is why it is the greatest folly of which a man can be capable to sit down with a slate and pencil to plan out a new social world.[95]

For Carter, evolutionary determinism was equally paramount. "Whatever is necessary in the scheme of the universe must be right, and society therefore is right and necessary and right."[96]

Custom as a Mediator Between Legislative Supremacy and Natural Rights Individualism

This invocation of custom as a standard of justice prior to law was widespread in late-nineteenth-century American social thought. In legal as in social thought, the deification of custom mediated a series of major intellectual and political tensions and contradictions. In particular, custom served both to defeat the democratic impulse for legislative supremacy and, at the same time, to avoid the potential anarchy of a common law based solely on individual natural rights.

At one end of the legal spectrum was continental positivism, which had flourished since the French Revolution and the Napoleonic Code.[97] It invoked popular sovereignty and legislative supremacy as the legitimate foundations of all lawmaking. In one way or another, it acknowledged the legitimacy and necessity of social coercion to maintain order and justice. Bentham, the arch-foe of the common law power of judges, and John Austin were the major English exponents of this position. In America, Bentham had become the intellectual fountainhead of the codification movement.[98]

Writers as distinguished as Sir Henry Maine[99] and as pedestrian as James Coolidge Carter deified custom largely in order to deny the positivism of Bentham, Austin, and the Continental jurists. In nineteenth-century America, customary law was employed as a conservative intellectual construct established in order to neutralize or delegitimize legislative authority and to defend the slow process of common law decision making under the guidance of judges.

At the opposite pole from legislative positivism was the highly individualistic natural rights philosophy that had reached its pinnacle at the time of the American Revolution. It emphasized the sovereignty of the individual will and the pre-political character of the right to property. As applied to contract law, for example, an emphasis on natural rights led to an insistence on a subjective interpretation in order to find the real will of the parties.

Amid the widespread fear of social disintegration in the late nineteenth century, conservative social thinkers wished to deny highly individualistic and utopian natural rights modes of thought as much as they feared the majoritarian power of the legislature. Carter, for example, observed that if each individual were to pursue that conduct

> which he deemed to be intrinsically right in itself . . . there would be every variety of difference of opinion, and consequently, every variety of action. . . . It is therefore manifest that some rule other than the individual sense of right should be adopted for the government of conduct. . . . The notion that each individual should be left to follow the dictates of his own conscience must be at once abandoned.[100]

Having thus acknowledged that if obedience to individual conscience were the norm "disputes and collisions . . . would mark all social intercourse,"[101] Carter simultaneously sought to deny that legislative regulation of conflicting interests was the inevitable solution.

It was here that custom served its most essential late-nineteenth-century function of mediating between an anarchically individualist natural rights philosophy and a potentially coercive legislative sovereign. Customs, Carter wrote,

> being common modes of action, are the unerring evidence of common thought and belief, and as they are the joint product of the thoughts of all, each one has his own share in forming them. In the enforcement of a rule thus formed no one can complain, for it is the only rule which can be framed which gives equal expression to the voice of each. It restrains only so far as all agree that restraint is necessary.[102]

Custom, according to Carter, was no less than consent. It was the means by which he and many other late-nineteenth-century social thinkers legitimated social coercion without having to acknowledge that it was coercive. It satisfied the conservative desire for order and stability while perpetuating the idea that each person nevertheless had consented. Though Carter constantly emphasized that resort to individual conscience would produce inevitable conflict, custom allowed him to dissolve all conflict by identifying customary rules with "the sense of justice" and then to "tacitly assum[e] that the sense of justice is the same"[103] in all persons.

I have focused at length on Carter's jurisprudence primarily because it represents in a clear and unsubtle manner the intellectual paradigm for virtually all orthodox late-nineteenth-century legal theory. On the one hand, custom was employed for the purpose of overthrowing post-revolutionary natural rights individualism, which represented an anarchic threat to order. On the other hand, custom was used in order to deny the legitimacy or necessity of most legislative and social coercion.

Custom thus represented a Rorschach blot onto which conservative social thinkers could project their fantasies of a naturally harmonious society free from the twin dangers of anarchy and coercion, yet capable of organic change and growth.

It is only with this background in mind that seemingly irreconcilable contradictions in the thought of Oliver Wendell Holmes, Jr., can be understood.

Strict Liability versus Negligence

Just as natural rights individualism threatened all order and stability by allowing private and subjective appeals to conscience and morality, continental positivism raised the threat of legislative tyranny, of dangerous equalitarian passions, and of attacks on the common law system. Like the writings of James Coolidge Carter, Holmes's lectures on *The Common Law* were also efforts to find a middle position through the mediating notion of custom. Holmes's focus on the issue of subjective versus objective standards in the law can best be understood as precisely such an effort to split the difference between the unpalatable extremes of natural rights and legislative positivism.

Holmes rejected subjective standards because, being too individualistic and moralistic, they inevitably led to subversion of all certainty and predictability in law. But why then were not legislative rules the most supremely objective standards, dispensing with all need for common law rule-making? Why didn't the rejection of a subjective standard force Holmes into the camp of codification?

Holmes, his biographer informs us, several times "revealed the gravest distrust of [the] presuppositions" of the codification movement. Insisting that "law is not a science, but is essentially empirical," Holmes applauded the reluctance of the common law to put its trust in "any faculty of . . . generalization, however brilliant."[104] It is a particular merit of the common law, he concluded, "that it decides the case first and determines the principle afterwards."[105] Besides, Holmes was no democrat. "I loathe the thick-fingered clowns we call the people," he proclaimed in 1862, "—especially as the beasts are represented at political centres—vulgar, selfish and base. . . ."[106]

To put Holmes's dilemma another way, let us turn to his complex views on negligence versus strict liability in the law of torts. Ranking second in significance to his advocacy of objective external standards is Holmes's well-known opposition to strict liability and his defense of a negligence standard.

From at least 1840, the negligence standard had begun to displace strict liability as the norm in English and American tort law. But, as we have seen, there were many important areas, such as common carrier liability and the vicarious liability of masters for the torts of their servants, that remained resistant to the engulfing sweep of negligence liability. Beyond that, strict liability seemed to correspond to a traditional understanding that a person should compensate for any injury he or she caused. Negligence, by contrast, was the doctrine of an emerging entrepreneurial class that argued that there should be no liability for socially desirable activity that caused injury without carelessness.

After more than a generation of widening victories, the negligence principle was decisively challenged in 1868 in a decision of the English House of Lords in *Rylands v. Fletcher.*[107] Holding that a landowner was liable without regard to negligence when his leaking dam permitted water to flood a neighboring coal mine, the Lords seemed to reassert the traditional presumption of compensation for injuries.

Most American courts immediately resisted this new major barrier to the triumph of the negligence principle.[108] Strict liability, they argued, was an amoral doctrine that imposed liability on a person regardless of whether he or she was blameworthy. Without a requirement of moral fault, they saw, there was no limitation on imposing liability in order to bring about a redistribution of wealth from the active to the inactive or from rich to poor.

But moralism itself had increasingly come under criticism for promoting redistributive tendencies in the law. As we saw earlier, attacks on the institution of punitive damages and on a three-tier classification of negligence were all predicated on the assumption that if juries were permitted to use the tort law in order to punish (and not simply to compensate) for gross negligence, the legal system would easily lend itself to systematic persecution of the rich.

It was in the midst of this intellectual disarray that Holmes wrote *The Common Law* and took upon himself the heroic task of finding "[s]ome middle point . . . between the horns of [a] dilemma"[109]—of defending the negligence principle at the same time as he tried to banish moral fault as a necessary ingredient of negligence.

Holmes joined in the general rejection of strict liability, basing his objections on two grounds. First, it threatened to bring about arbitrary redistributions of wealth by "undertaking to redistribute losses simply on the ground that they resulted from the defendant's act. . . ."[110]

> The state might conceivably make itself a mutual insurance company against accidents, and distribute the burden of its citizens' mishaps among all its members. . . . The state does none of these things, however, and the prevailing view is that its cumbrous and expensive machinery ought not to be set in motion unless some clear benefit is to be derived from disturbing the status quo. State interference is an evil, where it cannot be shown to be a good.[111]

In addition, Holmes argued, strict liability was open to a "still graver" objection,[112] that "of offending the sense of justice."[113] It was a "coarse and impolitic principle"[114] that failed to "require that people should not be made to pay for accidents which they could not have avoided."[115]

Holmes thus required a liability-limiting criterion independent of causation of harm in order to avoid the pernicious implications of strict liability. The obvious choice was an evaluation of the moral quality of the defendant's action. But that evaluation could not be based on subjective, and hence idiosyncratic and unpredictable, assessments of the actor's state of mind. Nor could it be supported directly by considerations of policy, as to do so would deprive common law judges of their claim to be discovering rather than making the law. Holmes's solution to the dilemma was to base liability on the violation of customary norms. Holmes's negligence standard limited liability by imposing it only in cases where harm was caused by deviation from customary standards of reasonableness.

In *The Common Law*, objective standards are treated as equivalent to customary standards, not as coercive impositions of a sovereign state. Even the view Holmes expressed in *The Common Law* that law "is legislative in its grounds"[116] did not contradict this customary law perspective, but meant only that law is "at bottom the result of more or less definitely understood views of public policy."[117] A conception of custom, he then believed, could mediate successfully between the subjective individual and the coercive legislature. For Holmes, as for many other contemporary thinkers, custom reconciled individual and social morality. It avoided the extreme implications both of potentially anarchic individualism and of the threat of tyrannical state power.

In 1881, Holmes did not yet presuppose social engineering by a coercive state. Instead, he saw the evolution of law as "the unconscious result of instinctive preferences and inarticulate convictions."[118] By the time Holmes wrote "The Path of the Law" in 1897, however, the power of custom as a mediating category had begun to disintegrate amid social conflict and class struggle.[119] Now Holmes was no longer prepared to denounce strict liability for "offending the sense of justice."[120] Instead, he saw conflict between strict liability and negligence as expressing "a concealed, half conscious battle on the question of legislative policy, and if any one thinks that it can be settled deductively, or once for all, I only can say that I think he is theoretically wrong, and that I am certain that his conclusion will not be accepted in practice. . . ."[121] Custom could no longer provide a cushion of immanent rationality between state and society.

No longer having access, in their own experiences of the world, to a sense of an autonomous realm of custom, legal thinkers in the early twentieth century were caught once more on the horns of the dilemma that Holmes had originally thought he could reconcile. The negligence principle, they began to maintain once more, could be defended only on the grounds that it was unjust to punish a person who was not morally at fault.[122] The move away from a subjective standard of personal fault, they realized, had caused them to abandon the original natural rights justification for negligence. Objectivism had in fact authorized the state to impose liability on a person who was not at fault. The only ground for opposing strict liability, then, was by a return to an individualistic morality.

In an article in the *Harvard Law Review* in 1909 entitled "Law and Morals," James Barr Ames revived a moralistic attack on strict liability, contrasting it to "a rule of liability based upon moral culpability."[123] The rule of strict liability, he argued, exhibited "the unmoral character of the early common law as an instrument of injustice, as permitting unmeritorious or even culpable plaintiffs to use the machinery of the court as a means of collecting money from blameless defendants."[124] "The law of today, except in certain cases based upon public policy, asks the . . . question, 'Was the act blameworthy?' The ethical standard of reasonable conduct has replaced the unmoral standard of acting at one's peril."[125]

Though he confusedly invoked the standard of reasonable conduct, Ames clearly took his stand against strict liability on the grounds that it was immoral to punish "blameless defendants." For he realized that only a standard of personal blameworthiness could provide the necessary foundation for a moralistic attack on strict liability. By excluding personal blameworthiness from his system, Holmes had deprived the defenders of negligence of their most powerful weapon—the tradition of natural rights individualism.

While legal theorists who defended the negligence standard came more and more to justify it in terms of moralistic principles of personal fault,[126] most of the case law, dominated by practical problems of industrial society, had moved in the opposite direction. And proponents of strict liability had begun to see that objectivism had already cleared away the most powerful individualistic objections to strict liability.

"I find it impossible," Nathan Isaacs wrote in the *Harvard Law Review* of 1918, "to fence off a field of law in which liability is based exclusively on fault. In the first place, even in those cases in which fault is admittedly the basis of liability, it is not the individual fault of the particular culprit, but rather a type of culpable conduct that must be considered."[127] He then quoted Holmes on the objective standard. "In other words," he continued, "even within the realm of fault cases, the law cannot stop to take into consideration all of the peculiarities of the individual case to determine whether there is actual fault. It must classify and classify more or less roughly."[128] And finally, he concluded, strict liability was precisely "a case of rough classification" of hazardous conduct "as a result of which the innocent must suffer with the guilty."[129]

In 1927, Warren Seavey attacked the whole theory of objectivism in the law of negligence. He wrote:

> [I]t would appear that there is no standardized man; that there is only in part an objective test; that there is no such thing as reasonable or unreasonable conduct except as viewed with reference to certain qualities of the actor—his physical attributes, his intellectual power, probably, if superior, his knowledge and the knowledge he would have acquired had he exercised standard moral and at least average mental qualities at the time of action. . . .[130]

The only coherent conception of negligence, Seavey saw, was based upon some version of subjectivism. "It is quite true that negligence does not depend upon moral fault," he wrote, acknowledging the orthodox view, but "it is equally true that it does not depend upon fault even in a legal sense. It is not true, however, that there can be an objectively negligent act, unless we create for 'objective' a special meaning to be used only in negligence."[131]

Having shown that the only plausible meaning of fault implied an impracticably particularistic subjective test, he moved on to the next step: "Whether it would be better to determine liability without reference to the qualities of the actor is a different question." [132] Under primitive law, strict liability was regarded as "just" [133]:

> [I]n the age of economic expansion and individualism, it was "just" that the burden of loss should be shifted only where the cause of the harm was a knave or a fool. With a mechanistic philosophy as to human motives and a socialistic view-point as to the function of the state, we may return to the original result of liability for all injurious conduct, or conceivably have an absence of liability for any conduct, with the burden of loss shifted either to groups of persons or to the entire community. The lawyer cannot determine that our rules of liability for negligence are either just or unjust, unless he has first discovered what the community desires (which determines justice for the time and place), and whether the rules are adapted to satisfying those desires (which I assume to be the end of law). [134]

The leading legal thinkers of the next generation, in short, rejected Holmes's effort to distinguish strict liability from objectivism, grounding the latter in a non-coercive system of customary law. For those who followed Holmes, there was little choice except between an ever more anachronistic individualism and dangerous varieties of statism and collectivism.

Indeed, by the time he wrote "The Path of the Law," Holmes himself came to accept such a limited choice, and as a result, he abandoned his faith in the common law as a repository of determinate solutions to specific legal questions. Never again would he experience common law adjudication as a process capable of grounding judicial decision-making in anything other than direct policy analysis. Indeed, Holmes anticipated much of Legal Realism when he proclaimed the death knell of legal doctrine: "For the rational study of the law the black-letter man may be the man of the present, but the man of the future is the man of statistics and the master of economics." [135] All of the law is no more than "a concealed, half conscious battle on the question of legislative policy." [136] This profound loss of faith in traditional doctrine ultimately caused Holmes to abandon his youthful determination to unite justice and rationality in the law in favor of the detached olympian skepticism that was to characterize him for the rest of his life. [137]

I now wish to illuminate the forces behind this transformation and to explain how it developed, particularly in the years between the publication of "Privilege, Malice and Intent" in 1894 and "The Path of the Law" in 1897.

"The Path of the Law" represents Holmes's full acknowledgment that law is a social creation. His earlier effort in *The Common Law* to tie law to custom—to turn from an autonomous "logic" to social "experience"—created a picture of law as simply a mirror or reflection of unconsciously evolving social conventions. Law thus continued to be thought of as independent of human will and as not susceptible of being transformed by social engineering.

This picture of law began to unravel for Holmes in "Privilege, Malice and

Intent." [138] "The time has gone by when law is only an unconscious embodiment of the common will," he wrote. "It has become a conscious reaction upon itself of organized society knowingly seeking to determine its own destinies." [139] Yet, as we shall see in a moment, Holmes's return to common law modes of thought in "Privilege, Malice and Intent" is an example of how difficult it was to abandon completely traditional sources of legal meaning and to acknowledge fully the demise of the law-politics distinction.

We saw earlier how, from the beginning of his intellectual career, Holmes sought to attack the natural rights basis of law. By the time he wrote *The Common Law*, he had begun to understand that much of American legal thought was ultimately dependent on natural rights theories of property. Absolute conceptions of property, he realized, were the logical starting point for most orthodox analyses of legal rights and duties. In order to deny natural rights theories, it was therefore necessary that the justification for the institution of property be sought "outside the Bill of Rights or the Declaration of Independence. . . ." [140]

Holmes's only systematic attack on natural rights thinking is put forth in the chapter on "Possession" in *The Common Law*. Here he puts at center the age-old legal-philosophical conundrum: "Why is possession protected by the law, when the possessor is not also an owner?" [141]

His purpose was to use this example to challenge the natural rights justification for property put forth in German philosophy: "The freedom of the will, Kant said, is the essence of man. It is an end in itself; it is that which needs no further explanation, which is absolutely to be respected, and which it is the very end and object of all government to realize and affirm." [142]

Since the will of the owner justified the right to property in Kantian thought, the fact that most legal systems, including the German, often recognized a mere possessory interest against ownership seemed to contradict the principle of freedom of the will. Even a leading Kantian jurist, Holmes reported with some satisfaction, "says . . . that this is a sacrifice of principle to convenience." [143] Holmes's conclusion is that the natural right of the owner in this case is sacrificed to the utilitarian goals of stability and predictability. "I cannot see what is left of a [natural rights] principle which avows itself inconsistent with convenience and the actual course of legislation." [144] A justification must then be found in social utility, "outside" the natural rights philosophy of "the Bill of Rights or the Declaration of Independence. . . ." [145]

After attacking the natural rights framework of post-revolutionary American law, Holmes sought to reverse the relationship between rights and duties that had emerged from that framework. "Let us begin afresh. Legal duties are logically antecedent to legal rights. . . . Legal duties then come before legal rights." [146] Legal duties, Holmes had emphasized earlier, were not derived from a set of pre-political rights. They were social constructs from which rights themselves were often derived and thus defined. Now Holmes went still further and insisted that the role of duty was "to limit freedom of action or choice on the part of a greater or less number of persons in certain specified ways." [147] "[A] right corresponding to [a] burden, is not a necessary or universal correlative,"[148] Holmes concluded. In other words, the law had often imposed duties and restricted freedom without creating any correlative rights. Here one can find the original inspiration for Hohfeld's great 1913 article challenging the natural rights foundation of American law.[149]

Holmes began his attack on absolute property rights in *The Common Law* with the original and fertile recognition that they stood in conflict with the premises of a competitive market economy. "The absolute protection of property," he wrote, "however natural to a primitive community more occupied in production than in exchange, is hardly consistent with the requirements of modern business."[150]

Holmes was the first thinker to see that the legal assumptions behind the existence of a competitive regime were fundamentally incompatible with conceptions of absolute property rights. And more than any other set of issues, the conflict between competition and property influenced the fundamental structure of Holmes's legal thought during the 1890s.

When Holmes wrote *The Common Law*, orthodox legal thought was growing ever more conceptualist. The aspiration of judges and jurists was to develop a small group of fundamental conceptions—fault, will, property rights—from which one could logically deduce virtually all legal rules and doctrines. When Holmes proclaimed in *The Common Law* that "[t]he life of the law has not been logic: it has been experience,"[151] he was directly confronting this growing tendency toward conceptualism.

Holmes's first attack on conceptualism had been made a year earlier when he acidly described Harvard Law School Dean Christopher Columbus Langdell as "the greatest living legal theologian."[152] But the most important of his anti-conceptualistic aphorisms was his declaration that "General propositions do not decide concrete cases."[153] As prevailing legal thought came to be based on a series of supposedly logical deductions from an abstract conception of absolute property rights,[154] Holmes's attack on the absoluteness of property was also a challenge to the dominant form of deductive legal reasoning. If property rights were not absolute, but relative, if the right to property had to be weighed against other competing claims, it was no longer possible to engage in legal discourse as if it were syllogistic reasoning.

The typical structure of argument in *The Common Law* for Holmes is to identify two intellectual extremes or poles in a particular field of law, to show why some small group of cases falls within one or the other extreme, and then to demonstrate that the rest of the cases—most of the significant everyday stuff of the law—falls on the continuum between the extremes. The problem for the legal thinker was how to locate legal problems on the spectrum between the extremes.

While rejecting conceptualism, Holmes nevertheless seemed quite confident in *The Common Law* that there was an underlying rational basis for the distribution of different legal rules and doctrines along the spectrum. Viewed from the vantage point of a legal anthropologist, one could demonstrate how the doctrines developed and how their placement on the continuum was related to the function that the doctrine was called on to serve. With some exceptions, therefore, the evolution of law by and large proceeded according to functional rationality.

By the time we come to "Privilege, Malice and Intent" and "The Path of the Law," however, all that is left are the contradictions between the poles. There is no longer an organic customary principle to mediate the contradictions. Turning his back on his own quest in *The Common Law*, Holmes regarded it as "theoretically wrong"[155] to believe, for example, that the conflict between strict liability and negligence is capable of logical solution. Now it could be solved only by "a concealed, half conscious battle on the question of legislative policy. . . ."[156] "Such matters," he concluded, "really are battle grounds where the means do not exist for determinations that shall be good for all time, and where the decision can do no more than embody the preference of a given body in a given time and place."[157] For Holmes the customary theory of law had collapsed. Law is the product of social struggle. Nothing stands between the state and the individual.

Let us turn to the first crucial moment in Holmes's shift—his essay "Privilege, Malice and Intent" (1894).[158] The essay has been largely ignored because it seems merely technical and because, to the practical minded, it deals only with ancient controversies that have been relegated to pre-history, to the period before the Wagner Act of 1935 removed labor law from common law control. In "Privilege, Malice and Intent," Holmes posits the existence of a fundamental contradiction in the law between the accepted notions of property and competition and, for the first time, expresses doubt whether there is any methodology capable of rationally reconciling the two.

The specific subject of the most important part of his essay was a series of late-nineteenth-century labor cases in which the English courts had limited the right of unions to engage in various forms of economic struggle.[159] The problem had been "suggested, and brought to greater prominence," he wrote, by cases dealing with "boycotts, and other combinations for more or less similar purposes. . . ."[160] It was the legal response to the struggle between labor and capital that produced Holmes's essay.

Holmes had addressed this problem before, in more general terms, as the conflict between absolute property rights and competition. In fact, immunity from liability for competitive injury provided Holmes with one of the important conceptual "extremes" in his organization of legal ideas in *The Common Law*. It was an example—at first glance paradoxical—of a situation in which "the law does not even seek to indemnify a man from all harms. . . . He may establish himself in business where he foresees that the effect of his competition will be to diminish the custom of another shop-keeper, perhaps to the ruin of him."[161] Here, the law permits competitive injury to property on grounds of "policy without reference to any kind of morality."[162] Competition was the most prominent example in *The Common Law* of a legal system's allowing a person to injure another's property, even intentionally, with impunity.

But the problem of competitive injury was only a minor theme in *The Common Law*. By the time he wrote "Privilege, Malice and Intent," the general question of the nature and limits of economic struggle had moved to the center of his consciousness due to two major developments.

The first arose from the question of economic concentration. To what extent was the rapid organization and concentration of economic power in both England and America legitimate and to be supported by law? In this connection, were there ways in which common law judges could (or should) distinguish fair from unfair competition based on the size or power of the units of competition?

A second and more immediate question involved the growing struggle between labor and capital. To what extent was labor organization the same as (or different from) business concentration? Should legal rules pertaining to business competition be applied to economic struggles between labor and capital?

In his section on "privilege," Holmes first spelled out those reasons of public policy that he had said in *The Common Law* justified allowing injury from competition as well as other privileges to injure. Judicial determinations of when to allow privileges to inflict harm could not be arrived at by "merely logical deduction"[163] from absolute conceptions of rights, Holmes declared. Since rights were in conflict, decisions must inevitably be based on "distinctions of degree."[164] The two rights "run against one another, and a line has to be drawn."[165]

Notice the structure of his argument. A balancing test must replace syllogistic reasoning because there is a conflict between property and competition. Whenever the rights of capital conflict with those of labor, "a line has to be drawn" based on "distinctions of degree." While this analysis of when to permit a privilege to inflict injury was simply a reaffirmation of the external standard proposed in *The Common Law*, it did constitute a far more developed attack on prevailing theories of absolute property rights. Above all, it is the first time, I believe, that a fully articulated balancing test has entered American legal theory.[166] Because of this development, perhaps it is the moment we should identify as the beginning of modernism in American legal thought.

After 1910 in many fields of law, a balancing test overthrew the earlier system of legal reasoning based on logical deduction from general premises.[167] The triumph of the balancing test marks the demise of the late-nineteenth-century system of legal formalism. And more than any other figure, it was Holmes who provided the intellectual ammunition for the subversion of the earlier dominant system of thought. Moreover, now for the first time, Holmes also sought to define the limits of the scope of legitimate economic struggle, prompted, as he said, by the decisions of the English courts outlawing the labor boycott.

He turned to the recent English boycott case of *Temperton v. Russell* (1893),[168] in which members of a trade union had struck after their employer had supplied goods to a non-union buyer. The buyer-plaintiff successfully sued the officer of the union. "So," Holmes concluded with some irony, "the right to abstain from contracting is not absolutely privileged as against interference with business."[169] There were, he was insisting, legal rights on both sides, including the right of the union members to refuse to work. Yet one year earlier in the *Mogul Steamship Company Case*,[170] the English judges had allowed a cartel of merchants to offer unprofitable rates and rebates to their customers on the condition that the latter would not deal with a competitor. "The defendants" in *Mogul Steamship*, Holmes wrote, "meant to benefit themselves by making the plaintiff submit, just as, in the other case [of the labor boycott], the defendants meant to benefit themselves by driving the plaintiff away."[171]

How could the English courts have reached such different conclusions regarding two so similar forms of economic coercion? "The ground of decision," Holmes wrote,

> really comes down to a proposition of policy of rather a delicate nature concerning the merit of the particular benefit to themselves intended by the defendants, and suggests a doubt whether judges with different economic sympathies might not decide such a case differently when brought face to face with the issue.[172]

Here, for the first time, Holmes suggests that there may be no neutral way of deciding between the claims of labor and of capital.

There was also a similar problem "in distinguishing between the combination of great powers in a single capitalist, not to speak of a corporation, and the other form of combination,"[173] the labor union. These distinctions involved "very serious legislative considerations which have to be weighed," with "[t]he danger . . . that such considerations should have their weight in an inarticulate form as unconscious prejudice or half conscious inclination."[174]

Here was the problem that a completely external or objective standard presented. How could judges, without a theory of absolute rights, and absent evidence of general customary norms, decide these "distinctions of degree" on any other basis but their preference for labor or capital? Since all forms of economic struggle are inherently coercive,[175] what criteria could distinguish legitimate from illegitimate forms of coercion?

Holmes continued to hold out the unexplained hope that through "training which the practice of the law does not insure"[176] as well as "freedom from prepossessions which is very hard to attain,"[177] "the highest powers of a judge"[178] might still be called forth. Yet he now recognized for the first time the problem inherent in an external standard—that judges might be forced simply to choose between labor and capital. Three years later, Holmes picked up this theme in "The Path of the Law":

> When socialism first began to be talked about, the comfortable classes of the community were a good deal frightened. I suspect that this fear has influenced judicial action both here and in England, yet it is certain that it is not a conscious factor in the decisions to which I refer.[179]

Attempting to mitigate this problem, Holmes sought in the concept of "malice" a mediating force that custom could no longer provide. In so doing, he retreated substantially from his insistence on objective external standards in law.

The basic position of "Privilege, Malice and Intent" is that sometimes, though rarely, the privilege to injure expresses a clear right on one side with no corresponding right on the other. Such a situation represents an easy though infrequent case, where an external standard can decide whether the defendant is privileged to invade the plaintiff's right. But once rights are regarded as relative, Holmes declared, "[i]t is entirely conceivable that motive . . . should be held to affect all, or nearly all, claims of privilege."[180] "There is no general policy in favor of allowing a man to do harm to his neighbor for the sole pleasure of doing harm."[181]

This position represented a complete about-face for Holmes. In *The Common Law*, he had consistently denied that malicious motives were relevant to finding legal liability. His chapter on "Fraud, Malice, and Intent" was, above all, designed "to prove that actual wickedness . . . is not an element in the civil wrong to which the words are applied."[182] Indeed, he specifically denied that "the plaintiff may meet [that is, defeat] a claim of privilege . . . by proving actual malice, that is actual intent to cause the damage complained of."[183] Holmes had even gone so far as to maintain that the frequent use of the word "'malice' in the law, including the criminal law, had "not the same meaning as in common speech";[184] it meant neither "actual intent to cause the damage complained of" nor "malevolence."[185] Instead, it could be reduced to "foresight of consequences"—what the reasonable man, as judged by external standards, could foresee.[186]

Clearly, Holmes's acceptance of the malice test in "Privilege, Malice and Intent" marks a major retreat from the idea of the external objective standard that Holmes had always regarded as his major contribution to legal theory. Only the most pressing intellectual conflict could have produced such a reversal.

Just after "Privilege, Malice and Intent" was published, Holmes was presented with a suit for a labor injunction that permitted him to elaborate his legal theories in one of his most famous dissenting opinions. *Vegelahn v. Guntner* (1896)[187] was an appeal from a narrowly drawn injunction that Holmes had issued against labor picketing. The employer charged that the strikers "have conspired to prevent the plaintiff from getting workmen, and . . . carrying on his business"[188] unless he agreed to a schedule of wages. While Holmes agreed to enjoin the workers from making "threats of personal injury or unlawful harm . . . to persons seeking employment or employed,"[189] he refused to bar peaceful picketing that produced "persuasion and social pressure"[190] even though it might be "sufficient to affect the plaintiff disadvantageously. . . ."[191]

A majority of the Supreme Judicial Court of Massachusetts overturned Holmes's injunction on the ground that "[i]ntimidation is not limited to threats of violence or of physical injury to person or property. It has a broader signification, and there also may be a moral intimidation."[192]

In his dissent, Holmes treated the majority opinion as an example of an unsound conception of absolute rights. He wrote:

> [I]n numberless instances, the law warrents the intentional infliction of temporal damage because it regards it as justified. . . . [T]he policy of allowing free competition justifies the intentional inflicting of temporal damage, including the damage of interference with a man's business . . . as an instrumentality in reaching the end of victory in the battle of trade.

I have seen the suggestion made that the conflict between employers and employed is not competition. But I venture to assume that none of my brethren would rely on that suggestion. If the policy on which our law is founded is too narrowly expressed in the term free competition, we may substitute free struggle for life. Certainly the policy is not limited to struggles between persons of the same class competing for the same end. It applies to all conflicts of temporal interests.[193]

Finally, Holmes argued that competition was not limited to struggle between individuals:

[I]t is plain from the slightest consideration of practical affairs, or the most superficial reading of industrial history, that free competition means combination, and that the organization of the world, now going on so fast, means an ever increasing might and scope of combination. It seems to me futile to set our faces against this tendency. Whether beneficial on the whole, as I think it is, or detrimental, it is inevitable. . . .[194]

This opinion, which perhaps more than any up to that point made Holmes a hero to the Progressives, explicitly emphasized one group of the views he had articulated in "Privilege, Malice and Intent"—the attack on absolutist conceptions of rights. Though it was implicit in the lines he had drawn in the injunction, Holmes had no occasion to mention that malice could defeat the privilege to picket. Indeed, his dissenting colleague, Chief Justice Field, took the far more radical position, eventually adopted by the English House of Lords,[195] that picketing is not enjoinable "whatever the motive may be."[196] But Holmes remained troubled about defining the legal limits to economic struggle, and it began to dawn on him that the problem was made more acute by the collapse of deductive and self-executing conceptions of absolute rights.

Five years after publishing "Privilege, Malice and Intent," Holmes commented again on the English labor cases.[197] The decision banning a union boycott in *Temperton v. Russell*, he declared, "confirms opinions which I have had occasion to express judicially, and commands my hearty assent."[198] Still, he continued, the "discussion which took place" was "inadequate."[199]

[E]minent judges intimated that anything which a man has a right to do he has a right to do whatever his motives, and this has been hailed as a triumph of the principle of external standards in the law, a principle which I have done my best to advocate as well as to name.[200]

But Holmes remained skeptical. "Now here the reasoning starts from the vague generalization Right, and one asks himself at once whether it is definite enough to stand the strain."[201]

If the scope of the right is already determined as absolute and irrespective of motive, *cadit quaestio*, there is nothing to argue about. So if all rights have that scope. But if different rights are of different extent, if they stand on different grounds of policy and have different histories, it does not follow that because one right is absolute, another is—and if you simply say all rights shall be so, that is only a pontifical or imperial way of forbidding discussion.[202]

Holmes was articulating the reasons that led him to retreat to motive in "Privilege, Malice and Intent." Without a conception of bright-line boundaries based on pre-existing absolute rights or empirically determinable customary norms, it was difficult, if not impossible, to construct external standards to distinguish between legitimate and illegitimate forms of competition. As Holmes had observed, to the extent that clear boundaries existed, an inquiry into motives was unnecessary for determining the extent of a privilege to coerce. But where coercion is recognized as an inevitable and legitimate part of economic struggle for which one can only identify "distinctions of degree,"[203] privileges can be assigned in either of two ways.

Judges might be left unconstrained to follow their personal assessments of the relative merits of the parties' claims. But, especially in labor cases, this approach "suggests a doubt whether judges with different economic sympathies"[204] will be able to avoid simply choosing between labor and capital. Likewise, in cases involving restraint of trade, "[i]t is a question of degree at what point the combination becomes large enough to be wrong. . . ."[205]

So a second possibility that would restrict these dangerous tendencies toward judicial legislation presented itself. Allow the privilege to injure whenever the defendant is furthering his own interests through economic struggle, but deny the privilege where harm is inflicted simply for the purpose of injuring the plaintiff. Malice—a subjective standard—becomes an additional basis for distinguishing between legitimate and illegitimate forms of coercion.

From the beginning, economic struggle was, for Holmes, the best example of the weakness of a theory of rights. Yet the collapse of a theory of rights, accompanied by the collapse of customary norms, eventually raised for him a more troubling question about whether objective or external judicial standards were "definite enough to stand the strain"[206] of conflicting political and economic views.

"Privilege, Malice and Intent" sought to define limits on judicial interference with the process of economic struggle by attacking theories of rights that gave courts great confidence that there were clear bright-line boundaries that could not be crossed with impunity. Holmes put forth the model of competition to demonstrate not only that public policy often permitted injury to property, but that competition was in principle no less coercive than other forms of economic struggle.[207] Though he realized that "a line has to be drawn"[208] that would distinguish theft, bribery, and intimidation from legitimate forms of economic warfare, he was not confident that this would be easy. Without a theory of rights, objective criteria might not be available or would degenerate into "unconscious prejudice"[209] based on "different economic sympathies."[210] So he returned to the traditional common law subjective tests of "malice" and "intent" as ways of compensating for the ambiguity of external standards.

Like most of Holmes's writings, "Privilege, Malice and Intent" sought to find a middle point between two extreme legal positions. On the one hand, its analysis of rights was consistent with the general insight of *The Common Law* that "[t]he absolute protection of property . . . is hardly consistent with the requirements of modern business."[211] Competition and property were conflicting legal categories. Economic and social struggle undermined and eroded all efforts to find clear external bright-line boundaries between right and wrong. Compared to the prevailing judicial theory of rights, this approach permitted much greater scope for economic struggle, especially for labor unions, since it required a finding of actual intent or malice. Since most legal restrictions on labor unions derived from a conception of absolute property rights, Holmes deserves to be seen as the preeminent figure in dismantling the system of legal thought based on absolute rights. To that extent, he was justly a hero to the next generation of Progressive social reformers.

On the other hand, Holmes never reached the conclusion, often intimated in his writing, that the relativity of rights meant that all non-violent forms of economic struggle were legitimate. That is what the English House of Lords finally decided in *Allen v. Flood* (1898).[212] Instead, his purpose in writing "Privilege, Malice and Intent" was to attempt to reinstate motive as a basis for confining the scope of legitimate conflict.

After all is said and done, the most interesting observation about "Privilege, Malice and Intent" is that Holmes felt that the disintegration of a theory of rights placed his advocacy of an external standard in jeopardy. Why did he seem to lose confidence in his long-standing view that when two rights "run against one another . . . a line has to be drawn"[213] that could be derived from external considerations of "policy"? Why should the collapse of rights theory have presented him with any more difficulty later than it did in *The Common Law*?

The answer, I believe, is that in *The Common Law* there was something of a symbiotic relationship between the orthodox theory of rights and Holmes's advocacy of external standards. The process of line drawing first advanced in *The Common Law* was ultimately dependent on external criteria. For Holmes, some conception of the "average," the "normal"—in short, some conception of custom— lay in the background of his early thought. Natural rights conceptions, by contrast, he originally identified with the dominant Germanic emphasis on subjective theories of will. He therefore wrote *The Common Law* on the assumption that the shift to an external standard was equivalent to an attack on natural rights theory itself.

But as Holmes came to see later, objective standards were by no means incompatible with all appeals to natural rights. In fact, natural rights theories of property could actually be employed to buttress a legal theory based on external standards. Indeed, during the 1870s there was a shift to objective or external standards in common law cases dealing with property rights. The argument centered on none other than the question of the place of malice in the law.

One typical class of cases involved the problem of the "spite fence."[214] The defendant had erected a fence on her own land that interfered with her neighbor's quiet enjoyment of his land. All courts agreed that without malice the defendant was entitled to build a fence within her boundaries. The only disagreement centered on whether a court could inquire into the defendant's motives. What if her only reason for building the fence was a desire to make her neighbor miserable?

In 1879 Justice Thomas Cooley published his influential *Treatise on the Law of Torts*, which established the orthodox proposition that in determining legal liability "the good or bad motive which influenced the action complained of is generally of no importance whatever."[215] "One of the major themes of Cooley's treatise was that moral considerations should not determine legal relations. Spite fence cases were central to this argument. Beginning with the first pages of his treatise on torts, Cooley endeavored to separate legal and moral obligations."[216]

After Cooley, the overwhelming trend in the cases was a refusal to inquire into the defendant's state of mind. One of the most important opinions supporting Cooley's views on the role of motive in spite fence cases was decided by Justice Holmes in 1889. In *Rideout v. Knox*,[217] Holmes declared:

> It has been thought by respectable authorities, that even at common law the extent of a man's rights in cases like the present might depend upon the motive with which he acted. . . . We do not so understand the common law, and we concede further, that to a large extent the power to use one's property malevolently, in any way which would be lawful for other ends, is an incident of property which cannot be taken away even by legislation.[218]

Holmes thus continued to support an objective or external standard based on the view that a landowner was sovereign within the boundaries of his or her property. Indeed, there was much talk by other judges about how the right to property would be subverted if motives or states of mind could be judicially explored.[219]

The crystallization of a natural rights theory of property during the second half of the nineteenth century was thus further strengthened by the turn to external standards for regulating land use. During this period the dominant tendency in English and American law was to identify natural rights with sovereignty over property. Objective bright-line boundaries actually became the basis for legal definitions of the right to property.[220] But competition, whether between cartelized business or between labor and capital, subverted this bright-line definition of the natural right to property. Only in "Privilege, Malice and Intent" did Holmes begin to discover the dependence of his own conception of external standards, as developed in *The Common Law*, on definitions of bright-line boundaries as created by natural rights judges. Holmes took this idea to its logical conclusion in 1918 when he stated explicitly that property was no more than a "creation of law."[221]

Customary law and natural rights theories thus marched hand in hand during the late nineteenth century. When he retreated to the subjective standard of malice, Holmes acknowledged that it was because of the collapse of a believable conception of boundaries. As he grew more skeptical about a determinate realm of custom that had established the normative framework of *The Common Law*, Holmes finally began to lump together customary and natural rights theories. Social struggle demonstrated that appeals either to custom or to natural rights were simply "pontifical or imperial way[s] of forbidding discussion."[222] Policy was no longer derivable from customary norms but was a coercive imposition of the state.

It is appropriate at this stage to review briefly the process by which Holmes came to occupy a position in 1894 that appeared not only to contradict the most basic tenets of orthodox legal thought, but also to reverse what he himself regarded as his own greatest contribution to legal theory.

We have seen how, in *The Common Law*, Holmes advocated objective rules as a foundation for the stable and predictable legal framework necessary to support a rapidly changing economy. In espousing an objective standard, Holmes was forced to confront individual natural rights theory, which forbade the imposition of the coercive power of the state upon an individual who was personally free from blame.

The manner in which Holmes framed his original objection to subjective rules revealed his early rejection of the notion that law could be understood as the result of judicial application of principles of natural right. He contended that any right of an individual to be assessed according to his own peculiar state of mind simply did not exist. A legal "right," insofar as it made sense to use the term at all, was no more than a legal conclusion: It was simply an expression of the practical consequences of particular rules on particular individuals. Legal rights, Holmes recognized in *The Common Law*, are intellectual constructs used to describe the consequences of the imposition of legal obligations. As he puts it, "legal duties are logically antecedent to legal rights."

The transition from subjective to objective standards was replicated within natural rights theory by a parallel shift away from a concern with individual will. Orthodox legal thinkers during the late nineteenth century gradually surrendered Germanic theories of the will, substituting traditional notions of absolute property rights.[223] As exemplified by the spite fence cases, the refusal to inquire into personal motives was thought to express the absolute right of an individual to control his or her property.[224] The triumph of objective rules in orthodox legal thought was not, however, accompanied by a corresponding rejection of the view that legal rights were analytically prior to legal rules. Orthodox thinkers continued to regard natural rights as prior to and properly determinative of the law.[225]

While Holmes was induced to reject subjective standards by the realization that legal rights took their form from legal rules, orthodox thinkers continued to view objective rules as defined by pre-existing natural rights, such as the right to the quiet enjoyment of one's property. These opposite conceptions of the proper analytic priority of rights and duties set the conceptual stage for the revolutionary change that was to occur in Holmes's thought shortly before the turn of the century. The background condition was a dramatic increase in social and economic change resulting from massive immigration, corporate cartelization, economic depression, and labor unrest.

The radical social and economic conflicts of the 1890s disrupted the legal order in two related ways. First, judges were no longer able to anchor objective rules to the legitimating force of what were thought to be widely shared customary norms. Second, natural rights discourse began to lose its legitimating power as the emergence of fundamentally new problems underlined the indeterminacy of natural rights concepts. For example, natural rights constructs could not provide determinate solutions to the problems posed by economic concentration or the growing confrontation between capital and labor. In addition, as we shall see in the next chapter, the shift from landed to intangible property exposed the socially created and hence disputable character of all property boundaries.

As these issues came to dominate legal discourse, the internal inconsistency of natural rights conceptions became visible, and orthodox legal thinkers were gradually forced to confront Holmes's question posed in "Law in Science": "Now here the reasoning starts from the vague generalization Right, and one asks himself at once whether it is definite enough to stand the strain." By the mid-1890s, Holmes was gradually becoming aware that the objective standard he had advocated so forcefully in *The Common Law* as an alternative to the natural rights emphasis on individual will was in practice actually dependent on natural rights assumptions about property.

Holmes thus saw his greatest contribution to *The Common Law* under siege on two fronts. First, the breakdown of customary norms seemed to leave judges without an external guide as to where to draw objective boundaries. Second, and perhaps even more distressing, Holmes realized that the objective standard had been co-opted by late-nineteenth-century legal thinkers as a way of defining the boundaries of pre-existing natural rights to property. As these natural rights conceptions broke apart under the strain of social and economic change and the dephysicalization of property, the objective standard was gradually sapped of its vitality.

Holmes's solution was simply to abandon purely objective standards where they no longer served to provide determinate solutions to legal questions. Hence the unabashed consideration of motive in "Privilege, Malice and Intent" as a legitimate factor in determining the resolution of labor disputes. As the revolutionary social and economic changes of the late nineteenth century operated to deprive objective rules of their stable external anchors in custom, Holmes gradually abandoned objectivism. By 1894, he was willing to accept the uncertainty inherent in all inquiries into subjective states of mind in order to preserve the integrity of common law adjudication.

But Holmes's reliance on the concept of malice to provide some determinacy to judicial decision making was really no more than a retreat to formalistic application of traditional common law rules of pleading. By the time Holmes wrote the "Path of the Law" three years later, he had finally abandoned any conviction that common law categories were capable of providing neutral constraints on judicial decision making.

"The Path of the Law," written when Holmes was fifty-six, was his last serious effort at systematic legal theory. Though he lived for almost four more decades and made many contributions to legal thought as a judge, one can find within the substance of this last essay many clues about why he seems to have given up on systematic thought.

"The Path of the Law" reflects both a new synthesis and a major stopping point in Holmes's intellectual journey. It is an important measure of how far he had traveled from a youthful rationalism marked by an earnest faith that legal contradiction could be overcome by thought and hard effort. No longer does he seek to "twist the tail of the cosmos," as he put it. Instead, we see clearly the detached olympian skepticism that was to characterize him for the rest of his life.

With the collapse of a customary theory of law amid social and economic struggle, Holmes abandoned the search for a middle position between the state and the individual. Custom was no longer the buffer between consent and coercion. A judicial balancing test not free of economic prejudice might be impossible to construct. All of my previous efforts, he seemed to be saying, at finding a plausible and believable distinction between law and politics have collapsed. The main message of "The Path of the Law" is that there is no basis in reason for deciding which of two contradictory legal doctrines is correct.

To elaborate this message, Holmes first turned to the distinction between law and morals. While the law-morals distinction had not been central to *The Common Law*, the book's contrasts between logic and experience and between subjective and objective standards did implicate the law-morals question. Yet these dichotomies were offered primarily in order to capture the divide between common law and custom, on the one hand, and natural law or natural rights, on the other. Now in "The Path of the Law" the law-morals issue is placed at center stage, and is daringly and originally presented in terms of Holmes's "prediction theory": "The prophecies of what the courts will do in fact, and nothing more pretentious, are what I mean by the law." [226] If law is prophecy, Holmes continues, we must reject the view of "text writers" who tell you that law "is something different from what is decided by the courts of Massachusetts or England, that it is a system of reason, that it is a deduction from principles of ethics or admitted axioms or what not, which may or may not coincide with the decisions." [227] He provocatively introduces "the bad man" who "does not care two straws" about either the morality or the logic of the law. For the bad man, "legal duty" signifies only "a prophecy that if he does certain things he will be subjected to disagreeable consequences by way of imprisonment or compulsory payment of money." [228] The bad man concerns himself only with "material consequences."

"The Path of the Law" marks the first clear articulation of legal positivism— that is, an insistence on a sharp distinction between law and morals—by any American legal thinker. I do not mean that Holmes reversed himself in "The Path of the Law." His position is certainly consistent with his earliest efforts to separate law and morals even before *The Common Law*, reflecting the original influence of the English philosopher John Austin on his thought during the 1870s.

Yet in "The Path of the Law" there is a new urgency to distinguish sharply between law and morals. In my view, the issue of legal positivism—indeed, of positivism in general in American thought—becomes central only after the decline of Darwinism. For Darwinism in law held out the hope that custom could merge fact and value, law and morals. Just as its demise created an unbridgeable chasm between the state and the individual, so too did it separate power and morality.

If Holmes's first object in "The Path of the Law" is to distinguish law from morality, his second is to reiterate the contrast between logic and experience that he originally proclaimed in *The Common Law*. But the meaning of the distinction has changed dramatically.

Holmes continues to criticize "the fallacy . . . of logical form" and the view that law "can be worked out like mathematics from some general axioms of conduct."[229]

> [T]he logical method and form flatter that longing for certainty and for repose which is in every human mind. But certainty generally is illusion, and repose is not the destiny of man. Behind the logical form lies a judgment as to the relative worth and importance of competing legislative grounds, often an inarticulate and unconscious judgment, it is true, and yet the very root and nerve of the whole proceeding.[230]

While Holmes's criticism of formalism is not new, his association of logic with a "longing for certainty and for repose" is. Moreover, while it has been frequently observed that Holmes's own rendition of *The Common Law* was itself deeply rooted in formalism,[231] "The Path of the Law" is, by contrast, decisively anti-formalist.

It is not logic but experience that is dramatically reconceived in "The Path of the Law." In *The Common Law*, Holmes managed to achieve a subtle balance between the "analytical" and "historical" elements of law, between policy and purpose, on the one hand, and historical change and contingency on the other. Because of the mediation of Darwinism, Holmes experienced no ultimate contradiction between the two. In "The Path of the Law," however, policy—the analytical—virtually obliterates history in Holmes' conception of "the rational study of law." "We . . . must remember that . . . our only interest in the past is for the light it throws upon the present,"[232] Holmes declares. "I look forward to a time when the part played by history in the explanation of dogma shall be very small, and instead of ingenious research we shall spend our energy on a study of the ends sought to be attained and the reasons for desiring them."[233] History is necessary only because "it is the first step toward an enlightened scepticism, that is, towards a deliberate reconsideration of the worth of . . . rules."

> When you get the dragon out of his cave on to the plain and in the daylight, you can count his teeth and claws, and see just what is his strength. But to get him out is only the first step. The next is either to kill him, or to tame him and make him a useful animal. For the rational study of the law the black-letter man may be the man of the present, but the man of the future is the man of statistics and the master of economics. It is revolting to have no better reason for a rule of law than that . . . it was laid down in the time of Henry IV.[234]

Just as history is no longer associated with progressive evolution, the source of experience has shifted from custom to policy. The conflict over workers' compensation reflects "a concealed, half conscious battle on the question of legislative policy" that cannot be settled either "deductively, or once for all. . . ."[235] More generally, all policy reflects trade-offs. We need to learn "that for everything we have we give up something else," and we need to be "taught to set the advantage we gain against the other advantage we lose. . . ."[236]

With "The Path of the Law" Holmes pushed American legal thought into the twentieth century. It is the moment at which advanced legal thinkers renounced the belief in a conception of legal thought independent of politics and separate from social reality. From this moment on, the late-nineteenth-century ideal of an internally self-consistent and autonomous system of legal ideals, free from the corrupting influence of politics, was brought constantly under attack.

"The Path of the Law" appeared just one year before the publication of William James's path-breaking first essay on pragmatism, announcing that the only test of any idea is in its "practical consequences."[237] Indeed, Dorothy Ross shows that by this time John Dewey had begun to embrace the view that "the only test of action, in ethics as in knowledge, was whether or not it worked."[238] With "The Path of the Law" both American legal theory and philosophy marched hand in hand to embrace consequentialism.[239] In this sense, "The Path of the Law" is but one part of a deep sea change in American consciousness that one might broadly describe as a fundamental break with theological and doctrinal modes of thought.[240]

It is at this moment that the idea that law is discovered and not made was dealt its most powerful blow in American thought. Only a short time later, Charles Beard extended these demystifying premises to the Constitution itself. The result was an intellectual alliance between social reform and a view of law as socially created. Those Progressive writers during the decade before World War I who elaborated a "social engineering" view of law would come to treat "The Path of the Law" as an inspired text.

It is only at this point, I believe, that Holmes takes on the mantle of judicial self-restraint for which he became famous eight years later in *Lochner v. New York*.[241] For judicial restraint follows from the collapse of his search for immanent rationality in customary law. If law is merely politics, then the legislature should in fact decide. If law is merely a battleground over which social interests clash, then the legislature is the appropriate institution for weighing and measuring competing interests. By the time "The Path of the Law" was written, the focus of Holmes's Darwinism had shifted from courts to legislatures, and interest group conflict had replaced historical evolution as the key to understanding the law.[242]

Though I have dwelt at great length on intellectual history, I hope I have not presented the misleading message—regularly conveyed by students of jurisprudence in England and America—that the history of philosophy is the story of a gradual unfolding of better and better ideas that prevailed simply because they were correct. Indeed, I believe that the widespread experience of Americans during the 1890s that the country was falling apart is perhaps the most important key to understanding the shift in thought not only in law but in virtually every field of intellectual inquiry. It is this experience that Holmes, more than any other legal thinker, was able to capture and to work back into the technical structure of the law.*

---

* After the above text was completed, I learned of the existence of a collection of letters written by Justice Holmes to Lady Clare Castelton, an Irish aristocrat, whom he met in Ireland during the summer of 1896. Copies are held in the Harvard Law School Library. I am grateful to the Harvard Law School for permission to quote from these letters.

Between August 22, 1896, and May 19, 1899, when their correspondence lapsed for fifteen years, Holmes wrote around one hundred letters to Lady Castelton. He was fifty-five years old, she forty-three, when they met. Some of these letters have been published in the *Boston Sunday Globe Magazine* of March 24, 1985, by John S. Monagan under the title *Secret Love of Oliver Wendell Holmes*, and in his book, *The Grand Panjandrum: Mellow Years of Justice Holmes* (University Press of America, 1988). Many have been quoted in Chapter 15 of S. Novick, *Honorable Justice: The Life of Oliver Wendell Holmes* (Little, Brown, 1989).

The letters clearly indicate that Holmes was smitten by the lady and offer unmistakable evidence of a man deeply in love.

Holmes indicates in some of his letters that he has burned all of Lady Castelton's letters, and on May 20, 1897, he asks: "Do you burn my letters?"

My own interest in this correspondence is that Holmes wrote "The Path of the Law" during the fall of 1896 under the immediate glow of this new relationship. It was delivered as an address at Boston University on January 8, 1897.

On September 17, 1896, Holmes, who had been sent a photograph by Lady Castelton, wrote: "Tonight I ought to go to work on a discourse on Legal Education—but I like it a might better sitting here at home with you looking at me and your eye breaking all over your face. I will stop however, [illegible] with rose scented hair I wonder if you know how you delight me?"

On October 7, 1896, Holmes wrote: "You speak of my touch of isolation in some of my speeches. It has reference to my work. One cannot cut a new path as I have tried to do without isolation. I have felt horribly alone. But the result has been far more immediate than I have dared dream of its being and the real danger perhaps is that when one has been for a moment in the lead he should wrap himself in his solitude and sit down, and before he knows it instead of being in advance the procession has passed him and his solitude is in the rear."

On January 11, 1897, three days after he delivered the address, Holmes wrote: "On Friday I fired off my long projected discourse—on the law—with unexpected success. I had so much to say that I read it in order to get it inside an hour—and to read instead of speaking is bad for the hearers." Even though "the room was crowded the air not too good" and his speech "was preceded by more than an hour of prayer and discourse on the finances of the institution . . . until I saw the listeners eyes begin to roll with poisoned slumber . . . to my great satisfaction I had them all wide awake pretty soon and kept them so."

On February 11, 1897, Holmes wrote: "I have now dispatched my address about the law to you and lay it at your feet. Look out or it will kiss them. The Boston University printed it—I think rather decently though I should prefer brown cover to the virgin white put on in my honor. But what's the use of being good if it is not signalized by appropriate symbols."

Before I had read any of this, I had felt strongly that "The Path of the Law" represented an astonishing intellectual leap for Holmes. I supposed that the best way to understand it was "only" as intellectual history. Now one must ask whether and to what extent it was the discovery of some deep—and previously unfulfilled—love that produced in Holmes what Freud called an "oceanic" feeling, inducing him to transcend the prior categories of his thought.

One of the best accounts of the influence of a love relationship on intellectual activity is in R. Steel, *Walter Lippmann and the American Century*, chapter 28 (Little, Brown, 1980).

FIVE

The Progressive Transformation in the Conception of Property

Redefining the Nature of Property

The basic problem of legal thinkers after the Civil War was how to articulate a conception of property that could accommodate the tremendous expansion in the variety of forms of ownership spawned by a dynamic industrial society. At a time when legal conceptions were still overwhelmingly derived from ideas about landed property, new forms of property developed and expanded that were increasingly difficult to fit into the conventional categories. The rise of the business corporation generated a number of novel questions about property rights, in terms both of constitutional protection of corporate property and of shareholders' property rights in the corporation. The enormous expansion in the variety of commercial instruments produced new forms of ownership in need of legal classification.

Above all, the prevailing emphasis in traditional law had been on a "physicalist" definition of property derived from land. Property thus was usually understood in terms of a tangible parcel with clear boundaries. Trespass to land was the essence of legal interference with property rights. But how could a physicalist and concrete definition of property incorporate new, abstract, and intangible forms of wealth such as business goodwill or copyright and patent rights?[1] During the course of the nineteenth century, there was a consistent tendency toward generalization and abstraction of the idea of property in order to accommodate these new and intangible interests. And as the abstraction of the legal idea of property reached its culmination near the end of the century, it became more and more vulnerable to certain fundamental contradictions that the earlier, more modest, physicalist understanding of property had been able to conceal or suppress.

"Property is everything which has exchangeable value," declared Supreme Court Justice Noah H. Swayne in his dissent in the *Slaughterhouse Cases* (1873).[2] As

John R. Commons has shown, Swayne's statement was one of the earliest post-bellum efforts to abstract and generalize the conception of property in American constitutional law. This minority conception thereafter "began to creep into the constitutional definitions given by state and federal courts, as indeed was inevitable and proper if the thing itself was thus changing. Finally, in the first *Minnesota Rate Case*, in 1890, the Supreme Court itself made the transition and changed the definition of property from physical things having only use-value to the exchange-value of anything."[3]

This shift, Commons saw, had been foreshadowed by Justice Stephen Field's dissent in *Munn v. Illinois* (1876),[4] which upheld state regulation of grain elevator rates against a due process attack. "There is, indeed, no protection of any value under the constitutional provision," Field declared, "which does not extend to the use and income of the property, as well as to its title and possession."[5] At last, as Commons noted, the Court held in the first *Minnesota Rate Case*[6] "that not merely physical things are objects of property, but the *expected earning power* of those things is property; and property is taken from the owner, not merely under the power of *eminent domain* which takes *title* and *possession*, but also under the police power which takes its *exchange-value*."[7]

Eminent Domain

One of the most dramatic examples of the move away from a physicalist conception of property during the late nineteenth century can be seen in the law of eminent domain.

For the purpose of determining when a taking of property has occurred sufficient constitutionally to require just compensation, post-revolutionary judges had developed a distinction between "direct" (compensable) and "consequential" (uncompensable) injuries.[8] The effect of this distinction was to restrict severely the obligation of the state—as well as that of state chartered railroad corporations—to pay damages for activity that, while concededly reducing the value of land, nevertheless did not amount to a physical trespass.

By the middle of the century, the distinction between direct and consequential injuries had been further extended. As cities began to develop more extensive controls over land use, courts held that public regulation that reduced the value of land by restricting various uses was not a taking because it did not physically appropriate the land.[9] Restrictions on land use were thus also brought within the uncompensated category of mere consequential injuries.

Until the 1870s, the law of eminent domain turned on various judicial definitions of what sorts of physical intrusions constituted a taking. Above all, it was well recognized that the state or its agents were legally immune from paying compensation for many of the forms of interference with land for which a private person would unquestionably have been required to pay.

As the varieties of commercial and intangible property grew during the nineteenth century, land slowly receded as the model for property conceptions. As the most significant forms of new property were incorporeal, judges were pressed to redefine the nature of interference with property rights more abstractly, not as an invasion of some physical boundary but as any action that reduced the market value of property.

The effort to generalize and abstract the idea of property in terms of market value brought to the surface some of the most significant contradictions concerning any legal definition of property and, at the same time, destroyed the power of the mechanisms existing within the previous system of thought for obscuring and concealing those contradictions. Abstraction, in short, rendered the system both more vulnerable to attack and more difficult, eventually, to defend.

This shift in law away from physicalist conceptions of property based on land began to take shape during the last quarter of the nineteenth century. One of the most self-conscious and influential efforts to redefine these ideas was John Lewis's *Treatise on the Law of Eminent Domain in the United States* (1888). Lewis was "convinced that the earlier cases as to what constitutes a taking were based upon a radically defective interpretation of the constitution. . . ."[10] This interpretation "denied the right to compensation in many cases where it ought to be given. . . ."[11] These erroneous doctrines arose, Lewis observed, because "[t]hese early cases attacked the question wrong end first, so to speak, through the word *taken* instead of through the word *property*."[12] "We must . . . look beyond the thing itself, beyond the mere corporeal object, for the true idea of property. . . . The dullest individual among the *people* knows and understands that his *property* in anything is a bundle of rights."[13] Thus property does not consist of mere physical invasion but should be understood "to include every valuable interest which can be enjoyed as property and recognized as such."[14]

> If property, then, consists, not in tangible things themselves, but in certain rights in and appurtenant to those things, it follows that, when a person is deprived of any of those rights, he is to that extent deprived of his property . . . though his title and possession remain undisturbed. . . .[15]

By insisting that "based upon the nature of property itself" every interference with "the possession, use or enjoyment" of property must be compensated, Lewis thus delivered a major challenge to existing legal doctrine.[16]

As late as the time of the Civil War, it was still regarded as settled that a taking meant that "property must be actually taken, in the physical sense of the word."[17] Yet, even this restrictive definition of eminent domain had been criticized for demonstrating "[t]he tendency under our system . . . to sacrifice the individual to the community."[18] A strong shift to individualism during the 1870s eventually combined with a gradual move away from tradition physicalist definitions of property to produce a major judicial expansion in constitutional doctrine. Lewis thus was aided in his own reformulation by what he called these "radical changes" in judicial attitudes during "the last few years."[19]

In the leading case of *Eaton v. Boston, Concord & Montreal R.R.* (1872),[20] the New Hampshire Supreme Court decided that any action by the state that interfered with the *use* of land was constitutionally a taking. The view that only a physical appropriation constituted a taking, the court declared, "seem[s] . . . to be founded on a misconception of the meaning of the term 'property'. . . ."[21]

> In a strict legal sense, land is not "property," but the subject of property. The term "property" . . . "means only the rights of the owner in relation to it." "It denotes a right . . . over a determinate thing." "Property is the right of any person to possess, use, enjoy, and dispose of a thing."[22]

This abstraction of the conception of property made sense as new varieties of legal interests, different from land, began increasingly to force themselves on the attention of courts. "A refusal to pay a debt is an injury to the property of the creditor," the New Hampshire Supreme Court noted two years later in explaining the *Eaton* case.[23]

> A patent right, a copyright, a right of action, an easement, an incorporeal heredi-tament, may be property as valuable as a granite quarry; and the owner of such property may be practically deprived of it,—such property may be practically taken from its owner,—although it is not corporeal. So those proprietary rights, which are the only valuable attributes or ingredients of a landowner's property, may be taken from him, without an asportation or adverse personal occupation of that portion of the earth which is his. . . . Property is taken when any one of those proprietary rights is taken, of which property consists.[24]

The case that was most influential in highlighting this dephysicalized defini-tion of property was *Pumpelly v. Green Bay Co.*,[25] decided by the U.S. Supreme Court in 1871. *Pumpelly* involved the question of compensation for the destruc-tion of property due to flooding caused by a governmentally authorized dam. In rejecting the traditional distinction between direct and consequential damages, Justice Samuel F. Miller wrote that "[i]t would be a very curious and unsatisfac-tory result, if . . . the government . . . can destroy [property's] value entirely, can inflict irreparable and permanent injury . . . without making any compen-sation, because, in the narrowest sense . . . it is not *taken* for the public use. . . ."[26]

Though the broadest implications of *Pumpelly* only gradually emerged, the case immediately presented a challenge to the prevailing idea that a taking consti-tuted either a physical trespass or appropriation of title. Instead, it soon came to stand for the increasingly prevalent proposition that all restrictions on the use of property that diminished its market value were takings in the constitutional sense. By 1893, *Pumpelly* was being cited to support the expansive conclusion that any interference with the future income stream of an owner constitutes a taking of property.[27]

Property and Expectations

As legal thinkers sought to move away from physicalist definitions of property, they found it necessary to find some more abstract measure of interference with those "bundles of rights" that legal writers and judges now identified with increasing frequency as constituting property. They tended, therefore, to turn to "market value" as the common denominator for measuring whether an interference with property represented a taking.[28] Indeed, there seems to have been a convergence between writings in law and those in economics, which with increasing regularity identified "market price" as the closest practical measure of objective value.[29]

The abstraction of property into market value at once freed the legal system from an increasingly archaic emphasis on physical invasion and brought to the surface many more fundamental difficulties that a concrete and tangible conception of property had been able to avoid.

With the development of the market value theory of property, legal thinkers were forced to face a basic contradiction in all legal theories of property built upon market value. How does one avoid the conclusion that any governmental activity that changes expectations and hence lowers the value of property constitutes a taking? While this question had emerged very early in American constitutional history, the legal conceptions then prevailing made it possible to avoid seeing its full implications.

At the heart of the post-Revolutionary American constitutional system was the principle that all retroactive lawmaking was an interference with property rights. The story of precisely how this principle was worked into American constitutional doctrine is long and complex. The problem appeared for the first time in the very early case of *Calder v. Bull* (1798)[30] in which the U.S. Supreme Court wrestled with the constitutional status of an act by the Connecticut legislature ordering a court to grant a new trial to a losing litigant. The case is famous for the Supreme Court's determination that the constitutional bar on ex post facto laws was limited to crimes and hence did not apply to the Connecticut legislature's actions. Since the meaning of the ex post facto clause was the only question formally submitted to the Court, the judges' more general unease with non-criminal retroactive laws did not find focused constitutional expression. Nevertheless, Justice James Iredell's defense of the constitutional validity of civil retroactive laws was perhaps the earliest expression of the fear that such a restriction would bring all governmental change to a halt. "The policy, the reason and the humanity of the prohibition" against retrospective criminal laws, Iredell wrote,

> do not . . . extend to civil cases that merely affect the private property of citizens. Some of the most necessary and important acts of legislation are, on the contrary, founded upon the principle, that private rights must yield to public exigencies. Highways are run through private grounds; fortifications, light-houses, and other public edifices, are necessarily sometimes built upon the soil owned by individuals. In such, and similar cases, if the owners should refuse voluntarily to accommodate the public, they must be constrained, so far as the public necessities require; and justice is done, by allowing them a reasonable equivalent. Without the possession of this power, the operation of government would often be obstructed, and society itself would be endangered.[31]

At this very early point in American constitutional history, the dilemma was clearly stated. How could one bar all retroactive laws while still managing to avoid the absurd conclusion that every governmental action that interferes with settled expectations is unconstitutional?

Within two decades after *Calder v. Bull* was decided, the contracts clause of the Constitution came virtually to serve as a civil anti-retroactivity provision.[32] Through a series of distinctions thereafter developed under the contracts clause, however, the Supreme Court managed to avoid having to face the basic contradiction that if property rights consist of stable expectations, all changes in legal rules can be regarded as governmental interference with property.

Ultimately, it was the dominant physicalist conception of property that muted the contradiction during the antebellum period. Its most significant application under the contracts clause was the distinction between "vested" and "non-vested" rights. Drawing on the law of landed estates, the constitutional distinction sought to establish a delimited category of vested rights that the state could not retroactively change. No other expectations were constitutionally protected against changed legal rules.[33]

For our purposes, the most important aspect of the vested rights doctrine was that it enabled courts to avoid the *reductio ad absurdum* that every change in legal rules constituted an interference with property rights. Yet since the vested rights doctrine itself was founded by analogy to the vesting of landed property by way of title, it became increasingly difficult to decide whether other, more abstract and intangible property interests had also been vested. Indeed, the problem was already foreshadowed as early as 1827 in the great case of *Ogden v. Saunders*.[34] In that case, by a four to three vote, the U.S. Supreme Court decided that a state insolvency law that affected future debts was not unconstitutional. Eight years earlier, the Court had held unconstitutional an insolvency law discharging debtors from obligations previously incurred.[35]

Ogden v. Saunders was decided just as the nature of property was in the process of substantial transformation. In 1789, no one would have doubted that a vested right to property meant, above all, fee simple ownership of land. But during the intervening forty years, a dazzling variety of abstract and intangible property claims had developed out of an increasingly commercial society. Vested rights therefore could no longer be defined simply in terms of concrete and universally recognized interests in land. It was now necessary to decide whether corporate charters, stock ownership, contractual debts, and a host of other abstract and intangible commercial interests should also be counted as vested property. The question thus began to turn on attempting to define a more abstract, arguable, and elusive set of expectations that government was bound to respect. As it became necessary in these increasingly novel areas to define vested rights more abstractly, legislative claims to interfere with the very definition of property posed a correspondingly greater threat.

In *Ogden v. Saunders*, the majority simply reaffirmed what had by now become a conventional formal distinction between prospective and retrospective laws. But Chief Justice John Marshall, in dissent, argued for the first time that *all* statutory interferences with a contractual obligation were in fact retrospective laws.

According to Chief Justice Marshall as well as to Justice Joseph Story, all state bankruptcy laws, whether they operated on past or future contracts, were unconstitutional. Marshall maintained that virtually all established expectations, including the expectation of the power to contract in the future, were vested property rights. The obligation of a contract was not "the mere creature of society, . . . deriv[ing] all its obligation from human legislation." Some argued that contractual obligation "is not the stipulation an individual makes which binds him, but some declaration of the Supreme power of a State to which he belongs, that he shall perform what he has undertaken to perform." "On the contrary," Marshall argued, contract establishes "a pre-existing intrinsic obligation which human law enforces." Contracts exist "anterior to, and independent of society . . . [and] like many other natural rights, . . . although they may be controlled, are not given by human legislation." [36]

This was Marshall's only dissent in a constitutional case. That he could not bring a majority with him underlines how, from its earliest decisions, the Supreme Court had struggled to avoid the conclusion that every change in the laws that adversely affected the value of property constituted either an unconstitutional taking or, as its closest functional equivalent under the antebellum federal Constitution, an interference with the obligation of contract. [37] By confining the prohibition on state retroactivity within the limits of vested rights and by attempting to define the vesting of those rights by analogy to the law of real property, the Court sought to create manageable and practical limits on the confiscatory power of the state.

The gradual collapse of a physicalist definition of property after 1870 revived all of the contradictions that had been barely suppressed in traditional doctrine. For as the definition of a property right became divorced from concrete physical objects with bright-line boundaries and came to turn more and more on abstract ideas of individual expectations of stable market values, the very conception of property became infinitely expandable. The result was that during the 1880s and 1890s a variety of new property interests for the first time received recognition by American courts. These property interests were endowed with what, by traditional standards, can only be called extravagantly expanded prerogatives. During this period, American courts came as close as they had ever had to saying that one had a property right to an unchanging world.

But the very abstraction in the conception of property during the last two decades of the nineteenth century was ultimately the source of its own undoing.

Hohfeld's Influence on Legal Thought

If abstraction threatened to "propertize" the entire world of legal relations, it also encouraged the earliest efforts to undermine and subvert the extreme conceptualism of orthodox legal thought. Every move of intellectual integration eventually encountered an equally powerful movement aimed at resisting any imperial idea of property. Every attempt at construction of a systematic conception of property based on market value generated an effort at deconstruction thus sought to demonstrate the tautological and all-consuming character of the concept. Each effort at aggregation of the multiple and varied areas of property doctrine under the concept of "right" produced a reaction aimed at disaggregating the very idea of property itself.[38]

One of the most influential figures in the Progressive assault on the conceptualism of the old order was Yale Law Professor Wesley N. Hohfeld, whose analytical system of "jural relations" had an electrifying impact on some of his most brilliant contemporaries.

In a famous 1913 article,[39] Hohfeld set forth his two tables of eight "fundamental legal conceptions":

Jural Opposites

right	privilege	power	immunity
no right	duty	disability	liability

Jural Correlatives

right	privilege	power	immunity
duty	no right	liability	disability

The problem of recapturing the political and theoretical significance of Hohfeld's categories is not without its difficulties. For while it has become "a staple of academic legal culture," Hohfeld's system "survives, like a sack of dried beans, unesteemed by those who have lost the recipe for its use. . . . By today's law students (not to speak of their teachers), Hohfeld is often envisaged as a chap with a scholastic passion for terminological nicety—at worst a carping bore, at best an authentic, if pedantic exemplar of the academic virtue of precision."[40]

To understand where Hohfeld was "coming from," we need first to place him squarely within pre–World War I Progressive legal culture. Hohfeld's speech before the Association of American Law Schools in 1914 captures his relationship to the Progressive movement.[41] Hohfeld endorsed President Woodrow Wilson's call for a "fresh and critical analysis" that would lead to "nothing less than a radical reconstruction" of American society. "Society is looking itself over in our day from top to bottom," Hohfeld quoted Wilson as saying. Then he asked: "Have our university law schools been giving full recognition to what Mr. Wilson calls the conscious struggle for change and readjustment which characterizes our era?"[42]

Within this political context, Hohfeld explained the need for a "Formal, or Analytical, Jurisprudence" that would provide "an accurate and intimate understanding of the fundamental working conceptions of all legal reasoning." It was "not . . . a mere matter of juridical ornament or intellectual delight. On the contrary, it would be difficult to overestimate the economic and social value" of such an undertaking.[43]

While analytical jurisprudence appealed to logical consistency, another branch, critical or teleological jurisprudence, sought "a more comprehensive, coordinated and synthetic consideration of the underlying psychological, ethical, political, social and economic causes and purposes of the various branches and specific rules of the law."[44] Hohfeld clearly regarded his own efforts at analytical jurisprudence as a preliminary step toward understanding how law related to what he called society's "underlying policies and purposes."[45]

Here he stood in a line of analytical jurisprudence that had begun in England with Jeremy Bentham and John Austin and was made prominent in America by Oliver Wendell Holmes, Jr., as well as by that obscure classifier, Henry Terry. In late-nineteenth-century England, academic jurisprudence was dominated by Austin's disciples Thomas Holland and John Salmond.[46]

What of the actual system Hohfeld created? It appears to be one of the pioneering attempts by a Progressive legal thinker to deconstruct the abstract character of orthodox conceptions of property.[47] Hohfeld seems to have had two broad intellectual strategies in mind in creating his tables of jural "correlatives" and "opposites." Each of the correlatives was, in effect, no more than a tautology. Each of the opposites was, in effect, a contradiction. By showing, for example, that rights and duties were correlatives, Hohfeld reintroduced a theme highlighted by Holmes forty years earlier.

The question of whether to have a jurisprudence of rights or of duties had been one of the classical issues in analytical jurisprudence, beginning with Bentham. It resurfaced as a central preoccupation of Anglo-American legal theory only with the posthumous 1863 publication of the complete edition of John Austin's *Lectures on Jurisprudence*.[48] Austin, an intimate of Bentham and of James and John Stuart Mill, had originally given his lectures at the University of London in 1828 and had published some of them in 1832. Yet "no notice was taken" of the book, and "it was never reviewed in any learned journal."[49] Indeed, Sarah Austin, who arranged for the publication, observed that her husband had lived "a life of unbroken disappointment and failure." Yet, because of her efforts, "within a few years of [Austin's] death, it was clear that his work had established the study of jurisprudence in England."[50]

"Right, like Duty, is the creature of Law, or arises from the command of the Sovereign,"[51] Austin wrote. "[T]he term 'right' and the term 'relative' duty' are correlating expressions. They signify the same notions, considered from different aspects, or taken in different series."[52]

"Law is the Command of the Sovereign" is a traditional positivist formula that begins with Thomas Hobbes, appears in both Blackstone and Bentham (notwithstanding Bentham's vicious attack on Blackstone),[53] and is repeated by Austin. How much of Austin's positivism derived from Bentham's attack on the "anarchical" implications of the French Declaration of the Rights of Man,[54] and how much from Bentham's radical schemes of legislative codification[55] and his corresponding contempt for the common law and its "fundamental law" tradition,[56] is very difficult to measure.

Austin's positivism seems to have resonated with Holmes's own post–Civil

War fears of the anarchical implications of the abolitionists' use of natural rights theories.[57] In 1870, Holmes joined in the revival of Austin's jurisprudence. "Duties precede rights logically and chronologically," Holmes declared in the first systematic essay he ever published.[58] Though less famous than many of his aphorisms, it was perhaps his most revolutionary statement.

The rediscovery of Austin tells us much about the need of late-nineteenth-century legal thinkers for a systematic and integrated system of jurisprudence. Even more significantly, it underlines the widespread desire to attack any system of law built on a foundation of natural rights. In England, with its relatively weak natural rights assumptions, such a turn could easily be assimilated into the dominant tradition of parliamentary supremacy. In America, however, Holmes was declaring his opposition to perhaps the most basic element of political and legal culture. To import Austin into America was, therefore, to challenge the most fundamental underlying premise of American law.

What was Progressive about analytical jurisprudence when Hohfeld reintroduced it in America in 1913? We have seen that it contributed to the subversion of absolute property rights and substituted a vision of property as a social creation.[59] From the 1870s, we have seen as well, a de-physicalized conception of property had vastly expanded the outer limits of the right to property.[60] During the 1880s, the federal courts had begun to use the idea of interference with these more abstract and intangible property rights to generate the labor injunction.[61] Some courts expanded the idea of business goodwill well beyond its traditionally narrow usage, so that every form of coercive labor union activity was defined as an interference with property. Others concluded that any organized labor activity that reduced the market value of a business could be treated like a common law nuisance.[62] The breathtaking speed with which the federal courts instituted the labor injunction was partly a function of this propertizing conceptual move. To the extent that courts conceived of unions as inflicting damage on property no differently from a common law nuisance, they were more than ready to deploy one of the traditional weapons against a nuisance—the injunction. Indeed, in their passion to legitimate the non-discretionary character of the labor injunction, some courts in this period generalized the principle and saddled American law with the formalistic doctrine that whenever a nuisance is found, an injunction must be issued as a matter of course.[63]

Holmes began to resist the propertizing move in the labor cases around 1895, in his famous dissent in *Veghelan v. Guntner*[64] and his article "Privilege, Malice, and Intent."[65] The main thrust of his effort was to challenge the dominant rights-based theory of the labor cases. In this sense, he was re-connecting with the Austinian interests of his youth. The labor cases were also closely related to the issue of "competitive injury," which raised the question of whether property rights were compatible with the right to inflict injury on one's competitors.[66]

We have seen that the question of competitive injury—of the relationship between the right to property and the legitimacy of injurious competition—was one of the dominant intellectual issues in the law during the 1890s. It appeared in constitutional challenges to the Sherman Act, as well as in common law discussions of whether cartelization was a legitimate form of competition. Finally, it was Holmes who insisted in the labor cases that the struggle between labor and capital was but another version of competition and should be understood in the same way.[67] In framing the issue as one of competition versus property, Holmes was erecting a challenge to orthodox rights-based conceptions of legal reasoning. Hohfeld appears to have understood and carried forward this Holmesian move.

Late-nineteenth-century courts were "conceptualistic" in the sense that they believed that one could derive particular legal rules and doctrines from general concepts such as property.[68] And they were formalistic in believing that one could logically deduce these rules from the nature of property itself. Property, then, was thought to have an essence or a core of meaning, even if there could be legitimate argument about what was to be included at the periphery. Moreover, the orthodox idea of property was that it was a pre-political, Lockean natural right not created by law, though all lawyers recognized that the law might be needed to specify rights for the hard cases at the periphery of the concept.[69]

In late-nineteenth-century orthodox legal thought, it was thus possible to make statements such as "a labor boycott is inconsistent with the right to property" or "coercive picketing violates the employer's property rights and therefore should be enjoined." What workers could and could not legitimately do was thought to follow logically from the very definition of their employers' property rights.

By calling rights and duties "correlatives," therefore, Hohfeld sought to subvert the privileged position that rights had occupied as the starting point for orthodox legal analysis. He thus wished to relativize rights discourse by emphasizing that one might just as logically begin such an analysis with the concept of a duty created by law. A right therefore became simply the legal enforcement of a socially created duty.

Equally important was Hohfeld's classification of "privilege" as not logically entailing a right. "The lesson is that there is no logically necessary bond between a right over some act . . . and a privilege over that same act . . ., no logical reason why having the right must go with having the privilege, or vice-versa."[70]

Hohfeld's analytic scheme seemed to have had an electrifying influence on his Yale Law School contemporaries, Walter Wheeler Cook and Arthur L. Corbin, who were struggling to break out of the prevailing orthodoxy of rights discourse in their respective fields, conflicts of laws and contracts. Indeed, in his devastating analysis of the *Hitchman Coal Case* (1917),[71] published shortly after Hohfeld's tragically premature death, Cook self-consciously offered the only extant example of an application of Hohfeldian analysis to an actual legal problem.[72]

In the *Hitchman Coal Case*, the U.S. Supreme Court held that an employee's agreement with his company not to join a union created a right in the company to enjoin a union organization drive. The fact that the company had the *privilege* of employing non-union labor—that is, the state did not bar such activity—did not mean that it also had a *right* to prevent unionization, Cook showed. "So far, therefore, as the learned justice meant to say that the *right* of the plaintiff to protection *necessarily* followed as a matter of mere logical inference from the *privilege* to make the agreements . . ., the reasoning is clearly fallacious," Cook concluded.[73]

The most important consequence of Hohfeld's system of classification was that it carried through the radical implications of a de-physicalized system of property.[74] Property consisted of abstract legal relations, not physical things, Hohfeld showed. As Arthur L. Corbin put it in 1922, "Our concept of property has shifted; incorporeal rights have become property. And finally, 'property' has ceased to describe any *res*, or object of sense, at all, and has become merely a bundle of legal relations—rights, powers, privileges, immunities."[75]

The idea that property consists merely of "a bundle of legal relations" is perhaps the most radical and far-reaching implication of Hohfeld's system. "By breaking property into its constituent parts, Hohfeld both demonstrated that property does not imply any absolute or fixed set of rights in the owner and provided a vocabulary for describing the limited nature of the owner's property."[76]

The Higher Law Basis of Classical Legal Thought

The struggle over whether there should be a jurisprudence of rights or of duties highlights one of the most complex questions about how to understand Classical Legal Thought. A pervasive Progressive criticism of Classical Legal Thought charged orthodox jurists with having imported natural law into constitutional interpretation. The "revival of natural law concepts" came to be treated as one of the major explanations of how the Supreme Court during the *Lochner* era was able to write its own views of the Constitution into law.[77] The charge is also closely related to criticism of the emergence of so-called substantive due process during the twenty years before *Lochner*.[78]

Much of the confusion over this question derives from lack of clarity about how late-nineteenth-century lawyers thought about the character of higher law. At the time of the drafting of the Declaration of Independence, there was confusion over four different conceptions of higher law.[79] The first was medieval Thomistic natural law, with its premise that any positive law that violated natural law was void.[80] While this view had never been as influential in England as it was on the Continent, by the late eighteenth century it had been largely marginalized by English jurists.[81]

The communitarian and hierarchical character of traditional natural law also began to be transformed by the emergence of individualistic ideas of natural rights in seventeenth-century social contract theories. Emphasizing the primacy of pre-political rights in nature, the liberal social contract thinkers believed that positive law, especially laws dealing with property, should reflect those natural rights that individuals retained when they agreed to enter into civil society. Unlike traditional natural law, natural rights theories were centered on conflict between the individual and the state.[82]

In the period leading up to the American Revolution, these two very different versions of higher law were perhaps overshadowed in English and American constitutional thought by the notion of fundamental law, which usually referred to the "immemorial rights of Englishmen" or some other conception of immemorial custom.[83] Jefferson's great accomplishment was that he managed to weave all of these different strands of higher law thinking into the Declaration, adding perhaps a fourth variation as traditional natural law ideas were slowly reformulated into a Newtonian vision of universal moral laws.[84]

The Progressive charge that legal orthodoxy illegitimately turned to natural law in the late nineteenth century was built on several foundations. Beginning with the early Supreme Court case of *Calder v. Ball* (1798),[85] there had been a running debate in early American constitutional history over whether it was appropriate for judges to go outside of the specific provisions of a written constitution to invoke higher law principles. And while judges and jurists of the *Lochner* era were virtually unanimous in concluding that it was inappropriate to go outside of the Constitution, the charge that they did so nevertheless has been widely shared among constitutional historians.

The first count in the historians' indictment derived from what Edward S. Corwin called the "doctrine of implied limitations."[86] As we saw earlier,[87] late-nineteenth-century courts were willing to hold that, for example, an unequal tax "impliedly" violated a state constitutional provision requiring separation of powers because only taxation for revenue, not for purposes of redistribution, was a legislative act. Using similar reasoning, antebellum state courts had struck down uncompensated takings, even without a specific just compensation provision.

The question of how much one can legitimately imply from a provision in a contract, statute, or constitution has been a perennial issue in legal theory. It appeared early in American constitutional history in debates over Jeffersonian strict constructionism, as well as in Chief Justice John Marshall's expansive conception of the implied powers of the national government in *McCulloch v. Maryland*.[88] Similarly, in the late nineteenth century, we saw, the scope of implication in contract law was a major subject of controversy.[89]

The debate over the legitimate scope of implication was closely related to the more general Progressive challenge to the breadth of legal reasoning in Classical thought. As we shall see,[90] to the extent that Progressive jurists insisted that analogical reasoning needed to be restricted because analogies were productive of judicial legislation, they would similarly be suspicious of any claims about the neutral or necessary character of legal implication. If general propositions could not decide concrete cases, it was unlikely that one would believe that legal implication from highly abstract conceptions could be non-discretionary. If, by contrast, a concept was thought to have a fixed essence or core of meaning, it was correspondingly easier to derive particular sub-rules or doctrines from more general principles. Much of the Progressive charge that the *Lochner* court turned to higher law was really an expression of Progressive disbelief in the claimed power and scope of traditional legal reasoning.

The other, more obvious source of the Progressive charge that legal Classicists turned to natural law focuses on the question of the rise of substantive due process after the Civil War. In my judgment, this argument was largely a fabrication of Progressive thought, designed to delegitimate the *Lochner* court by arguing that it had taken a completely unprecedented turn in the late nineteenth century. In fact, under the due process clause of the Fourteenth Amendment, the Supreme Court after the Civil War promulgated doctrines not very different from those that had previously been developed under, for example, the contracts clause or state just compensation provisions. While there was considerable debate among *Lochner* court judges over whether the Civil War amendments should result in a vastly more interventionist federal constitutional system—a debate that included the very important claim that the amendments were meant to be limited to the protection of newly freed blacks—the controversy did not significanlty turn on whether due process had previously been restricted to a procedural meaning. It was easy to confuse the controversial expansion of federal judicial power under the Fourteenth Amendment with a supposed change in constitutional methodology from "procedural" to "substantive" due process. That confusion was largely produced by later critical Progressive historians intent on delegitimating the *Lochner* court.

While natural rights conceptions were extremely important in shaping the character of Classical Legal Thought, they did not usually operate as higher law principles that alone could determine the validity or invalidity of positive law. Rather, natural rights discourse structured legal argument by suggesting starting points, background assumptions, presumptions, or first principles in the law.

Perhaps the best way to see this is by turning to Robert M. Cover's discussion of the influence of natural rights ideas on anti-slavery judges before the Civil War. In a typical expression, one of these judges declared in 1845:

> Slavery is wrong, inflicted by force and supported alone by the municipal power of the state or territory wherein it exists. It is opposed to the principles of natural justice and right, and is the mere creature of positive law. Hence, it being my duty to declare the law, not to make it, the question is not, what conforms to the great principles of natural right and universal freedom—but what do the positive laws and institutions . . . command and direct.[91]

As Cover indicates, this statement captures the place of natural law/natural rights doctrines in the structure of antebellum constitutional discourse. He writes:

> [T]he courts uniformly recognized a hierarchy of sources of law . . . in which "natural law" was subordinate to constitutions, statutes, and well-settled precedent. This hierarchy was clearly established and unambiguously articulated by the courts. The reason for natural law's subordinate place was a thoroughgoing positivism concerning the origin of "law." Law was perceived as operative and valid because of a human constituent process and by virtue of valid lawmaking processes in pursuance of that Constitution. It was the will of men that gave law its force. But men look

to various sources for the content of their law. And one very important kind of source is that which declares what is right and just. Most of the jurists of this period felt comfortable designating this tradition as "natural law" and finding it in books and maxims that were self-styled statements of the law of nature. This body of principles and rules was conceived of as "existing," though without authority, apart from its incorporation, by virtue of men's wills, in the "law" of a particular state. Natural law was, indeed, a subject for study by the lawyer or law student because it was helpful in understanding the principles underlying so much of a rational legal system. It was also one potential source for formulating new rules or modifying old ones.[92]

Cover's understanding is confirmed by virtually all Classical legal thinkers. For example, Christopher G. Tiedeman, whose influential A *Treatise on the Limitations of the Police Power in the United States* (1886) was a major building block of laissez-faire constitutionalism, has been regularly portrayed as a natural law thinker.[93] Yet Tiedeman began his treatise by rejecting Justice Chase's early view in *Calder v. Bull* that it was appropriate to appeal above the Constitution to natural law principles. "[T]he current of authority, as well as substantial constitutional reasoning, is decidedly opposed to the doctrine," Tiedeman proclaimed.

> It may now be considered as an established principle of American law that courts, in the performance of their duty to confine the legislative department within the constitutional limits of its power, cannot nullify and avoid a law, simply because it conflicts with judicial notions of natural right or morality, or abstract justice.[94]

Like Cover's anti-slavery judges, Tiedeman was willing to appeal to higher law principles in the interpretation and "reasonable construction" of positive law. "[A]lthough these fundamental principles of natural right and justice cannot, in themselves, furnish any legal restrictions upon the governmental exercise of police power . . . yet they play an important part in determining the exact scope and extent of constitutional limitations."[95]

Nor was Tiedeman unique in his views. The other great exponent of laissez-faire constitutionalism, Judge Thomas M. Cooley, was equally clear in his *Treatise on the Constitutional Limitations Which Rest Upon the Legislative Power of the States of the American Union* that a court could not declare a statute unconstitutional "solely on the ground of unjust and oppressive provisions or because it is supposed to violate the natural, social, or political rights of the citizen. . . ."[96]

For Progressive jurists bent on de-legitimating the claimed autonomy of orthodox legal reasoning, any distinction between judicial interpretation and construction, on the one hand, and judicial lawmaking, on the other, simply represented an effort to disguise the appeal to natural law principles. Yet just as anti-slavery judges acknowledged that these ideas restricted the scope of what they could legitimately do as judges, so too is there no reason to doubt that Classical legal thinkers felt just as constrained by their own positivistic framework. It is that framework that Progressive constitutional historians ultimately failed to acknowledge.

Rate Regulation

Legal positivism combined with the de-physicalization of property to produce dramatic legal changes in the area of judicial oversight of the "reasonableness" of governmentally regulated rates. The process of overseeing the reasonableness of rates forced courts to articulate abstract conceptions of property, and especially of value, that constituted a sharp departure from the emphasis on physical intrusions across boundaries that had marked earlier legal definitions of interference with property. Moreover, the rate cases impelled most courts to think in terms of the "market value" of property for the first time. This process of abstracting the idea of property into market value was not only dangerously over-inclusive—it made virtually every change in government policy that caused a decline in market value potentially a taking—it also eventually exposed the circularity in the very conception of property, a circularity that had been hidden from view by the traditional land-centered distinction between direct and consequential injuries.

Perhaps the best way to see the influence of judicial oversight of rate making on the conception of property is to turn to the intense debate during the 1920s about value in determining the base from which to judge the fairness of a public utility's rate of return.

From the moment that the U.S. Supreme Court imposed a reasonableness requirement as a check on confiscatory rates, the definition of the value of property became a major question of federal constitutional law. In *Smyth v. Ames* (1898),[97] the Court sought to establish a test to determine the reasonableness of rates. "The conflicting desires which plagued the Supreme Court in the [rate] cases were reconciled by the unanimous adoption of a formula which conceded what the majority of the court desired, the power to regulate, and yet guarded against what the minority feared, confiscation."[98]

Whether the Court's decision in *Smyth v. Ames* should be given its traditional reading as establishing a set of multiple (and hence difficult to administer) factors to be considered in determining the fair value of property or, as one scholar has argued,[99] be read as in fact adopting a "reproduction cost" standard, everyone agrees that somewhat later, during the 1920s, the Court did finally fix upon reproduction cost as the required constitutional measure of value.[100]

By this time, reproduction cost had begun to be extremely controversial, since it had only recently become extraordinarily favorable to railroads and other utilities as a result of war-induced inflation. While "[o]ver the first decade and a half after *Smyth v. Ames* the price level slowly rose," between 1913 and 1920 prices increased by almost 150 percent. Suddenly, "[t]he relative equivalence of historic and present costs was broken; decidedly different results once again followed from whether reproduction [or historical cost] set the limits on government rate regulation."[101] The standard for measuring value suddenly became both a central issue of public policy on which millions of dollars turned and a fundamental theoretical question about the nature of property. Beginning in 1920, a number of prominent legal scholars addressed these questions.[102] They showed how, by the time *Smyth v. Ames* was decided, the idea of reasonableness in rate regulation and come to rest "on the analogy of the law of eminent domain."[103]

It had not always been so. Justice John Marshall Harlan had proposed analyzing rate regulation under a contract theory by which the corporate charter had impliedly required reasonable rates.[104] Even Justice David J. Brewer, who eventually became the leading proponent of a property theory that analogized the problem to eminent domain law, had seemed to propound the contract theory as late as 1901. "[I]s there not force in the suggestion," Brewer wrote, "that as the State may do the work without profit, if he voluntarily undertakes to act for the State he must submit to a like determination as to the paramount interests of the public?"[105]

The debate over contract versus property theories symbolized much deeper conflicts over basic ideas about property. The analogy to eminent domain law—the property conception—was correctly charged with having a bias in favor of higher valuations. As Donald R. Richberg wrote in 1927:[106]

> In the public utility field, monopoly (partial or complete) is accepted as a desirable condition. But for many centuries such monopolies have been subject to regulation in order to prevent the charging of unreasonable rates. The charging of unreasonable rates, if skillfully imposed, undoubtedly would enhance the value of the property used. Thus we find that the very purpose and necessary effect of public regulation is to diminish the value that otherwise might be realized.[107]

The Court, in insisting on reproduction cost as the measure of value, Richberg wrote, was assuming, by contrast, "that the private owner of public utility property should be given the same value for his property that it would possess if it were being used in private business."[108] The Supreme Court's adoption of reproduction cost grants the utility its "monopoly value," not its competitive value, Richberg charged:

> The theory of the opinion . . . permits the utility to disregard its implied promise . . . that the private operation of the public service should not be used as the means for compelling the public to pay rates grossly in excess of those which could be secured for the public by public operation of public service. Public competition has been prevented by assurance that the benefits of "free competition" would be preserved. Essentially the demand of the utilities for a monopoly value is a breach of faith.[109]

The Supreme Court's adoption of the eminent domain theory represented an acceptance of the view that the natural starting point for analysis was private, not governmental, ownership and that rate regulation was thus essentially confiscatory. Richberg had begun to develop the alternative Legal Realist view—given its classic formulation the very same year by Morris R. Cohen in "Property and Sovereignty"[110]—that property constituted a delegation of state power to private individuals. And more specifically, Richberg was part of a movement that emphasized that the measure of value was not simply a factual or scientific question but also one deeply embedded in controversies about the nature and purpose of property.

The Supreme Court's rate-making decisions, Gerard Henderson saw in 1920,[111] were regularly shrouded in an aura of science—he called it "the illusion of juristic necessity." "[T]he [C]ourt has been trying to ascertain not a rule of policy, but a discoverable fact. The question has been, not what is it wise to allow the company to earn, but what is the value of the property on what it must be allowed to earn a return."[112]

Why invoke the authority of science, of the "conception that there is a fact which can be discovered . . . and which, once it is found, will provide a mathematical solution of all rate-making problems . . . ?"[113] Henderson answered:

> Above all, the judges must have been anxious to avoid the suspicion that they were substituting their own discretion for the will of the legislature. . . . What the value of a railroad was, seemed on the surface to be a pure question of fact. . . . A judge who upset a state statute on the ground that it failed to allow a reasonable return on the fair value of the property seemed protected against any charge of usurping legislative power.[114]

The brilliant and extensive technical writing on the measure of value in rate-making seems clearly to have inspired some of the more general theoretical Legal Realist literature on the nature of property. Not only do both bodies of writing share a common hostility to "the illusion of juristic necessity"—to the substitution of scientific for political discourse—but each sought to demonstrate how de-physicalization encouraged the view that the legal conception of property was completely circular. Just as the shift in the eminent domain cases from physical invasion to reduction in market value threatened to "freeze" the world by "propertizing" expectations of stable market values, the identification of value with market value in the rate cases created a similar dilemma.

The first thinker to see the relationship between the de-physicalization of property and its abstraction into market value was the great Wisconsin institutional economist John R. Commons. His penetrating—though often obscure—*Legal Foundations of Capitalism* (1924) traced the late-nineteenth-century judicial shift to a market value standard. The Rate Cases, in particular, allowed Commons to appreciate that it was the guarantee of a *future* income stream that determined the *present* value of property. "All value is expectancy," Commons proclaimed.[115] In rate-making cases, "market value is the present value of the expected rates. If the rates are unreasonable, so is the market value."[116]

Judges who believed that reasonable rates could be deduced from fair market value were "reasoning in a circle," Commons declared.[117] He relied on Gerard C. Henderson's extraordinarily brilliant demonstration of circularity four years earlier.[118] Henderson had imagined a dialogue between an economist and a lawyer before a rate-setting commission:

> The company's attorney . . . suggests that it be allowed always a certain percentage on the value of the property. If value goes up, rates should go up proportion-

ately. But the economist points out that the only accepted and sensible meaning of the word "value" is "value in exchange,"—the amount which the property would bring at a free sale, and that obviously this depended mainly on earnings. "But earnings," he said, "will depend partly on what we allow you gentlemen to charge the public. If we reduce your rates, your value goes down. If we increase them, it goes up. Obviously we cannot measure rates by value, if value is itself a function of rates.[119]

Henderson's demonstration of the circularity of prevailing notions of value was widely accepted. Indeed, it may have provided the model from which Commons succeeded in generalizing the point to cover all forms of property. Commons was thus able to claim not only that the shift from landed to intangible forms of property required an increasingly abstract idea of property, but also that it made any distinction between present market value and future income entirely circular.

If, as Commons argued, "all value is expectancy," it pushed the legal idea of property to the verge of the *reductio ad absurdum* that antebellum land-based ideas had for so long succeeded in obscuring. Since any prospective change in the law that reduced future income necessarily also reduced the property's present market value, it seemed to mean nothing less than a constitutional guarantee that the future should remain unchanged. Antebellum physicalist ideas had long managed to avoid this dilemma.

The next step in the developing critique of the property idea was taken by Robert L. Hale, an extraordinarily fertile economist on the Columbia Law School faculty. In "Rate Making and the Revision of the Property Concept" (1922),[120] Hale argued that the developing analysis of value in the public utility area needed to be generalized to all property.

A "monopoly" analysis of the justification of public utility regulation was too restrictive. "There is scarcely a single advantage possessed by a business affected with a public use which cannot be matched in the case of some unregulated concern. . . . [T]here is not a single income-yielding property right, inside or outside the utility field, which can be enjoyed on equal terms by *everyone*. To speak of equal rights of property is ridiculous."[121]

The truth which most rate bodies lack the courage to face is, that in regulating the rates of utilities the law is trying the experiment in one limited field of turning its back on the principles which it follows elsewhere. The experiment may perhaps be extended to other fields if successful. We are experimenting with a legal curb on the power of property owners. In applying that curb, we have to work out principles or working rules—in short a new body of law. Those principles will necessarily differ from the ones upon which the law acts in other fields—for in other fields it acts on the assumption that whatever income a property owner can get without fraud by virtue of his ownership is legitimately his. In the utility field, standards of what it is proper for an owner to get out of his ownership have to be worked out *de novo*. Because, therefore, the law permits various kinds of income outside the regulated field, it does not follow that similar forms are to be approved within the regulated field. The revision of property rights worked out within the utility field may very well serve as a model, wherever applicable, for the revision of other property rights.[122]

Next, Hale used Hohfeld's analytical scheme to reach a striking conclusion:

> The right of ownership in a manufacturing plant is, to use Hohfeld's terms, a *privilege* to operate the plant, plus a *privilege* not to operate it, plus a *right* to keep others from operating it, plus a *power* to acquire all the rights of ownership in the products. The analysis is not meant to be exhaustive. Having exercised his power to acquire ownership of the products, the owner has a *privilege* to use them, plus a much more significant *right* to keep others from using them, plus a *power* to change the duty thereby implied in the others, into a privilege coupled with rights. This power is a power to release a pressure which the law of property exerts on the liberty of the others. If the pressure is great, the owner may be able to compel the others to pay him a big price for their release; if the pressure is slight, he can collect but a small income from his ownership. In either case, he is paid for releasing a pressure exerted by the government—the law. The law has delegated to him a discretionary power over the rights and duties of others.[123]

Hale's conclusion that "the law has delegated" to property owners "a discretionary power over the rights and duties of others" represented a major analytical breakthrough that should perhaps be considered one of the moments at which Legal Realism separated itself from Progressive jurisprudence. It not only laid the foundation for one of the great classics of Legal Realism, Morris Cohen's "Property and Sovereignty" (1927);[124] it also anticipated Hale's own original gem, "Coercion and Distribution in a Supposedly Non-Coercive State" (1923).[125]

Hale not only totally reconceptualized property as a delegation of state power to private individuals but also pushed this conclusion still further. "Ownership is an indirect method whereby the government coerces some to yield an income to the owners. When the law turns around and curtails the incomes of property owners, it is in substance curtailing the salaries of public officials or pensioners."[126]

> Frequently the owner can only exercise his power of coercion as a result of having rendered in the past some service in the production of wealth, or of having abstained from consuming all the wealth which he might lawfully have consumed. For this and other reasons of policy it would be as bad to abolish all incomes arising from ownership as it would be to abolish all salaries and pensions. On the other hand it would be as absurd to justify any particular utility values on the ground that their legitimacy is generally recognized in other fields, as it would be for a municipal administration to justify a salary of a sinecure on the ground that some other administration of some other city still pays that sort of salary. Any value which is still to be allowed to a utility company must be justified on some independent ground of policy.[127]

Property as Public Law

With the relativization of the concept of property, Progressive legal thinkers pushed on to challenge the distinction between public and private law as it applied to property.

By and large, Progressives of Brandeis's generation had great difficulty in transcending the great gulf posited by the legal system between public and private law. Instead, they tended to conceptualize most legal questions as involving the need to strike a balance between private property and the public interest. Thus, while they seemed to accept the private law character of property, they agreed that it might be modified constitutionally in the case of "businesses affected with the public interest."

The really radical reconceptualization of property that I would identify with Legal Realism is associated with a far more fundamental challenge to the private law status of property ideas. The most prominent example is the great article "Property and Sovereignty" (1927), in which the philosopher Morris Cohen offered a major contribution to the disintegration of the orthodox distinction between public and private law.[128]

"Th[e] distinction between public and private law is a fixed feature of our law-school curriculum," Cohen began.[129] First, he emphasized what Hohfeld and Hale had begun to make clear. "Whatever technical definition of property we may prefer, we must recognize that a property right is a relation not between an owner and a thing, but between the owner and other individuals in reference to things."[130] Next, he challenged the unbounded claims of legal orthodoxy to protect all forms of property. "[I]n all civilized legal systems there is a great deal of just expropriation or confiscation without any direct compensation."[131] The abolition of slavery and the prohibition of liquor were two examples. "We may go farther and say that the whole business of the state depends upon its rightful power to take away the property of some (in the form of taxation) and use it to support others."[132] Here we see clear evidence of the dramatic defeat that ratification of the Income Tax Amendment in 1913 represented for the orthodox goal of creating a clean distinction between a tax and a taking. Not only had the constitutional legitimacy of the progressive income tax muddied that distinction but, even more important, it had discredited the Classical notion that a neutral state entailed opposition to redistribution.

Finally, under the heading "Property as Power," Cohen challenged the Classical private law definition of property. "The character of property as sovereign power compelling service and obedience may be obscured for us in a commercial economy by the fiction of the so-called labor contract as a free bargain and by the frequency with which service is rendered indirectly through a money payment."[133] Here Cohen was summarizing almost a generation of American legal and social thought emphasizing the coercive character of property.

Since at least the turn of the century, Progressive economists had highlighted the coercive character of property. As early as 1903, for example, in a book dedicated to Justice Holmes, the Progressive economist Richard T. Ely emphasized that an increasingly concentrated and unequal distribution of wealth had resulted in "the coercion of economic forces."[134] "The coercion of economic forces is largely due to the unequal strength of those who make a contract, for back of contract lies inequality in strength of those who form the contract."[135]

Beginning with the founding of the American Economic Association in 1885, anti-laissez-faire economists had developed arguments either for public ownership or for regulation of monopoly, as well as for governmental intervention to improve working conditions, to prohibit child labor, and to allow concerted action by labor unions.

Perhaps the most influential Realist work to highlight the connection between property and power for an entire generation was *The Modern Corporation and Private Property* (1932), by Adolph A. Berle and Gardiner C. Means. Its famous distinction between absentee shareholder ownership and management control of the property of the modern public corporation captured the imagination of a wide array of scholars of law and economics.

Berle and Means argued, "The shifting relationships of property and enterprise in American industry . . . raise in sharp relief certain legal, economic, and social questions which must now be squarely faced." Under "the traditional logic of property" the shareholders—the legal owners—were entitled to the entire profits of the enterprise. But "since the powers of control and management were created by law, in some measure this appeared to legalize the diversion of profit into the hands of the controlling group." Under the traditional logic of property, "it is clear that these powers are not absolute" but rather "are powers in trust" for the legal owners, the shareholders. "Yet, while this conclusion may result inevitably when the traditional logic of property is applied to the new situation, are we justified in applying this logic? . . . [M]ust it *necessarily* follow that an owner who has surrendered control of his wealth" by becoming "a supplier of capital, a risk-taker pure and simple . . . should likewise be protected to the full?"[136]

The economist starts from different premises than the lawyer, Berle and Means maintained.

> He is preoccupied not with the rights of property but with the production of wealth and distribution of income. To him property rights are attributes which may be attached to wealth by society and he regards them and their protection, not as the inalienable right of the individual or as an end in themselves, but as a means to a socially desirable end. . . .[137]

The separation of ownership and control therefore creates a situation under which shareholders,

> by surrendering control and responsibility over the active property, have surrendered the right that the corporation should be operated in their sole interest,—they have released the community from the obligation to protect them to the full extent implied in the doctrine of strict property rights. . . . They have placed the com-

munity in a position to demand that the modern corporation serve not alone the owners or the control [group] but all society.

More than any other development, the separation between ownership and control in the modern corporation became the catalyst for the legal realist reconceptualization of private property rights. The large national corporation not only drew into question the orthodox separation between public and private law but it also challenged the notion that modern property could continue to be represented as a pre-political right and not as a creature of social choice.

SIX

Defining Legal Realism

From the beginning of the twentieth century, Classical Legal Thought found itself confronted by an increasingly powerful critique of its basic premises. In one legal field after another, Progressive thinkers challenged both the political and moral assumptions of the old order and the structures of legal doctrine and legal reasoning that were designed to represent those assumptions as neutral, natural, and necessary. What is the relationship between Legal Realism and this Progressive critique?

Legal Realism was neither a coherent intellectual movement nor a consistent or systematic jurisprudence. It expressed more an intellectual mood than a clear body of tenets, more a set of sometimes contradictory tendencies than a rigorous set of methodologies or propositions about legal theory.

Indeed, defining Legal Realism with precision is not all that easy. It usually refers to the body of legal thought produced for the most part by law professors at Columbia and Yale Law Schools during the 1920s and 1930s. Some of the great names are Karl Llewellyn and Robert Lee Hale at Columbia and Walter Wheeler Cook and Arthur L. Corbin at Yale.

The first problem with this definition is that it draws too sharp a distinction between the Progressive legal thought that began to crystallize after the *Lochner* decision in 1905 and later post-World War I legal thought.[1] For many purposes, it is best to see Legal Realism as simply a continuation of the reformist agenda of early-twentieth-century Progressivism. Too much has been made of the distinction between Legal Realism and what Roscoe Pound had called "sociological jurisprudence" before World War I. When Pound delivered his famous 1931 criticism of Realism, as we shall see,[2] it was not that Realism had come to represent some heretical deviation from the core insights of Progressive legal thought but that Pound himself had begun to change. There is much more continuity than discontinuity between Realism and the underlying critical inspiration of Charles Beard's *An Economic Interpretation of the Constitution* (1913) or of Hohfeld's "Fundamental Legal Conceptions" (1913) or, indeed, of Pound's great pre-war writings.

The effort to portray Legal Realism as a sharply delineated body of legal theory confined to the 1920s and 1930s is usually accompanied by an effort to represent Realism as either representing some distinctive new methodology or embodying a serious systematic jurisprudence. Not only does this interpretation tend to suppress the obvious contradictions within Realism; it also renders Realism too "academic" and not sufficiently connected to real political struggles. For, above all, Realism is a continuation of the Progressive attack on the attempt of late-nineteenth-century Classical Legal Thought to create a sharp distinction between law and politics and to portray law as neutral, natural, and apolitical.

But there are also enough important discontinuities—or, at least, changes in emphasis—between pre– and post–World War I Progressive legal thought to permit us to treat Legal Realism as a distinct intellectual outlook. While pre-war reformist legal thought tended to be court-centered—with the dramatic exception of the movement for workers' compensation[3]—Legal Realism concentrated much of its energy in arguing for statutory or administrative change. Legal Realists, especially after the New Deal came to power, were also much more self-conscious than their Progressive predecessors in attempting to legitimate social reform and social engineering in the emerging regulatory state.

Perhaps the most significant difference between Realism and its pre-war reformist predecessors can be expressed in terms of skepticism about reason and morality. Like their European counterparts, American post–World War I intellectuals experienced a sense of doubt, if not despair, about the possibilities of realizing the Enlightenment's ideal of reason.[4] Pre-war Progressive intellectuals represented what might be called a Victorian world view, one that, while often deeply skeptical of revealed religion, was nevertheless self-confident about the ability of reason to arrive at civilized and humanitarian values.[5] The Realist generation, by contrast, had lost much of the pre-war faith in reason, both as a reliable source of moral understanding and as a powerful internal guide to law.[6]

Realist skepticism produced what is probably its most lasting contribution: its critique of the claims of orthodox legal reasoning to be able to provide neutral and apolitical answers to legal questions, answers that were said to be neutral because they were determinate and non-discretionary.

The Emergence of Realism

Nothing has so shaped—and distorted—our picture of Legal Realism as the famous exchange over Realism between Karl Llewellyn and Roscoe Pound in 1930–1931. The list of twenty Realists compiled by Llewellyn in response to Pound's criticism has completely dominated historians' subsequent understanding of the meaning and significance of Legal Realism.[7] It is one of the ironies of legal history that the person who eventually became the undisputed guru of Realism, Karl Llewellyn, should also have been the leading inspiration for a picture of Legal Realism that is far too narrow and confined, and far more systematic and dogmatic, than anything the intellectually pluralistic and methodologically catholic Llewellyn could ever have desired.

Legal Realism received both its name and its designation as an intellectual movement when Llewellyn, a thirty-seven-year-old Columbia law professor, published an article in the *Columbia Law Review* of April 1930 entitled "A Realistic Jurisprudence—The Next Step."[8] Realism became famous when, a year later, the sixty-one-year-old dean of Harvard Law School, Roscoe Pound, at the height of his reputation as the only world-class American legal thinker since Holmes, deigned to criticize Realism.[9] And Llewellyn, in the midst of a failed marriage and perhaps seized by fear that the Pound article might damage a budding academic career or, more likely, seeing the opportunity to gain almost instant recognition as the leader of a movement, prepared a rigid and dogmatic reply that was very much out of character with the normally non-sectarian nature of his thought.[10] The reply included his famous "sample" of twenty Realists, a list that, despite Llewellyn's statement that "there are doubtless twenty more," has been taken by all subsequent historians as the core material for studying Realism, to be slightly altered, if necessary, by adding two or three names, but essentially containing the particulars from which any general picture of Realism would need to be drawn.[11] Now, thanks to N. E. H. Hull, who has recently discovered a more elaborate unpublished list of Realists compiled by Llewellyn and sent to Pound in the midst of the controversy, we can see Llewellyn's own attempt to create a somewhat more pluralistic picture of Realist thought.[12] This list, of course, has never been known by historians, and one might speculate on how Realism might have looked if this second list had become the starting point for a definition of Realism. But, even so, I wish to show that in 1931 Llewellyn was in no special position to define Realism and that both his own still limited intellectual horizons and his powerful intellectual prejudices produced a way of thinking about Realism that has distorted our understanding of its significance ever since.

I wish to make three points. First, because Llewellyn's debate was with Pound, the leading figure of pre–World War I Progressive or sociological jurisprudence, historians have been misled into looking for sharper distinctions between sociological jurisprudence and Legal Realism than are justified.[13] For most purposes, I would suggest, both intellectual movements should be understood as subcategories of pre– and post–World War I Progressive legal thought, and Legal Realism needs to be seen primarily as a continuation of the reformist attack on orthodox legal thought.

Second, Llewellyn's list has produced a distorted picture of the meaning and significance of Realism. It is important to realize that, until 1929, when Llewellyn first delivered the paper that provoked Pound's reply, "jurisprudence came a poor second to commercial law" in Llewellyn's intellectual work.[14] Indeed, only two years earlier, after eight years in law teaching, Llewellyn for the first time began "to take a sustained interest in the nature of the appellate judicial process and of case law."[15] "In fact he published relatively little before 1930"[16]—the year his first marriage ended after his wife left him for another man—and "several of his most promising lines of inquiry had not yet been worked up into publishable form."[17] In 1930–1931, Llewellyn was no more qualified to offer a general survey or synthesis of American legal thought than any number of law professors. He did not, in fact, really understand the existing state of American legal thought.

One can only speculate on the relationship between the apparent chaos in Llewellyn's personal life and his sudden move to jurisprudence. Did Llewellyn suddenly need an excessively systematic orientation—did he exaggerate the "scientific" as well as the methodological aspects of Realism—in order to reassert control over his own life?

Third, Llewellyn's effort to define Realism in terms of a relatively coherent and systematic methodology has resulted both in a de-emphasis of the substantive political commitments of the Realists—their connection to the movement for political reform—and in a substantial over-emphasis on a now largely discredited strand of positivist and behavioralistic social science that has deprived us of the true richness of the intellectual and political heritage of Realism.

The Controversy

Llewellyn's "A Realistic Jurisprudence—The Next Step" was published in the *Columbia Law Review* in April 1930. Llewellyn had previously presented this paper at the Round Table on Current Trends in Political and Legal Thought of the American Association of Political Science in December 1929. Its original title was "Modern Concepts of Law."

Reflecting the influence of his teachers (and former colleagues) at Yale, as well as his experiences of the Columbia curricular battle of 1928, it is the work of a brilliant novice and a fast learner. Llewellyn had studied with Hohfeld, Cook, and Corbin at Yale; and his Columbia colleagues Douglas, Oliphant, Moore, and Yntema had just resigned to join Cook at the newly established Johns Hopkins Institute devoted to law and behavioral social science.[18]

Llewellyn's "A Realistic Jurisprudence" is, in a word, an intellectual "cut and paste" job reflecting some existing tendencies in American jurisprudence read in conjunction with his newly acquired knowledge of German "free law" jurisprudence.[19] The ideas in the paper were clearly not represented as original, nor were they stated in an especially arresting or provocative manner. Llewellyn's biographer, William Twining, calls the essay "a *pot pourri* of interesting ideas, some of them as yet only half formed . . . it is not to be recommended to someone who seeks a coherent introduction to realism."[20]

What induced Pound to reply, if that is what it was? "The Call for a Realist Jurisprudence," published in March 1931, is an extraordinarily interesting document for anyone who wishes to situate Pound in relation to Progressive jursiprud-ence. By the time the New Deal came to power two years later, Pound seemed ready to begin his move both to more eccentric varieties of legal theory and to reactionary politics, culminating in his intemperate 1938 attacks on the adminis-trative state.[21]

But Pound's "Call for a Realist Jurisprudence" is neither intemperate, eccen-tric, nor reactionary. In tone, at least, it is a respectful and even admiring parental admonition to young scholars, urging them not to be unbalanced, excessive, and, above all, dogmatic. Moreover, Pound emphasized that his intentions were not polemical. "It is much more important to understand than to criticize," Pound wrote, and he emphasized that too much criticism "achieve[s] an easy victory over straw men. . . ."[22] "In a letter to Llewellyn," Twining informs us, Pound "congratulated himself on his long record of abstention from polemical jurispru-dence."[23]

And yet Pound's criticism has rightly been labeled by Twining as "scholarly in conception but unscholarly in execution."[24] Pound himself later admitted that it was written in haste at a time when he was burdened with other duties. Even so, what is it about the article that so "distressed" Llewellyn?

First, it is, as Twining says, "a typical Poundian hotch-pot"[25] filled with olym-pian generalities that had always been present in Pound's writing but that seemed to have gained the upper hand with his growth in eminence. The strand in Pound's intellect of Polonius-like tendentiousness appears to have begun to dominate his thinking at around this time. There is not one specific reference to a work of Realist jurisprudence in Pound's entire article. Perhaps he simply assumed that an impersonal tone could not be regarded as polemical. But for Llewellyn and his collaborator in response, Jerome Frank, Pound had done just what he denied doing—he had set up intellectual "straw men" since, as Llewellyn put it, "we knew of hardly anyone whom one might fairly suspect of holding any of the views critici[z]ed."[26]

What was bothering Pound? Simply stated, from the very first page, Llewel-lyn's piece reads like an attack on Pound. The one major idea in Llewellyn's article is a slight variation on Pound's famous and important distinction between law in books and law in action.[27] But Llewellyn used this reference to Pound's authorship to attack him. "Only a man gifted with insight" could have created the distinction. "But only a man partially caught in the traditional precept-thinking of an age that is passing" would have still maintained respect for the law in books. Then: "I have no wish to argue the point. It will appeal, or it will not, and argument will be of little service."[28]

Pound thus would have had every reason to feel personally slighted and even abused by Llewellyn. And Llewellyn? Why does he so peremptorily close off the argument? Is there some other arena in which he experiences the "real" issue taking place, so that "argument will be of little service"?

But this was mild stuff compared to Llewellyn's page-length footnote attack on Pound. Pound's distinction, Llewellyn wrote, "is as striking in its values as in its limitations. It is full to bursting of magnificent insight. . . . I am not concerned here with whether prior writers may have contributed to, or anticipated, some or all of these ideas. Pound saw them, he formulated them, he drove them home. *But these brilliant buddings have in the main not come to fruition.*"[29]

> "'Balancing of Interests" remains with no indication of how to tell an interest when you see one, much less with any study of how they are or should be balanced. "Sociological jurisprudence" remains bare of most that is significant in sociology. "Law-in-action" is left as a suggestion. . . . "The limits of effective legal action". . . is left without study of the society to which law is supposed to have relation.[30]

The insight in Pound's writings "always . . . fails to penetrate . . . to the more systematic set-up of the material."

> One is tempted to see in the thinking of the one man and of the American school of sociological jurisprudence a parallel to the development of case law as a whole: accepting in the main what has been handed down; systematizing compartmentwise; innovating where need shows . . . but *ad hoc* only, with little drive toward or interest in incorporating the innovation. . . .[31]

One is "embarrassed by the constant indeterminacy of the level of his discourse. At times the work purports clearly to travel on the level of considered and buttressed scholarly discussion; at times on the level of bed-time stories for the tired bar; at times on an intermediate level, that of the thoughtful but unproved essay . . . [sometimes] on the level of the after dinner speech. . . ."[32]

"There is value in this," the young law professor concluded. "There is value, even, in the legal bed-time story. But there is greater value to be had. What would one not give for the actual appearance of the long-awaited *Sociological Jurisprudence*, if its author would integrate [into] it . . . those pioneering thoughts of his. . . ."[33]

Thus, Pound could reasonably have read Llewellyn's article not only as impertinent but also as an ungenerous attempt to obscure Llewellyn's own reliance on Pound's ideas. Llewellyn's reference to the "long-awaited *Sociological Jurisprudence*"—a work that continued to be awaited for another thirty years[34]—must have cut Pound deeply. And Llewellyn's very telling mockery of Pound's pontifical style—after-dinner speeches and legal bedtime stories for a tired bar—contained a set of demeaning and provocative images not only about Pound's ideas—which "have in the main not come to fruition"—but also about his increasingly pandering relationship to the established bar.

Above all, I believe, Llewellyn meant to deliver an attack on Pound's abandonment of any commitment to reform. Pound's attachment to the law in books, Llewellyn wrote, was "*central* to his thinking about law" and showed "a tendency toward idealization of some portion of the *status quo* at any given time." He was "a man partially caught in the traditional precept-thinking of an age that is passing. . . ."[35]

What was the basis for Llewellyn's belief that Pound tended "toward idealiza-tion . . . of the *status quo*"? Llewellyn must have heard academic gossip about the growing rift between Frankfurter and Pound over the Harvard faculty appoint-ments of Nathan Margold and James Landis.[36] The Pound-Frankfurter rift appears to have begun in 1927 when the Italian-American anarchists Sacco and Vanzetti were executed after a commission headed by Harvard President A. Lawrence Lowell whitewashed the accusations of unfairness prominently ex-pressed by Frankfurter, among others.[37] While Pound privately thought that Sacco and Vanzetti had been unfairly convicted, "his refusal to speak out against what many regarded as a new nadir in American law" contributed, his biographer tells us, to a growing sense that Pound had lost his commitment to reform. In the controversial faculty appointments that followed, Pound was regarded as doing Lowell's bidding, and "nothing created more bitterness than Pound's uncharacter-istic timidity in response to President Lowell's periodic acts of anti-Semitism."[38]

By 1928, after Sacco and Vanzetti had been executed, Llewellyn accepted an invitation to join the council of the recently formed Sacco and Vanzetti National League, which was devoted to establishing their innocence and to working for reforms in the criminal justice system.[39] It is reasonable to suppose that Pound's silence affected Llewellyn's determination to characterize him as "a man partially caught in the traditional precept-thinking of an age that is passing" and one who showed "a tendency toward idealization of some portion of the *status quo*."

It is at this point that Llewellyn strangely declined: "I have no wish to argue the point. It will appeal, or it will not, and argument will be of little service." His point, I surmise, is that while it was still impossible on the public record to show that Pound had changed, those who understood the significance of his failure to take a stand on Sacco-Vanzetti, as well as of his subsequent role in Harvard Law School politics, would realize that Pound had become a conservative. And now the task was to explain why the leader of the pre-war Progressive movement for legal reform had abandoned the cause.

Llewellyn's article, standing alone, was probably not enough to provoke Pound's reply. The final straw was the publication in the same year of Jerome Frank's radioactive *Law and the Modern Mind* (1930) and of a symposium on the book, apparently organized by Llewellyn, in the *Columbia Law Review* of January 1931 two months before Pound's reply appeared.[40]

Law and the Modern Mind was published at a pivotal moment in the forma-tion of the Legal Realist movement. If Llewellyn had coined the term "Realism" only a few months before, Jerome Frank needs to be credited with first using the name "Legal Realism" in his book. It was through the collaboration between Llewellyn and Frank that a decision to proclaim the arrival of a new movement in legal thought crystallized, even as some of the named members of the move-ment refused to be drawn into any collective self-identification.[41]

Law and the Modern Mind produced a flurry of furious criticism and was undoubtedly the precipitating event in Pound's decision to criticize Realism. For a long time thereafter it remained the most popular and widely read piece of

Realist literature,[42] especially because its accessible and provocative style made legal controversy comprehensible to a lay public. Within professional and academic circles, however, it quickly led to the marginalization—and perhaps even the blackballing—of Frank, and it became a favorite vehicle for discrediting the Legal Realist movement.[43] For years, the only notion that many educated people associated with Realism was that it asserted that a judge's decision could be traced to what he ate for breakfast.

In truth, *Law and the Modern Mind* is a brilliant book that, after more than a half century, still manages to communicate the irreverent excitement of one brand of Realism. While its bold and simplistic psychoanalytic strokes are what made it famous—and infamous—its criticisms of formalism—what Frank aptly called "legal fundamentalism"—remain a much better summary of the accumulated intellectual assaults on the old order than any of Llewellyn's simultaneously ponderous renditions. But Frank clearly went too far in the judgment of his more respectable contemporaries, and he became, at age forty one, the *enfant terrible* of the movement, not without some clear satisfaction to his own exhibitionist tendencies.[44]

"A precocious child," his biographer informs us, Frank at age twenty-three had graduated with the highest grades ever achieved at the University of Chicago Law School.[45] "Although he had become a lawyer at his father's insistence, he still dreamed of writing fiction." He later remembered an unfinished novel as "a neurotic effort."[46] "The perennial bags under his eyes," which gave "him a burned-out appearance, came from mental rather than physical over-indulgence."[47]

The future judge of the Second Circuit Court of Appeals, widely regarded as the most impressive bench of federal judges in America, began writing *Law and the Modern Mind* in the midst of his own psychoanalysis. He had begun seeing a New York psychiatrist who had already been treating Frank's daughter for intermittent psychosomatic paralysis of the legs.

> Frank took such a liking to Dr. Glueck that he considered undergoing analysis himself, but insisted on reducing the doctor's usual term of treatment from a year to six months. Dr. Glueck told him that a shorter period would be quite impossible, but Frank persevered, suggesting that they meet twice a day. Dr. Glueck reluctantly agreed and the hurried sessions began.[48]

Law and the Modern Mind reads like the work of a recent convert, notwithstanding Frank's repeated insistence that he was offering only "a partial explanation."[49] Its dramatic and simple vision is proclaimed as if the writer is offering a blinding new truth to a humanity in darkness. Yet, his main message continues to be filled with insight.

> That religion shows the effects of the childish desire to recapture a father-controlled world has been often observed. But the effect on the law of this childish desire has escaped attention. And yet it is obvious enough: To the child the father is the Infallible Judge, the Maker of definite rules of conduct. He knows precisely what is right and what is wrong and, as head of the family, sits in judgment and punishes

misdeeds. The Law—a body of rules apparently devised for infallibly determining what is right and what is wrong and for deciding who should be punished for misdeeds—inevitably becomes a partial substitute for the Father-as-Infallible-Judge. That is, the desire persists in grown men to recapture, through a rediscovery of a father, a childish, completely controllable universe, and that desire seeks satisfaction in a partial, unconscious, anthropomorphizing of Law, in ascribing to the Law some of the characteristics of the child's Father-Judge. That childish longing is an important element in the explanation of the absurdly unrealistic notion that law is, or can be made, entirely certain and definitely predictable.[50]

There were several intertwined messages in Frank's book. First, to appropriate terms from the future, Frank was offering what one might call a "modernist" or "existentialist" message. The insistence on the uncertainty and indeterminacy of law involved not only many internal technical challenges to claims of the non-discretionary and self-executing character of legal reasoning. The book also mockingly questioned one of the few remaining sources of objectivity or certainty in a post-religious age. Frank shrewdly understood the fear of a standardless universe that religious and legal fundamentalism shared. Indeed, he suggested that law had come to replace religion as the main focus of the yearning for certainty.

Among American legal thinkers only Holmes perhaps qualified in this sense as an existentialist. "[C]ertainty generally is illusion, and repose is not the destiny of man," he proclaimed more than once.[51] Many of these themes were also prominent in the career of Holmes's contemporary, the philosopher William James, as Frank noted. He recounted James's youthful terrors at "the insecurity of life," his near mental breakdown, and his sudden "cure."[52] "And the cure," Frank wrote, consisted in a "sudden shift from panic fear of insecurity to a deep enthusiastic bliss in the absence of security [that] marked for James the advent of emotional adulthood."[53] But existential doubt has never been welcome within the oracular culture of American legal discourse. Jeremiads against subjectivity have constituted a recurrent theme in the literature of the law.

Jerome Frank's challenge not only to the possibility but even the desirability of legal certainty was received by the legal profession with as much enthusiasm as Darwinism had been greeted by Protestant ministers seventy years earlier.[54] The legal profession also has had its abundance of William Jennings Bryans ready to insist, as in the *Scopes* trial, that any departure from fundamentalism meant that everything would be set adrift.[55]

If Frank's existentialism ran against the grain of American legal culture, his irreverence was virtually unique. None of his contemporaries except perhaps Llewellyn and Thurman Arnold[56] would have dared to mockingly label legal fundamentalism "Bealism" (in contrast to Realism), after the esteemed Harvard formalist Joseph Beale.[57] While Frank was condemned for his bad manners in making an *ad hominem* argument, the real point was that he was engaged in a form of cultural politics against an earnestly serious and intensely rationalistic legal culture. Frank's irreverence was everywhere experienced as being in bad taste, which is precisely why it seems so alive to us today.

But Frank's irreverence was experienced as outright rebelliousness because of its challenge to rationalism itself. Before Frank, there is no other important book by an American lawyer on legal theory that deals so derisively with the legal profession. And, like Llewellyn, Frank felt called upon to devote a special chapter to attacking Dean Pound.

But all of these forms of irreverence paled before the psychological claims that made the book so arresting and ultimately so infuriating. There is "The Basic Legal Myth"[58] that law is certain. This is "deceptive" as well as undesirable. "Why do men crave an undesirable and indeed unrealizable permanence and fixity in law?"[59] Does the legal profession engage in "professional hypocrisy"[60] when "the generality of lawyers insist that law should and can be clearly knowable and precisely predictable although, by doing so, they justify a popular belief in an absurd standard of legal exactness?"[61] When they "fail to recognize fully the essentially plastic and mutable character of law," lawyers "are not *consciously* deceptive." Rather, they are attempting to fulfill "childish longings" for "a father controlled world."[62]

Of all Frank's impieties, perhaps the greatest was his survey of "Certain Brilliant Legal Thinkers"[63] to determine how legally "adult" they were. Pound he accuses of childish thinking. "Pound has never completely freed himself of rule-fetishism."[64] While "aware of the judicial realities," he was nevertheless "reluctant to relinquish entirely the age-old legal myths."[65]

In a chapter shrewdly entitled "The Candor of Cardozo,"[66] Frank observed that "it would seem" that Cardozo "has reached adult emotional stature," because "unlike some of the other thinkers that we have discussed"[67] he was willing to share his belief in legal uncertainty with the public. "No one has expounded more elaborately than Cardozo, for the benefit of the bar and the laity, the fact that law is uncertain and must be uncertain, that overeagerness for legal certainty and denials of legal contingency are harmful."[68] Yet, "he makes it plain that he has learned to accept this belief only with bitterness. . . . [h]e implies that, one day, when 'a deeper insight is imparted to us,' we will need no longer to be content with 'makeshift compromise,' and truths that are 'merely approximate and relative,' and can then satisfy our 'yearning for the absolute' and be done forever with the curse of 'fluidity.' "[69]

Finally, with trumpets sounding, Frank presents "Mr. Justice Oliver Wendell Holmes, The Completely Adult Jurist."[70] "He has put away childish longings for a father-controlled world. . . ."[71] "He has attained an adult emotional status, a self-reliant, fearless approach to life, and . . . he invites others to do likewise. We might say that, being rid of the need of a strict father, he can afford not to use his authority as if he, himself, were a strict father."[72] One cannot avoid suspecting that Frank's own psychoanalysis had something to do with these observations.

How are we to react to all of this today? None of it seems capable of being proven true or false. Actually, legal anthropology, in its infancy when Frank began writing, sought to illuminate some of these issues. But perhaps this is beside the point. Frank was engaged in a kind of cultural polemic that has been rare in the law. "Without straining too hard," Bruce Ackerman has written, "one can discern parallels to the thought of Frank and his fellow Realists in twentieth-century art and science. Stravinsky, Picasso, Joyce, Einstein, and Freud each radically challenged the effort to structure objective reality into a single determinate rationalizable order."[73] Indeed, after more than a half century of Freudian culture, we can hardly be shocked by any of Frank's assertions. They seem plausible, interesting, some perhaps even intuitively correct. Yet to Frank's contemporaries in 1930, they could only have come as a shocking and intemperate message from an alien culture. In successfully opposing Frank's appointment to the Yale Law School faculty in 1935, Arthur L. Corbin declared: "His well-known book seems to me to have fundamental defects that invalidate his major conclusions and will prevent it from having any permanent influence."[74]

Law and the Modern Mind provided the opponents of Realism with the perfect target with which to tar the entire movement. Llewellyn's endorsement helped. Though he was quite skeptical of Frank's psychoanalytic explanations of the yearnings for legal certainty, he nevertheless roundly endorsed the book. "The book excites; it illuminates; it breaks new ground; it is an important contribution," Llewellyn concluded with his typically undogmatic generosity.[75]

Along with Llewellyn's endorsement, the symposium in the *Columbia Law Review* contained the first of many attacks on Frank. The philosopher Mortimer Adler, who under the twin banners of Aristotelianism and Thomism was beginning the restoration of philosophical conservatism at the University of Chicago, enthusiastically undertook the task of discrediting Frank and Realism, indulging, with a kind of nasty delight, in the tactic of intellectual guilt by association. "I gladly accept Mr. Llewellyn's opinion that [Frank's] treatment is realistic in the best sense of the word, because it lends weight to my thesis that this book can be taken as representative of the school of legal thought which has raised so much dust in jurisprudential controversy in this country in the last twenty-five years." In criticizing Frank, Adler noted, he was also criticizing various Realists, as well as "to a lesser extent, Pound, Cardozo and Holmes."[76] "If, as Mr. Llewellyn suggests, *Law and the Modern Mind* is a praiseworthy exhibition of realistic jurisprudence," Adler concluded, "it is also a composite picture of the confusions and failures in analysis which have pervaded the writings of Mr. Frank's oft-quoted doctrinal affiliates and chosen authorities, in philosophy and science as well as in jurisprudence." The trouble with the legal writers was "their philosophical incompetence and naivete, and the uncritical transference of their authoritarian habits of thought" from law to philosophy.[77]

Whether this was true, Frank was clearly obsessed with, as one of his chapter titles put it, "Getting Rid of the Need for Father-Authority."[78] One of these father-authorities was Roscoe Pound. Pound was clearly appalled by *Law and the Modern Mind*, and his wish bluntly to dissociate himself from it may have been prompted by Adler's sinister effort to use it against him.

As Llewellyn was considering a reply to Pound's criticisms of Realism, he resumed his correspondence with Pound, who was friendly and conciliatory in reply. "I am sorry," Pound wrote, "if my attempt to understand and set forth a possible program for a group of thinkers with whom I have a great deal of sympathy should have appeared to be controversial."[79] "If ever one scholar had offered an olive branch to another," N. E. H. Hull wisely concludes, "this was the moment."[80]

But Llewellyn also informed Pound that "Jerome Frank had promised to go halves with me" on the planned reply to Pound, and that was enough to trigger Pound's alarm. "Something had turned Pound against Frank since their polite correspondence only six months before," Hull writes. "That something was undoubtedly the fact that Pound had finally read Frank's book. . . ."[81] Pound wrote Llewellyn:

> I must confess I am troubled about Jerome Frank. When a man puts in quotation marks and attributes to a writer things which he not only never put in print any where, but goes contrary to what he has set in print repeatedly, it seems to me to go beyond the limits of permissible carelessness and to be incompatible, not merely with scholarship but with the ordinary fair play of controversy. . . . I cannot afford to discuss anything with one who uses such tactics, and should like to suggest to you whether you can afford to identify yourself with him.[82]

Llewellyn immediately told Pound that he had informed Frank of the accusations. And Pound's criticism set off a manic flurry of activity by Frank that was slightly terrifying. "[B]oiling with indignation"[83] over Pound's charges, Frank besieged the dean with a series of telegrams, letters, long lists of citations and quotations, all for the supposed purpose of correcting any misquotations before the impending second printing of the book. Pound's evasions and silence drove Frank to enlist intermediaries such as Felix Frankfurter, Thomas Reed Powell, and Judge Julian Mack. To Mack, for example, he wrote: "Would it be possible for you to write to Pound? After all, you were my sponsor and his vicious slaps at me does [sic] somewhat reflect on your judgment."[84]

Over a two-month period between March and May 1931, then, Jerome Frank appears to have become somewhat unhinged by Pound's accusation. One wonders whether he really ever understood that the source of Pound's anger was not some isolated misquotation but rather the disrespectful treatment Pound had received at Frank's hands. "Getting Rid of the Need for Father-Authority" clearly lay behind the behavior of Frank—and I suspect, Llewellyn too—in their encounters with Pound.

Llewellyn's List

Llewellyn's 1931 list of twenty Realists—the starting point for all previous discussion of Realism—has resulted in some fundamental misunderstanding of the meaning and significance of the Realist movement. The list does not reveal wide reading in or understanding of the currents of American legal thought. Ten of the twenty were either teachers of Llewellyn's at Yale or subsequently colleagues at Yale or Columbia. From the perspective of more than a half century, only eight or nine can be regarded as having been at the forefront of legal thought. In my judgment, six were not sufficiently important or distinguished as scholars even in 1931 to have made the list. The list shows not only how ill equipped Llewellyn was at that time to represent new trends in legal thought but also how narrow his conception was.

The core group on Llewellyn's list—Clark, Moore, Oliphant, Yntema, Douglas and Cook—were all deeply involved in the relationship between law and the social sciences;[85] some even represent what seems, from our contemporary perspective, the narrowest and most naively behavioralist versions of positivist social science.[86] Pound's criticism of Realism for its positivism, dogmatism, and reductionism was able to capture quite well the severe limitations in this prominent strand of Realist work.

But Llewellyn chose to over-emphasize this group not only because his own institutional affiliations limited his intellectual horizons, and not only, as we shall see, because his working knowledge of intellectual developments in law was concentrated in his own specialized areas of legal scholarship, but also because Llewellyn's eccentric views of Realism shaped the list. As Llewellyn stated many times, Realism was a "method" or "technology" not grounded in historical or political or ideological controversies.[87] It entailed no substantive content.

Llewellyn's own subsequent work was greater than that of most of the scholars on the list, in part, because the tremendous variety of perspectives that he generated in the course of his own scholarly career reflected a staggeringly diverse range of methodologies. The eccentric and poetic sides of his intellect usually conspired to prevent his positivist methodological inclinations from producing mechanical or reified insights. In practice, he usually ignored the arid dogmatism of his view of methodology as technology because of his everyday pluralist tolerance of ambiguity and contradiction. Indeed, his own "institutionalist" and "evolutionist" perspectives were ways of infusing supposedly descriptive statements with undisclosed normativity. Yet, this passionate and intense man chose to represent his movement as primarily creating a technology.

Not only was the admirable Progressive support for reformist social science unfairly downgraded by Llewellyn's having reduced it to mere technology, but he also simultaneously contributed to the identification of Realism with the most intellectually regressive forms of behavioral and value-free social science. As a result, the now standard picture of Legal Realism needs to be corrected twice over. First, it needs to be reconnected to earlier forms of social science that were anything but value-free; and second, because it has often been identified exclusively with positivist social science, the most significant legacy of Realism has all but been ignored. American Legal Realism was perhaps the earliest intellectual expression in America of cultural modernism or what Peter Novick calls "cognitive relativism." In their extraordinarily fertile critique of legal reasoning, Realists drew into question traditional foundations of thought and structures of under-standing. Their intense interest in the socially constructed character of frames of reference, categories of thought, and legitimating concepts was closely linked to their passionate desire to challenge the claimed objectivity of deductive and ana-logical reasoning. This critical thrust of Realism has been virtually smothered by the exaggerated emphasis placed on the Realist turn to social science. The result has been virtually to ignore a central element of the Realist legacy—its interpretive or hermeneutic understanding of reality.

This emphasis on the cognitive relativism of Realism is offered as a corrective to the usual picture of Realists as ethical positivists or moral relativists. In fact, many Realists were passionate about values and had no problem in identifying social injustice. Nevertheless, many of their statements about cognitive relativism were mistaken by a highly moralistic culture as affirmations of moral relativism. Indeed, once we take account of the considerable overt hostility to ethical positiv-ism among some prominent Realists, it becomes clear that we must take Llewel-lyn's unfortunate identification of Realism with value-free social science with a grain of salt.

Who Were the Realists?

What was omitted from Llewellyn's picture of Realism?

First, and perhaps most important, he virtually ignored the body of brilliant criticism of Classical Legal Thought that had already become part of pre–World War I Progressive legal consciousness. Just as Holmes was an acknowledged in-spiration for the new jurisprudence, so too were John Chipman Gray[88] and Pound,[89] Brandeis[90] and Cardozo,[91] Hohfeld,[92] Learned Hand,[93] and Harlan Fiske Stone.[94]

Other than Llewellyn's Yale teachers, the only pre-war thinker to make the list was Walter Bingham, certainly not a major figure. Hohfeld, whom he would surely have listed, had already been dead for twelve years.

A second influential group that Llewellyn virtually ignored were the great in-stitutional economists, the first generation of whom founded the American Eco-nomics Association in 1885.[95] Two of the important figures who wrote on legal subjects were Richard T. Ely and John R. Commons.[96] In the controversies over rate making and the theory of value during the 1920s, they were joined by Gerard Henderson, Robert Lee Hale, and James Bonbright, the latter two of Columbia.[97] The most influential legal work by an institutionalist, published one year after Llewellyn's list appeared, was Adolph A. Berle's *The Modern Corporation and Private Property* (1932), co-authored with Gardner Means.[98] The book highlighted for an entire generation the separation between ownership and control in the modern corporation. The monumental edition of the *Encyclopedia of the Social Sciences*, published between 1930 and 1935, represents the most successful collab-oration of institutional economists and Legal Realists.[99]

The institutionalist perspective of the *Encyclopedia* highlights a form of social science that, while careful to speak in tones of scientific expertise, was also proud to acknowledge its very close connection to Progressive social reform. It would have been impossible, after reading the *Encyclopedia*, to describe it as simply applying a value-free method or as just representing a technology.

A third group were the philosophers John Dewey[100] and Morris Cohen, as well as his son Felix Cohen, whose scholarly career had just begun its tragically short but spectacular ascent in the same year that Llewellyn's list of twenty appeared. Each of these writers opposed Llewellyn's insistence on separating facts and values, and devoted their scholarly careers to opposing the sort of positivism that it produced. Dewey, in particular, elaborated a pragmatic, experimental, and dynamic vision of value formation, dependent on regular interactions between theory and practice.[101]

Fourth were the sophisticated and critical doctrinal writers.

> Llewellyn often complained that the critics of realism had overlooked the theoretical significance of some of the best works by realists because of a tendency to draw artificial distinctions between "jurisprudential" and "substantive" legal writings. . . . Thus Llewellyn's final position appears to have been that the Realist movement should be judged mainly by its influence on detailed work in various spheres of legal activity.[102]

Yet Llewellyn's list of twenty in many ways significantly contributed to the generalist and jurisprudential bias of subsequent interpretations of Realism.

His limited knowledge of work outside of his own fields of contracts and commercial law is quite apparent in the list. While, of course, he included the greatest of the new doctrinal writers, his "father in the law," Arthur L. Corbin, he failed to include many other important doctrinalists. In torts, though he listed Leon Green, he failed to include Francis Bohlen,[103] Jeremiah Smith, Fleming James, the original and penetrating torts-contracts scholar Nathan Isaacs, or even the wide-ranging Englishman, Harold Laski.[104] If the torts writing of Harvard's Warren Seavey tended to be old school, some of his greatest work in agency law was quite critical and very much in the spirit of earlier work begun by Walter Wheeler Cook.[105]

Llewellyn's 1931 list could not, of course, have been able to capture subsequent Realist doctrinal work in the 1930s, which remains a prominent part of the Realist legacy. Much of the most important and lasting Realist writings were technical doctrinal articles written in criticism of the work produced under the auspices of the American Law Institute, which was founded in 1923.[106] During the early 1930s, the first restatements in various fields began to appear, each of them an attempt to reassert the formalism and conceptualism of the legal thought of the old order.[107] Lon Fuller and John Dawson, for example, wrote important articles criticizing the first restatement of contracts.[108] And in criticizing Joseph Beale's first restatement, David Cavers continued the Realist revolution in conflict of laws originally launched by Walter Wheeler Cook.[109]

The anti-formalist doctrinalists often did not think of their work as political.

Lon Fuller's co-authored 1936 article, "The Reliance Interest in Contract Damages,"[110] remains perhaps the single most influential piece of Realist doctrinal work, though it was written by a scholar whose own jurisprudential work had already begun to target Legal Realism. How does one account for this seemingly striking contradiction?

Written in the midst of an impending constitutional challenge to the Norris-LaGuardia Act (1932)[111] barring the labor injunction in federal courts, Fuller's article applied the same kind of analysis to contract law that the draftsman of the act, Felix Frankfurter, had hoped would save its constitutionality. Frankfurter had maintained that because "remedies" were independent of "rights," legislatures were free to change them on the basis of considerations of social policy.[112] This idea originated in Walter Wheeler Cook's 1918 application of Hohfeld's ideas to the labor injunction and continued to be elaborated in various constitutional defenses of state laws barring the labor injunction.[113] Similarly, Fuller began by insisting that there was no way logically to derive contract remedies from the will of the parties or the "nature of contract." The choice among contract remedies was to be determined, not by some deduction from the parties' rights, but rather by the social purposes it would serve.

The most visible influence of Fuller's article—and perhaps the most tangible indication of the influence of Legal Realism on legal education—was that the entire next generation of law school contracts casebooks reversed the traditional order of presentation and now began teaching remedies before rights.[114] If the message of legal orthodoxy had been that "rights determine remedies," the new message appeared to be that "remedies determine rights." Thus, rights themselves were now conceived of as, derivatively, social creations.

"The Reliance Interest in Contract Damages" is the most prominent example of a form of doctrinal writing that was focused, localized, and technical in its primary orientation. It embodied an anti-formalist critical spirit that it brilliantly deployed against one of the dominant formalistic paradigms of the old order—the view that remedies logically flow from the nature of rights. Its critical moves demonstrated how pervasively anti-formalism had penetrated sophisticated legal consciousness, even among one whose more general jurisprudential and political perspective was, in many respects, hostile to Realism. Fuller's strategy of disaggregating and contextualizing the question of contract damages, as well as the consequentialist policy orientation he brought to the question, were part of a generational revolt against formalism that was still capable of producing revolutionary technical insights whose political significance he may never have realized.

The last group Llewellyn ignored were the administrative lawyers, Frankfurter and Landis, both of whom did appear on the longer unpublished list Llewellyn sent to Pound. In one of Llewellyn's most misleading asides justifying the composition of his original list of twenty, he wrote: "Frankfurter we do not include; he has been currently considered a 'sociological jurist,' not a 'realist.' "[115] Whatever one might say in justification of such a distinction, it does nevertheless clearly underline the distortion produced by Llewellyn's attempt to reduce Realism to particular methodological commitments. For as we shall see in Chapter 8, admin-istrative law is in many ways the culmination of the crisis of legitimacy that Realist criticism produced. It reflects the successful Realist attacks on the naturalness of the market and on the sharp classical division between public and private law. It expresses the decline in legitimacy of court-centered conceptions of law and the emergence of a social engineering perspective out of the ruins of doctrinal for-malism.

But Llewellyn's technological view of Realism encouraged him to miss the significance of the relationship between Legal Realism and its efforts, especially after the New Deal, to legitimate the new bureaucratic, regulatory state.

Legal Realism and Iconoclasm

Llewellyn always thought of himself as "a rebel, a freak, a non-conformist." [116]

> Queerness of view and action seems to be in my blood. My great-grandmother in her eightieth year became a Seventh Day Adventist, and every Sunday, seated in blazing sunlight in her parlor window, jaw set and knitting needles flying, rebuked the unenlightened as they passed to church. My grandfather lent help and counte-nance to the then looked down upon Salvation Army, and was a woman suffragist in the 'seventies. My mother reads Ellen Key, works for birth control, votes for Debs, and distributed peace leaflets at the Democratic convention in New York. Through college I conformed so little that I did not discover until after graduation what a Big Man was; my uncut thatch became a byword in my law school days; and the canons of etiquette which I have left unbroken include few things but eating with the knife. My views have been, and are, as curious as my clothes. With a few more years, and more experience, I have gained some respect for most of the accepted ways of action, but little respect indeed for most of the accepted ways of thought about such action. [117]

The "tradition of militant non-conformism on his mother's side" [118] seems to have been matched by a down-to-earth pragmatism on his father's. On graduation from Yale College in 1915, he wrote, "I had become clear that I wanted to teach, but had gotten no further towards picking a field than a general interest in Latin. My father's urging got me into law, and my own inclinations got me back into teaching." [119] Of his teachers at Yale Law School, Llewellyn often referred to Corbin as his "father in the law" and, in fact, addressed him in private as "Dad." [120]

As his biographer concluded, "there can be little doubt that in his career as a jurist he owed more to [Corbin] than to any other single person." [121] Since "Cor-bin's most striking characteristic was the patient relentlessness of his scholar-ship," [122] it is not surprising that Llewellyn "often used Corbin as an *exemplar* of his ideal of 'the legal craftsman.' " [123]

> Llewellyn's fondness for praising what he would refer to as "good, clean, solid work" must have seemed strange to those who saw him as a volatile genius, bub-

bling over with brilliant insights, but slapdash in execution. But much of Llewellyn's work is marked by painstaking efforts of careful scholarship which seem out of character with some of his more freewheeling writings . . . a tension between his spirited and imaginative insight and the "craftsmanship" that he so much admired in Corbin, between his own inclination and his scholarly ideal.[124]

Of Llewellyn's other teachers at Yale Law School, the most important influence was Wesley N. Hohfeld. Hohfeld had come to be viewed by "the better students" with "a combination of awe and evangelical enthusiasm," and Llewellyn was "one of his most ardent admirers." Llewellyn's own praise for Hohfeld "stressed the breadth of Hohfeld's learning and his vision of the law as a whole more than the more prosaic virtues of clarity and precision."[125] After Hohfeld's early death, Llewellyn, along with his fellow students, regarded him "as a prophet tragically cut off in his prime."[126]

The polarities in Llewellyn's personality and intellect seem especially striking in their intensity. Though "an emotional and intuitive . . . person"[127]—"someone with poetic tendencies"—he loved "technical complexity"[128] in the law and chose to work in commercial law, often regarded as one of the most "prosaic and technical . . . subject[s.]"[129] His writing style "fascinates some readers, repels others and perplexes most."[130] The "strangeness," "erratic" and "idiosyncratic" character of his mode of expression seems to reflect a tormented and "volatile genius."[131] His three marriages, during an era when divorce was extremely rare, and his lifelong problem with alcoholism seem to confirm this picture of a soul in conflict.[132]

Though he had an "intensely religious nature," he was fanatically hostile to "contemporaneous polysyllabic professionalized academic" philosophy.[133] "What the hell has Kant to do with my course on Jurisprudence?" he thundered at a student who submitted a paper on the Kantian distinction between the "is" and the "ought."[134] Rather, he maintained that his jurisprudence course was "the best bread-and-butter course" and "the one with the most immediate practicality" of any taught at the Law School.[135] It was this slightly philistine attitude towards jurisprudence—perhaps justified by the blatantly apologetic character of most traditional jurisprudential writing—that shielded Llewellyn from the strongly anti-positivist messages of John Dewey, Morris Cohen, and Roscoe Pound, as well as the even more eloquent later warnings of Felix Cohen.[136]

Llewellyn's frequently expressed hostility to fancy "academic" work seems to have pushed him into rebelliously non-conformist modes of informal expression, including stylistic monstrosities and somewhat shocking colloquialisms. His stylistic informality led him to coin phrases like "situation sense" and "law-stuff,"[137] which occasionally illuminate but more often communicate a certain suffocating technocratic or scientistic sensibility. Realism was "a sound, horse sense technology."[138] "What realism was, and is, is a method, nothing more. . . ."[139] Even though as he grew older, he wrote at age thirty-one, "I grow no less a rebel, a freak, a non-conformist,"[140] were it not for his study of the social sciences, "I should by now hold some obnoxious fighting faith and be stump-speaking a vigorous progress into jail." Social sciences both kept rebellious impulses in check and permitted their displacement onto more legitimate forms of cultural eccentricity. In what his biographer calls "a particularly revealing document" in which Llewellyn draws analogies between law and religion, he criticized St. Paul for straying from Jesus's teachings. "I find I feel about Paul the same way I feel about great lawyers whom I think to have gone sometimes off track. He over-intellectualized so far as he *wrote.* . . . Let me then stay as close as I may to Jesus' and to Paul's living rather than—or better, together with—his writing." Llewellyn concluded: "With this, 'rebel' and 'non-rebel' begin to line up. I observe with amusement that I am duplicating in religion a twenty-year road in legal work." [141]

Llewellyn's meaning, I take it, is that the gap between the writing and teaching of these religious figures was, like the dichotomy between theory and practice or between law in books and law in action, also parallel to the rebellious/non-rebellious polarity within his own character. His rebellious side always turned against the abstract, the too theoretical, the academic—the law in books, if you will. By contrast, he had an instinct for the ordinary, the everyday, the down-to-earth. "[H]e would take an intense interest in the minutiae of even the most mundane transactions and he would enthusiastically praise as 'lovely' or 'beautiful' examples of [technical solutions such as] the functional 'beauty' of mill-race and turbine." [142] His non-rebellious side always tended to idealize the law in action—to endow custom with a perhaps undeserved normativity. Here he sought to express his compliant or apologetic side.

Llewellyn thus suggested that by following "Jesus' and . . . Paul's living rather than . . . writing" he could overcome any contradictions between the abstract and the concrete, between his rebellious and his compliant sides.

Jerome Frank certainly appealed to Llewellyn's rebelliousness. He was incorporated into the list of twenty by Llewellyn as one of the "men peculiarly vocal in advocating new or rebellious points of views" at the same moment as Llewellyn characterized himself as "both vociferous and extreme." [143] That Frank and Llewellyn together should have been the founders of the Legal Realist movement is one of the best indicators of its diversity—if not its schizophrenia. Intellectually, they had little in common except an irreverence for authority and a contempt for the platitudes of orthodox legal discourse. They appear to have been drawn to each other's emotional volatility, exhibitionism, and rebelliousness. They were lucky to have been present at a particular moment in history when the Great Depression and the early New Deal swept away the legitimating premises of the old order and made things seem possible that just a short time before seemed impossible, if not illegitimate. Rebellion could be tolerated for a time.

The Significance of Realism

All Realists shared one basic premise—that the law had come to be out of touch with reality. Holmes's statement that "the life of the law has not been logic, it has been experience" was its battle cry. Pound's distinction between the law in books and the law in action was its most famous academic formulation.

The perception that institutions were out of touch was not only a major theme of post-*Lochner* legal thought, but of American critical social thought generally. From Turner's 1893 frontier thesis to Beard's 1913 *An Economic Interpretation of the Constitution*, the search for social explanations of institutions (not religious destiny or inherent racial or national character) came to express a widening skepticism of the orthodox explanations of things, as well as a mode of criticizing the system of legitimacy from which those explanations had derived.[144]

The perception that law and life were out of sync produced many different forms of intellectual response. Many sought to show that while life had rapidly changed, law had lagged behind. Pound, for example, offered many versions of a cyclical theory within which legal systems fluctuated between generality and particularity, rule and discretion, and professional and lay norms of justice.[145] He seemed to suggest that the disparity between the law in books and the law in action was a temporary aberration, a lag, an abnormal departure from balance and equilibrium.

How one sought to explain the disparity between law and life was thus filled with unarticulated political premises. Did the disparity exist, as Pound had suggested, because legal learning continued to reflect the values and categories of an individualistic agricultural society that had evolved into an interdependent, urbanized, industrial society? Or was the problem, as Pound had also suggested, that a system of "mechanical jurisprudence" had moved law ever further away from society and that a better juristic method might have enabled law to stay in touch with life?[146] From the time Holmes wrote "The Path of the Law" in 1897, a major part of all critical jurisprudence had focused on this question of why legal thought had lost touch with reality. It produced a body of writing that cohered into an elaborate critique of the intellectual premises of Classical Legal Thought and represents some of the greatest contributions in all of American legal literature.

This attack on the juristic methods of the old order has been called the "revolt against formalism" or the shift to "scientific naturalism."[147] Both characterizations enable us to see the enormous similarities between the changes in the governing premises of philosophy, history, economics, and other social sciences around the turn of the century. But the emphasis on method often overstates these changes primarily as academic or intellectual discoveries unrelated to the enormous upsurge of social change and class struggle in the late nineteenth century and the crisis of legitimacy that it produced.

As we shall see in the next chapter,[148] the distinction between law in books and law in action also led directly to an alliance between Progressivism and reformist social science. For example, the "Brandeis brief" presented to the Supreme Court by Louis D. Brandeis in the case of *Muller v. Oregon* (1908) extensively cited social science research into working women's lives to defend successfully a constitutional challenge to a maximum hours law for women. This focus on social fact, it needs to be emphasized, represented another important form of critique of that "heaven of legal concepts," those otherworldly abstractions haunting Classical Legal Thought, that Felix Cohen portrayed as the reason for its being out of touch with reality. It is important to appreciate fully the critical intentions of these early social scientists, many of them women, whose desire to pierce the veil of conventional appearances and grasp reality sharply differed from later value-free social science. By insisting that detailed knowledge of social fact represented a healthy antidote to highly apologetic forms of discourse and judgment, Progressives treated social science research as providing a necessary demystifying first step toward the goal of social reform. In short, social science was another way of undermining disembodied formalism.

In fact, the battle against formalism was waged on many different fronts. It represented a broad attack on the claims of Classical Legal Thought to be natural, neutral, and apolitical, which is precisely what the Langdellian slogan "Law is a science" was meant to proclaim.[149] Some believed that, in principle, it was possible to create such a scientific system of neutral legal concepts, even though Classical legal thinkers had unfortunately allowed formalism to insulate the law from the pressures of reality. Therefore, the path of criticism of orthodoxy was to demonstrate how the incompetent legal reasoning of Classical thinkers had enabled legal thought to lose touch with reality. Hohfeld is such an example of the continuing hold of legal science over even the critics of orthodoxy.[150] When he died prematurely in 1919, he was the last Progressive system builder, the last reformist believer in the possibility of constructing a set of extremely abstract legal concepts and categories that could continue to be the basis for legal criticism.

But if no other Progressive sought to scale Hohfeld's grandiose heights, many nevertheless concentrated on showing that a better juristic method could produce more legitimate and more realistic results. Not only Pound but also Justice Benjamin N. Cardozo reflected this serene pre-war confidence that mechanical jurisprudence could be replaced by a better juristic method. Llewellyn's failure to include Justice Cardozo on his list of Realists offers an important clue to the way in which Llewellyn's version of Legal Realism was severed from its roots in Progressive Legal Thought.

Cardozo was one of the two greatest American common law judges of the twentieth century. Appointed to the New York Court of Appeals in 1914 and to the U.S. Supreme Court as Holmes's successor in 1932, he was, along with Roger Traynor of California a generation later, a leader in the progressive reorientation of private law doctrine.[151]

Cardozo's *The Nature of The Judicial Process* (1921), originally delivered as the Storrs Lectures at Yale Law School, remained perhaps the most widely read American work on legal thought for over a half century. No other book managed to capture the serene optimism of Progressive jurisprudence or to convey its reformist conviction that "the force which in our day and generation is becoming the greatest [influence] of them all, [is] the power of social justice. . . ."[152]

In his gentle confidence in the inevitability of reform, Cardozo thus seemed oblivious to the growing indications that post-war sentiment had turned sharply against "the power of social justice." As Frank and Llewellyn looked back a decade later, in the midst of the Great Depression, at Cardozo's contribution, it must have seemed to them to have been derived not from reason or analysis but from a generous but unrealistic faith in inevitable incremental progress.

Yet they failed to acknowledge how far Cardozo had gone in shifting the intellectual frame for talking about law—and how courageous he, a sitting judge, had been in publicly proclaiming that law "is not found, but made"[153] because "[e]verywhere there is growing emphasis on the analogy between the function of the judge and the function of the legislator."[154] "[T]he whole subject-matter of jurisprudence," Cardozo declared, "is more plastic, more malleable, the moulds less definitively cast, the bounds of right and wrong less preordained and constant, than most of us . . . have been accustomed to believe."[155]

Not only did Cardozo emphasize the pervasiveness of judicial discretion—"the demon of formalism tempts the intellect with the lure of scientific order"[156]—but he indicated that when judges "are called upon to say how far existing rules are to be extended or restricted, they must let the welfare of society fix the path, its direction and its distance."[157] He referred to Pound over and over again to argue that "in every department of the law . . . the social value of a rule has become a test of growing power and importance."[158] This Cardozo called the "method of sociology," after Pound's own Sociological Jurisprudence. "[T]he power of social justice . . . finds its outlet and expression in the method of sociology," Cardozo declared.[159]

The method of sociology was, above all, consequentialist. "[T]he final principle of selection for judges, as for legislators, is one of fitness to an end."[160] "[T]he end which the law serves" determines its value.[161]

> Not the origin, but the goal, is the main thing. There can be no wisdom in the choice of a path unless we know where it will lead. The teleological conception of his function must be ever in the judge's mind. This means, of course, that the juristic philosophy of the common law is at bottom the philosophy of pragmatism. Its truth is relative, not absolute.[162]

More eloquently than any other writer, Cardozo in *The Nature of the Judicial Process* managed to state the working premises of Progressive jurisprudence. Little of what he wrote was truly original, though he was able to draw very interesting comparisons among what he called four different judicial "methods"—(1) the method of philosophy or logic and analogy; (2) the method of history or evolution; (3) the method of tradition or custom; (4) and the method of sociology. Into the complex interplay among these four methods, he was able to pack many of the typical tensions and dilemmas of jurisprudence.

The confident ease with which Cardozo approached value questions captures one important tension within both pre–World War I Progressive jurisprudence and post-war Realism. In boldly disputing the legal positivism of Holmes (whom he did not mention) and the analytical philosophers Austin, Holland, and Gray (whom he did), he asserted that it "really matters" that

> the judge is under a duty . . . to maintain a relation between law and morals, between the precepts of jurisprudence and those of reason and good conscience. . . . The constant insistence that morality and justice are not law, has tended to breed distrust and contempt of law as something to which morality and justice are not merely alien, but hostile. . . . Not for us the barren logomachy that dwells upon the contrasts between law and justice, and forgets their deeper harmonies.[163]

No wonder that Cardozo did not fit into Llewellyn's program of reducing law to scientific methodology. This contrast between Cardozo and Llewellyn does highlight the fact that there was a major shift toward value skepticism after the First World War. Legal Realists generally did not express the sort of self-assurance about values that Progressives were able regularly to muster. "Many who had been rebellious optimists" before the First World War became "despairing nihilists . . . ," Henry F. May observed.[164] Yet, it is also true that some Realists were themselves deeply critical of Llewellyn's positivism. Felix Cohen, for example, also insisted in 1931 "that all valuations of law are moral judgments, that the major part of legal philosophy is a branch of ethics, that the problem which the judge faces is, in the strictest sense, a moral problem, and that the law has no valid end or purpose other than the maintenance of the good life. . . ."[165]

Perhaps it was Cardozo's own method of exposition that turned Frank and Llewellyn off. "For every tendency," he wrote in his introduction, "one seems to see a counter-tendency; for every rule its antinomy."[166] Throughout *The Nature of the Judicial Process*, one finds Cardozo stating a proposition and then its opposite, as if there were some obvious but unstated reconciliation waiting in the wings. "Adherence to precedent must . . . be the rule rather than the exception," he reiterates just after devoting his energies to demonstrating the malleability of legal rules.[167] While much of his work emphasized the "creative" element in judging—that judging is an "art"—he was prepared simultaneously to insist on the "narrow range of choice" available to the judge.[168] If with one hand he wrote of the judge as legislator, with the other he warned of the danger of discretion. At one moment, he emphasized that his "duty as judge" is "to objectify in law, not my own aspirations and convictions and philosophies, but the aspirations and convictions and philosophies of the men and women of my time."[169] At the very next moment, he insisted that "[h]ardly shall I do this well if my own sympathies and beliefs and passionate devotions are with a time that is past."[170]

Cardozo's charm as a writer and his influence as a judge was in his unequaled ability to sugar-coat whatever was unconventional in the message he was delivering or the doctrine he was creating. Immediately after proclaiming that "law . . . is not found, but made,"[171] he reassures the reader that "[t]here is in truth nothing revolutionary or even novel in this view of the judicial function."[172] Cardozo was not comfortable with the bold, broad strokes of a Holmes, whose daring aphoristic style precluded careful qualification. Nor did Cardozo share the genuine philosophical disposition of a Holmes, who usually began an inquiry by asserting some fundamental contradiction between principles. Instead, Cardozo portrayed judicial decision making as more like a "strange compound which is brewed daily in the caldron of the courts."[173] The task was to let the different "ingredients enter in varying proportions."[174] "Before we can determine the proportions of a blend," however, "we must know the ingredients to be blended."[175] The outstanding judge, therefore, is like "a wise pharmacist" who "can compound a fitting remedy." He "must balance all his ingredients . . . adding a little here and taking out a little there" in order to "determine, as wisely as he can, which weight shall tip the scales."[176] The judge's "conclusions must, indeed, be subject to constant testing and retesting, revision and readjustment . . ."[177] The pharmacist provides the central image of Cardozo's ideal of the incremental and experimental reformer as a common law judge. Perhaps he might, almost unnoticed, be able to slip a few more ingredients of "humanness" into the remedy, but it was not his job to reconsider the fundamental structure.

SEVEN

The Legacy of Legal Realism

Legal Realism is the culmination of the early-twentieth-century attack on the claims of late-nineteenth-century Classical Legal Thought to have produced an autonomous and self-executing system of legal discourse. The creation of a system of legal thought that could separate law and politics has been the leading aspiration of American legal orthodoxy since the Revolution. In a nation lacking either an established social order or an established church to produce the social cement of legitimate authority, from the beginning Americans turned the rule of law into a "civil religion."[1] And in this most democratic country in the world, Americans after the Revolution obsessed about the dangers of "tyranny of the majority" and about how a "government of laws, not of men" might spare them from its ravages. If in 1776 tyranny of the majority might well have meant sectarian religious tyranny, by 1830 it had come almost exclusively to represent fear of leveling, confiscation—fear of the redistribution of wealth or power from rich to poor. The desire to create an autonomous system of legal thought that would separate law and politics, and create a neutral and apolitical mode of legal discourse, has always been associated in American thought with preventing tyranny of the majority.[2]

The late-nineteenth-century system of Classical Legal Thought that Progressive jurisprudence after *Lochner* sought to dismantle was the culmination of a set of ideas that had gradually crystallized over the course of a century.[3] By the time *Lochner* was decided, these ideas had produced conceptions of law and legal reasoning that were designed to create a sharp separation between law and politics, and between legal reasoning on the one hand and moral and political reasoning on the other.

The most important legacy of Realism therefore was its challenge to the orthodox claim that legal thought was separate and autonomous from moral and political discourse.

The Realist Critique of the Naturalness of the Market

A conception of a self-executing, decentralized, competitive market economy was central to ideas of legitimacy in all areas of late-nineteenth-century American thought. It formed the foundation for ideals of social justice according to which individual self-interest and distributive justice could, "as if by an invisible hand," be harmonized. It was the source of the pervasive view that justice required only equality of opportunity—that everyone be enabled to begin the competitive race equally—and that any requirement of equality of condition or results certainly was illegitimate.[4] For it was well recognized that, given the unequal distribution of talent, energy, and luck, equality of opportunity inevitably resulted in organized inequality. As Justice Pitney put it in *Coppage v. Kansas* (1915):

> No doubt, wherever the right of private property exists, there must and will be inequalities of fortune; and thus it naturally happens that parties negotiating about a contract are not equally unhampered by circumstances. This applies to all contracts, and not merely to that between employer and employé. Indeed a little reflection will show that wherever the right of private property and the right of free contract co-exist, each party when contracting is inevitably more or less influenced by the question whether he has much property, or little, or none; for the contract is made to the very end that each may gain something that he needs or desires more urgently than that which he proposes to give in exchange. And, since it is self-evident that, unless all things are held in common, some persons must have more property that others, it is from the nature of things impossible to uphold freedom of contract and the right of private property without at the same time recognizing as legitimate those inequalities of fortune that are the necessary result of the exercise of those rights.[5]

The assumptions of a self-executing market economy thus ensured that unequal results were just because they reflected the unequal abilities that individuals brought to the competitive race. Every effort to interfere with outcomes—to judge overall social justice by results—inevitably subverted the legitimacy of the market process as a neutral and apolitical arbiter of the just distribution of wealth.

This vision of a self-executing, competitive market constituted the foundation of all efforts to create a sharp separation in legal thought between processes and outcomes, between means and ends, and between law and politics. Just as result-oriented economic policy was regarded as a non-neutral interference with the natural operations of the market, so too was orthodox legal thought stridently committed to avoiding political scrutiny of outcomes. The law of contracts, the legal paradigm of voluntary market relations, was, as we have seen, especially resistant to any attempts to judge the fairness of contracts by their results.[6]

The appearance of pragmatism in American philosophy around the turn of the century represents a challenge to the prevailing process-oriented conception of justice that had dominated late-nineteenth-century American thought.[7] This turn to consequentialism in social thought is an important expression of the gradual disintegration of the belief in neutral processes, especially a neutral market economy, as the legitimate distributor of just rewards. As American society grew more unequal and as the spectacular increase in corporate concentration undermined the belief in the naturalness of a decentralized, competitive market economy, social critics focused their attack on the assumptions behind an entirely process-oriented view of social justice.

Pound's picture of a glaring disparity between the law in books and the law in action was one expression of this turn to consequentialism.[8] It criticized a process of mechanical legal reasoning that was oblivious to the way law actually worked out in society. Thus, even before Realism had been proclaimed as a movement, the basic consequentialist critique of orthodox legal doctrine emphasized how unrealistic it was, because it had lost touch with the way things actually were.

The Realists of the 1920s and 1930s pursued their attack on the legitimacy of the market with a degree of insight, brilliance, and social passion that has never been equaled since. First, they emphasized that the market was not natural, but rather a social construct. And just at the moment that economic science had begun to reorganize its postulates to explain how a cartelized economy was not incompatible with axioms developed under a competitive and decentralized market regime—in other words, just as economists were attempting to reimpose an apologetic mode of natural equilibrium on the system—the Great Depression encouraged still further elaboration of the view that, far from being neutral and natural, markets were social constructs that could be judged only by their social consequences.[9]

If late-nineteenth-century social thought had insisted that the results of the market process were, by definition, legitimate, the critics sought to turn the tables and show that the premises that lay behind the organization of the market were themselves entirely debatable social choices that could not be justified in scientific terms. Here the great institutional economists[10]—Veblen, Ely, Commons—had left an anti-naturalist legacy that economic science has never managed to destroy.[11] Within Realism, their most influential heir was Robert Lee Hale of Columbia, both an economist and a lawyer.[12]

Hale's pathbreaking "Coercion and Distribution in a Supposedly Non-Coercive State" (1923) is the model for several Realist critiques of the premises of legal and economic orthodoxy.[13] First, it is one of the earliest rigorous criticisms of the orthodox ideal of voluntariness in market exchange. Since all market transactions are affected by the prior distribution of property and entitlements, Hale argued, the market was in fact an organized form of coercion of the weak by the strong. The decision to "withhold"—not to buy in the market or not to employ labor—was simply another form of assertion of economic power.

So far, Hale was elaborating themes concerning the unequal distribution of market power that had grown in volume since the founding of the American Economic Association in 1885 during the first phase of cartelization of the economy. Hale, however, understood that, for reformist lawyers, the most important task was to undermine the ideology of voluntariness that had formed the legitimating background of American private law, especially the law of contracts. He realized the moral significance of emphasizing the coercive aspect of markets, something that perhaps economists simply took for granted.

Because Hale's article was such a seminal work, we need to pause to understand its intellectual significance. Hale's basic goal was to attack the prevailing vision of the market as a system of free and voluntary exchange, and thereby to undermine the claim that the law should simply reflect the results arrived at in a neutral market. Instead, he wished to show that the market itself was a social creation, a creature of law, government, and prevailing conceptions of legitimate exchange. Many of Hale's arguments were more generally directed at these legitimating conceptions, especially the alliance between natural rights theory, formalism, and conservatism.

Hale sought to break down the bright-line distinction between voluntariness and coercion. He thus needed to portray the market as an interlocking system of power relations, not as some abstract voluntary meeting of minds or convergence of wills. His two central images are of the laborer who does not voluntarily choose to work, but rather is coerced into working for fear of starvation, and the factory owner whose "coercive power is weakened by the fact that both his customers and his laborers have the power to make matters more or less unpleasant for him— the customers through their law-given power to withhold access to their cash, the laborers through their *actual* power (neither created nor destroyed by the law) to withhold their services."[14]

"There is, however, a natural reluctance" to use the term "coercion," Hale wrote, as if he were a scientist unconcerned with its ordinary normative significance. "But were it once recognized that nearly all incomes are the result of private coercion, some with the help of the state, some without it, it would then be plain that to admit the coercive nature of the process would not be to condemn it."[15] Nevertheless, because "popular thought undoubtedly does require special justification for any conduct . . . which is labelled 'coercive,' " Hale sought to show that there was no privileged category of economic relations that could be regarded as purely voluntary.[16] There was no state of nature prior to law.

Here Hale deployed one of the most important intellectual strategies that Realism would borrow from Holmes—the characterization of differences of kind as differences of degree. In particular, he sought to show that since all market relations involved varying degrees of coercion, there could never be a state of nature in which a purely voluntary system of exchange existed. John Dawson would later refine this strand of Hale's argument in his important article on economic duress.[17] Late-nineteenth-century Classical Legal Thought, Dawson wrote, involved "a basic contradiction in the concepts of 'freedom' which were . . . at work."[18]

> On the one hand, doctrines of undue influence were attempting to "free" the individual by regulating the pressures that restricted individual choice; on the other hand, theories of economic individualism aimed at an entirely different kind of freedom, a freedom of the "market" from external regulation. It was not yet fully recognized that the freedom of the "market" was essentially a freedom of individ-

uals and groups to coerce one another, with the power to coerce reinforced by agencies of the state itself. Even though the larger implications of this idea were by no means understood, one simple and quite obvious deduction had already been made—that is, that if the "market" was to be free, any form of external regulation was objectionable. Regulation by court-enforced rules of private law seemed just as unwise and dangerous as regulation by statute or administrative action. From this point of view, where urgent need or special disadvantage compelled agreement to the terms proposed, these circumstances must be disregarded since they differed only in degree from the basic conditions which governed the exchange of goods and services throughout society. [19]

In depicting all market relations as inherently coercive, Hale realized that "the undoubtedly coercive character of the pressure exerted by the property-owner is disguised" by state-of-nature thinking. [20] Indeed, state-of-nature reasoning lay at the foundation of all Classical legal categorization and classification, as Holmes's *Lochner* reference to "Mr. Herbert Spencer's Social Statics" was intended to convey. [21] Hale in addition drew on Hohfeld's system of legal correlatives, which also denied any privileged status to natural rights starting points, in order to discredit assumptions of a privileged realm of voluntary market relations. Two of the most prominent background assumptions that supported ideas of such a natural realm were the dubious distinctions between acts and omissions and between a public and a private sphere. These legal distinctions were among the important intellectual divisions that disguised the all-pervasive nature of coercion in the market.

Hale's most original insight was the view that the market was the actual creator of property and entitlements rather than just being a neutral institution that reflected pre-existing Lockean property. The legal rules governing the market determined whether, for example, news was property, or whether employers have the power to fire workers, or whether economic coercion was legitimate—more like competition—or illegitimate—more like theft or duress. [22]

Since this idea was such a prominent part of the Realist de-legitimation of the market, we should pause for a moment and see where it came from. First, in law, the general attack began with the criticism of the *Lochner* court and the full realization of the incestuous relationship between orthodox legal thought and economic conceptions of a self-executing market economy. From that moment, critical legal thought sought to undermine both the claims of the market to be neutral and natural and of law to be simply a passive reflection or facilitator of a neutral market.

Simultaneously, the attack on the labor injunction seems to have influenced Hohfeld to deconstruct property conceptions and led Walter Wheeler Cook to apply the Hohfeldian system to the Supreme Court's conceptions of labor relations. [23] Cook's conclusion was that one could not logically derive the labor injunction from any general character of entrepreneurial property. Property was a bundle of often conflicting rights.

At the same time, Holmes and Brandeis were developing the view in the Supreme Court that, in Holmes's words, property was a "creation of law." [24] What formerly had been constitutionally treated as a taking, they tended to recategorize as regulation under the police power not requiring compensation.[25]

But the most important specific influence on Hale's views, as we saw in Chapter 5, were the arguments over rate making that began around 1920. There could have been no better case study of the social creation of property than these disputes over the constitutionality of rates set by regulatory commissions. We have already seen how Hale, among others, developed the view that the Supreme Court's analysis of how to determine value for rate-making purposes was circular. Indeed, the underlying premise of Hale's critique of the orthodox theory of value was that value was not an essence to be discovered but rather depended on the social purposes for which the concept was to be used.[26]

The rate-making cases enabled Hale to see that there was no real rate of return independent of value and no market value independent of prior legal norms. Just as the law created value in the rate cases, so too every market regime created property and entitlements, depending on its prior rules for regulating coercion.[27] Once it was understood that there could be no such thing as a completely *voluntary* market, there could also be no completely *neutral* market because, one way or the other, there needed to be rules on how to regulate (or not regulate) coercion.

That Hale's insight was shaped by the rate regulation controversy was no accident. Throughout American history, there had been a contest between a powerful Lockean ideology that insisted on the pre-political character of property and the existence of social facts that regularly demonstrated otherwise.[28] In the immediate post-revolutionary period, land grants and the regulation of inheritance were clear examples of the social creation of property. Later, franchises for roads, canals, and railroads underlined their political origins. Finally, until the naturalization of the corporation after 1900, the corporate charter stood as the most forceful reminder that law creates property.[29]

Yet, so powerful has been the yearning to find a natural and pre-political realm free from the threats of social choice that the Lockean vision of property has regularly reasserted its evocative power, never more so than in late-nineteenth-century orthodox legal thought. So when Hale challenged the neutrality of the market, he was not only insisting on the politically contingent character of all definitions of property, he was also questioning two prominent premises of Classical Legal Thought: the act-omission distinction[30] and the distinction between public and private spheres of action.

The Critique of Orthodox Legal Reasoning

The effort of late-nineteenth-century orthodox legal thinkers to create an autonomous system of legal doctrine was the most important expression of their desire to separate sharply law from politics. We have seen how they constructed a system of legal architecture whose very generality, abstraction, and systematization appeared to them to be the perfect expression of law as science. Above all, they sought to represent legal reasoning as fundamentally different from political or moral reasoning and professional reasoning as radically different from that of laypersons. If political reasoning was subjective, legal reasoning was objective; if the one was discretionary and a matter of opinion, the other was non-discretionary and not subject to the whims of the judge. The ideal—no one supposed it was the complete reality—was, in Holmes's critical words, to represent legal reasoning as capable of attaining the "certainty which makes [it] seem like mathematics."[31] Late-nineteenth-century legal thought has often been called formalistic because of its aspiration to be able to render one right answer to any legal question. In attacking deductive legal reasoning, Legal Realists made more original and lasting contributions to legal thought than in any other area. Yet the Realist critique of orthodox legal reasoning has often been understood too narrowly as simply an attack on a formalism that includes only deductive legal reasoning. In fact, like any powerful system of understanding, late-nineteenth-century conceptions of legal reasoning were rooted in much more complicated and multi-faceted systems of meaning.

Categorical Thinking

Perhaps the most fundamental architectural idea of legal orthodoxy was embodied in its faith in the coherence and integrity of bright-line boundaries.[32] Whether we look to direct-indirect tests involving causation or the reach of the commerce clause or, instead, to the way in which legal thinkers believed they could distinguish a tax from a taking or regulation from confiscation, we see what is really the most distinctive element of formalism.[33] In all areas of thought, early-twentieth-century thinkers challenged the naturalism and essentialism of existing social practices, as well as the categories that legitimated them.[34] Everywhere there developed a critique that sought to transform differences of kind into differences of degree and to see the world not as a series of mutually exclusive black-white bright-line boundaries requiring intellectual on-off switches but rather as a series of continua involving shades of gray requiring line drawing.

Perhaps it is the fate of the first generation of basically secular intellectuals— if that is the way we can think of the late-nineteenth-century American legal orthodox—that they cushion the terrors of unbelief by constructing a system of categories sufficiently rigid to alleviate their fear that only the threat of the hereafter can keep people from turning into beasts.[35] There seems to be an important relationship between the psychological inspiration for religious fundamentalism and similar underlying sources of legal fundamentalism. For the recently irreligious person, profession, or nation, does the secure rigidity of secularized categories substitute for those earlier stern substantive prescriptions grounded in religious truths?

Whatever one may make of the important relation between law and religion, it is quite clear that Legal Realism represents the culmination of early-twentieth-century assaults on legal fundamentalism and, in particular, on late-nineteenth-century categorical thinking.[36] Not only did Realists follow Holmes in conceiving of ordinary legal questions as questions of degree requiring line drawing and balancing tests but, more fundamentally still, they insisted that legal classifications and categories were not natural but social constructs. The way to determine whether a legal classification was good or not depended on the purposes for which the category was created, not on some measure of whether it fit or reflected a pre-existing natural category. Categories do not express pre-existing essences. Property, Holmes pointed out, is a "creation of law." Just as pragmatism had attacked the essentialist claims of philosophical idealism by insisting on a functionalist and consequentialist truth, so did the Realists treat the value of concepts and categories in terms of the results that they produced. This "cognitive relativism" of Realism has not been sufficiently appreciated; its "value relativism" has, by contrast, been exaggerated.[37]

There has been some confusion between the Realist insistence on the socially constructed nature of legal categories (and the still broader assertion of the socially contingent character of all legal architecture) and the somewhat different anti-conceptualism for which Legal Realism is also known.

Hostility to conceptualism was a hallmark of Legal Realist criticism. Deriving from the widely shared Realist view that orthodox legal thought had created an illusory sense of integration through a process of generalizing and abstracting concepts to cover an ever-widening range of legal relations, Legal Realists sought to explicate the famous aphorism from Holmes's *Lochner* dissent: "General propositions do not decide concrete cases."[38]

Realist anti-conceptualism developed into varieties of "rule skepticism," which denied that it was possible to reason downward in a non-discretionary and apolitical manner from very general concepts to more particular rules or doctrines and then, finally, to specific applications of these rules to concrete sets of facts. The demonstration that deductive logic could not provide a self-executing way to move from the general to the particular was among the most important contributions of Felix Cohen and the great philosopher John Dewey to the Realist critique.[39] It was the most influential source of Realist anti-conceptualism and the insistence on greater particularity and contextualism in legal thinking.

The Realist hostility to general concepts like "liberty," "will," "fault," and "property" led them to attempt to deconstruct what Felix Cohen derisively called the "heaven of legal concepts."[40] Indeed, their hostile attitude toward abstraction represents one of the most significant differences between Realism and earlier Progressive legal thought.

Until the Realists, critical thought about law had generally tended toward the abstract and the systematic. The brilliant system building of Bentham inspired almost a century of efforts of utilitarians to go behind the dense and unsystematic common law system in order to find more fundamental truths derived from utility.[41] The gradual collapse of the forms of action after mid-century unleashed a surge of efforts to discover underlying general principles of law, a perspective that had been virtually unknown among common lawyers for 500 years. For much of the nineteenth century, therefore, efforts at systematization and generalization carried the deeply subversive message that the existing common law system was at best incoherent and at worst irrational and illegitimate. A thin line, however, has always separated the apologists, who believed, like Blackstone, that a more abstract and systematic jurisprudence would reveal the deeper rationality of the common law, from the critics like Hohfeld, whose efforts at systematic jurisprudence were inspired by the belief that only a more abstract system of legal thought could expose the irrationality of common law modes of legal classification.[42]

The appeal of Austin's jurisprudence to Holmes, for example, was the appeal of the analytical system builder to the young, critically minded legal theorist. But the most important American example of abstraction and systematization in the service of reform was Hohfeld's 1913 and 1917 articles on fundamental legal conceptions.[43]

I attempted earlier to explain the critical and deconstructive strategy behind Hohfeld's work, which was clearly understood by his contemporaries at Yale, Arthur Corbin and Walter Wheeler Cook.[44] Less than a generation later, however, the method behind Hohfeld's categories was lost and his system of legal classification had become "a sack of dried beans" delighted in only by apolitical pedants.[45]

The most important reason for this turn is that the Realist generation after Hohfeld arrived at a virtually unanimous conviction that the old order had attained an undeserved legitimacy through abstraction, generalization, and systematization of legal categories, which (in the language of a later day) they believed "reified" reality and produced a false sense of order and security through suppression of anomalies.[46] "The present wave of nominalism in juristic science," Morris Cohen wrote in 1931, "is a reaction by younger men against the *abuse* of abstract principles by an older generation that neglected the adequate factual analysis necessary to make principles properly applicable."[47]

It is at this point that we need to pause and realize the full significance of the Realist assault on the abstraction and systematization of orthodox legal thought. The assault occurred at the very moment at which, after a century of development, the treatise tradition was finally able to confer legitimacy on systematic legal thought. For the first time in 500 years, Anglo-American legal thought had begun to move away from the common law's proceduralism and particularism to resemble more closely the flights of system building associated with the Continental pandectists.

The Realists charged the systematizers not only with distorting reality but also with using abstraction and generalization to cover up the conservative nature of their politics. They insisted, therefore, that only more specific, more concrete, and more contextual legal rules could actually fit reality. The Realists' rule skepticism[48] thus represented a protest against what today we would call the over- and under-inclusiveness of rules and doctrines in orthodox legal thought.[49]

But the Realist critique of categories was developed still further into what has been called "anti-conceptualism." As Lon Fuller pointed out in an extraordinarily perceptive 1934 article, many Realists seemed to accept the view that since *all* concepts inevitably distorted reality, the task of a Realist jurisprudence was somehow to root out concepts altogether and return to the raw material of reality.[50] They thus seemed to merge the critique of abstraction as over-inclusive and under-inclusive with a more antinomian hostility to all forms of categorization and classification. The question is whether this did not eventually produce an untheoretical and uncritical form of legal discourse.[51]

One can best see the practical consequences of the Realist critique of concepts by comparing its arguments against deductive reasoning—the vertical dimension—with those that criticized analogical reasoning—the horizontal dimension. We have seen that the Realist attack on the formalism of the old order denied the claim that legal reasoning could imitate syllogistic or geometrical forms of argument. General propositions could not decide concrete cases because, in reasoning downward from a concept to its application, there were multiple inferences to be made and thus multiple conclusions to be drawn. Depending on which major premise was deployed or which intermediate minor premise was assumed, there were an infinite number of potential conclusions that could be drawn. Hence deductive reasoning suppressed the inevitable moral or political choice among possible inferences. The more general the starting premise, the more indeterminate its particular applications.

Yet it should be emphasized that this critique of deductive reasoning does not question the necessity of using concepts to bring order to experience. Rather, it is critical of concepts only to the extent that they are so general as to be inherently random in their application. Otherwise, the critique simply denies the formalist assertion that it is possible to avoid *some* indeterminacy in the application of concepts, which was the point of the discussion of deductive reasoning in the first place. However, it was in the horizontal dimension of analogical reasoning that the true anti-conceptualism of some Legal Realists was revealed most clearly.

The capacious claims by Classical legal thinkers for the power of analogical reasoning were perhaps more important than any other in legitimizing the old order. Analogical reasoning—the ability to say that one case was like another—was central to all theories that distinguished legal reasoning from political reasoning or sought to show that judging was a function of reason, not will. All of the "discovery" and "finding" metaphors, developed to distinguish courts from legislatures, were heavily dependent on developing a conception of common law reasoning that would exemplify a government of laws, not of men. All theories of precedent designed to portray the judge as bound by prior rulings were similarly based on the ability to determine whether one case was like another.[52] Indeed, the most typical nineteenth-century defense of the common law against the charge of the codifiers that "judge made law . . . from its nature, must always be *ex post facto*"[53] was the reply that there really was no common law "case of first impression" because analogical reasoning from similar cases or principles provided a self-executing process of discovery, at least for those learned in the law.[54]

Because analogical reasoning carried such a heavy burden of justification under the common law system, it became a tempting target for those who wished to challenge the apolitical premises of Classical Legal Thought. One of the best examples of this challenge appears in the case of *International News Service v. Associated Press*, decided by the U.S. Supreme Court in 1918. The case involved the question of whether news was property and whether the Associated Press, the established news service, could enjoin a newly organized competitor from "stealing" news.

At one level, we saw earlier,[55] the case is a significant example of judicial efforts to come to terms with the de-physicalization of property and the implications for legal thought of a shift away from landed property to more highly abstract—and physically unbounded—forms of commercial property. Here I wish to emphasize the close relationship between the de-physicalization of property and the decline in the power of concepts deriving from property to generate a field of analogical discourse.

There were three opinions in the *INS* case. For the majority, Justice Mahlon Pitney seemed to believe that the case was an easy one for the plaintiff, who had put labor, money, and time into creating value. Appealing to a Lockean labor theory of value, he upheld the issuance of an injunction. His only apparent doubt was conveyed by the qualified reference to news as *"quasi* property," though that qualification was never explained.[56]

Justice Holmes concurred but issued his terse positivist proclamation about the nature of property: "Property, a creation of law, does not arise from value, although exchangable—a matter of fact."[57] This statement was designed to challenge the pre-political natural rights basis for property that underlay the majority opinion. For Holmes, there was no essence called property that existed prior to law. Instead, law defined whether something should be treated as property, which turned on questions of social policy.

Before we go further, we need to see how the positivist attack on natural rights theories of property was not only an attack on essentialism but, ultimately, a challenge to the power of analogical reasoning as well. Justice Pitney's majority opinion proceeded from the principle that anything that had market value was property, and that it was the task of the law to ratify what would have been true even in a state of nature. It was therefore also possible to reason at a very high level of abstraction about the nature of property. For Justice Holmes, by contrast, something may be called property to advance social purposes, not because it is endowed with some pre-existing essence of propertyness. If the judge is to look to precedent to decide whether news is property, he must analogize at a more concrete level of abstraction.

We can see all of this most clearly by comparing Holmes's solution to that of Justice Brandeis, who dissented in *INS*. "[T]he fact that a product of the mind has cost its producer money and labor, and has a value for which others are willing to pay," Brandeis wrote, "is not sufficient to ensure to it this legal attribute of property." How should a court decide whether or not to call news property? Proposing a radical analysis, Brandeis wrote:

> The great development of agencies now furnishing country-wide distribution of news, the vastness of our territory, and improvements in the means of transmitting intelligence, have made it possible for a news agency or newspapers to obtain, without paying compensation, the fruit of another's efforts and to use news so obtained gainfully in competition with the original collector. The injustice of such action is obvious. But to give relief against it would involve more than the application of existing rules of law to new facts. It would require the making of a new rule in analogy to existing ones. The unwritten law possesses capacity for growth; and has often satisfied new demands for justice by invoking analogies or by expanding a rule or principle. This process has been in the main wisely applied and should not be discontinued. Where the problem is relatively simple, as it is apt to be when private interests only are involved, it generally proves adequate. But with the increasing complexity of society, the public interest tends to become omnipresent; and the problems presented by new demands for justice cease to be simple. Then the creation or recognition by courts of a new private right may work serious injury to the general public, unless the boundaries of the right are definitely established and wisely guarded. In order to reconcile the new private right with the public interest, it may be necessary to prescribe limitations and rules for its enjoyment; and also to provide administrative machinery for enforcing the rules. It is largely for this reason that, in the effort to meet the many new demands for justice incident to a rapidly changing civilization, resort to legislation has latterly been had with increasing frequency.

> The rule for which the plaintiff contends would effect an important extension of property rights and a corresponding curtailment of the free use of knowledge and of ideas; and the facts of this case admonish us of the danger involved in recognizing such a property right in news, without imposing upon news-gatherers corresponding obligations. . . .

> Courts are ill-equipped to make the investigations which should precede a determination of the limitations which should be set upon any property right in news or of the circumstances under which news gathered by a private agency should be deemed affected with a public interest. Courts would be powerless to prescribe the detailed regulations essential to full enjoyment of the rights conferred or to introduce the machinery required for enforcement of such regulations. Considerations such as these should lead us to decline to establish a new rule of law in the effort to redress a newly-disclosed wrong, although the propriety of some remedy appears to be clear.[58]

Brandeis's opinion was one of the most important Progressive statements of the changing status of common law analogical reasoning. First, we see the influence of the Progressive attack on natural rights essentialism, so that "unless the boundaries of the right are definitely established and wisely guarded . . . recognition by courts of a new private right may work serious injury to the general public . . ." Once the concept of property is acknowledged to be a social creation whose boundaries are inevitably fluid and contingent, analogies also become more problematic. Second, Brandeis reflects the Progressive view that property law is not private but public law, since "with the increasing complexity of society, the public interest tends to become omnipresent. . . ." When contests over landed property were bipolar,[59] common law decision was satisfactory. "When the problem is relatively simple, as it is apt to be when private interests only are involved," analogical reasoning "generally proves adequate." But where recognition of a property right in a complex and interdependent society affects many different interests, resort to legislation or administrative regulation becomes increasingly necessary. At this point, analogical reasoning by common law courts has become plainly inadequate.

Brandeis's dramatic refusal to apply common law analogical reasoning to a dispute over property rights between private parties illustrates the extent to which the process of analogy itself had been drawn into question as fundamentally political. Compared to Brandeis, Holmes was willing to engage in some modest analogical reasoning about the nature of property on the basis of common law precedents. Holmes thus turned to the law of unfair competition, which was designed to protect consumers from having a product made by another "palmed off" as the seller's own. "[I]n my view," Holmes wrote, "the only ground of complaint that can be recognized without legislation is [an] implied misstatement," a form of common law misrepresentation.[60]

So, unlike Brandeis, who condemned all analogy as inherently political in this case, and unlike Justice Pitney, who confidently believed that common law analogy could operate at a very high level of generality to deal with virtually all contradictions, gaps, and ambiguities in the legal system, Justice Holmes turned to concrete and contextualized common law precedent to do the job of analogy. This more particularized inquiry, he thought, was capable of generalizing limited principles whose field of radiation would be inevitably quite narrow. Beyond that, he agreed with Brandeis that analogy was, in effect, judicial legislation.

We can best capture the change in the status of analogical reasoning by looking back to an earlier Brandeis, still comfortably acting within the world of Classical Legal Thought. In 1890, Brandeis became famous when, together with Samuel Warren, he published an influential Harvard Law Review article arguing for common law recognition of the right to privacy.[61] There is no better example of faith in the incredible power of analogical reasoning, no more perfect illustration of the legitimacy within Classical Legal Thought of argument from extremely abstract propositions about the supposed underlying principles contained within particular cases. Within two decades, however, the steady assault on conceptualism by Progressives drew into question the claims of analogical reasoning to be neutral and apolitical. Whether it is true, as most Realists came to believe, that abstraction necessarily tended toward reified concepts that inevitably lost touch with the complex currents of life continues to be a central question of social and legal theory. But whether it is possible to avoid such consequences without becoming untheoretical and anti-critical is an equally important question that Realism, by and large, did not address.[62]

The Public-Private Distinction

One of the most important contributions of Legal Realism was its challenge to the classical liberal division between public and private spheres.

Through legal doctrine, one can trace the steady growth during the nineteenth century of ever more formal versions of the public-private distinction.[63] It makes its first appearance in Justice Story's classification of public and private corporations in the *Dartmouth College Case* (1819).[64] By the time of the Civil War, it had already been extended to a rigid categorization of public versus private takings under state eminent domain provisions.[65]

A massive expansion of public-private rhetoric emerged after the Civil War under Fourteenth Amendment state action doctrine,[66] as well as under public versus private tests of the legitimacy of municipal taxation to satisfy bonds floated to build railroads.[67] A striking formalization of this distinction is also reflected in the postbellum cases eliminating punitive damages in tort because they mixed the functions of public and private law.[68] With the Supreme Court's intervention into the process of rate making by the end of the century, the distinction between legitimate regulation of public bodies and illegitimate regulation of private ones was mediated by a hybrid category of "business affected with the public interest."[69]

What was the significance of the growing separation between the public and private spheres? It expressed not only the increasingly separate spheres of men and women,[70] but also the growing separation between the market and the family[71] as the factory system and the division of labor compartmentalized existence.[72] It reflected, as well, the increasing power of laissez-faire ideology and its tendency to shrink the sphere of legitimate governmental regulation of the economy. Even pro-regulatory intermediate categories like business affected with the public interest had the effect of reinforcing an essentialist mindset, so that much political and legal thought was devoted to searching for supposedly inherent characteristics of public and private spheres.

A picture of a decentralized, competitive, and self-regulating market lay at the core of all efforts to define the public-private distinction. Just as the analogous division between public and private law pre-supposed that voluntary relations of market exchange would usually make coercive regulatory intervention unnecessary, the more general separation of activities into public and private spheres was also driven by a conception of a neutral, apolitical, and, above all, self-regulating economic realm.

The first challenge to the orthodox public-private distinction emerged in precisely the same area in which it had been originally formulated—the law of corporations. Seventy-five years after Justice Story deployed the public-private distinction to uphold the constitutional rights of business corporations, the private character of recently consolidated industrial enterprises was drawn into question, first in terms of railroad regulation, then in terms of economic regulation more generally.[73] In an era in which the financial resources of corporations vastly exceeded those of many state governments and at a time when the ability of these corporations to buy political officials was widely noted, it should have come as no surprise that Progressive legal thinkers were unprepared to treat these corporations as simply private entities.

The orthodox line between public and private spheres began to be challenged in many different realms. We saw earlier the ways in which Progressive thinkers after *Lochner* followed Holmes and attacked freedom of contract by arguing that private law was really a form of regulatory public law. The culmination of this view in the scholarly literature was Morris Cohen's assertion in "The Basis of Contract" (1933) that the power to contract was nothing more than a choice to delegate public power to individuals based on social considerations.[74]

The most dramatic example of the triumph of the Realist analysis occurred in *Shelley v. Kraemer* (1948), where the Supreme Court held that judicial enforcement of racially restrictive covenants was "state action" barred by the Fourteenth Amendment.[75] As has been argued many times since, if enforcement of private contracts is state action, then all private activity is public activity and all private law is public law.[76] That was precisely the conclusion to which the Realist critique led.

The trade association movement of the 1920s also played a critical role in undermining the public-private distinction.[77] Classical liberal thought, especially in America, had always found difficulty in conceptualizing intermediate groups that stood between the state and the individual.[78] We have seen the fantastic energy legal thinkers expended, beginning in the 1890s, in attempting to legitimate a non-individualistic entity theory of the corporation.[79] Similarly, during the 1920s, the trade association movement, advancing under the banner of economic cooperation as an alternative to cutthroat competition, sought to defend private lawmaking within various industries against the charge that it simply constituted price fixing or monopolistic control of output.

By the time of the New Deal, industrial self-regulation had also become an important element in efforts to combat the Great Depression.[80] In 1936, the Supreme Court in the *Carter Coal Case* struck down as an unconstitutional delegation of legislative power a provision of the Bituminous Coal Act that had permitted coal companies to regulate output.[81] The Court's analysis proceeded from traditional conceptions of the illegitimacy of delegating public power to private groups. In an article on the Court's decision, "Law Making by Private Groups," Louis Jaffe delivered one of the most trenchant Realist critiques of the public-private distinction.[82] After two decades of expansion of trade association regulation, as well as an enormous increase in group self-regulation through the power over licensing of professional and skilled crafts, Jaffe was able to offer a broad catalogue of coercive regulations by private groups that were supported by legal sanctions. His point was that it was no longer possible to distinguish sharply between public and private exercises of coercion. Just as Morris Cohen had recharacterized the power to enforce a contract as a delegation of public power, Jaffe saw lawmaking by intermediate groups as equally a symptom of pervasive delegation of state power. The disapproved delegation in the *Carter Coal Case*, he maintained, was no different from any of these.

The doctrine of unconstitutional delegation of legislative power made much more prominent one year earlier in the *Schechter Poultry Case* formally concerned the somewhat different question of legislative delegation to the executive.[83] In reality, however, *Schechter* and *Carter Coal* were virtually identical. The National Industrial Recovery Act, which *Schechter* struck down, also involved industrial self-regulation through the famous codes authorized under the act.[84] These codes acquired legal force when they were promulgated by presidential executive order, which was, in reality, simply a rubber stamp of whatever provisions the interest groups had previously agreed to. The case, nevertheless, was formally analyzed not as a delegation of lawmaking power to private groups, as in *Carter Coal*, but as a delegation of lawmaking power to the President.

The collapse of the delegation doctrine after *Schechter* and *Carter Coal* has perhaps more to do with the vast expansion of administrative regulatory power during the New Deal than with recognition of Jaffe's analysis of the pervasiveness of private lawmaking. Yet after Jaffe's attack on the public-private distinction, it became as difficult to think of an inherent category of exclusively legislative lawmaking as it was to continue to think of lawmaking as inherently public. Both moves were not only part of a general skepticism about essentialist categories but were also a reiteration of Hale's views on the pervasiveness of coercion. It was as difficult thereafter to conceive of all coercion as essentially public as it was to think of coercion as a monopoly of legislative power.

Realism: Critical or Scientific?

From the beginning, the Realist critique of the old order was filled with potential contradictions. There were those who criticized Classical jurisprudence for being too political—and for disguising its political preferences in abstraction and systematization. In much of the critical literature of Legal Realism, conceptualism is identified as the primary disease, accused of causing intellectual distortion in situations where there might otherwise be clear expressions of reality. The cure was to produce a better jurisprudence—one that was less formalistic and more contextual.

For others, however, the problem with Classical Legal Thought was not that it was illicitly political but rather that it expressed bad politics. Thus, whether the goal of Realism was to root out distorting juristic methods in order to create a purer and more neutral system of legal concepts or, instead, to acknowledge the necessarily political character of law and insist upon a better system of political values were differences that from the beginning produced contradictory analyses.

Another potential contradiction was contained within the Realist criticism that law had lost touch with life. With this criticism, Realism challenged the assertion of the autonomy of law that was at the core of all Classical legal ideas. Realists agreed that law needed to be brought back in touch with life, that legal categories needed to reflect better or express a more complex social reality. For some, the critique of autonomy meant that legal questions needed to be more closely rooted in the traditional inquiries of moral and political philosophy. For them, the central task was to shed moral light on the traditional questions of, for example, freedom, equality, and justice. If law lacked autonomy, they reasoned, this only meant that there was no fundamental divide between law and morals or between legal and political questions. Thus, the choices within law needed to be addressed within the discourse of moral and political philosophy. For many other Realists, however, the absence of legal autonomy meant that law became the dependent variable, society the independent variable. The task of bringing law back in touch with life meant that law needed to become a mirror of social relations. Since their goal was to develop a method that permitted the legal system to receive undistorted messages from reality, they turned to the social sciences to learn what that reality was.

This Realist turn to social science research was a direct extension of pre-war Progressive sociological jurisprudence. The famous Brandeis Brief submitted in *Muller v. Oregon* (1908) is a perfect illustration of the practical influence of sociological jurisprudence on legal understanding.[85] In that case, the U.S. Supreme Court was asked to decide whether maximum hour laws for women were unconstitutional under the ruling in *Lochner v. New York*. Containing two pages of legal argument and ninety-five pages of sociological and economic data about the conditions of working women's lives in factories,[86] the Brandeis brief, by highlighting social and economic reality, suggested that the trouble with existing law was that it was out of touch with that reality. It was at precisely this time that an alliance between the social sciences and the movement for legal reform was being forged under the theoretical umbrella of sociological jurisprudence.[87]

Two different faces of Realism—one critical, another reformist and constructive—emerged from these contradictory critiques of the old order.[88] Critical theory tended to dominate the earlier post-*Lochner* phase, while social science reformism, allied with administrative law, became a major Realist mode after the New Deal came to power in 1933. In its critical phase, Realism drew on a reservoir of political and moral outrage at the injustices of the old order. Barely concealing its political commitments, its debunking, deconstructive style sought to undermine the claim of the old order that its legal categories and modes of legal reasoning were natural, neutral, and necessary. Critical Realism remained not only passionate, but the most sophisticated version of cognitive relativism available in American thought.[89]

In its constructive mode, Realism subordinated political and moral passion to social science expertise.[90] In Llewellyn's famous phrase, Realism sought "[t]he *temporary* divorce of Is and Ought for purposes of study," thus postponing the question of appropriate values while concentrating on developing a rich collection of social science studies about the way society actually worked.[91] While Progressivism had initiated this distinctively modern emphasis on the legitimating role of expertise and professionalism,[92] it was this strand of Realism that pushed the behavioral social sciences in directions that ultimately dulled the critical edge of Realism itself.[93] Behavioral and value-free social science not only suppressed the moralism of early Progressive social science; it was also dependent on a completely naive view of social thought.

The social science methodology that Llewellyn sought to represent—incorrectly, I believe—as the essence of Realism has been something of an embarrassment among legal historians.[94] Virtually all agree that most of the social science research projects undertaken by Realists were either trivial attempts to prove the obvious through pseudo-scientific methodology or else naive and misconceived efforts at social science research.[95] Except perhaps as it fed into the developing administrative law theory of the regulatory state, this constructive strand of Realism was a failure even in its own terms.

But the question remains whether the turn to positivist social science was not also a political and moral failure because it not only suppressed the critical stand of Realism but also encouraged Realists to rely on a methodology that strongly tended to confer a privileged position on the status quo. To understand this point, we need to see why Llewellyn was happy to accept the "temporary divorce of Is and Ought."

The emergence of positivism within turn-of-the-century American social thought is a major development that has only recently begun to be explored. Though there is a close family relationship between legal, logical, and ethical positivism, it is only the last, emphasizing a separation between objective facts and subjective values, that I wish to focus upon here.[96] In America, as I pointed out earlier, positivism emerged amid the collapse of Darwinism and its desperate effort to maintain that evolution could combine the descriptive and the prescriptive, the Is with the Ought.[97] American intellectuals thus entered the twentieth century with a terrifying doubt about whether either religion or science could objectively justify values.[98]

Twentieth-century American social thought has thus been preoccupied with finding a method that can either determine values objectively or avoid the value question entirely. The turn to social science was part of this general effort to find alternative forms of legitimation amid the decline of religious belief and the disintegration of an orthodox Darwinian paradigm. When Holmes declared in 1897 that the man of the future would be the master of statistics and economics, he was abandoning an immanent evolutionary theory for modern social science methodology.[99] The best that one could now hope for was that law could be brought back in touch with society, not that it could continue to reflect an autonomous process of progressive moral evolution.

In the absence of any autonomous method for objectively determining values, secularly inclined social reformers turned to society to generate values. They maintained that what was wrong with Classical Legal Thought was not that it was based on bad values—for who could presume to defend the objectivity of any system of values?—but that it was simply out of touch with social reality. Social reality—the Is—became the source of the Ought. Description was privileged over prescription. Value was to be discovered from social fact. The turn to positivist social science was thus an attempt to evade the value question by substituting expertise and professionalism as the central forms of legitimation.

As early as 1934, Lon Fuller understood the political implications of the Realist turn to social science. "Why should realism," he asked, "which starts out as a reform movement, carry in its loins [an] essentially reactionary principle?"[100] The answer was that "the cleft between Is and Ought causes acute distress to the realist."[101]

> He sets about resolutely to eliminate it. There are two ways in which this may be done. The Is may be compelled to conform to the Ought, or the Ought may be permitted to acquiesce in the Is. There are enormous difficulties in the first course. Life resists our attempts to subject it to rules; the muddy flow of Being sweeps contemptuously over the barriers of our Ought. There is something even more disheartening. We find it impossible to say exactly what it is we wish life to conform to, what our Ought is. Life laughs at our rules, and even our rules betray us by refusing to reveal their nature to us. The easier course beckons temptingly, to let the Ought acquiesce in the Is, to let law surrender to life.[102]

The problem, Fuller saw, was that in attempting to have law simply mirror society, Realism ended up endowing the Is with normative content. He offered an illustration that appears, in light of Llewellyn's future involvement in drafting the Uniform Commercial Code, as nothing short of prophetic.

> If I have to choose someone to draft a statute regulating the banking business I may put a high value on a knowledge of banking practice. I may regard as the ideal man for the task the man who knows the practices of the banking world so thoroughly that he can predict with certainty the psychological reactions which the sight of a postdated check will invoke in any banking employee, from messenger boy to president. I may prefer him to a man who, though less familiar with the behavior of bank employees, has spent his life studying the history and theory of banks and banking law, and many hours in arm-chair reflection on the possible ways of organizing and controlling the banking business. I am entitled to my preference. But I am not entitled to escape responsibility for it by saying it involves no "value judgment," no philosophy of what ought to be.[103]

It has now become a familiar criticism of Llewellyn that in drafting the Uniform Commercial Code to reflect mercantile custom, he endowed economically dominant commercial practices with undeserved normativity.[104] So, for example, he chose to represent the custom of bankers, not of consumers, as representative of commercial custom.

The point is not that Llewellyn preferred bankers to consumers, but rather that inherent in the turn to society was the need to represent commercial custom as homogeneous. If one's central concern is to make law reflect society—in Fuller's language, to make the Ought acquiesce in the Is—then what does one do when the Is unfortunately offers conflicting messages because society expresses heterogeneous principles? If the motive for turning to society in the first place is to evade a paralytic choice among subjective values, then how can one choose between conflicting customs when that choice simply renews the question of value? To appreciate this dilemma is to see why the Realist turn to society carried within it a strong tendency to wish to portray the social—or commercial—world as homogeneous. Only a society without fundamental conflict could avoid a choice among values.

Here was the "reactionary principle" that Fuller insisted Realism "[carried] within its loins." Not only was there increasingly urgent pressure to make the status quo the benchmark for all criticism. The adoption of social science methodology also reproduced the same dilemma that customary law theorists like James Coolidge Carter encountered at the end of the nineteenth century. How was it possible to base law on custom when an increasingly heterogeneous society generated conflicting social customs? Like the customary law theorists, some Realists became committed to denying or suppressing any picture of sharp or irreconcilable social conflict as they renounced all efforts to assert a system of values independent of the existing structure of power. Realism thus became increasingly apologetic as it enthusiastically fit into the dominant forms of post–World War II consensus theory, also developed to evade the question of value.

EIGHT

Legal Realism,
The Bureaucratic State, and
The Rule of Law

It was a triumphant note that James M. Landis struck as he delivered the 1938 Storrs Lecture at the Yale Law School. Just a year earlier, Landis had resigned from the chairmanship of the Securities and Exchange Commission to return to Harvard Law School as the youngest dean in its history. Now Landis would articulate the New Deal's most penetrating and passionate defense of the dramatic growth in administrative regulation.

As Landis spoke, it appeared that the last barrier to New Deal regulation, the U.S. Supreme Court, had finally crumbled. Just two years earlier, the Court had compared the behavior of Landis's own Securities and Exchange Commission to "those intolerable abuses of the Star Chamber."[1] "The action of the Commission . . . is wholly unreasonable and arbitrary,"[2] wrote ("thundered," Landis said)[3] Justice George Sutherland. "It violates the cardinal precept upon which constitutional safeguards of personal liberty ultimately rest—that this shall be a government of laws. . . ."[4] Where "the mere will of an official . . . is permitted . . . to supplant the standing law as a rule of human conduct, the government ceases to be one of laws and becomes an autocracy."[5]

"Such an outburst," Landis observed, "indicates that one is in a field where calm judicial temper has fled."[6] Justice Sutherland's "invective" "was naturally seized upon by every opponent of security regulation. . . . If it is fair to apply the legal rule that one intends the natural and probable consequences of his acts, certainly the effect if not the purpose [of Sutherland's opinion] was to breed distrust of the administrative."[7]

But there was reason to hope for the future, Landis continued. "[A] world of difference in temper and in outlook separates the denunciatory fervor of Mr. Justice Sutherland . . . from the hope of the administrative process"[8] expressed in Justice Brandeis's opinion for the minority, Landis declared. "The minority is not only sympathetic with the administrative process; it hopes to encourage its capacity to dispose more effectively of the business entrusted to it."[9]

From its earliest embodiment in the Interstate Commerce Commission (1887), federal administrative regulation had met regular and persistent judicial efforts to confine its scope and limit its powers. The attack on administrative "autocracy" was often simply a stand-in for opposition to or fear of governmental regulation. The form was only incidental. But for others, the rise of the administrative state raised the most basic questions about the meaning and continuing viability of the "rule of law" in situations where unelected officials exercised enormous and unprecedented power to affect the lives and property of citizens.

Only three years before, in the midst of the Great Depression, the Supreme Court had unanimously struck down the National Industrial Recovery Act, the centerpiece of the first New Deal.[10] Yet there were now at least four justices on the Court who, Landis concluded, had already taken the pro-administrative position on "[t]he most disputed field of judicial review over administrative action today," the question of finality of administrative findings of constitutional or jurisdictional fact.[11] "In view of these divisions, the law as to what finality shall attach to administrative findings of fact is likely to reflect the minority's rather than the majority's view," Landis predicted.[12] "Because their reasoning seems more to accord with the temper of the times, it is they, rather than the majority, who are likely to gain adherents to this position."[13]

Landis left it to his audience to realize that his prophecy had already become reality. Not only had the Supreme Court appeared to have reversed its constitutional direction dramatically during the previous year, but in fact, one of the Court's conservative "four horsemen," Justice Van Devanter, had resigned, to be replaced by Hugo Black. By Landis's own count, there was now a pro-administrative majority on the Court.

Landis's lectures, entitled *The Administrative Process*, left little doubt that he believed his own views were in tune with "the temper of the times."[14] He declared:

> Despite [a] chorus of abuse and tirade, growth of the administrative process shows little sign of being halted. Instead, it still exhibits the vigor that attends lusty youth . . . its extraordinary growth in recent years, the increasing frequency with which government has come to resort to it, the extent to which it is creating new relationships between the individual, the body economic, and the state, already have given it great stature.[15]

Landis presented a more comprehensive defense of the growth of administrative agencies than any that had been offered up to that time. And since his vision began to come under attack almost as soon as it was presented, it would do well for us to pause for a moment and explore his thinking.

Landis's defense of the administrative process began with a classic synthesis of Progressive and Legal Realist attacks on the inefficiency of the judicial process and on the inability of judges trained in common law methods of thought to bring either consistency or deep social understanding to the task of regulation.

First, he catalogued fifty years of accumulated Progressive assaults on the idea that courts and judges were either institutionally, ideologically, or technically competent to promote justice or efficiency in economic regulation. The expansion of administrative agencies, he wrote, "sprang from a distrust of the ability of the judicial process to make the necessary adjustments in the development of both law and regulatory methods as they related to particular industrial problems." [16]

The institutional limitations of courts meant that judges were "jacks-of-all-trades and masters of none." [17] Regulation required not only "specialization" but "a method that calls upon other sciences to provide the norms." [18] Understanding business problems, for example, required knowledge of "incredible areas of fact" as well as "wisdom in the ways of industrial operations," none of which judges possessed. [19]

In regulatory fields such as unfair competition, monopoly, and labor, "there was widespread distrust of the courts' ability to evolve workable concepts to direct the economic forces which had posed these problems." [20] This distrust arose from a "belief that the men who composed our judiciary too often held economic and social opinions opposed to the ideals of their time. The distrust was not without foundation." [21]

Moreover, the common law system of case-by-case adjudication provided a too "slow and costly method of making law." [22] It left enforcement of regulations to inconsistent private initiative, based on the view that government was in "the position of an umpire deciding the merits upon the basis of the record as established by the parties." [23] But "the umpire theory of administrative law is almost certain to fail" where "the absence of equal economic power generally is so prevalent." [24] By contrast, since administrative regulation does entail "the power to initiate action," [25] it "permits the development of consistency" in the approach to complex regulatory problems. [26]

But beyond emphasizing the limited institutional ability of courts to apply consistent policy across a complicated, interdependent economy, Landis reiterated the Legal Realist attack on the formalism and conceptualism that orthodox judges had brought to their task.

> [T]here are certain fields where the making of law springs less from generalizations and principles drawn from the majestic authority of textbooks and cases, than from a "practical" judgment which is based upon all the available considerations and which has in mind the most desirable and pragmatic method of solving that particular problem. [27]

Progressive legal thinkers, Landis observed, had frequently pointed out that solutions to industrial problems "were determined much less by accepted 'legal principles' than by given political, economic and social considerations. . . . [T]hese juristic writers thereupon crossed the Rubicon of legal tradition to declare openly that judges made rather than discovered the law." [28] They had, in the process, sought to make social engineering through law legitimate.

But what gave unelected administrators legitimacy to engage in regulatory tasks? Expertise, Landis confidently declared. "With the rise of regulation, the need for expertness became dominant; for the art of regulating an industry requires knowledge of the details of its operation. . . ." Because of "the advantages of specialization," [29] "[e]fficiency in the processes of government regulation is best served by the creation of more rather than less [sic] agencies." [30]

Landis's *The Administrative Process* is a joyous celebration of the virtues of "expertness" in justifying the growth of the administrative state. This turn to expertise also represented an historic shift away from the delegation theory of administrative law that had legitimated the exercise of bureaucratic power during the previous fifty years.

The Delegation Theory

When the first institutionalization of the regulatory state, the Interstate Commerce Commission, was established in 1887, separation of powers theory created the framework for conceptualizing administrative action. Administrative officials were classified as part of the executive, whose function was to carry out the commands of the legislature. Under this view, the legislature would decide all questions of policy and establish clear standards and goals. The essential task of bureaucratic officials was to find the most efficient means to implement clear, legislatively elaborated ends. The courts' role was to police this relationship by limiting administrative authority to clear delegations of power from the legislature. [31]

The delegation theory reflected the dominance of the German bureaucratic ideal in the late nineteenth century and its twin assumptions that (1) general rules can effectively constrain bureaucratic action and (2) the relationship between bureaucratic means and legislatively established ends was essentially a technical or scientific question. [32] Landis was calling these assumptions into question.

The delegation theory had already been drawn into question by Legal Realists as part of their critique of orthodox legal reasoning. If general propositions did not decide concrete cases in the common law context, was there any greater reason to suppose that general statutory language could provide determinate limitations on administrative discretion?

The Interstate Commerce Act, with its lengthy and detailed grant of authority, had already exemplified the delegation theory's vision of the legislature as the jealous guardian of governmental power. Yet the subsequent experience of railroad regulation cast severe doubt on the ability of general rules or standards to provide serious guidance for the detailed and complex tasks involved in administrative regulation. Therefore, by the time the Federal Trade Commission was established in 1914, the agency received essentially a blank check authorizing it to eliminate unfair competition.

In his lectures, Landis contrasted the Interstate Commerce Act, whose detailed provisions gave it the appearance not of "a constituent document" but of "a regulative code," with the Securities Exchange Act of 1933, which vested "broad rule-making powers" in the Commission.[33] "Such [broad] delegation of power means, of course, that the operative rules will be found *outside* the statute book," Landis provocatively concluded.[34]

An important part of *The Administrative Process* was devoted to attacking the delegation theory. Landis derisively referred to the "political conceptualism"[35] that underlay every attempt to fit administrative agencies into traditional separation-of-powers thinking. Legislative efforts to create "Procrustean standards" that would limit administrative discretion were the unfortunate result.[36] He deplored a "legalistic approach that reads a governing statute with the hope of finding limitations upon authority" instead of "grants of power with which to act decisively."[37] Landis declared aggressively:

> One of the ablest administrators that it was my good fortune to know, I believe, never read at least more than casually, the statutes that he translated into reality. He assumed that they gave him power to deal with the broad problems of an industry, and upon that understanding he sought his own solutions.[38]

The "modern tendency" to reject sharp limits on legislative delegation was conducive to "flexibility—a prime quality of good administration."[39] However, while flexibility was a virtue in the hands of the administration portrayed by expertise theory, it also raised the specter of administrative arbitrariness and left the regulatory state open to consistent attack.

Pound's About-Face

Hardly had Landis completed his celebration of the growth of administrative power than he encountered a surprising but formidable adversary in Roscoe Pound, his predecessor as dean of Harvard Law School.

No other American could match Pound's international reputation as a legal scholar. His most original contributions, written primarily before the First World War, had had an enormous influence in shaping the Progressive ideal of social reform through law. Many of Pound's most important early writings were sympathetic to the growth of administrative regulation.

Pound's famous and controversial 1906 address to the American Bar Association on "The Causes of Popular Dissatisfaction with the Administration of Justice" attacked the adversary system for creating a "sporting theory of justice" and stated that many legal disputes could be more efficiently shifted from courts to administrative tribunals.[40]

Pound's earliest writings sought to move American jurisprudence away from an overly rule-bound and rigid attitude toward law that he had denounced as "mechanical jurisprudence."[41] His cyclical theories of legal history were developed to explain the process by which legal consciousness became too formalistic and rigid, as well as to show that "discretion" and freedom from rules had legitimate social and historical functions. There was always a conflict between "two antagonistic ideas, the technical and the discretionary," Pound had written. "From time to time . . . reversion to justice without law became necessary in order to bring the administration of justice into touch with new moral ideas or changed social or political conditions."

The advantages of administrative justice, Pound wrote in 1914, "are those which are claimed for justice without law: directness, expedition, conformity to the popular will for the time being, freedom from the bounds of purely traditional rules, freedom from technical rules of evidence and power to act upon the everyday instincts of ordinary men." Yet, significantly, he was careful to warn that although useful to revitalize a rigid, "law-ridden" system, "justice without law can be no more than a temporary expedient" in the modern state. [42]

Even as late as 1924, in an address entitled "The Growth of Administrative Justice," [43] Pound spoke enthusiastically of the rise of administration. He saw the rise of the administrative state not as "alarming phenomena, indicating a decay in our spirit of liberty" but as the "natural results of the evolution that we have been going through . . . economically and socially; an evolution that has changed us . . . from a predominantly rural agricultural society to a predominantly industrial society." [44]

Troubled by late-nineteenth-century conceptualism, Pound welcomed the fact-focused nature of the administrative process. He saw the rise of administration as part of a shift from nineteenth-century ideas of "abstract justice" to twentieth-century demands for "concrete justice." [45] "The last century thought of all legal precepts in terms of rules or principles or conceptions," Pound declared. [46] "Abstract justice of abstract rules as applied to abstract men was our whole concern. . . . [O]ur individualism of the last century was a theoretical individualism only." [47] The law concerned itself only with a "standard individual," "a theoretical individual up there in a vacuum." [48]

The rise of administration was "simply a part of that general movement in all human activities, to deal with the individual; not the abstract individual but the concrete human being in a society of human beings like himself." [49] Administrative law represented a groping "for methods of dealing with the actual case and not with a theoretical, standard, typical case." [50] Answering the desire "to deal with a special case, specially and peculiarly," the growth of administrative law thus challenged "our former methods of broad generalization." [51]

"The congestion of legislation and the lawlessness of administration are the text of pretty nearly every presidential address before bar associations today," Pound wryly observed. [52] However, the problem did not arise because of "materialism or paternalism, or a decay of the ancient faith, or a loss of fiber in the American public, or anything of that sort. It is simply this: . . . Our pioneer versatility does not suffice in the complex, intricate, economic industrial organization of today." [53]

We can see that Pound's attitude in 1924 toward the growth of administra-

tive law ("Let us think . . . in terms of 'can,' not of 'can't.' ")[54] still very much
expressed the optimistic and experimental mindset characteristic of his great pre-
war writing. Administration reflected the "natural . . . evolution" away from
nineteenth-century formalism and conceptualism.[55] Administrative regulation was
not bureaucratic or standardized justice but a superior form of justice in the individual case. What a far cry from Pound's later invocation of the judicial model
as the only legitimate expression of the rule of law!

Pound's 1924 address was part of a deeper, more long-standing conflict over
the meaning of the rule of law ideal. Progressive reformers, including Pound, had
for some time been challenging the nineteenth-century view that general and
abstract rules could produce the kind of certainty and predictability traditionally
identified with the rule of law. Pound was among the earliest thinkers to observe
that the broad generalizations that characterized nineteenth-century legal consciousness presupposed a homogeneous society with standardized transactions and
human interactions that could be generalized and abstracted into rules. The complexity of industrial society, however, undermined this traditional identification of
generality with predictability. Judicial regulation was notoriously slow and unpredictable, Pound insisted.

> Especially in the complicated economic organization of today the law cannot say
> to the business man, well, you guess; you employ a lawyer by the year to give you
> the best guess that he can, and then as the result of litigation we will tell you five
> years afterwards whether your guess as to the conduct of your business was the
> correct one or not.[56]

The solution was to create new forms of law that would disaggregate, sub-
categorize, particularize, and individualize rules and disputes.

> We are in a busy, crowded world, and when we do anything today we must spe-
> cialize. . . . We cannot waste our time and substance on the mere incidents of
> our life. . . . We try to tell men in advance what they may do and what they may
> not, as far as possible; and our administrative commissions are nothing but traffic
> officers, as it were, with signals to tell us when to cross and when not to cross, and
> where to cross.[57]

By 1938, however, Pound had made an abrupt about-face on the uses of
administrative justice. As Landis was appealing to "flexibility" and "the temper of
the times" in his defense of administrative growth,[58] Pound, who had singlehand-
edly proclaimed "social engineering" and "sociological jurisprudence" as the twin
goals of earlier Progressive reform, was devoting himself to denouncing the dangers flowing from "administrative absolutism."[59] "The reader of Pound's earlier
writings," Judge Jerome Frank observed, "rubs his eyes" upon encountering Pound's
recent denunciations and asks: "Can this be the same man?"[60]

In a report issued while he was chairman of the American Bar Association's
Special Committee on Administrative Law, Pound lent his enormous prestige to
an unmitigated denunciation of New Deal administrative practices. The "Pound
Committee Report," published in 1938, issued a call to arms to an establishment

bar, many of whose once powerful clients, demoralized by the Great Depression, had silently endured five years of New Deal social engineering. Now it was time to act. Unless "the bar takes upon itself to act, there is nothing to check the tendency of administrative bureaus to extend the scope of their operations indefinitely even to the extent of supplanting our traditional judicial regime by an administrative regime," Pound wrote.[61]

Pound warned of "the idea of administrative absolutism," which took the form of "a highly centralized administration set up under complete control of the executive . . . , relieved of judicial review and making its own rules."[62] "Those who would turn the administration of justice over to administrative absolutism," Pound declared, treated rule of law ideals as "illusory." "They expect law in this sense to disappear."[63] Referring to Felix Cohen's daring Legal Realist article, "Transcendental Nonsense and the Functional Approach,"[64] he announced: "This is a Marxian idea."[65] As if to leave no doubt about this charge, Pound noted that "the jurists of Soviet Russia" favored the end of law.[66]

Amid this overheated rhetoric, Pound also took on Landis's contrast between "the overheated atmosphere of litigation" and "the calm of scientific inquiry"[67] prevailing in administrative agencies. "Who indeed shall say that an inquiry before the National Labor Relations Board is not heated?" Pound asked.[68] "The postulate of a scientific body of experts pursuing objective scientific inquiries is as far as possible from what the facts are or are likely to be. . . ."[69]

How had Pound changed? The emphasis in his early writing on the excitement of social experiment and the need for legal flexibility had been replaced by a fear of social change. In 1905 Pound could ask how jurists might "lead our law to hold a more even balance between individualism and socialism."[70] In 1914 he maintained that while some people "went to one extreme and were bureauridden, we went to the opposite extreme and were law-ridden."[71] Throughout the 1930s, however, as the Great Depression contributed to the prostration of constitutional regimes and the rise of totalitarian dictatorships, Pound increasingly put his political faith in a traditional court-centered rule of law ideal. All of "his common law prejudices," his biographer wrote, were directed "against the administrative process."[72] An earlier complex understanding of the limits of formalism was replaced by simplistic pieties about the rule of law.

Pound's positions on administrative law contained a good deal of "careless and emotional"[73] posturing, his biographer noted. "Pound became increasingly vituperative, and the fantastic accusations that he hurled so effortlessly demonstrated his loss of proportion."[74] He degenerated into deploying "a rhetoric of mudslinging."[75]

Pound and Landis: Two Traditions Collide

The dramatic fluctuations in Pound's views symbolized the deep sense of ambivalence that the rise of the administrative state had produced. The tremendous growth in administration posed the dilemma of how to create a regulatory state without allowing it to become arbitrary and oppressive. This dilemma spawned theories of justification or restraint that drew on very different traditions of thought about administrative law. In the debate between Pound and Landis, two traditions, which I will call the "legalist" and "scientific" approaches, collided.

Pound drew upon a long-standing legalist suspicion of the rise of the administrative state that goes back to the enormously influential pronouncements of the English jurist A.V. Dicey on the intimate relationship between collectivism and administration. For Dicey, administrative law, perceived as a hotbed of discretion and coercion, posed a major threat to the rule of law ideal. With that insular arrogance that long characterized the common law tradition, the legalists were quick to dismiss the non-judicial focus that characterized the development of Continental administrative law as nothing less than a betrayal of the rule of law itself.

Landis, by contrast, drew on a well-developed Progressive belief that courts were ideologically and administratively incapable of handling the regulatory problems of a complex, interdependent industrial society. He offered instead a "scientific" alternative to judicial decision making. Though this anti-judicial perspective began to surface with the passage of the Interstate Commerce Act, the Commission established by the act was still justified primarily as a substitute for unwieldy legislative power to set rates, not as an attack on judicial competence. The critical view of courts as unfair and inefficient forums clearly took root after 1910 with the successful campaign to take worker injury cases out of common law courts, an effort closely linked to severe criticism of the insensitivity and incompetence of common law judges. Indeed, Theodore Roosevelt's 1912 campaign proposal for recall of judges was offered in reaction to judicial hostility towards workers' compensation statutes.[76]

The conflict between the legalist and scientific approaches needs first to be put in the context of American attitudes toward regulation, as well as ideals of the rule of law. We are accustomed to recognizing the enormous influence that law and lawyers have exercised in American society. Indeed, we are taught to appreciate the unusual power that courts have exercised in the American system of constitutional government. We are less likely, however, to see the disproportionately greater role that American courts have played historically compared to that of other institutions of government, especially the administrative ones. For more than a century after the American Revolution, ideals about the meaning of the rule of law were developed within an entirely judge- and court-centered system of thought.

The victory over the codification movement (1820–1848, 1870–1890) symbolizes the success of nineteenth-century legal orthodoxy in legitimating the role of common law judges in a democratic society. It created for judges and lawyers an autonomous system of legitimation as powerful as those of its traditional rivals—democracy, religion, science, and the market. It not only treated legislative initiatives with great suspicion ("statutes in derogation of the common law are to be strictly construed") but it reacted to the development of administrative regulation with a hostility reserved for an alien intruder.

Compared to European governmental structures, the American system was anomalous. As Stephen Skowronek has shown, most nineteenth-century European political theorists were struck with "the sense of statelessness" when viewing early-nineteenth-century American government. For Hegel, America could not be considered to be a "Real state" because "it had not developed the national governmental forms and orientations that distinguished the state realm in Europe." Among the most startling omissions was the absence of an "insulated bureaucratic class to give a distinct character to national administration."[77] "The combination of extremes—a highly developed democratic politics without a concentrated governing capacity—made early America the great anomaly among Western states."[78]

A system of "courts and parties" provided the basic institutional structure of governance. Courts "filled a governmental vacuum" left by the discrediting of active state intervention in the building of canals in the 1820s.[79] By the end of the nineteenth century, "the courts had become the American surrogate for a more fully developed administrative apparatus."[80] "Providing the national institutional capacities commensurate with the demands of an industrial society"[81] created pressure by the turn of the century for "a new governmental framework" that included national administrative power.

If the central problem of legal legitimacy in nineteenth-century America focused on the power and authority of judges, in the twentieth century the issue of legitimacy has centered on the authority of administrators and bureaucrats.[82] As new administrative agencies were created, they were not treated as coordinate or parallel governmental entities but instead were pressed to conform to court-centered conceptions of legitimacy. The rise of administrative regulation thus represented a renewed threat to common law conceptions of legality, which had already resisted the earlier challenge of codification. It also revived older fears of redistribution, statism, and centralization that had previously been directed at legislative action.

Courts not only brought these fears to their decisions regarding administrative action; they also sought to insist upon judicial ideals of justice in the individual case even for systems of economic regulation devised to provide only rough justice over a vastly expanded number of cases. Much of the struggle over administrative justice during the past century has derived from this challenge posed by the rise of administration to nineteenth-century conceptions of individually oriented justice.[83]

The Scientific Tradition

The passage of the Interstate Commerce Act marks the formal beginning of the struggle for primacy between courts and administrators. In response to the challenge of rate regulation, judges created strict doctrines about delegation of power in order to place substantial procedural and substantive limits on exercises of administrative discretion. These limits included judicial supervision of the substantive reasonableness of rates in order to prevent confiscation under the guise of regulation. Despite these restrictions, the scope of federal administrative regulation increased geometrically, first between 1887 and the Federal Trade Commission Act of 1914, and once again by the time of the New Deal. Administrative regulation increased massively at the state level as well, from the passage of the Granger laws to the rise of enormous state insurance, banking, and utility regulation and the establishment of workers' compensation systems.[84]

As a result of this expansion, it became impossible to use general legislative enactments as the basis of detailed control over the exercise of administrative power. Indeed, the last time the U.S. Supreme Court used delegation theory to hold a grant of legislative power unconstitutional was in 1935, when in *Schecter Poultry* it held the delegation in the National Industrial Recovery Act unconstitutional.[85] The delegation doctrine soon came to be regarded as too crude and formalistic to serve the function of limiting administrative discretion. It depended on a theory of language and legal reasoning that supposed that general propositions could actually decide concrete cases.

Progressives sought to discredit the delegation theory by claiming both the failure of general rules to limit administrative powers and the institutional incapacity of legislatures to create detailed and constantly changing regulations. While general rules could not effectively limit administrative discretion, Progressives asserted, the need for a multiplicity of specific rules to cover the full range of regulatory activity far exceeded any legislature's capacity in terms of time, knowledge, and attention.

By the time Landis wrote *The Administrative Process*, almost a half century of experience had cast doubt on the legalist premise that general rules could substantially limit administrative decisions. Rate making, for example, was widely conceded to be dependent on too many variables to be effectively limited by general criteria. One of the most frequently cited examples of the failure of rules to constrain discretion was the accumulating experience under the law of negligence. Instead of becoming more rule-bound, as Holmes had hoped, the law of negligence had succumbed to the reality that a multiplicity of factors ordinarily combined to produce accidents in a highly complex society. Indeed, the Legal Realists had argued that it had become virtually impossible to use general rules to limit jury discretion in negligence cases. In fact, one of the arguments for shifting worker injury cases to administrative adjudication derived from growing doubts about the efficacy of general rules.

John Dickinson saw in 1927 that the failure of courts to limit jury discretion in negligence cases lay in the overly general structure of rules. "How far legal rules are capable of development to govern such adjudications is . . . dependent . . . on the possibility of isolating facts pertinent to all the cases which may form the basis for a rule," Dickinson wrote.[86]

> The real reason for the special difficulty of developing legal rules in the field of economic regulation . . . is that the situations which form the subject matter of such regulation are generally so complex and unique that the factors which are determining in one case seldom repeat themselves in others.[87]

Legalists from Dicey to Pound have been reluctant to confront this difficulty that traditional rule of law ideas were dependent on a conception of legal generality that could flourish only in relatively simple and homogeneous societies.

The collapse of the delegation theory after *Schechter Poultry* in 1935 occurred because of a conjunction between Legal Realist theoretical attacks on the claims of legal reasoning to move from the general to the particular with an accumulation of experience that demonstrated the difficulty of constraining administrators effectively through general rules. For many, the highly general language of the Federal Trade Commission Act of 1914 represented the first moment of recognition. For most, the broad legislative delegations to New Deal regulatory agencies settled the issue.

The delegation theory was thus among the most important casualties of the Legal Realist assault on formalism and conceptualism. But its demise raised questions about the rule of law in an administrative state in which legislative rules could no longer serve as a serious check on the exercise of administrative authority. It was in this context that the Progressives developed the scientific or expertise justification of administrative power as an alternative to traditional ideas of legality.[88]

As early as 1905, one Progressive thinker, Frank Goodnow, drew on Continental ideas to create a non-court-centered theory of administrative law. At its core was the assertion of a sharp distinction between "Politics and Administration." The first constituted "the expression," the second "the execution" of "the state will."[89] If politics consisted of choices among social ends, administrative activity was "scientific" or "technical." "[T]he discharge of its functions . . . should be uninfluenced by political considerations, else the work will be done inefficiently or partially, and it may be corruptly. The more politics gets into [administration], the less effective and less impartial will the work . . . be. . . ."[90]

Goodnow thus sought to articulate the Progressives' increasing admiration of the professional expert whose skill, neutrality, and impartiality formed an alternative to both the demagoguery and corruption of American democratic politics and the unmitigated self-interest of marketplace ethics. He drew inspiration from the efforts begun in 1883 to reverse the Jacksonian hostility to a professional civil service, as well as from the Progressive campaign to cure the endemic corruption of American municipal politics through the appointment of professional city managers.[91]

Goodnow's admiration for the neutral expert reflected important social trends of the era. A five-fold increase in the professional middle class between 1870 and 1910[92] was accompanied by efforts to identify and elaborate internal professional norms based on skill and craft. In his famous lectures on professional ethics in 1898–1900, the French sociologist Emile Durkheim found in the rise of professionalism the potential for re-creating new, "organic" guild norms that, on the one hand, would substitute for declining religious constraints and, on the other, would serve as an alternative to the reign of unrestrained self-interest in the market.[93] By the time Durkheim made these observations, the turn to neutral professionalism was already underway in the United States.

The growth of professional education at Harvard and Johns Hopkins after 1870, together with the emergence of professional social science by 1900, produced a corps of experts on a scale unknown just a generation earlier. Scholars at the forefront of emergent disciplines sought to wrap themselves in the additional mantle of scientific expertise. The prestige of the natural sciences was apparent both to Langdell, who sought to model a science of law on the physical sciences,[94] and to the founders of positivist social sciences such as economics, sociology, and behavioral psychology.[95]

As the Progressive disenchantment with the competence of courts to perform social engineering tasks combined with a loss of faith in the sensitivity of judges to questions of social justice, the effort to replace courts with administrative experts became more pronounced. Increasingly, those concerned with social engineering came to regard the rule of law as an archaic set of ideas that exalted private rights over the public interest and procedural red tape over substantive policy. By the time Landis and Pound split over New Deal administrative regulation, the two positions had become sharply defined. The legalist position embodied in the delegation theory was treated by its opponents as merely a cover for reactionary positions on social policy; the anti-legalist scientific position, based upon several varieties of expertise theory, was viewed by its opponents as an effort to eliminate all legal restraints standing in the way of statism and collectivism.

The Legalist Tradition

In striking contrast to Landis's views, Pound drew on a powerful tradition of hostility to administrative law that, a half century earlier, had suddenly acquired the status of sacred dogma through the writings of A. V. Dicey, the Vinerian Professor of Law at Oxford. Dicey's *Law of the Constitution*[96] (1885) became instantly famous not only for coining the phrase "the rule of law," but also for positing an irreconcilable conflict between the traditional ideal of the rule of law and the emergence of a modern system of administrative regulation.

Dicey had drawn a sharp distinction between the French system of *droit administratif* and the English system of judicial determination of the power of administrators through decisions concerning the "regular law."[97] In France, he wrote, "the relations of the government and its officials towards private citizens are regulated by a whole body of special rules . . . which differ from the laws which govern the relations of one private person towards another."[98] The French administrative tribunals were composed of "persons who, if not actually part of the executive, are swayed by official sympathies, and who are inclined to consider the interest of the state or of the government more important than strict regard to the legal rights of individuals."[99] By contrast, the English rule of law required "the predominance of regular law as opposed to the influence of arbitrary power" and "exclud[ed] the idea of any exemptions of officials or others from the duty of obedience to the law which governs other citizens or from the jurisdiction of the ordinary tribunals."[100]

That Dicey evidenced "a thorough misinterpretation of French law" has been demonstrated many times. "[M]odern constitutional scholars," his biographer concludes, "have shown striking unanimity in their condemnation of Dicey."[101] Nevertheless, his influence "long threw a chilly shadow over administrative law"[102] and for the next fifty years managed to persuade Anglo-American lawyers that administrative law was simply "a misfortune inflicted upon the benighted folk across the Channel."[103]

Law of the Constitution went through eight editions over the next thirty years, and Dicey's conception of the rule of law acquired a permanent place in all subsequent discussions of the growth of the administrative state. While his political and economic views were muted in the original formulations, they eventually became more explicit, as he increasingly linked the growth of administration with the decline of individualism and with the corresponding rise of collectivism and socialism.

Dicey combined the laissez-faire hostility of nineteenth-century Manchester Liberals toward the emergent English welfare state with the nineteenth-century English Whigs' identification of common law courts as the foundation of constitutional government. He brought to the rise of administration all of the conservative common lawyer's antipathy to public law as coercive, political, and redistributive. His great ideological—and intellectual—achievement was in successfully asserting the existence of a conflict between the rule of law and the rise of administrative regulation. He succeeded not only in identifying all forms of regulation with socialism but also in representing the administrative state as a continuing enemy of legality.

In *Law and Public Opinion* (1905)[104] Dicey associated his anxieties for the rule of law with his fear and loathing of the rise of collectivism. Delivered first as lectures at Harvard Law School in 1898, his attack on the English factory laws as harbingers of socialism was greeted by orthodox American legal opinion as a strong authority for the emerging *Lochner* era in the U.S. Supreme Court. For an American legal establishment in the midst of the *Lochner* era, Dicey's praise for a lost age of laissez-faire individualism was warmly received in the only Western society where that doctrine continued to dominate public philosophy.[105]

By 1914, as Dicey's "fears of socialism" became "more intense," his introduction to *Law and Public Opinion* degenerated, his biographer observed, into "a political diatribe that had not the slightest veneer of objectivity or scholarship."[106] "I have lived on into a generation which is not my own," Dicey confided in a letter. "[M]y last words are the voice of 1886 heard in 1913."[107]

Rooted in his laissez-faire vision, Dicey's conception of the rule of law was simply irreconcilable with the emerging welfare-regulatory state. It created, in the minds of both proponents and opponents of the regulatory state, the conviction that rule of law ideals could be nurtured only in a political culture whose values were fast coming to be regarded as unacceptable. For more than a half century after Dicey first wrote, then, the rule of law ideal came to be increasingly regarded as inseparable from reactionary political and social views.

Condemnation of administrative power did, however, come from influential voices less extreme than Dicey. The Chief Justice of England, Lord Hewart, also wrote deploringly about the growth of administration in *The New Despotism* (1929). "Parliamentary institutions and the rule of law have been tried and found wanting, and . . . the time has come for the departmental despot, who shall be at once scientific and benevolent, but above all a law to himself. . . ."[108]

Hewart treated Dicey's analysis with some ambivalence. On the one hand, he followed Dicey in seeing "the sharpest possible contrast."[109] between administrative law and the rule of law. He agreed that it makes "all the difference"[110] that under the English Constitution there are not separate courts, one for actions against officials, another for ordinary litigation between citizens. And like Dicey, he deplored the rise of the executive, extending his analysis to the recent growth of cabinet government, which had eroded parliamentary supremacy. On the other hand, Hewart departed from Dicey's most extreme pronouncements and conceded that, "rightly understood, [the French] 'droit administratif' is a definite system of law, the rules and principles of which . . . [constitute] true 'administrative law,' administered by a tribunal which applies judicial methods of procedure."[111] In contrast to France, the emerging "despotism" in England actually presented the greater danger of "administrative lawlessness"[112] in that it did not involve even this "application of known rules and principles, and a regular course of procedure."[113] Instead, it represented an "indescribably more objectionable method" than French administrative law in its delegation to bureaucrats of unreviewable power to make law.[114]

Hewart embraced Dicey's stringent common law view that the supremacy of law "means something more than the exclusion of arbitrary power, and something more also than the equality of all citizens before the ordinary law of the land administered by the ordinary Courts." It means, wrote Hewart, "that in this country, unlike some foreign countries, the principles of the Constitution are, in Dicey's phrase, inductions or generalisations based upon decisions pronounced by the Courts as to the rights of particular individuals."[115] Beyond his plea for judicial review of administrative action, then, Hewart also reiterated Dicey's insistence upon treating determinations of the validity of administrative regulation as no different from any other individualized common law determination of rights. Above all, he continued to insist that administrative law should be derived from private law.

In his 1938 attack on "administrative absolutism,"[116] Pound invoked the full weight and rhetorical fervor of Dicey and Hewart. If Hewart sought to restore parliamentary supremacy by entrenching in England the principle of judicial review of administrative action, that principle had already been established in America. Pound's main debt to Hewart was therefore to borrow the latter's call for "judicial procedures" in administrative determinations "to achieve a workable balance between the judicial and the administrative processes which will be effective for the ends of the legal order."[117] Thus, Pound sought the additional bulwark of traditional common law process in administrative justice.

Attacks on the administrative state came also from the Continent. Outside of the common law countries, the writings of Dicey and Hewart were limited as general theory because of their Anglo-Saxon parochialism. Their identification of the rule of law with regular case-by-case determinations of common law courts was not likely to be of paramount interest to Continental legal theorists, who identified the rule of law with European codes promulgated by parliaments. On the Continent, instead, nineteenth-century liberalism had embraced the ideals of generality and predictability of rules as the essence of a government of laws. Indeed, European liberals regularly questioned whether the common law system was itself compatible with the rule of law. It was one of those liberals, Friedrich von Hayek, who delivered one of the most formidable attacks on the growth of the administrative state.

Hayek showed how intimately connected were the laissez-faire political and economic ideals of nineteenth-century liberalism and its commitment to the rule of law. In *The Road to Serfdom* (1944), he delivered a scathing attack on the rise of socialism as incompatible with legality and as not fundamentally different from the worldwide threat of totalitarianism.

Dedicated to "The Socialists of All Parties," *The Road to Serfdom* is the *cri du coeur* of a nineteenth-century Viennese liberal against the worldwide drift toward dictatorship and totalitarianism.

> It is necessary now to state the unpalatable truth that it is Germany whose fate we are in some danger of repeating. . . . [S]tudents of the currents of ideas can hardly fail to see that there is more than a superficial similarity between the trend of thought in Germany during and after the last war and the present current of ideas in the democracies. . . . [I]n Germany it was largely people of good will, men who were admired and held up as models in the democratic countries, who prepared the way for, if they did not actually create, the forces which now stand for everything they detest. . . . [T]he rise of fascism and nazism was not a reaction against the socialist trends of the preceding period but a necessary outcome of those tendencies.[118]

The problem with socialism, Hayek wrote, was that to achieve legitimate ends it needed to use dubious means through "which the entrepreneur working for profit is replaced by a central planning body."[119]

But centralized socialism was not Hayek's only target. Even "some middle way between" "the extreme decentralization of free competition" and "the complete centralization of a single plan" "means that neither will really work and that the result will be worse than if either system had been consistently relied upon."[120]

Centralized planning and competition were fundamentally incompatible forms of social organization.

For Americans debating the merits of the growth of administration, the most influential part of Hayek's book was his chapter on "Planning and the Rule of Law." [121] First, he dismissed Dicey's work, suggesting that Dicey's focus on the indispensability of common law courts was irrelevant for Continental jurists, for whom "[t]he wider and older meaning of the [rule of law] concept" was associated with the early nineteenth-century German *Rechtsstaat*. [122]

"Stripped of all technicalities," Hayek wrote, the rule of law "means that government in all its actions is bound by rules fixed and announced beforehand—rules which make it possible to foresee with fair certainty how the authority will use its coercive powers in given circumstances, and to plan one's individual affairs on the basis of this knowledge." [123] Generality of rules barred "*ad hoc* action." [124] Rules "could almost be described as a kind of instrument of production, helping people to predict the behaviour of those with whom they must collaborate, rather than as efforts toward the satisfaction of particular needs." [125]

Economic planning, by contrast, "cannot tie itself down in advance to general and formal rules which prevent arbitrariness. It must provide for the actual needs of people as they arise and then choose deliberately between them." [126] Decisions in concrete cases therefore had to be left "more and more to the discretion of the judge or authority in question." [127] The result is

> that formal equality before the law is in conflict, and in fact incompatible, with any activity of the government deliberately aiming at material or substantive equality of different people, and that any policy aiming directly at a substantive ideal of distributive justice must lead to the destruction of the Rule of Law. [128]

This distinction between "formal law or justice and substantive rules" was, for Hayek, "the same as that between laying down a Rule of the Road, as in the Highway Code, and ordering people where to go; or, better still, between providing signposts and commanding people which road to take." [129]

Hayek was correct, I believe, in seeing the intimate connection between formal and general rules and the rule of law tradition. Whether he successfully established a similar connection between planning, on the one hand, and particularity and individualization, on the other, is a more difficult question. In England and America, administrative regulation was often justified as importing generality into what otherwise would have been a particularized, case-by-case adjudication of common law courts.

The core of Hayek's analysis focused on a fundamental conflict between a regime of formal and impersonal rules and one that sought to achieve substantive ends. He therefore did not limit his critique to administrative discretion. He equally deplored long-standing judicial tendencies to move from strict rules to vague standards—"to qualify legal provisions increasingly by reference to what is 'fair' or 'reasonable.'" [130] It was thus not only the growth of administrative regimes dedicated to economic planning or social welfare to which Hayek objected. More fundamentally, he challenged the pervasive attack on formalism that was part of the movement for social reform not only in the United States but also in pre-Nazi Germany.[131]

Hayek put forward the most cogent statement of the classical rule of law ideal. He showed how powerfully that ideal was connected, first, to the classical liberal laissez-faire tradition and, second, to a conception of an autonomous realm of law and legal reasoning. Impersonal general rules applied neutrally and apolitically by independent judges would assure citizens certain and predictable consequences wherever they acted. Law was to perform the neutral umpire role that classical liberalism had assigned to the night-watchman state. In Hayek's view, any activist, interventionist state was incompatible with the rule of law ideal.

Emerging from a very different intellectual, political, and social milieu than that of the Legal Realists, Hayek's critique ignored the insights of the Realist attack on formalism. Hayek sought to draw on a rule of law tradition that identified predictability with generality. The Legal Realist critique had shown, however, that considerable political discretion entered into the application of highly general formal rules to concrete cases. Hayek's views failed to take account of dramatic changes in theories of language and legal reasoning that cast doubt on the determinacy of formal and general rules. If one accepted the Legal Realist internal critique of formalism, Hayek's vision was no longer viable.

Moreover, the Legal Realists had claimed that while formal and general rules may have produced relatively little injustice in an earlier homogeneous society, the problems of over- and under-inclusiveness of rules grew more severe as society became more heterogeneous and variegated. Hayek insisted that the rule of law required ignoring "particular needs of different people"[132] at the very moment that these differences were growing more striking. One was reminded of Anatole France's remark that the rule of law equally prohibited the rich and the poor from sleeping under bridges.

Indeed, if Legal Realism was essentially correct, the real problem now became one of creating a certain and predictable legal regime after the demise of a nineteenth-century formalist world view. In a post-formalist era, particular and concrete rules, sub-categorized to deal with a variety of highly differentiated economic and social problems, may have offered the best hope of legal predictability. Yet it was the legalist approach, extolling general rules, that would soon prevail in the legislature.

The Renewed Struggle Over the Regulatory State

The legalists' attack on the regulatory-welfare state, begun by Pound and the American Bar Association in 1938, finally bore fruit with the passage of the Administrative Procedure Act (APA) of 1946.[133] Because it was passed without any discernible opposition in Congress, in "unquestioning—we might even say uncritical—unanimity," as Justice Frankfurter put it,[134] the act has often been mis-read as simply codifying a consensus on administrative law and therefore as a continuation of pre–World War II administrative theory. In fact, as I hope to show, the APA is one of many expressions of a post-war resurgence of a legalist mentality, in this case riding the wave of renewed political opposition to the New Deal regulatory-welfare state. The act represented the triumph not of all the spe-cific proposals in the "Pound Report" of 1938 but of its legalist mindset, which New Dealers had been vigorously resisting in one official report after another ever since Pound first launched his attack.

From the time of the "Pound Report" until the passage of the APA six years later, disputes over questions of administrative law became thoroughly intertwined with raging political struggles over the legitimacy of the regulatory state. When Congress enacted the APA, the terms of the struggle had already been transformed, and a truce had been finally negotiated.

Fashioned amid a surge of conservative post-war hostility to the New Deal as well as bewilderment over the horrors inflicted by totalitarian regimes, the terms of the truce were extremely favorable to the critics of administrative regulation. Even if many of their specific proposals were ignored, the triumph of their legalist mindset successfully reversed the New Deal vision of the appropriate relationship between courts and administrative agencies.

In order to understand the ideological significance of the APA, we must first recapture the bitterness of the preceding struggle. The "Pound Report" directly spawned the Walter-Logan Bill of 1940, which was passed by both houses of Congress but was vetoed, amid intense controversy, by President Franklin D. Roosevelt. Pro–New Deal lawyers widely denounced the bill for forcing adminis-trative agencies, in the words of the Association of the Bar of the City of New York, "into a single mold which is so rigid, so needlessly interfering, as to bring about a widespread crippling of the administrative process."[135]

For a time, the battle over administrative procedure was nothing less than a struggle over the legitimating premises of the New Deal.

Nothing better captures the gulf that existed between the proponents and op-ponents of this "high water mark of judicialization"[136] of the administrative pro-cess than President Roosevelt's powerful veto message of the Walter-Logan Bill in 1940. Roosevelt wrote:

[A] large part of the legal profession has never reconciled itself to the existence of the administrative tribunal. Many of them prefer the stately ritual of the courts, in which lawyers play all the speaking parts, to the simple procedure of administrative hearings which a client can understand and even participate in. Many of the law-yers prefer that decision be influenced by a shrewd play upon technical rules of evidence in which the lawyers are the only experts, although they always disagree. Many of the lawyers still prefer to distinguish precedent and to juggle leading cases rather than to get down to the merits of the efforts in which their clients are engaged. For years, such lawyers have led a persistent fight against the administra-tive tribunal.[137]

Only three years after his own bitter struggle with the Supreme Court, Roosevelt's message not only reiterated the traditional Progressive suspicion of the efficiency of the courts, but also powerfully restated Landis's identification of administrative regulation with social reform. Roosevelt continued:

> In addition to the lawyers who see the administrative tribunal encroaching upon their exclusive prerogatives there are powerful interests which are opposed to reforms that can only be made effective through the use of the administrative tribunal. Wherever a continuing series of controversies exist between a powerful and concentrated interest on one side and a diversified mass of individuals, each of whose separate interests may be small, on the other side, the only means of obtaining equality before the law has been to place the controversy in an administrative tribunal. . . . Great interests, therefore, which desire to escape regulation rightly see that if they can strike at the heart of modern reform by sterilizing the administrative tribunal which administers them, they will have effectively destroyed the reform itself.[138]

One of Roosevelt's stated reasons for vetoing the Walter-Logan Bill was that his Attorney General's Committee on Administrative Procedure was about to issue its own report, one that was "more eagerly awaited by the administration that commissioned it" than any other on administrative law had ever been.[139] Roosevelt applauded its vindication of New Deal administrative procedure, declaring that it "confirmed my belief that the Walter-Logan Bill was an abortive attempt to hamstring many progressive administrative agencies."[140]

Yet, it was the minority report of the Attorney General's Committee, quite critical of existing administrative forms, that was to have greater influence on the underlying assumptions of the APA. The most significant structural difference between the majority and the minority was over the question of whether a general code of administrative procedure would straitjacket the agencies. The majority report is remembered, above all, for rejecting any general code as an unnecessary interference with agency flexibility and creativity. By contrast, it seems clear that the APA "reflect[ed] the minority position" on questions of structure.[141] Indeed, at a still deeper ideological level, the divisions within the Attorney General's Committee were basically a repeat performance of the original split between Landis and Pound.

In light of this history, it is difficult to accept Verkuil's conclusion that the APA represented "compromise without retrenchment" or, even more extravagantly, that it moved administrative law permanently away from "automatic and unexamined reliance upon the judicial model" and into a "third and mature phase" of "concern with administrative procedure as an independent model."[142] However, Verkuil's observation that, "[o]n the face of it, [the APA] looked like a victory for the old Walter-Logan forces"[143] continues to ring true. "Since some had considered the 1941 minority report an extension of Walter-Logan," Verkuil acknowledged, "it was not difficult to view the APA, which reflected the minority position, as a code inspired by Walter-Logan."[144]

Not only did the minority's conception of a general code prevail in the APA.

More basically, the legalist mentality that Pound had effectively revived became the accepted framework for drafting the APA.

The Re-emergence of Proceduralism

The APA is a prominent example of the dialectical relationship between expertise theory and proceduralism in twentieth-century American legal thought. In the period of its greatest strength, between 1910 and 1940, the expertise justification of authority resulted in the elimination of elaborate procedural protections in judicial proceedings. A declining faith in the ability of experts to produce scientific, neutral, and apolitical solutions to social and legal questions led in turn to a re-emergence of proceduralism.

One of the best examples of this shift away from confidence in experts is the dramatic reversal of the premises that have governed juvenile delinquency proceedings. Separate juvenile courts were created during the Progressive era out of a conviction that the adversary system prevailing in regular criminal cases, with its elaborate procedural protections against a hostile state, were inappropriate to juvenile proceedings. Juvenile delinquency was often spoken of as a "social disease," requiring experts such as social workers and criminologists to advise judges on the appropriate individual cure.[145] The state was viewed as benevolent and paternalistic, and professional advisors as capable of providing the best solution to the juvenile's problems.[146] Elaborate procedures, by contrast, presupposed the gamesmanship of the adversary system, not the scientific deliberation of the trained professional. What was needed was the flexibility of the social engineer, not the rigidity of legal procedures that inevitably distorted the complexities of life. As the U.S. Supreme Court declared in 1967:

> The early reformers were appalled by adult procedures and penalties and by the fact that children could be given long prison sentences and mixed in jails with hardened criminals. They were profoundly convinced that society's duty to the child could not be confined by the concept of justice alone. They believed that society's role was not to ascertain whether the child was "guilty" or "innocent," but "What is he, how has he become what he is, and what had best be done in his interest and in the interest of the state to save him from a downward career." The child—essentially good, as they saw it—was to be made "to feel that he is the object of [the state's] care and solicitude," not that he was under arrest or on trial. The rules of criminal procedure were therefore altogether inapplicable. The apparent rigidities, technicalities, and harshness which they observed in both substantive and procedural criminal law were therefore to be discarded. The idea of crime and punishment was to be abandoned. The child was to be "treated" and "rehabilitated" and the procedures, from apprehension through institutionalization, were to be "clinical" rather than punitive.[147]

Dominant for half a century, this vision was abruptly rejected by the U.S. Supreme Court in *In re Gault* (1967), which insisted that juveniles be accorded the same procedural protections as adults in criminal proceedings.[148] The decision reflected almost a generation of growing disillusionment with expertise, particularly with the professional claims of social scientists.[149] Without the legitimacy of science, the state's apparatus was no longer experienced as benevolent but once more as potentially oppressive. As claims of professionalism to scientific legitimacy grew weaker, as their ability to provide objective solutions was increasingly called into question, courts reverted to traditional legalist protections against arbitrariness.[150] As the Supreme Court declared:

> It is these instruments of due process which enhance the possibility that truth will emerge from the confrontation of opposing versions and conflicting data. "Procedure is to law what scientific method is to science."[151]

A similar shift away from expertise occurred much more rapidly in the realm of judicial definitions of insanity. The monumentally important 1954 opinion by Judge David Bazelon in *United States v. Durham*[152] is a clear example of the influence on our law of a generation of Legal Realist claims for the social sciences, especially for the scientific status of psychiatry. Eighteen years later, however, in the face of mounting attacks on the neutrality and scientific status of psychiatry, Bazelon's own court reversed the *Durham* rule.

The original opinion, filled with appeals to the "modern science of psychology"[153] and "scientific knowledge,"[154] rejected the traditional M'Naghten Rule, which determined whether a criminal defendant was insane by whether he or she could distinguish right from wrong. Supplemented by the "irresistible impulse" test, the M'Naghten Rule had been almost universally adopted by American courts at the time *Durham* was decided.[155]

Using advances in science as justification, the *Durham* court developed a new test: whether the "unlawful act was the product of mental disease or mental defect." Indeed, Judge Bazelon's opinion characterized the earlier history of the insanity defense as an initial refusal to change "[d]espite demands in the name of scientific advances,"[156] followed by a late addition of the irresistible impulse test "in response to 'the cry of scientific experts.' "[157]

Eighteen years later, recognizing the accumulated scholarly and judicial criticism of the *Durham* rule, the full bench of the U.S. Court of Appeals for the District of Columbia, including Judge Bazelon, unanimously voted to overrule *Durham* and substitute still another formulation proposed by the American Law Institute.[158] "A principle reason" for the change, the court declared, was "undue dominance by the experts giving testimony"[159] on the issue of insanity, especially on the twin questions of whether there was a "mental disease or defect"[160] and whether the crime was the "product"[161] of that disease. The *Durham* rule, the court declared, had "opened the door to 'trial by label.' "[162]

In a defensive partial concurrence, Judge Bazelon conceded that *Durham* relied too heavily on expert opinion. He took pains to emphasize the *Durham* left ultimate decisions as to criminal responsibility in the jury's hands. He maintained that *Durham* itself was originally promulgated "largely in response to the plea of behavioral scientists that they did not want to decide ultimate questions of law and morality, but wanted only an opportunity to report their findings as scientific investigators without the need to force those findings through the prism of M'Naghten."[163] From the beginning, he argued,

> Durham challenged the experts to provide the information they had long promised. We expected, perhaps naively, that the presentation of this new information would permit—indeed require—the jury to undertake a much broader inquiry and to rely less on the ultimate conclusions of the experts. But it quickly became apparent that . . . it did not do nearly enough to eliminate the experts' stranglehold on the process.[164]

Frankfurter and the Changed "Mood" in Congress

The erosion of the legitimating power of expertise theory, and the consequent re-emergence of legalism and proceduralism, best explain the significance of the APA of 1946.

After 1946, political attacks on the regulatory state and intellectual challenges to social science claims of objectivity marched hand in hand. Every triumph of proceduralism occurred at the expense of professionalism.

In the immediate post–World War II period, it was conservatives who challenged expertise theory, not only through the APA but, even more dramatically, in legal attacks on the authority of the National Labor Relations Board as a result of the passage of the Taft-Hartley Act (1947).

In the *Universal Camera* case (1951),[165] the Supreme Court was asked to decide whether the Taft-Hartley Act had expanded the scope of judicial review of Labor Board decisions, thus reversing traditional judicial deference to administrative findings based on "substantial evidence." The Act, passed over President Harry S. Truman's veto by the first Republican-controlled Congress since the New Deal, was the product of a decade of conservative attacks on the pro-labor ideology of the Labor Board. More than any other New Deal administrative agency, the Labor Board had become a lightning rod for conservative skepticism about claims to administrative expertise.[166] By expanding the scope of review of Labor Board decisions, conservatives hoped both to reduce judicial deference to claims of agency expertise and to re-legalize the process of administrative regulation.

In *NLRB v. Universal Camera*, the Court of Appeals, per Judge Learned Hand, held that the Taft-Hartley Act had not expanded the scope of review, but had simply codified the traditional relationship between courts and administrative agencies.[167] But the Supreme Court, in an opinion by Justice Felix Frankfurter, reversed, asserting that the Taft-Hartley Act actually reflected a changed "mood" in Congress concerning the appropriate relationship between courts and administrative agencies.[168]

Frankfurter maintained that the act's new language—"substantial evidence on the record considered as a whole"—was in fact a new formula, meant to expand the scope of judicial review. But he conceded that he was hardly compelled to reach that conclusion, since, as he pointed out, the congressional committee reports seemed only to wish to make the statute "conform" to the established "substantial evidence" test.[169]

Frankfurter chose to give the new language a broad reading based on his observation that under the Wagner Act, courts had "by imperceptible steps" come to defer to Labor Board fact finding where any evidence in the record, even "when viewed in isolation, substantiated the Board's findings."[170] Thus, "the belief justifiably arose" that the Court had "so contracted [its] reviewing power"[171] as to lead, in effect, to "an abdication of any power of review."[172]

Frankfurter pointed out that the new formula "ma[de] its first appearance"[173] in the minority report of the Attorney General's Committee of 1941, and that it was rejected by the New Deal majority on the ground that "[i]t would destroy the values of adjudication of fact by experts or specialists in the field involved."[174] Thus, despite a lack of "clarity of purpose" in the congressional changes,[175] Frankfurter correctly identified the change in mood as a decisive shift away from those presuppositions about agency expertise that had been central to the pre-APA conception of the administrative process.

The more general significance of the question before the Court lay in the fact that the APA had also used the "substantial evidence . . . [on] the whole record" formula.[176] Therefore, the Court was, in effect, deciding that the APA itself had significantly expanded the scope of judicial review of *all* administrative determinations.

Frankfurter's opinion is filled with historical ironies. As a law professor before his appointment to the Court, his influence on legal thought and on the Harvard curriculum had been to move the center of intellectual gravity away from an exclusive emphasis on nineteenth-century private law subjects toward a twentieth-century public law focus. In addition to being trained in the common law, students, he wrote in 1927, "must have a sympathetic understanding of the major causes which have led to the emergence of modern administrative law, and must be able to move freely in the world of social and economic facts with which administrative law is largely concerned."[177] The administrative state needed both "a highly professionalized civil service" and "a flexible, appropriate and economic procedure."[178] Caught up in Progressive hopes for social reform through law, he was the first person to teach administrative law at Harvard. After Frankfurter's departure for Washington, two of his students, James M. Landis and Louis L. Jaffe, continued the close connection between the New Deal and public law scholarship at Harvard.[179]

Before his appointment to the Court, Frankfurter was one of the most vocal advocates of administrative solutions to social problems. A prominent proponent of expertise theory, he expressed his faith in administrative expertise most directly as the hope that America would develop a group of professional administrators modeled on the English civil service. In *The Public and Its Government* (1930) Frankfurter emphasized, as his biographer put it, "the crucial role that could be played in modern government by trained experts recruited from the nation's universities and professional schools."[180] While the political conflicts of the nineteenth century "thrived in the main, on the levels of feeling and rhetoric," Frankfurter maintained, the critical problems of modern industrial society remained "deeply enmeshed in intricate and technical facts" that had to be freed from "presupposition and partisanship." It was thus necessary "to contract the areas of conflict and passion" and to expand "the areas of accredited knowledge as the basis of action."[181] Thus Frankfurter issued the call for rational, neutral inquiry by experts into the proper course of national affairs.

Frankfurter acknowledged that many policy questions went "beyond the authority of engineer or economist" into "the realm of judgment regarding values as to which there is as yet no voice of science." And he denied that he was advocating "a new type of oligarchy, namely, government by experts." "The expert should be on tap, but not on top," he concluded.[182]

Yet, as Michael Parrish perceptively observed, "[a] certain insouciance . . . characterized [Frankfurter's] belief that these intellectual mandarins would remain subject to popular, democratic controls. In a decade that produced the first edition of the *Encyclopedia of the Social Sciences*, however, his confidence and myopia were hardly unusual."[183]

Thus, when twenty years later Frankfurter confronted a vehement congressional attack on the expertise of the Labor Board, whose own roots go back to Frankfurter's involvement during World War I in the problems of labor unrest,[184] he must have been struck by the erosion of faith in expertise and the return to "presupposition and partisanship" that it represented.

For those who had carefully followed the views on administrative law of Professor and then Justice Frankfurter, his shift to a legalized and judicialized approach in the late 1940s and early 1950s came as quite a surprise. Two years before *Universal Camera*, his former student, Professor Louis L. Jaffe, noted "a strange and unexpected hyperbolism" that had appeared in a dissenting opinion Frankfurter had joined.[185] Its Poundian rhetoric and its invocation of administrative lawlessness startled Jaffe. "One remembers Mr. Justice Frankfurter's respect for 'expertise,' his reluctance even to review the agencies, and his assertion that they as well as the courts must be trusted to observe the law. It is as if here he had become momentarily seized with the chilling thought that he had been coddling a monster."[186]

Louis Jaffe's Pilgrimage

Perhaps it was Jaffe himself who began to fear he had been "coddling a monster," for his own general disillusionment with the New Deal's administrative law vision began to emerge at about this same time. A former law clerk to Justice Louis Brandeis and an ardent New Dealer, he became, surprisingly, one of the most prominent scholars to cast doubt on wide-ranging expertise justifications for administrative action. He began to embark on what he was later to call his own intellectual "pilgrimage" away from a strong attachment to the Landis model of his youth and back to Pound's more legalistic and proceduralized vision of the administrative process.

Rooted in a strong commitment to the New Deal, Jaffe's earliest writings were careful but powerful defenses of the administrative state. "The social legislation" of the New Deal, he wrote in 1941, had "brought to the boiling-point the long-simmering agitation" over the administrative process.[187] Earlier, he had lamented the absence of serious factual investigation of the charges of administrative arbitrariness and injustice, noting that "invective" had drowned out "ingenuity and goodwill" in recent studies.[188] In particular, Pound's 1938 American Bar Association report had gone on a "spree" that Jaffe termed "the most unfortunate event" in the Association's series of studies of administrative law.[189] The Walter-Logan Bill, inspired by the "Pound Report" and later vetoed by President Roosevelt, Jaffe mocked as "A Bill to Remove the Seat of Government to the Court of Appeals for the District of Columbia."[190] Another report critical of New Deal agencies he found "unwise and irresponsible"[191] and filled with "violent, unmeasured condemnation of the independent commissions."[192]

The pro-New Deal 1941 "Report of the Attorney General's Committee on Administrative Procedure" was, for Jaffe, "a heartening document."[193] He could find "nothing [in the "Report"] to justify the fears of Dean Pound"[194] of "administrative absolutism." Rather, it was simply the extension of administration "into fields of hotly-contested measures of economic control" that had "intensified . . . objections" to administrative procedures.[195] "The attack pressed by those hostile to the legislative purposes . . . was usually indiscriminate and argued for a wholesale condemnation of the entire corpus [of regulation] based on its departure from the assumed norm of a common law litigation."[196]

Yet now, for the first time, Jaffe struck an unexpected note of impartiality.

> [T]hose jealous for the preservation and extension of the new reforms [were] apt to be nearly as indiscriminate in [their] suggestion either that there were no grounds whatsoever common to administrative and judicial procedure, or that in any case there were no abuses or no abuses other than were likely to occur in any system of administration. In response to this somewhat unyielding attitude the conservative forces and their lawyers devised [the Walter-Logan bill, which sought] to reform the entire system of administration . . . by hasty and ill-digested generalizations.[197]

Still the New Dealer, however, Jaffe also observed that the "Attorney General's Committee Report" "issues out of a caldron of hot controversy, a controversy that has its roots deep in class struggle, a controversy which is concerned with the basic direction and purposes of government."[198] It was amid these circumstances that the "Report," "balanced and firmly reasoned," was viewed as a "heartening document."

By 1942, in a review of Pound's book on administrative law, Jaffe declared that "[i]t is time to shrink the proportions of this controversy."[199] "The depth of controversy is attested by the violence and distortion which it generates."[200] If since 1938 "invective" had come to prevail in administrative law debate, "[n]ot the least offender, both by reason of intellectual eminence and the extent of his transgression, is Dean Pound . . . [who] might well deflate the substance and the form of his attack."[201] For the first time, however, Jaffe perceived a "sound kernel" in Pound's criticism and found himself "essentially in agreement," despite Pound's "immoderate and unprofessional manner."[202]

> Judges, despite the growing number of liberal men who have been elevated to the bench, are still regarded as a hostile conspiracy against administration. A judge bold enough to reverse an administrative determination is presumptively either stupid or reactionary. The related assumption is that the administrator is invariably right because he is an "expert" and "makes policy."[203]

By 1943, Jaffe emphasized that

> [t]here is no longer need for violent recrimination; those who still decry the administrative process are relics of a battle now being conceded by their more sensible fellows. Nor is there [any] longer need of overlabored, ultradefensive justifications of the administrative process in which its expertness and capacity is given credit beyond its claim on our common and individual humanity. It is time for at least a truce.[204]

By 1949, Jaffe had clearly joined the legalist camp. In that year, he published a comprehensive appraisal of Justice Frankfurter's judicial opinions in which he stated a number of propositions to which he repeatedly returned in later articles. Two of the most important were that administrative agencies must be governed by an overarching "rule of law" rather than their own "expertise," and that "rationalism" stripped of custom jeopardizes the fragile bonds of society.[205]

Amid "the disintegration of faiths" and "the great social turmoil of the times," Jaffe had "come to doubt that rationalism can forge the bonds of society or endow it with energy." A stable society "derives its coherence from its history, its customs and its symbols."[206] Echoing Edmund Burke's denunciation of the French Revolution, Jaffe now observed that "rationalisms take as many forms as the self-interest which they so often mask." And echoing the many contemporaneous associations of rationalism with totalitarianism, he declared: "[T]he truth that prevails in the market place may rest on a pedestal of corpses. 'Appetite, a universal wolf' may 'make perforce a universal prey, and last eat up himself.' "[207]

By the time he wrote "The Effective Limits of the Administrative Process" in 1954,[208] Jaffe's pilgrimage away from the Landis model was essentially complete. He now observed that a "Great Disillusion" with the administrative state had begun to develop.[209] His own critique combined earlier Poundian pessimism with a new conviction that a regulatory bureaucracy inevitably developed "arteriosclerosis."[210]

Meanwhile, his faith in the judiciary gradually became unqualified. Judicial review, he wrote as early as 1949, "protects the agencies themselves against the temptation of absolutism."[211] Now he also disagreed even more broadly with Landis's objection to judicialized procedures in the administrative process.[212] A new dimension of Jaffe's critique questioned the capacity of regulation to remain innovative and energetic. Indeed, he was perhaps the first New Dealer to identify a tendency toward "industry-orientation" as "a condition endemic in any agency" that attempted industrial planning and supervision.[213]

"[O]ur generation—that of Landis and myself—" he wrote in his memorial to James Landis in 1964, "judged the administrative process in terms of its stunning performance under the New Deal."[214] But they had failed to take account of "the dynamic of history,"[215] "the unique concatenation of circumstances" that gave encouragement to the "galvanic forces" unleashed by the Great Depression.[216] History had left the New Deal era behind and made the Landis model obsolete.

In a later, still more disillusioned article, Jaffe explained that he had first come to doubt the Landis model because it was established on the foundation of two crucial assumptions: "the existence in each case of relevant, value-free concepts, and an administration located at any given moment of time outside the political process, that is to say, outside or insulated from the power structure."[217] The dynamism and autonomy of the model, he saw, derived from a conception of scientific method operating on neutral principles and from the presumption that teams of specialists could implement a comprehensive body of expert knowledge to forge solutions to economic and social ills. Because no "autonomy of systems of expert judgment" exists, Jaffe wrote in 1955, Justice Jackson's "warning . . . against the loose application of the concept of expertness was warranted and timely."[218]

"One Man's Delay Is Another Man's Due Process"

The cold war marked a new era in attitudes toward the deference due agencies and the value of procedures. In 1956, Walter Gellhorn, former research director of the Attorney General's Committee, noted the sudden reversal of liberal and conservative positions on questions of judicial and procedural restraints. With deliberate irony, he observed that the staunchest supporters of restraints during the APA debates began arguing for unrestrained agency powers in the interest of national security. The former advocates of individual rights and due process suddenly became enthusiasts for vesting administrative agencies with discretionary authority to censor publications, ban foreign periodicals, supervise and register private organizations, deport legally resident aliens after denying them formal hearings, and adjudicate in less formal, administrative tribunals the loyalty and dangerousness of U.S. citizens.

> During the period in which these and other new powers have been granted or old ones fortified, the former friends and the former detractors of the administrative process have been circumnavigating the globe of government, traveling in opposite directions. The friends, starting from a point on the globe that might be labeled extreme support, have now traveled all the way to the station of extreme fear. The

detractors, starting from extreme fear, have seemingly reached the point from which the friends had so recently departed.[219]

Formerly, Gellhorn observed, liberals and conservatives could be charted in terms of their attitudes toward administrative bodies. "By and large the liberals believed that administrators could be relied upon for wise and just decisions, and that, as a corollary, they should as far as possible be free from judicial supervision that might rigidify administrative procedures or supplant the informed administrative conclusions."[220] In the midst of McCarthyism, however, liberals "now feel that what were mainly imaginary dangers have become real—and frightening,"[221] that is, a "real danger exists that an entirely fictitious expertness may limit the review of administrative rulings in a way that to all intents and purposes gives sanction to administrative fiat."[222]

If McCarthyism had begun to undermine the New Dealers' cavalier attitude toward the rule of law in the administrative state, it took some time before it produced a generalized distrust of expertise among liberals, who had devoted several decades to cementing the connection between social science and social reform. During the 1960s and 1970s, criticism of administrative expertise continued to shift leftward on the political spectrum, fueled by political and scholarly claims that, during the Eisenhower administration, administrative agencies had been "captured" by the very interests they had been expected to regulate. In fact, the charge of agency capture was first given public prominence by a remarkable spokesman, none other than James M. Landis himself.

In a 1960 report commissioned by President-elect John F. Kennedy, Landis expressed the disillusionment of even ardent New Dealers with administrative regulation. "A common criticism" of administrative agencies, Landis wrote, was that they had developed a tendency toward "industry orientation . . . frequently expressed in terms that the regulatees have become the regulators."[223] The Civil Aeronautics Board had consistently sided with the established commercial airlines against both unscheduled airlines and all-cargo air carriers. "[T]he Interstate Commerce Commission has frequently been characterized as railroad-minded, the Federal Communications Commission as dominated by the networks, while the actions of the Federal Power Commission speak for themselves."[224] Landis had already described how "ineffective administration" and a pro-industry orientation had made the Federal Power Commission "the most dismal failure in our time of the administrative process."[225]

The theme of agency capture produced an extensive body of scholarly literature during the 1960s and 1970s that contributed to still further delegitimation of the expertise theory, if not of the administrative state itself.[226] By the late 1960s and early 1970s, the war in Vietnam had produced still deeper cultural changes that undermined the expertise theory from the left.[227] For the first time since the turn of the century, the party of reform had turned against science and technological rationality as instruments of humanitarian change. Books such as Thomas Kuhn's enormously influential *The Structure of Scientific Revolutions* (1962) gave credence to claims that science itself was political and that even scientific systems required "subjective" starting points or first principles. But above all, disillusionment with the "best and brightest," those arrogant technocrats who had confidently predicted a quick victory in Vietnam, produced a deep reaction against claims of expertise.

One can see this shift in attitude most dramatically in the environmental law decisions of the Court of Appeals for the District of Columbia, which because of its special jurisdiction has been the paramount administrative law tribunal in the United States for the past half century. Dominated by New Deal liberals until the mid-1980s, its decisions during the 1960s and 1970s express a change in attitude regarding the benevolence of many kinds of regulation. In 1974, Harold Leventhal, one of those New Deal judges, emphasized the activist role that the courts had begun to play in "environmental decisionmaking."

> Judicial review . . . is not to be denied or tightly confined by the doctrine of deference to executive officials. That deference is appropriately generous under the rule of administrative law when there is a technical matter within the special competence of the official or agency. But when an essentially nonenvironmental agency has made a determination downplaying the environmental consequences of its action, the court may cock a skeptical eye and insist on [a special] kind of justification. . . .[228]

Leventhal spoke of "[t]he solicitude which has generally characterized judicial review of environmental issues" and pointed to the leading D.C. Circuit Court opinion in *Environmental Defense Fund Inc. v. Ruckelshaus* as the decision where that solicitude "was perhaps most openly expressed."[229] Chief Judge Bazelon's declaration in that case that "[w]e stand on the threshold of a new era in the history of . . . administrative agencies and reviewing courts"[230] was, for the less lyrical Leventhal, an example of the fact "that in the environmental field the courts so far have been, if anything, fully vigilant to exercise rather than abdicate their supervisory role."[231] During this period, one sympathetic scholar noted, "[t]he environmentalists' crusade had the courts as its gods and agencies such as the Federal Power Commission and the Atomic Energy Commission as its devils."[232] Writing in 1977, he remarked that "in much of the important environmental litigation [of the previous decade] the courts exercised special solicitude in behalf of environmental interests."[233] But with the creation of the Environmental Protection Agency and its special stake in environmental issues, he observed a return to "a more traditional, limited role of judicial review"[234] and a "narrowing gap between the standards of judicial review of environmental decisionmaking and other forms of agency decisionmaking."[235]

The Supreme Court's 1978 decision in *Vermont Yankee Nuclear Power Corp. v. Natural Resources Defense Council*[236] decisively marked such a return to "a more traditional, limited role of judicial review." There the Court dealt a sharp and contemptuous rebuke to a decade of D.C. Circuit Court decisions that had forged procedural restraints on agency rule-making powers, primarily in the environmental field. The decision was heralded by conservatives such as then Professor Antonin Scalia as no less "than a major watershed"[237] in freeing agency policymaking from judicially created constraints. Since the Court of Appeals "was in the process of replacing the rudimentary procedural mandates of the Act . . . with a much more elaborate, 'evolving,' court-made scheme," Scalia wrote, *Vermont Yankee* constituted a welcome reversal of the D.C. Circuit Court's "progressive evisceration of the APA."[238]

Why should conservatives now have wished to reduce judicial review to what Scalia called the APA's "rudimentary procedural mandates," when only a generation earlier they had pressed even more elaborate procedural constraints on administrative policymaking? Scalia was quite explicit about the reasons.

The most fundamental question, Scalia wrote, was "the indissoluble link between procedure and power, which must determine when and how procedures are made."[239] While he was "willing to stipulate, for the sake of argument," that Congress could do "a superb job" if it focused on revising the APA itself,[240] "[i]n fact, however, that is not the context in which the 'legislative thinking' which has produced the continuing statutory erosion of the APA has occurred."[241] Instead, Congress was constantly "tinkering with administrative procedures in every major regulatory statute that is passed," and it was not likely to stop.[242] Thus, despite his praise for *Vermont Yankee* as returning the courts to the "intent" of the legislature that passed the APA, Scalia was not eager to encourage legislative "tinkering with administrative procedures" in regulatory statutes themselves. During deliberations over those regulations, he asserted,

> [t]he principal issue—the issue to which all the lobbying and horse trading which are an indispensable part of representative democracy were directed—was not, for example, "What are the most fair and efficient procedures for the Federal Trade Commission's adoption of trade practice rules?" but rather, "Should the Federal Trade Commission have rulemaking authority?" and, if so, how actively do we want it exercised?" Not, for example, "What are the most fair and efficient procedures for Consumer Product Safety Commission rulemaking?"; but rather, "Should there be a Consumer Product Safety Commission and, if so, how intensively do we want it to regulate?"[243]

In lobbying before congressional committees concerned with the substance of regulation, "[p]rocedural efficiency and fairness are a side issue—and at least the first of them is inevitably regarded as negotiable in the interest of obtaining what are, in the context presented, more basic goals."[244]

> An interest group which cannot achieve its goal of eliminating FTC rulemaking authority may, quite rationally, settle for imposition of cumbersome procedures that at least reduce the extent to which rulemaking can occur.[245]

Scalia "fear[ed] that repeated Congressional attention to administrative procedure as a mere subsidiary issue in the context of more important substantive controversies" would lead to "the balkanization of administrative law."[246] "[T]he fundamental point" he wished to emphasize was "that one of the functions of procedure is to limit power . . . the power to act at all."[247] Procedural limitations are "principally a restriction" on the power of courts and agencies "impairing (however crudely) their ability and thus their inclination to make social policy."[248] There is a strong tendency "to alter procedures as a means of altering power."[249]

Scalia was perhaps the first conservative to give expression to the relationship between procedure and power that had once been a New Deal monopoly. Indeed, his message seemed but an echo of James M. Landis's complaint that "the complexity and prolixity of . . . existing procedures redound to the benefit" of those who "have a vested interest in the status quo."[250] In a 1961 address before the American Bar Association, Landis denounced "Alice-in-Wonderland procedures, reminiscent of the vested interest that the bar of the eighteenth century had in the procedures then prevalent in England," which enabled lawyers to "drag out proceedings" and "draw out issues beyond all reasonable bounds."[251] In the distribution of television frequencies, for example,

[t]he substance of the matter is simple. . . . [T]he problem of government is to see that they are used as effectively as they can be used in the public interest rather than being employed in the interest of some purveyor of toothpaste or a deodorant. But this basic issue was concealed beneath an unreal procedural battle [that invoked] slogans, such as "czarism" . . . and even "sovietizing our government."[252]

As another example of "[t]he same situation—a desire that the administrative process should not work efficiently,"[253] Landis cited the defeat of a reorganization plan for the National Labor Relations Board. The defeat was "due to considerations having no relationship to the improvement of the administrative process but having a relationship to two factors, first political opposition pure and simple, and secondly the desire to thwart the basic principle" of the Labor Act that collective bargaining "should be the foundations of labor-management relations in our economy."[254] Landis concluded: "As one witness for the National Association of Manufacturers bluntly put his reasons for opposing the plan: 'One man's delay is another man's due process.' "[255]

Landis's lesson was not very different from that of Scalia almost twenty years later. Proceduralization of the administrative process "derive[s] more from opposition to the substantive laws entrusted to administrative agencies rather than any genuine opposition to the betterment of administrative procedure."[256] Delay brought about through increasing proceduralization "is . . . equally an element of the lack of due process" because "the lag in the administrative disposition of its business approaches a national scandal, whose impact affects not merely individuals but the health and well-being of vast industries."[257]

What had changed in the interim to lead Scalia also to protest the increasing proceduralization of the administrative process? For one thing, the advantages of delay had begun to shift to newly organized welfare and environmental groups. Until the 1960s, the structure of regulation had remained within the New Deal framework—private industry using legal procedures to resist implementation of governmental restrictions on their power. Procedural restraints had traditionally been defended in the name of protecting private property rights against essentially confiscatory governmental policy. But the emergence during the 1960s of environmental organizations seeking to restrict or delay governmental action created a new set of beneficiaries of procedural delay. In addition, the vast expansion of the welfare state during Lyndon Johnson's presidency, together with the establishment of a legal services bar, created a new constituency for procedural regularity.[258]

One of the most famous efforts to elaborate the effect of these changes on legal theory was Charles Reich's path-breaking 1964 *Yale Law Journal* article, "The New Property."[259] "One of the most important developments in the United States during the past decade has been the emergence of government as a major source of wealth," Reich began.[260] Government largesse in the forms of "money, benefits, services, contracts, franchises and licenses" was "steadily taking the place of traditional forms of wealth—forms which are held as private property."[261] "Only by making such benefits into rights," Reich argued, "can the welfare state achieve its goals of providing a secure minimum basis for individual well-being and dignity in a society where each man cannot be wholly master of his own destiny."[262]

Reich first criticized the ideology of "the public interest state" according to which "the wealth that flows from government is held by its recipients conditionally, subject to confiscation in the interest of the paramount state."[263] He called this "The New Feudalism,"[264] which resulted in a "dependent position of the individual and [a] weakening of civil liberties."[265]

Next, he attacked the traditional chasm between property rights and governmentally created privileges. Here he drew on the Realist critique of property as a pre-political natural right in Classical Legal Thought. "The chief obstacle to the creation of private rights" in governmental benefits is "the fact that it is originally public property, comes from the state, and may be withheld completely. But this need not be an obstacle. Traditional property also comes from the state. . . ."[266] Thus, neither "old" nor "new" property is a "natural right but [instead] a deliberate construction by society. If such an institution did not exist, it would be necessary to create it, in order to have the kind of society we wish."[267] The post-Realist creation of rights in "new property" would not depend on traditional natural rights ideas but on the positive creation of procedural limitations on governmental power.

Reich's conception was developed in reaction to governmental abuse during the McCarthy era. The largest group of cases he refers to are examples of denials or revocations of benefits and licenses to persons accused of Communist associations,[268] including the infamous case of *Fleming v. Neston*,[269] in which the U.S. Supreme Court upheld a law that retroactively deprived a former Communist of social security benefits that had accrued after nineteen years of pension contributions.

Reich's ideas were soon to be applied in a somewhat different context—the development of a general right to welfare that had just begun to emerge. Its most famous expression is the decision of the U.S. Supreme Court in *Goldberg v. Kelly* (1970), which prominently relied on Reich's new property to establish a constitutional right to an evidentiary hearing before welfare benefits could be terminated.[270]

This association of the expansion of welfare rights with widening procedural guarantees shattered the traditional Dicean connection between conservatism and proceduralism in the administrative state. It is one prominent reason why conservatives such as Professor Scalia began to re-emphasize the distinction between old and new property through resistance to expanding procedural guarantees. In the process, conservatives began to see what James Landis had always understood— that there has always been a trade-off between substance and procedure, and that one man's due process is another man's delay.

NINE

Post-War Legal Thought
1945–1960

Post–World War II legal thought was shaped by three broad sets of influences. First were the varying reactions to the unsettling legacy of Legal Realism that encountered the persistent pressure of professional orthodoxy to restore a sharp distinction between law and politics. Second were the varying interpretations of and reactions to the horrors of fascism, Nazism, and Stalinism. The emergence of totalitarianism abroad not only revived broad interest in the meaning of the rule of law; it also rekindled thought about the relationship between democratic political culture and legal theory. An even more specific result of the rise of totalitarianism was the astonishing spread of McCarthyism, a form of anti-Communist authoritarianism that came to represent not only a major domestic political response to the cold war but also a powerful catalyst to political repression in post-war culture. Finally, post-war legal thought was powerfully shaped by efforts to square the Supreme Court decision in *Brown v. Board of Education*[1] (1954) with the half-century-old, post-*Lochner*, Progressive commitment to judicial restraint.

Llewellyn's Retreat

During the 1950s, after a decade of rancorous and mean-spirited attacks directed against him, Karl Llewellyn began his retreat from some of the ideas of his youth. From the Nazi-Soviet Pact and the invasion of Poland in August and September 1939 through the Japanese attack on Pearl Harbor in December of 1941, discussions of totalitarianism, as Edward A. Purcell, Jr., has shown, had been "transformed . . . into a national debate that reached frenzied proportions."[2] Argument over the nature of law also "had reached its most intense phase."[3] At a special conference of over 500 American intellectuals gathered in New York City in September 1940, Mortimer Adler had snidely observed that since

> [w]ith a few notable exceptions, the members of this conference represent the American academic mind, . . . [it was] unnecessary, as well as unwise, for me to make any effort in the way of reasoning." Charging American academics with embracing a skeptical positivism that corroded all ideals, he accused them of being largely responsible for the political crisis that had culminated in World War II. "For all of these reasons, . . . [Adler had declaimed] I say we have more to fear from our professors than from Hitler.[4]

Amid the resulting "intensity and extremism of debate," it had become common to "charg[e] realism with everything from atheism to communism to nihilism."[5]

When Llewellyn republished his 1930 book, *The Bramble Bush*, in 1951, he acknowledged in the foreword that while he was "[c]orrecting an error" in his earlier version, he was also intent on protesting the invective that had been unfairly directed against him.[6] The "error" could be found in the "thirteen short words" that had become a prominent point of attack after the original publication. He had written: "What these officials do about disputes is, to my mind, the law itself."[7]

These were "unhappy words when not more fully developed," he acknowledged. "[T]he words fail to take proper account" of the nature of a legal institution "as an instrument for conscious shaping or . . . as a machinery of sometimes almost unconscious questing for the ideal. . . ."[8] He should not have forgotten "that one inherent drive which is a living part of even the most wrongheaded and arbitrary legal system . . . [is] to make the system . . . more closely realize an ideal of justice." Nevertheless, "the history of these thirteen short words," Llewellyn concluded, "sheds troubling light on the methods, manner and ethic of a style of controversy in jurisprudence which is now happily waning but against which it still pays to warn."[9]

Still, it was becoming increasingly difficult to insist on a view of law as a social creation, which was the main point of those words. Together with Llewellyn's later advocacy of a "temporary divorce" between the empirical and the normative,[10] Legal Realism had been drawn into arguments about whether natural law or positivism best encouraged or resisted totalitarianism. As early as 1940, Llewellyn had conceded that "the heart and core of jurisprudence" was the problem of ethical purpose in the law. "I for one am ready to do open penance for any part I may have played in giving occasion for the feeling that modern jurisprudes or any of them had ever lost sight of this," Llewellyn declared.[11]

Even as sober an intellectual as the journalist Walter Lippmann had lost patience with the debate about the social origins of law. He wrote in *The Public Philosophy* (1955):

> The crucial point, . . . is not where the naturalists and the supernaturalists disagreed. It is that they did agree that there was a valid law which, whether it was the

commandment of god or the reason of things, was transcendent. They did agree that it was not something decided upon by certain men and then proclaimed by them. It was not someone's fancy, someone's prejudice, someone's wish or rationalization, a psychological experience and no more. It is there objectively, not subjectively. It can be discovered. It has to be obeyed.[12]

As if to underline the authoritarian implications of his words, Lippmann chillingly warned:

> There are limits beyond which we cannot carry the time-honored method of accommodating the diversity of beliefs. As we know from the variety and sharpness of the schisms and sects of our time, we have gone beyond the limits of accommodation. We know, too, that as the divisions grow wider and more irreconcilable, there arise issues of loyalty with which the general principle of toleration is unable to cope.[13]

Indeed, just before Llewellyn's confident assertion that "our methods, manners and ethic of controversy in jurisprudence have tremendously improved,"[14] Senator Joseph McCarthy had delivered his notorious 1950 Wheeling, West Virginia, speech inaugurating what came to be known as the McCarthy era.[15] And Llewellyn simultaneously had begun to move away from the critical tradition of Realism.

"[I]f these lectures were being done over," Llewellyn wrote in his afterword to *The Bramble Bush*, "I am clear that their focus would shift materially off of 'the law' as lawyers understand that term. . . ."[16] Instead, the emphasis would shift to legal institutions "and what the part is—the noble and needed part—which the various major crafts of law play. . . ."[17] Here Llewellyn introduced what would become the central theme of his last book, *The Common Law Tradition* (1960).[18]

Realism, Llewellyn observed, had been "made the scape-goat for all the sins (real and supposed) of administrators and autocrats and the ungodly in general." The "irresponsibility" of the accusations "reads like rather grotesque farce."[19] Yet, perhaps the cumulative nastiness of the attacks on Realism had finally taken their toll.

The Common Law Tradition opens with Llewellyn's agreement with a generation of critics of Realism that "we face a crisis of confidence" in appellate courts that has produced "a new corrosiveness" of belief. "[O]ne great group at the bar are close to losing their faith" in the "reckonability" of the work of appellate courts. "[T]he man at the bar must have *confidence* on pain of feeling his own sustaining faith in his craft, in his craftsmanship, in his very office and utility as a lawyer, . . . ooze and seep away from him until he stands naked and hollow, helpless and worthless, a nothing, or a medicine man who has discovered his medicine to be a cheat."[20]

The Common Law Tradition was written to combat "the cynicism about the appellate courts that is stock conversation of the semi- or moderately successful lawyer in his middle years" and to show the "skilled craftsman" that it was really possible "to make usable and valuable judgments about likelihoods, and quite sufficiently to render the handling of an appeal a fitting subject for effective and satisfying craftsmanship."[21] Thus, in his last work, Llewellyn ardently sought to emphasize the virtues of "stability," "predictability," "tradition," and professional "craft," all values that Realism had once called into question because of their inherently conservative tendencies.

In much the same way that scholarly fields as disparate as literary criticism and philosophy turned inward to technical questions of professional craft and technique, Llewellyn appears to have continued to do "open penance" for the destabilizing consequences of Realism. In a period in which it was common to deplore the loss of a sustaining faith in legal objectivity, Llewellyn offered a new basis for belief in professional craft as the source of stability and predictability in law.

The Pattern of Post-War Thought: An Overview

American legal thought after World War II shared a strikingly similar agenda with many other areas of social thought. There was more similarity of approach between the different branches of thought during this period than at any time since the decade before the First World War. Then the issues generated by industrial capitalism had formed the central agenda for all categories of social thought. After World War II, much of the American intellectual outlook was shaped in reaction either to the trauma of Nazism or to continuing encounters with the savagery of Stalinism.

As Edward Purcell has shown,[22] much of post-war American thought was obsessed with identifying the "lessons" to be learned from the the spread of totalitarianism. While one school of thought, mainly Catholic, sought to blame moral relativism for the spread of a "might makes right" philosophy, others wished to show instead that an absolutist mindset was actually more conducive to the growth of totalitarianism.[23] Similarly, while some thinkers wished to insist that an emphasis on "ideology" produced a fanatical frame of mind,[24] others devoted themselves to warning that it was rather the absence of an ideology that encouraged nihilism, which, in turn, could easily degenerate into totalitarianism. The question as to whether moral certainty enhanced or retarded the rise of totalitarianism was thus at the center of many debates over the lessons to be learned.

The emphasis on morality highlighted a crisis of authority that classical positivism encountered in the post-war environment. Could the devotees of ethical positivism continue to maintain a sharp distinction between objective facts and subjective values[25] in a world in which political morality was said to require commitment to a "fighting faith"?[26] Could the philosophical cousins of the ethical positivists, the legal and logical positivists, likewise continue to expound their versions of the fact-value distinction? For the logical positivists,[27] the question was whether there was anything left for philosophy beyond reducing all expressions to clear, scientific, value-free statements that could be tested like propositions in the natural sciences. For the legal positivists,[28] the claim of a separation between law and morality, or between positive law and natural law, was dramatically called into question not only by the decision in *Brown v. Board of Education* but also by the Nuremberg and Tokyo trials of Nazi and Japanese leaders for crimes against humanity. The desire to distinguish between justice and the vengeance of the victors led to many arguments over whether it was fair to impose criminal punishments without a pre-existing statutory prohibition.[29]

There were two schools of thought on the reasons why the free world had not succumbed to totalitarianism. For one group of thinkers, the explanation derived from one or another version of consensus theory, which sought to portray the existence of a basic societal consensus on fundamental values.[30] Another group of thinkers emphasized not consensus but rather some version of an equilibrium theory that posited that agreement would emerge after trading among different and competing groups. These interest group pluralist theorists thus sought to create a conception of a political market analogous to economic markets.

Each of these theories aspired to accommodate the powerful claim of positivism that values were incapable of being objectively determined. Both consensus and equilibrium theories were efforts to escape from the dilemma that the fact-value distinction had imposed on social thought.

Consensus thinkers followed the same intellectual strategy pursued by customary law theorists from Oliver Wendell Holmes, Jr., and James Coolidge Carter[31] to Karl Llewellyn[32] and Benjamin Cardozo.[33] By attempting to locate norms in widely shared customs and conventions, they sought to impute value to social facts.[34] They always tended, therefore, to suppose that the way things are is the way they were meant to be. Indeed, in its earliest incarnations, nineteenth-century positivism had sought to attack precisely this conservative merger of fact and value.

The equilibrium theorists, by contrast, tended to see a multiplicity of interests and values in society, not some homogeneous system of social consensus. While the interest group pluralists tended to regard the search for consensus as perhaps encouraging a coerced uniformity,[35] consensus thinkers often denounced the pluralists for proposing an amoral, market-oriented vision of politics. Yet, both theories shared a picture of public policy as benevolently reflecting the outcome either of homogeneous customs or of market-oriented political trading among competing interest groups. In some formulations, in fact, both consensus and equilibrium theories might converge, as the interest group pluralists conceded that what underlay the substantive conflict over ends was a more fundamental agreement about processes. If, for example, the consensus theorists sought to find the basic difference between democracy and totalitarianism in whether there was an agreement on democratic values among members of the society, the pluralists located their consensus in a "morality of process."[36] If the advocates of consensus insisted that widespread agreement on procedure actually reflected a deeply substantive consensus—for otherwise nobody would acquiesce in an unfavorable outcome—the equilibrium theorists tended to emphasize value-free "neutral principles" that could legitimate decisions independent of results. For them, the legal Realists represented a result-oriented jurisprudence that needed to be combatted in the name of neutral principles.

Constitutional Politics: 1937–1962

The story of the split within the New Deal majority on the Supreme Court has been told many times.[37] Just one year after a New Deal majority was finally consolidated in 1937, Justice Harlan Fiske Stone set the stage for future divisions with his famous *Carolene Products* footnote,[38] which sought to legitimate judicial activism in the area of civil liberties while reiterating the Progressive commitment to judicial restraint in review of economic regulation. The Court first divided along these lines in its dramatic 1943 reversal of a three-year-old decision upholding a compulsory flag salute. Written in the midst of a wartime atmosphere in which the the justices of the Supreme Court were clearly conscious of the need to articulate the fundamental differences between democratic and totalitarian values, the second *Flag Salute Case*[39] became the focal point for post-war debates about whether there was a "preferred position" for civil liberties in the American constitutional scheme and whether there was a principled basis for distinguishing between judicial protection of personal and property interests.[40] At just the moment that McCarthyism was emerging as a major domestic reaction to the deepening cold war, the New Deal justices split over protection of civil liberties, with a solid majority, led by Justice Felix Frankfurter, denying that there was any basis in the Constitution for special protection of civil liberties.

It was just at this time that a unanimous Supreme Court, led by its new Chief Justice, Earl Warren, decided *Brown v. Board of Education*, declaring school segregation unconstitutional and unleashing ever more far-reaching pressures for fundamental social change.[41]

While *Brown v. Board of Education* is justly regarded as the most important and influential decision of the Warren Court, its significance for post-war legal thought needs to be analyzed more discretely. Until Arthur Goldberg was appointed by President John F. Kennedy in 1962 to replace Justice Frankfurter, there was no clear liberal majority on the Supreme Court. Indeed, as Justice Hugo Black began increasingly to separate himself from the liberal majority, it was perhaps not until the appointment of Thurgood Marshall in 1967 that a strong Warren Court majority actually was consolidated. Only one year later, after an abortive attempt to elevate Justice Abe Fortas as Earl Warren's successor as Chief Justice, President Lyndon B. Johnson's term ended, enabling President Richard M. Nixon to appoint Warren Burger. Finally, the forced resignation of Justice Fortas for conflict-of-interest charges transformed the composition of the Burger Court.

For about two decades after the end of World War II, the central ideological question before the Supreme Court was whether judicial activism was compatible with earlier Progressive commitments to judicial restraint in the name of democracy. It was only during the 1960s that the Supreme Court began a determined effort to dismantle its own post-war judicial acquiescence in McCarthyism, and not until *Mapp v. Ohio* (1961)[42] did it initiate a steady process of incorporating the Bill of Rights into the Fourteenth Amendment as a restriction on the power of the states. *Brown v. Board of Education* thus became a lightning rod not only for the "massive resistance" of Southern segregationists but also for old Progressives who had become deeply wedded to the view that judicial review violated democratic principles.[43]

Until the consolidation of the Warren Court majority, legal thinkers thus spent a remarkable amount of intellectual energy attempting to reconcile *Brown v. Board of Education* with much earlier Progressive commitments to judicial restraint.

Legal Process and Neutral Principles

The single dominant theme in post-war American academic legal thought is the effort to find a "morality of process" independent of results. This theme not only represented a reaction to the Legal Realist subversion of the law-politics, substance-procedure dichotomy, but it also paralleled remarkably similar themes in many other post-war academic disciplines.

From analytical philosophy to logical positivism and behaviorism in the social sciences[44] to New Criticism in literature,[45] post-war academic thought sought to repress politics by devoting its energies to form instead of substance and to technical accomplishment at the expense of social or political insight. In fields such as sociology and economics, the emphasis on value-free social science subordinated or obscured conflicts over values.

The historian Carl Schorske has written of the general "intellectual situation" he encountered in America during the 1950s.

> In the fields of greatest importance to my concern—literature, politics, art history, philosophy—scholarship in the 1950's was turning away from history as its basis for self-understanding. At the same time, in a parallel movement, the several academic disciplines redefined their intellectual functions in ways that weakened their social relatedness. Thus, for example, the New Critics in literature, as they came to power in the academy, replaced the practitioners of literary historicism who had prevailed in English departments before World War II with scholars committed to an a-temporal, internalistic, formal analysis. In political science, as the New Deal receded, the normative concerns of traditional political philosophy and the pragmatic preoccupation with questions of public policy began to give way to the a-historical and politically neutralizing reign of the behaviorists. In economics, mathematically oriented theorists expanded their dominion at the expense alike of the older, socially minded institutionalists and of policy-oriented Keynesians. Even in such a field as music, a new cerebrality inspired by Schoenberg and Schenker began to erode musicology's historical concerns. Above all in philosophy, a discipline previously marked by a high consciousness of its own historical character and continuity, the analytic school challenged the validity of the traditional questions that had concerned philosophers since antiquity. In the interest of a restricted and

purer functioning in the areas of language and logic, the new philosophy broke the ties both to history in general and to the discipline's past.

"In one professional academic field after another," Schorske concluded, academic specialization subverted "unifying premises" and "principles of coherence" and "reinforced the culture's pluralism. . . ."[46]

The most influential and widely used text in American law schools during the 1950s was *The Legal Process* by Henry Hart and Albert M. Sacks. Much has already been written about the legal process school as an expression of a distinctive post-war perspective on law.[47]

The legal process school sought to absorb and temper the insights of Legal Realism after the triumph of the New Deal. Its most important concession to Realism was in its recognition that doctrinal formalism was incapable of eliminating discretion in the law. The task was instead to harness and channel that discretion through institutional arrangements.

The focus on "institutional competence" as the basis for the distribution of legal tasks among various legal actors was one of the most distinctive reflections of the New Deal sympathies of its authors. Hart and Sacks sought to move academic legal thought away from its almost exclusive pre–New Deal focus on the common law and instead to emphasize the major roles that statutory and administrative law had come to play in the regulatory state. Indeed, the explosion of law as a result of regulation meant that it was first necessary to have "a better understanding of law generally rather than of any particular field of law."[48]

"[T]he most fundamental of the conditions of human society," Hart and Sacks asserted, was that "people are continuously and inescapably dependent upon one another." Interdependence required "affirmative and knowledgeable cooperation," not forms of competition deriving from atomistic individualism. Because of "interdependence with other human beings and the community of interest which grows out of it," groups are formed "for the protection and advancement of their common interests . . . which, because of that interdependence, transcend necessarily their points of difference." "[I]nterdependent living is collaborative, cooperative living," and "[p]eople need understandings . . . about the kinds of affirmative conduct which is required if each member of the community is to make his due contribution to the common interest."[49]

But any consensus about what constitutes the common interest fails because "[a]bstract understandings . . . will necessarily be indeterminate in many respects." Indeed, "*substantive* understandings . . . about how the members of an interdependent community are to conduct themselves in relation to each other and to the community" derive from "the existence of what may be called *constitutive* or *procedural* understandings . . . about how questions . . . are to be settled."

> These institutionalized procedures and the constitutive arrangements establishing . . . them are obviously more fundamental than the substantive arrangements in the structure of a society. . . . The principle of institutional settlement expresses

the judgment that decisions which are the duly arrived at result of duly established procedures of this kind ought to be accepted as binding upon the whole society unless and until they are duly changed.[50]

The Legal Process materials symbolize the moment in post-war history at which the New Deal lawyers' conception of the "common interest" came to be thoroughly transformed from one of substance to one of procedure. Whether due to fear of conservative attacks on the ideal of "collaborative, cooperative living" or anxiety that any substantive conception of the common interest might degenerate into totalitarianism,[51] *The Legal Process* expresses the belief of a dominant post-war generation of elite legal thinkers that "procedures . . . are obviously more fundamental than . . . substantive arrangements. . . ."[52]

After the collapse of European democracies, it was to be expected that Americans would focus upon questions dealing with the nature of democracy. During the post-war period, in fact, writings on democratic theory played a central role in shaping the legal and political culture of the period. Among the most significant contributions were efforts to elaborate a process-oriented theory of democracy free of any substantive commitments to particular values such as equality.

The book that provided the intellectual foundation for post-war democratic theorizing was originally written in 1942 by Viennese-born Joseph A. Schumpeter, who became professor of economics at Harvard. In *Capitalism, Socialism and Democracy*,[53] Schumpeter offered a minimalist theory of democracy that created the framework for process-oriented theories of law and politics that would come to dominate American intellectual life in the 1950s. His book was in effect a dialogue between a post-war Europe, most of whose prominent intellectuals believed not only that socialism was inevitable in post-war democracies but that it was also the logical fulfillment of democratic values, and an American society, where cold war rhetoric emphasized the fundamental incompatibility between democracy and socialism. Critical of socialism for what he thought were inherent bureaucratic tendencies that dampened innovation, Schumpeter nevertheless offered a theory of democracy that was compatible with either capitalism or socialism.

Democracy entailed no substantive commitments, particularly to equality, Schumpeter argued. It was simply a set of rules of the game for preserving political competition, so that the "outs" could throw out the "ins." In a period in which one-party Eastern European states under Soviet domination were producing grim repressive regimes, this minimalist definition of democracy was not without value. Moreover, the conclusion that democracy and socialism were compatible was, coming from someone basically hostile to socialism, an important statement in post-war America, where, increasingly, democratic socialism and Stalinist Communism were purposefully confused. But equally—and perhaps more importantly for Schumpeter—he wished to inform his social democratic European friends that there was no necessary relationship between political and social equality. He began with an attack on what he called the "classical doctrine of democracy."

In Schumpeter's famous definition, democracy was an "institutional arrangement for arriving at political decisions in which individuals acquire the power to decide by means of a competitive struggle for the people's vote." Democracy thus only entailed "competition for political leadership."[54] "The principle of democracy . . . merely means that the reins of government should be handed to those who command more support than any of the competing individuals or teams."[55] Schumpeter offered a definition of democracy that sought to eliminate all notions that democratic governments express either some abstract "will of the people" or any particular commitment to equality.

Indeed, political theorists during the 1950s followed Schumpeter's lead with enthusiasm. "[D]emocracy has sometimes been defended," Henry B. Mayo wrote, "by reference to its extra-political egalitarian tendencies—social equality, for instance—but it need not be: the political equality and the free participation make up the proper logic of the system."[56] "[M]ixing the notion of political and legal freedoms with that of possession of the economic means to exercise these liberties" produced "confusion," Mayo concluded.[57]

Absolute equality "leads straight to the concentration camp, where it is most fully realized," the political theorist J. Rolland Pennock wrote in *Liberal Democracy* (1950). Even the prime value of relative equality "will end up by putting people where they belong for their own good or for the good of society. . . ."[58]

Schumpeter's analysis was followed by perhaps the most influential book on democratic theory during the post-war period, Robert Dahl's *A Preface to Democratic Theory* (1956).[59] Like Schumpeter, Dahl wished to discredit the classical theory of democracy, or what Dahl called "populist democracy." At the same time, American historians were discovering various sinister strands in the history of populism.[60]

Dahl sought to show that popular sovereignty and political equality were not sufficient ends of democratic government, specifically because they failed to ensure the protection of minorities. But, in fact, Dahl asserted, the American political system tended to produce responsible government because it consisted of competition among interest groups—"not minority rule," in Dahl's famous phrase, "but minorities rule."[61] It was Dahl who articulated what came to be called the "interest group pluralist" theory of American democracy that would dominate American political thought during the 1950s. All that was necessary was a prior commitment to rules of the game for resolving group conflict. Dahl's vision went hand in hand with Daniel Bell's picture of an "end of ideology" in which politics was confined to the question, as Harold D. Lasswell had put it, of "who gets what, when, how."[62] Non-ideological politics was thought to involve only technical disagreement over the best means of arriving at agreed-upon ends.

Democratic politics, Dahl wrote, actually represents "merely the chaff. It is the surface manifestation, representing superficial conflicts."

> Prior to politics, beneath it, enveloping it, restricting it, conditioning it, is the underlying consensus on policy that usually exists in the society among a predominant portion of the politically active members. Without such a consensus no democratic system would long survive endless irritations and frustrations of elections and party competition. With such a consensus the disputes over policy alternatives

are nearly always disputes over a set of alternatives that have already been win-
nowed down to those within the broad areas of basic agreement.[63]

Thus, Dahl continued, "so far as there is any general protection in human
society against the deprivation by one group of the freedom desired by another, it
is probably not to be found in constitutional forms. It is to be discovered, if at
all," Dahl concluded two years after *Brown v. Board of Education*, "in extra-
constitutional factors."[64]

One of the reasons why tyranny of the majority is controllable primarily through
extra-constitutional means, Dahl explained, is that "a central guiding thread of
American constitutional development has been the evolution of a political system
in which all active and legitimate groups in the population can make themselves
heard at some crucial stage in the process of decision."[65] But what about the
influence of racial or political persecution in determining who were the "active
and legitimate groups in the population"?

> [I]f a group is inactive, whether by free choice, violence, intimidation, or law, the
> normal American system does not necessarily provide it with a checkpoint any-
> where in the process. By "legitimate," I mean those whose activity is accepted as
> right and proper by a preponderant portion of the active. In the South, Negroes
> were not until recently an active group. Evidently, Communists are not now a
> legitimate group. As compared with what one would expect from the normal sys-
> tem, Negroes were relatively defenseless in the past, just as the Communists are
> now.[66]

One now wonders about Dahl's original insistence on the "underlying consensus" that makes political conflict "superficial," as well as about his assurance that
this "enveloping" consensus produces extra-constitutional checks far superior to
constitutional rules. Can it be that this consensus is defined as simply what remains after dissenting groups become "inactive, whether by free choice, violence,
intimidation, or law . . ."?

But why were the ends agreed upon? Here we see the close relationship between interest group pluralist theories of politics modeled on equilibrium theories
in economics and consensus theories that sought to find fundamental agreement
over ends and values. Whether rooted in a picture of a relatively conflict-free
American history or of a non-ideological "American mind," consensus theories
buttressed the view either that there could be agreement on rules of the game
independently of ends or else that all politics involved simply the non-ideological
question of the most efficacious means for arriving at undisputed ends.

The one area in which consensus theories seemed most obviously inadequate
was race. It was a common observation that consensus historians downplayed the
significance of slavery and the Civil War in their historical interpretations.[67] Indeed, just as consensus theorists were forced to ignore the meaning of the existing
racial caste system enforced by Southern segregation laws, interest group pluralist
theorists were likewise required to avoid the question of why certain groups were
excluded from the democratic political process entirely.[68]

Brown v. Board of Education was thus deeply unsettling to the picture of American society that the dominant version of postwar social thought had presented. As America rediscovered poverty with the publication of Michael Harrington's influential *The Other America* (1962)[69] and the civil rights movement surged with Martin Luther King, Jr.'s, 1963 "I Have a Dream" speech,[70] the web of denial that value-free and non-ideological post-war thought had spun concerning fundamental questions of social justice began to unravel.

Learned Hand's Bill of Rights

Brown v. Board of Education produced a sharply critical reaction among elite legal thinkers,[71] for it challenged at the deepest levels their efforts to re-establish a neutral, value-free system of constitutional doctrine. Could the *Brown* decision be kept from spilling over into other areas involving minority rights? For at the same time as a majority of the Supreme Court was justifying its capitulation to McCarthyism in the name of judicial restraint and democracy, a dissenting minority was insisting that civil liberties occupied a preferred position in the American constitutional scheme.

Brown v. Board of Education thus became the lightning rod for the emerging split within Progressive jurisprudence during the sixteen years since Chief Justice Stone's *Carolene Products* footnote. If a majority of the Supreme Court in *West Virginia v. Barnette* (1943) had seemed to accept the distinction between economic and personal rights, according the latter a preferred position in the constitutional scheme, by the time *Brown* was decided, a new majority was insisting that the Court's capitulation to McCarthyism was required by judicial restraint and deference to democratic principles. Thus, *Brown* was received by many legal thinkers as a test of their commitment to judicial restraint.

Two of the most prominent critics of the *Brown* decision were Judge Learned Hand and Columbia Law Professor Herbert Wechsler, who delivered consecutive Holmes Lectures at Harvard Law School in 1958 and 1959. Each of these lectures was widely discussed in legal circles, and indeed, they expressed a number of the themes prominent in post-war American legal thought.

Learned Hand's lectures, entitled *The Bill of Rights* (1958),[72] constituted a bold and uncompromising challenge to all constitutional review of legislation. "Particularly at the present time,"[73] he wrote four years after *Brown*, the question of "when a court should intervene" was important enough to re-examine. He then proceeded to offer a thorough review and critique of the justifications for judicial review. He first agreed with the earlier Progressive contention that there was "nothing in the United States Constitution that gave courts any authority to review the decisions of Congress," and he insisted that "it was a plausible—indeed to my mind an unanswerable—argument" that such an authority was incompatible with the separation of powers.[74]

Having fundamentally challenged the legitimacy of judicial review, Hand next turned to a discussion of the conflict that had emerged within the New Deal majority since the second *Flag Salute Case* over whether "a stiffer interpretation" of the Constitution was appropriate "when the subject matter is not Property but Liberty."[75] He concluded that any distinction between personal and property rights "would have seemed a strange anomaly" to the framers of the Constitution.[76] Having thus cast doubt on the preferred position argument, Hand immediately focused on the *Brown* decision itself.

> [This] question arose in acute form in "The Segregation Cases." In these decisions did the Court mean to "overrule" the "legislative judgement" of states by its own reappraisal of the relative values at stake? Or did it hold that it was alone enough to invalidate the statutes that they had denied racial equality because the [Fourteenth] amendment inexorably exempts that interest from legislative appraisal? It seems to me that we must assume that it did mean to reverse the "legislative judgement" by its own appraisal. . . . There is indeed nothing in the discussion that positively forbids the conclusion that the Court meant that racial equality was a value that must prevail against any conflicting interest, but it was not necessary to go to such an extreme.[77]

Hand could not see how the Court, in purporting to distinguish, not overrule, *Plessy v. Ferguson*,[78] could still defend "the notion that racial equality is a paramount value that state legislatures are not to appraise and whose invasion is fatal to the validity of any statute."[79] Therefore, after *Brown*, he concluded, "the old doctrine seems to have been reasserted" that personal rights had a preferred status over economic rights,[80] a view he had already done his best to criticize.

Hand ended his discussion of *Brown* by saying that he could not "frame any definition that will explain when the Court will assume the role of a third legislative chamber and when it will limit its authority. . . ." As to the former, "I have never been able to understand on what basis it does or can rest except as a *coup de main*."[81]

Because *Brown v. Board of Education* has become so incontrovertible a part of the legal landscape, one is surprised to realize how problematic it appeared to someone of Judge Hand's towering reputation. And because constitutional theorists have subsequently separated the preferred position issue from questions of racial equality, one is reminded that for many post-war legal thinkers the *Brown* case *was* the central challenge to their justifications for judicial restraint. For example, one month after *Brown v. Board of Education* was decided, Justice Felix Frankfurter wrote to Judge Hand: "You know my deep sympathy with your outlook on the XIV Amendment. I once shocked Cardozo by saying that I would favor the repeal of that Amendment—and had wished that only the XIII and XV had issued from the Civil War. But since we have it, we have it—and I literally go through torture, from time to time."[82] Four years later, after informing Hand of "the accounts that have come from Cambridge of the impressive success of your Lectures," Frankfurter recalled "that Cardozo's espousal of the value of the Fourteenth Amendment led to a correspondence between us in the course of which I told him that on the balance I wished that when the Amendment first came before the Court it had concluded that it was too vague, too much open to subjective interpretation for judicial enforceability."[83]

Judge Hand spoke amid the greatest crisis over school desegregation since *Brown* was decided. The governor of Arkansas, implementing the declared Southern policy of massive resistance to school desegregation, had disobeyed a federal court desegregation order by preventing black children from integrating an all-white school. At the same time as Judge Hand was casting doubt on the legitimacy of the *Brown* decision, federal troops, sent by President Dwight D. Eisenhower, were patrolling the grounds of Little Rock's Central High School. Hand not only questioned the general authority of the Supreme Court to engage in judicial review, but he also suggested that the Court had acted like "a third legislative chamber" in adopting the "extreme" view "that racial equality was a value that must prevail against any conflicting interest. . . ."[84]

How could one of the giants of pre–World War I Progressivism have averted his eyes so completely as to avoid seeing the significance of the Supreme Court's effort to end this long-standing institutionalization of systematic social injustice?

Before we attempt an answer, we need to set Hand's 1958 lectures in the context of the Supreme Court's contemporaneous efforts at dismantling the widespread institutionalization of attacks on civil liberties during the McCarthy era. Only one year earlier, in a series of major decisions, the Court first signaled a turn away from its virtually complete deference to cold war governmental measures designed to punish political dissent.[85]

The most important of these cases was *Yates v. United States* (1957),[86] in which the Court reversed the Smith Act convictions of fourteen second-string leaders of the American Communist Party and indicated that it would be reluctant to sustain future convictions under the act. Distinguishing between advocacy of abstract doctrine and advocacy of action, the Court held that there was insufficient evidence of the latter to support a conviction.

In his lectures, Judge Hand criticized the *Yates* distinction as unsound and urged that a court should always bow to the legislative judgment "unless . . . [it] is satisfied that it was not the product of an effort impartially to balance the conflicting values."[87] Moreover, at a time when the Holmes-Brandeis interpretation of the "clear and present danger" test represented the chief intellectual bulwark against complete deference to legislative restrictions on unpopular speech,[88] Judge Hand pronounced: "I doubt that the doctrine will persist. . . ."[89] Indeed, Judge Hand had already done his best to subvert the clear and present danger test in his influential circuit court opinion in *Dennis v. United States* (1950),[90] upholding the prosecution of the top leaders of the Communist Party. Chief Justice Vinson's incorporation of Hand's version of that test[91] is often thought to represent the post-war nadir of Supreme Court protection of free speech.[92]

Thus, when the Supreme Court reversed the second set of convictions under the Smith Act the year before Judge Hand delivered his Holmes Lectures, he might well have had reason to feel criticized. Indeed, when one recalls that four decades earlier, in the midst of war, Hand himself had delivered a strong and unprecedented defense of unpopular speech in the *Masses* case,[93] one is left wondering what had become of Learned Hand's commitment to free speech.[94]

Hand's views on *Brown v. Board of Education* and the Bill of Rights generally are representative of the demise of a critical vision to which Progressive jurisprudence succumbed after World War II. In developing its critique of the *Lochner* Court, Progressivism had originally overstated the contradiction between democracy and judicial activism,[95] which eventually culminated in Hand's assertion in *The Bill of Rights* of the virtual illegitimacy of judicial review. As the conception of democratic process became increasingly divorced from any notion of democratic *culture*, Progressives increasingly came to define judicial review as contrary to democratic principles. In addition, the introduction of balancing tests by Progressive legal thinkers as a way of undermining the confident formalism, conceptualism, and fundamentalism of Classical Legal Thought eventually also undermined Progressivism's own confidence in the validity of its social vision.

By the time Hand wrote, his school of pre-war Progressivism had come to focus upon adherence to judicial restraint as the paramount test of whether a judge was principled or opportunistic.

One can best capture the stakes in this issue by looking back twelve years earlier to Judge Hand's 1946 eulogy of Chief Justice Harlan Fiske Stone.[96] As the post-war division within pre-war Progressivism grew, one of the most prominent forms of debate involved argument over whether earlier revered figures such as Holmes, Brandeis—and now Stone—would have accepted or rejected a preferred position for civil liberties. Never so much as mentioning either Stone's *Carolene Products* footnote or his solitary dissent in the first *Flag Salute Case*, Hand nevertheless claimed Stone for his, the anti-preferred position, camp.

Hand's eulogy enables us to capture his justification for judicial restraint at a time before the sides became bitterly divided during the 1950s. Presenting a now standard Progressive version of the New Deal triumph over the *Lochner* Court, Hand declared that when Stone was appointed to the Supreme Court in 1925, "there had for long been a cleavage, deep though somewhat vague in its boundaries . . . chiefly in the interpretation of the Bill of Rights. . . ."

> With the extraordinary industrial expansion which followed the Civil War, there came in the seventies and eighties acute industrial and agrarian tensions, which, though in kind they were not new and indeed went back to the beginning of the republic and earlier, had not theretofore been thought to call for much affirmative governmental regulation. Beginning in the eighties the states strove to relieve these by statutes whose passage the propertied interests, on whom they impinged, were powerless to prevent.
>
> They appealed to the Fourteenth Amendment on the score that these measures invaded just those rights of property which the Amendment had been designed to prevent. There was no doubt that they did invade those rights as they had theretofore been enjoyed and understood; and the judges, having been for the most part

drawn—as was inevitable—from the group whose interests were affected, in entire good faith found ample warrant for the position that such enactments were contrary to the fundamental presuppositions of a society based upon that system of free enterprise which the Bill of Rights guaranteed.

It was during the nineties that this movement was in its heyday; perhaps it reached its most extreme expression in the Income Tax Decision, in spite of the fact that that involved the Bill of Rights, if at all, only very obliquely.[97]

Then, while Stone was a law student "there were questionings," and Professor James Bradley Thayer at Harvard had already become the "prophet of a new approach."[98] By the time Stone became dean at Columbia Law School, "the difference was articulate and strident and he made no secret where his choice lay."[99] As justice, he sided "with that minority of brethren"—Holmes and Brandeis—"who made up for their small number by the weight of their authority."[100]

> Their notion was that the Bill of Rights could not be treated like ordinary law; its directions were to be understood rather as admonitions to forbearance; as directed against the spirit of faction when faction sought to press political advantage to ruthless extremes. These men believed that democracy was a political contrivance by which the group conflicts inevitable in all society should find a relatively harmless outlet in the give and take of legislative compromise after the contending groups had had a chance to measure their relative strength; and through which the bitterest animosities might at least be assuaged, even though that reconciliation did not ensue which sometimes follows upon an open fight. They had no illusion that the outcome would necessarily be the best obtainable, certainly not that which they might themselves have personally chosen; but the political stability of such a system, and the possible enlightenment which the battle itself might bring, were worth the price.[101]

"All this," Hand concluded, Stone, "whether as judge or as teacher, believed with deep conviction and supported with undeviating loyalty. After many years of discouragement, he saw his school apparently triumphant."[102]

But at the very moment of triumph there appeared "a logical dilemma, which like other political dilemmas, would not be suppressed as new problems arose. The battle had been fought almost exclusively over the institution of property; and, although the changes effected were revolutionary, they had been gradual, and they had not gone beyond what the prevailing fashions had demanded, here and even more in Europe."[103]

Despite the New Deal triumph, Hand ominously acknowledged, "the losing school occupied a position from which logically it was hard to dislodge it."

> It argued that the interpretation of the winners was in effect an abdication of the admitted premise that the Bill of Rights was law, and not merely a counsel of perfection and an ideal of temperance: always to be kept in mind, it is true, but whose infractions were to be treated only as matter for regret. If all it forbade were statutes or administrative excesses which were so utterly outrageous that nobody could give any rational support, it was an idle gesture, for it is nearly always possible to find a plausible justification for supporting any measure that has com-

manded enough popular support to get itself enacted. The winners answered that, however that might be, it was apparent that any more stringent doctrine than they were willing to admit made the courts a third camera—in fact final arbiters in disputes in which everybody agreed they should have no part. Unless they abstained, the whole system would fall apart; or, if it did not, certainly the judges must be made sensitive and responsive to the shifting pressures of political sentiment, a corrective which few were prepared to accept. Therefore, they argued, theirs was the only possible canon, let political logic find in it what flaws it would.[104]

Hand's eulogy, written under the immediate glow of the astonishing constitutional revolution of 1937, was addressed above all to his victorious Progressive allies. One can still feel his sense of wonder that, after a half century of struggle against the constitutional doctrines of the old order, victory had finally been achieved. At this moment of Progressive celebration, Hand turned to history to explain the meaning of its triumph.

The triumph of the Progressive position on limiting property rights, Hand suggested, was achieved only through a kind of quid pro quo, in effect an agreement on across-the-board constitutional disarmament of the Supreme Court. For otherwise, the defenders of property, who "occupied a position from which logically it was hard to dislodge" them, might return to "the admitted premise that the Bill of Rights was law, and not merely a counsel of perfection and an ideal of temperance."[105] The only way to check the legal fundamentalism of the old order, with its legitimate predisposition in constitutional matters toward an absolutist protection of property, was to undermine in the first place the law-like character of constitutional prohibitions. For "unless [the judges] abstained, the whole system would fall apart. . . ."[106]

Hand's candid discussion of the ideological premises behind the New Deal triumph took place before legal Progressivism sharply split into warring camps and before the most pious and unhistorical claims in favor of judicial restraint came to monopolize the airwaves. Hand's version of history, we should note, accepted the Beardian vision of a property-centered Constitution that needed to be defanged in a more democratic age. The holders of property, he reminded his listeners, "in entire good faith found ample warrant for the position that [regulatory] enactments were contrary to the fundamental presuppositions of a society based upon that system of free enterprise which the Bill of Rights guaranteed."[107] The only way to neutralize these pro-property constitutional norms, then, was through "the notion . . . that the Bill of Rights could not be treated like ordinary law; its directions were to be understood rather as admonitions to forbearance. . . ."[108]

Those who insisted on treating the Bill of Rights as real legal prohibitions, therefore, risked this carefully constructed constitutional compromise. "Even before Justice Stone became Chief Justice" in 1941, Hand wrote, "it began to seem as though, when 'personal rights' were in issue, something strangely akin to the discredited attitude towards the Bill of Rights of the old apostles of the institution of property, was regaining recognition."[109] Why property rights were not also personal rights "nobody took the time to explain," Hand complained, and "the fact remained that in the name of the Bill of Rights the courts were upsetting statutes which were plainly compromises between conflicting interests. . . ."[110]

Hand thus enlisted Stone's name against the revival of the "discredited" doctrines, concluding with the assurance that anyone acquainted with Stone's "robust and loyal character" would know that he would not engage in any such "opportunistic reversion at the expense of his convictions. . . ."[111] Stone "could not understand how . . . the courts should have a wider latitude" in enforcing personal rather than property rights. "There might be logical defects in his canon, but it deserved a consistent application or it deserved none at all. . . ."[112]

Hand's effort to enlist Chief Justice Stone's reputation against a preferred position stance seems astonishing in its failure to acknowledge Stone's important contributions to actually shaping such a position. Is it possible that the positions were still not clearly enough defined in 1946 for Hand to recognize the significance of Stone's *Carolene Products* footnote?

In any case, we do see that Hand had already developed the extreme version of judicial restraint that he would later articulate in his Holmes Lectures. Unless there was "a consistent application" of the principles of judicial restraint, there could be no "tradition of detachment and aloofness without which, I am persuaded, courts and judges will fail."[113]

What is most surprising about Hand's history is the apologetic tone he uses in describing the New Deal triumph. There is no substantive defense of the Progressive constitutional position about property. Rather, all that seems to be said in favor of the constitutional revolution is that it was necessary because the property doctrines of the old order were out of touch with fashion.

Consistency thus became central to Hand precisely because he seemed to feel unable substantively to justify New Deal redistributive doctrines. Because he believed that, at its core, the Constitution actually did protect absolute property rights, he could only defend the New Deal in terms of judicial method. The basic source of the fixation on consistency, uniformity, and neutral principles in post–World War II constitutional thought may have been precisely this lingering doubt among many Progressives about whether they had won an illegitimate constitutional victory during the New Deal.

By the time *Brown v. Board of Education* was decided, Judge Hand had staked so much of his justification of the New Deal triumph on methodological grounds that he was no longer able to articulate any substantive conception of distributive justice in the Constitution.

In his Holmes Lectures, Hand endorsed Professor Paul Freund's criticism of the clear and present danger test as "an over-simplified judgment" because there was no "substitute for the weighing of values."[114] The clear and present danger formula, Freund continued, conveyed "a delusion of certainty when what is most certain is the complexity of the strands in the web of freedom that the judge must disentangle."[115] Yet, it was precisely to criticize such "weighing of values" that Judge Hand had challenged the Supreme Court for assuming the illegitimate role of "a third legislative chamber" in *Brown v. Board of Education*. Was it not, in fact, because he felt that any such weighing of values by judges was illegitimate that Hand was able to characterize as "extreme" the view "that racial equality was a value that must prevail against any conflicting interest. . . ."?[116]

Was there any alternative to the weighing of values other than complete judicial abdication of a constitutional role? Scattered throughout *The Bill of Rights* are value suggestions of an alternative. In one place, Hand refers to "that temper of detachment, impartiality, and an absence of self-directed bias that is the whole content of justice."[117] In another, he argues for judicial deference to the legislature "unless the court is satisfied that it was not the product of an effort impartially to balance the conflicting values."[118] "In the end," he suggests at another point, "all that can be asked on review by a court is that the appraisals and the choice shall be impartial."[119] The judge, he adds at still another point, "is charged with freeing himself as far as he can from all personal preferences, and that becomes difficult in proportion as these are strong."[120] "Impartiality," "detachment" and the absence of "strong . . . personal preferences" appear to be Hand's implicit alternatives to a simple balancing of values.

Whatever the content of such a position, it seems clearly to exclude the judge who passionately sees injustice in racial segregation or in the suppression of minority opinion. And without such a vision, is judicial capitulation to dominant opinion not virtually guaranteed?

Along with Learned Hand's *The Bill of Rights*, the second representative expression of post-war constitutional thought was the series of Holmes Lectures delivered by Professor Herbert Wechsler of Columbia. His lectures, published as "Toward Neutral Principles of Constitutional Law,"[121] continue, after thirty years, to be the second most often cited law review article ever written.[122]

Wechsler's lectures were written in clear response to Hand's. First, Wechsler denied Hand's challenge to the historical legitimacy of judicial review. Next, he sought to justify the Court's ruling in *Brown v. Board of Education*. Finally, through the concept of "neutral principles," he attempted to spell out the ideas that Hand had been groping towards with words like "impartiality" and "detachment."

For Wechsler, the fact that "the Court has been decreeing value choices"[123] did not, as it did for Judge Hand, seem to end the inquiry and establish the illegitimacy of judicial intervention. Rather, value choices were legitimate if they could be justified by neutral principles. "[T]he courts ought to be cautious to impose a choice of values," Wechsler continued, and they should do so "only when they are persuaded, on an adequate and principled analysis, that the choice is clear. That I suggest is all that self-restraint can mean and in that sense it always is essential, whatever issue may be posed."[124]

The question, of course, was what was the content of neutral principles and principled analysis that could legitimate clear value choices? "A principled decision," Wechsler continued, ". . . is one that rests on reasons with respect to all the issues in the case, reasons that in their generality and their neutrality transcend any immediate result that is involved."[125] The key was whether there was a workable idea of "reasons that in their generality and their neutrality transcend any immediate result. . . ." A result-oriented person, Wechsler emphasized, "may not . . . realize that his position implies that the courts are free to function as a naked power organ [and] that it is an empty affirmation to regard them . . . as courts of law."[126]

So unless there were "reasons that in their generality and neutrality transcend any immediate result," a court that reacted against McCarthyism or racial segregation was behaving like "a naked power organ." Any person who "disapproves of a decision when all he knows is that it has sustained a claim put forward by a labor union or a taxpayer, a Negro or a segregationist, a corporation or a communist . . . acquiesces in the proposition that a man of different sympathy but equal information may no less properly conclude that he approves."[127] Value differences were mere difference of "sympathy' that could not be legitimately resolved by "*ad hoc* evaluation."

Wechsler quoted at length from a Harvard alumni history that suggested that Justice Curtis had contradicted himself when, six years after he dissented in the *Dred Scott Case*, he delivered a private opinion that Lincoln's Emancipation Proclamation was unconstitutional. "How simple the class historian could make it all," Wechsler declared, "by treating as the only thing that mattered whether Mr. Justice Curtis had, on the occasions noted, helped or hindered the attainment of the freedom of the slaves."[128] Why freedom from slavery was not a sufficiently neutral principle he did not explain.

Finally, Wechsler turned to recent Supreme Court decisions involving racial equality, "the decisions that for me provide the hardest test of my belief in principled adjudication."[129] While these decisions, he wrote, "have the best chance of making an enduring contribution to the quality of our society of any that I know in recent year," they "are entitled to approval" only insofar as "they rest on neutral principles. . . ."[130]

First, he directed strong criticism against the cases that had outlawed the "white primary" and racially restrictive covenants, concluding that they were simply "*ad hoc* determinations of their narrow problems, yielding no neutral principles for their extension or support."[131] Then he returned to *Brown v. Board of Education*, "which for one of my persuasion stirs the deepest conflict I experience in testing the thesis I propose."[132] The judgment, he wrote,

> must have rested on the view that racial segregation is, in principle, a denial of equality to the minority against whom it is directed; that is, the group that is not dominant politically and, therefore, does not make the choice involved. For many who support the Court's decision this assuredly is the decisive ground. But this position also presents problems. Does it not involve an inquiry into the motive of the legislature, which is generally foreclosed to the courts? Is it alternatively defensible to make the measure of validity of legislation the way it is interpreted by those who are affected by it? In the context of a charge that segregation *with equal facilities* is a denial of equality, is there not a point in *Plessy* in the statement that if "enforced separation stamps the colored race with a badge of inferiority" it is solely

because its members choose "to put that construction upon it?" Does enforced separation of the sexes discriminate against females merely because it may be the females who resent it and it is imposed by judgments predominantly male? Is a prohibition of miscegenation a discrimination against the colored member of the couple who would like to marry?[133]

Why does Wechsler find inadequate "the view that racial segregation is, in principle, a denial of equality to the minority against whom it is directed [because] the group . . . is not dominant politically and, therefore, does not make the choice involved"? Why does he characterize the assertion of systematic white domination not as a statement of social reality but rather as an impermissible "inquiry into the motive of the legislature"? Indeed, does Wechsler show any real understanding of the bitter reality of racial domination when he declares that there is "a point" in the statement in *Plessy v. Ferguson* that if "enforced separation stamps the colored race with a badge of inferiority" it is because its members choose "to put that construction upon it"? Likewise, he finds it equally difficult to imagine that "enforced separation of the sexes is discriminatory . . . merely because it may be the females who resent it and it is imposed by judgments predominately male." And why should he have had any doubt about whether a prohibition against miscegenation discriminated "against the colored member of the couple who would like to marry"?

From the perspective of a generation later, Wechsler's difficulties in holding racially discriminatory statutes unconstitutional have that inaccessible quality of ancient structures of understanding derived from a time when a fundamentally different moral order seemed to prevail with assurance. Indeed, his conclusion that "the question posed by state-enforced segregation is not one of discrimination at all"[134] seems positively astonishing. Was there something about neutral principles analysis that produced such a startling conclusion?

If discrimination of whites against blacks did not provide a neutral principle for Wechsler, "freedom of association" might, he argued. "I think, and I hope not without foundation, that the Southern white also pays heavily for segregation, not only in the sense of guilt that he must carry but also in the benefits he is denied,"[135] Wechsler wrote. In other words, unless the Southern white "also pays heavily for segregation," there is no sufficiently general principle to condemn segregation. "But if the freedom of association is denied by segregation, integration forces an association upon those for whom it is unpleasant or repugnant. . . . Given a situation where the state must practically choose between denying the association to those individuals who wish it or imposing it on those who would avoid it, is there a basis in neutral principles" for barring segregation? Wechsler asked. And he concluded: "I should like to think there is, but I confess that I have not yet written the opinion."[136]

A second consecutive Holmes lecturer had ended in doubt about the legitimacy of the *Brown* decision.[137]

Why did Wechsler find "freedom of association," not "discrimination," the appropriately neutral framework for evaluating the segregation cases? Though he was never entirely explicit, Wechsler seems to have believed that only something approaching unanimous agreement—that is, consensus—constituted a sufficiently general and neutral basis for making a value choice. Discrimination analysis entailed choosing between victims and victimizers—in other words, being forced to choose between conflicting moral positions. Yet freedom of association analysis also failed because it too could not be generalized, since it "forces an association upon those for whom it is unpleasant or repugnant." There was no basis for choosing on neutral grounds between denying or imposing freedom of association because Wechsler offered no basis for concluding that whites had been systematically wronging blacks. If there was a "point" in the *Plessy* view that blacks had chosen their "badge of inferiority," there could, of course, be no such basis. The moral claims of whites and blacks could only be prima facie equal.

Like the consensus theory from which it was drawn, the neutral principles school sought to avoid ever having to decide whether one group was victimizing another, since that inevitably involved substantive evaluation of the justice of their respective claims. The emphasis on generality foreclosed any intervention to reform unjust social practices in precisely those cases in which the dominant groups had the greatest stake in justifying the status quo. By abstracting the question of segregation from its concrete historical meaning in order to avoid being accused of having a result orientation, Wechsler achieved neutrality through formalism—that is, by simple assuming the equal legitimacy of both groups' desire to choose freely with whom to associate. In its unhistorical abstractness, neutral principles analysis combined with ethical positivism to produce a new conservative formulation in orthodox legal thought.

Conclusion

Why have I ended the story around 1960, when the full flowering of the civil rights movement and the war on poverty, as well as a large proportion of significant decisions of the Warren Court, still were in the future? How could I have concluded without taking account of the breathtaking changes in postwar academic legal thought, as the virtual hegemony of the Legal Process School until the mid-1960s was followed by a swift decline of its influence during the next decade? The short answer is that, for the historian, a degree of perspective and distance remains essential if history is not to become simply an extension of current controversies about law. I wish to conclude, therefore, with a brief sketch of contemporary trends within legal theory, while acknowledging that, in the perspective of time, they may come to look very different from the ways I see them today.

Three different intellectual movements have struggled for ascendancy following the demise of the Legal Process School. The first movement has represented an extension of the postwar return to rights theories. Rights theories have developed both in reaction to the horrors of totalitarianism as well as out of admiration for the Warren Court's apparent success at disentangling rights theories from their traditional links to defenses of property and inequality. Whereas until 1940 the overwhelming majority of American Progressive legal thinkers were legal positivists who identified all talk of natural rights with the defense of unequal wealth and privilege, many of the most important progressive decisions of the Warren Court were derived from natural rights conceptions. At the same time, a parallel right-wing libertarian legal philosophy has demonstrated the malleability of rights discourse by reviving the property-centered version of rights that was a staple of Classical Legal Thought.

The two other intellectual tendencies that emerged out of the ruins of the Legal Process School are Law and Economics and Critical Legal Studies, both of which claim to be the rightful heirs to Legal Realism. This is not the place to elaborately analyze their relationship to Legal Realism; however, one important set of claims is intimately connected to several major arguments presented in this book.

The frequent assertion that the politically conservative Law and Economics movement is the true heir of Legal Realism because both share an instrumentalist and consequentialist approach to law can be accepted only if Legal Realism is treated, in Karl Llewellyn's words, as a "methodology" or "technology" entirely divorced from its connections to Progressive moral and political goals. In light of the Realists' brilliant analyses of the underlying social and political premises of the market, it would be particularly ironic if the Law and Economics movement should succeed in reestablishing Classical Legal Thought's reified picture of the market as neutral, natural, and necessary.

Even the narrower claim of Law and Economics to be the legitimate methodological successor to Legal Realism rests, in the final analysis, on understanding the connection of Legal Realism to the social sciences. Here our conclusions must be nuanced because the story, we have seen, is quite complex.

Some of those who called themselves Realists did in fact seek to substitute the behavioral social sciences for the discredited doctrinal "legal science" of Classical Legal Thought. Many explanations for the decline of Legal Realism identify this move as the fatal flaw that ultimately contributed to the demise of Realism. But this picture needs to be corrected in several respects. First, the Realists absorbed many of the earlier versions of the social sciences that did not adopt either the impoverished behavioral methodological apparatus of logical positivism or the sharp distinction between facts and values characteristic of ethical positivism. Neither turn-of-the-century institutional economists nor Progressive social and legal reformers divided their efforts to understand modern industrial society from their commitments to social justice. Second, there was an entire body of Legal Realist work that explicitly rejected both ethical positivism and the alliance between Legal Realism and value-free social science. As I have sought to demonstrate, historians have been misled into portraying Legal Realism much too narrowly because they have been seduced by Karl Llewellyn's early efforts to legitimate Realism through the prestige of science.

The most important reason why it is misleading to identify Law and Economics with Legal Realism is that, in my view, the greatest and most enduring contribution of Realism was its early recognition of the implications of cultural modernism and, in particular, of cognitive relativism for legal thought. Deriving from their attacks on the claimed objectivity of legal reasoning within Classical Legal Thought, some Realists were among the earliest American thinkers to understand the social and historical contingency of structures of thought. As they sought to delegitimate the powerfully interlocking categories of Classicism, they began to explain things in language not dissimilar from what would eventually be called the sociology of knowledge or the hermeneutic understanding of reality. It is this strand of cognitive relativism that Critical Legal Studies revived and extended in its own post—1960s critique of the Legal Process School's revival of "neutral principles."

The 1950s search for "neutral principles" was just one more effort to separate law and politics in American culture, one more expression of the persistent yearning to find an olympian position from which to objectively cushion the terrors of social choice. The search for neutral principles has always been the secular alternative in religiously pluralistic American society to a direct resort to religious authority. Yet it has served similar dogmatic and legitimating functions. One of its most important influences has been to encourage the production of abstract jurisprudential debate divorced from more particular (and inevitably controversial) political and moral visions. These abstract jurisprudential controversies have repeatedly served as snares and delusions to generations of legal thinkers, misled into believing that the previous generation's jurisprudential controversies necessarily continue to have the same political and moral significance.

The standard dichotomies of jurisprudence—judicial activism versus judicial restraint, democracy versus judicial review, positivism versus natural law, utilitarianism versus natural rights—have been argued about without the slightest acknowledgement of the fickle hold they have had on successive generations of American jurists. The idea that something concrete really follows from one's abstract position on, say, natural rights versus positivism is widely believed. Yet in American history natural rights has equally served both abolitionists and the defenders of the rights of ownership in human and non-human property. Progressive legal theory has been advanced both by the positivist view of the Realists that property is a social creation and by the emancipatory natural rights vision of the Warren Court. Conservative judicial views seem to be promoted equally well by the utilitarianism of Judge Richard Posner and the natural rights philosophy of Professor Richard Epstein of the University of Chicago. So why has legal theory continued to be discussed as if "general propositions" do indeed "decide concrete cases"?

Nowhere has the process of reification been more pronounced than in American legal theory. One of the most discouraging spectacles for the historian of legal thought is the unselfconscious process by which one generation's legal theories, developed out of the exigencies of particular political and moral struggles, quickly come to be portrayed as universal truths good for all time. This process of reification draws deep sustenance from a religious and unhistorical American culture. Thus, for example, "result oriented" jurisprudence is regularly equated with opportunism, and principled jurisprudence with sticking to one's principles regardless of their consequences. Only pragmatism, with its dynamic understanding of the unfolding of principle over time and its experimental appreciation of the complex interrelationship between law and politics and theory and practice, has stood against the static fundamentalism of traditional American conceptions of principled jurisprudence.

Until we are able to transcend the American fixation with sharply separating law from politics, we will continue to fluctuate between the traditional polarities of American legal discourse, as each generation continues frantically to hide behind unhistorical and abstract universalisms in order to deny, even to itself, its own political and moral choices.

NOTES

Introduction

1. The term "Classical Legal Thought" was originally coined by Duncan Kennedy in his manuscript "The Rise and Fall of Classical Legal Thought." A small portion of that manuscript has been published as *Towards an Historical Understanding of Legal Consciousness: The Case of Classical Legal Thought in America, 1850–1940*, 3 RES. LAW & SOC. (1980). Kennedy was the first scholar to attempt to elaborate a structure of late-nineteenth-century legal thought, from which I have extensively borrowed. He should also be credited with having first identified the history of American legal thought as a coherent scholarly field separate from constitutional history.

Chapter 1

1. *See* C. COOK, THE AMERICAN CODIFICATION MOVEMENT (Greenwood Press 1981); P. MILLER, THE LIFE OF THE MIND IN AMERICA: FROM THE REVOLUTION TO THE CIVIL WAR (Harcourt, Brace & World 1965); Gordon, *The American Codification Movement: A Study of Antebellum Legal Reform*, 36, VAND. L. REV. 431 (1983).

2. *See* M. HORWITZ, THE TRANSFORMATION OF AMERICAN LAW, 1780–1860, at 17–18, 257, 258 (Harvard Univ. Press 1977).

3. THE FEDERALIST No. 10, at 131 (J. Madison) (B. Wright ed., Harvard Univ. Press 1961). *See generally* J. NEDELSKY, PRIVATE PROPERTY AND THE LIMITS OF AMERICAN CONSTITUTIONALISM (Univ. of Chicago Press 1990).

4. J. KENT, COMMENTARIES ON AMERICAN LAW (4 vols, O. Halsted 1826–1830).

5. *See* M. HORWITZ, *supra* note 2, at 253–66; G. E. WHITE, TORT LAW IN AMERICA: AN INTELLECTUAL HISTORY 20–62 (Oxford Univ. Press 1980); Gordon, *Legal Thought and Legal Practice in the Age of American Enterprise, 1870–1920*, in PROFESSIONS AND PROFESSIONAL IDEOLOGIES IN AMERICA 70, 82 (G. Geison ed., Univ. of North Carolina Press 1943).

6. *See* Usher, *James I and Sir Edward Coke*, 17 ENG. HIST. REV. 664 (1903); T. HOBBES, A DIALOGUE BETWEEN A PHILOSOPHER AND A STUDENT OF THE COMMON LAWS OF ENGLAND (J. Cropsey ed., Univ. of Chicago Press 1971).

7. R. WIEBE, THE SEARCH FOR ORDER, 1877–1920, at 81–83, 92–93, 117 (Hill & Wang 1967).

8. *See* E. GENOVESE, ROLL, JORDAN, ROLL: THE WORLD THE SLAVES MADE (Pantheon 1974).

9. *See* M. TUSHNET, THE AMERICAN LAW OF SLAVERY, 1810–1860: CONSIDERATIONS OF HUMANITY AND INTEREST 63–64, 71–73 (Princeton Univ. Press 1981).

10. *See The Public/Private Distinction*, 130 U. PA. L. REV. 1289, 1423–28 (1982).

11. Dartmouth College v. Woodward (Story, J., concurring), 17 U.S. (4 Wheat.) 518 (1819).

12. *See* C. HAINES, THE REVIVAL OF NATURAL LAW CONCEPTS 88–95 (Harvard Univ. Press 1930).

13. *See* M. HORWITZ, *supra* note 2, at 63–66.

14. *See infra* text accompanying note 81.

15. *See* 6 C. FAIRMAN, RECONSTRUCTION AND REUNION, 1864–88, at 918–1116 (Macmillan 1971).

16. *See* C. DEGLER, AT ODDS: WOMEN AND THE FAMILY IN AMERICA FROM THE REVOLUTION TO THE PRESENT 26–29 (Oxford Univ. Press 1980); Delamont & Duffin, *Introduction* to THE NINETEENTH-CENTURY WOMAN: HER CULTURAL AND PHYSICAL WORLD at 19–21 (S. Delamont & L. Duffin eds., Barnes & Noble 1978); C. LASCH, HAVEN IN A HEARTLESS WORLD: THE FAMILY BESIEGED 6–8 (Basic Books 1977); N. COTT, THE BONDS OF WOMANHOOD: "WOMAN'S SPHERE" IN NEW ENGLAND, 1780–1835 (Yale Univ. Press 1977); E. ZARETSKY, CAPITALISM, THE FAMILY, AND PERSONAL LIFE (Harper & Row 1976).

17. *See* Benedict, *Laissez-Faire and Liberty: A Re-Evaluation of the Meaning and Origins of Laissez-Faire Constitutionalism*, 3 LAW & HIST. REV. 293 (1983).

18. "Public wrongs, crimes and punishments, depend on the legislative will for their existence as such: private rights and private wrongs are founded on and measured by the immutable principles of natural law and abstract justice." J. GOODENOW, HISTORICAL SKETCHES OF THE PRINCIPLES AND MAXIMS OF AMERICAN JURISPRUDENCE (J. Wilson 1819), *cited in* M. HORWITZ, *supra* note 2, at 246.

19. *See* W. NELSON, AMERICANIZATION OF THE COMMON LAW: THE IMPACT OF LEGAL CHANGE ON MASSACHUSETTS SOCIETY, 1760–1830, at 69–88 (Harvard Univ. Press 1975).

20. *See* Kennedy, *The Structure of Blackstone's Commentaries*, 28 BUFFALO L. REV. 209, 233 (1978–1979).

21. *See* W. NELSON, *supra* note 19, at 85–88.

22. J. STORY, SELECTION OF PLEADINGS IN CIVIL ACTIONS (Barnard B. Macanulty 1805).

23. N. DANE, A GENERAL ABRIDGEMENT AND DIGEST OF AMERICAN LAW (9 vols., Cummings, Hilliard 1823–1829).

24. F. HILLIARD, THE LAW OF TORTS vii ((Little, Brown 1859).

25. *Id.; see also* G. E. WHITE, *supra* note 5, at 11.

26. F. HILLIARD, *supra* note 24, at iv.

27. T. SHEARMAN & A. REDFIELD, A TREATISE ON THE LAW OF NEGLIGENCE iv (1st ed., Baker, Voorhis 1869).

28. T. SHEARMAN & A. REDFIELD, A TREATISE ON THE LAW OF NEGLIGENCE iii (3d ed., Baker, Voorhis 1874).

29. *See* Holmes, *Codes, and the Arrangement of the Law*, 5 AM. L. REV. 1 (1870).

30. *See infra* ch. 2.

31. *See* J. Perilleux, *Some Reflections on Causation and the Law of Torts in Nineteenth Century Common Law* 234–54 (unpublished S.J.D. dissertation, Harvard Univ. 1981); Holmes, *The Theory of Torts*, 7 AM. L. REV. 652, 660–63 (1873).

32. *See* O. W. HOLMES, THE COMMON LAW 63–103, 115–29 (M. Howe ed., Harvard Univ. Press 1963).

33. Holmes, *supra* note 31.

34. *See* Brown v. Collins, 53 N.H. 442 (1873); Losee v. Buchanan, 51 N.Y. 476 (1873); Rylands v. Fletcher, L.R., 3 E. & I. App. (H.L.) 330 (1868); C. Dalton, Losing

History: The Case of *Rylands v. Fletcher* (unpublished manuscript); G. E. WHITE, *supra* note 5, at 16–18.

35. O. W. HOLMES, *supra* note 32, at 160–161. *See* M. HORWITZ, *supra* note 2, at 204–7.

36. Holmes, *Agency* (pts. 1 & 2), 4 HARV. L. REV. 345 (1891), 5 HARV. L. REV. 1, 14 (1891).

37. *See* M. HORWITZ, *supra* note 2, at 264.

38. W. KEENER, A TREATISE ON THE LAW OF QUASI-CONTRACTS (Baker, Voorhis 1893).

39. *See infra* ch. 5.

40. 157 U.S. 429, *aff'd on rehearing*, 158 U.S. 601 (1895); *see also* discussion *infra* text accompanying notes 61–105.

41. 198 U.S. 45 (1905).

42. *See* J. SHKLAR, LEGALISM (Harvard Univ. Press 1964).

43. The debate over whether there was a harmonious and gapless fit between the doctrines of law and equity became one other arena of challenge to the perfectionist claims of Classical Legal Thought. *See* Cook, The Place of Equity in Our Legal System, 3 AM. L. SCH. REV. 173 (1912); Hohfeld, *The Relations Between Equity and Law*, 11 MICH. L. REV. 537 (1913) (criticizing Maitland and Langdell).

44. *Compare* United States v. E. C. Knight Co., 156 U.S. 1 (1895) *with* Swift v. U.S., 196 U.S. 375 (1905) and Stafford v. Wallace, 358 U.S. 495 (1922).

45. Munn v. Illinois, 94 U.S. 113 (1876).

46. *See* Beale, *The Proximate Consequences of an Act*, 33 HARV. L. REV. 633, 646 (1920).

47. *See* United States v. Trans-Missouri Freight Ass'n, 166 U.S. 290, 328 (1897).

48. *See infra* ch. 6, text accompanying notes 110–114.

49. *See infra* text accompanying notes 63–79.

50. *See infra* text accompanying notes 72.

51. For the eminent domain power, see M. HORWITZ, *supra* note 2, at 49–50, 65. For the taxing power, see *infra* text accompanying note 81.

52. *See* Standard Oil of New Jersey v. United States, 221 U.S. 1 (1911).

53. *See* Rose v. Socony-Vacuum, 54 R.I. 411, 173 A. 627 (1934). For injunctions against nuisances, the balancing test came into being much earlier. *See* Kurtz, *Nineteenth Century Anti-Entrepreneurial Nuisance Injunctions—Avoiding the Chancellor*, 17 WM. & MARY L. REV. 621 (1976); Halper, *Nuisance, Courts and Markets in the New York Court of Appeals, 1850–1915*, 54 ALB. L. REV. 301 (1990).

54. The classic statement for the law of negligence is found in Terry, *Negligence*, 29 HARV. L. REV. 40, 42–44 (1915). It is the basis for the Learned Hand test elaborated in United States v. Carroll Towing, 159 F.2d 169 (2d Cir. 1947).

55. *See* Pennsylvania Coal Co. v. Mahon, 260 U.S. 393 (1922).

56. *See* Schenck v. United States, 249 U.S. 47 (1919).

57. Pound, *A Theory of Social Interests*, 15 PAPERS & PROC. AM. SOC. SOC'Y 16 (1921), published (with revisions) as *A Survey of Social Interests*, 57 HARV. L. REV. 1, 7 (1943). *See also* Aleinikoff, *Constitutional Law in the Age of Balancing*, 96 YALE L.J. 943, 959 (1987).

58. 157 U.S. 429, *aff'd on rehearing*, 158 U.S. 601 (1895).

59. *See* L. LEVY, THE ESTABLISHMENT CLAUSE 25–62 (Macmillan 1986).

60. *See* Nelson, *Changing Conceptions of Judicial Review: The Evolution of Constitutional Theory in the States, 1790–1860*, 120 U. PA. L. REV. 1166 (1972).

61. *See* L. FRIEDMAN, A HISTORY OF AMERICAN LAW 126–27, 371 (2d ed., Simon & Schuster 1985). By 1890, about two-thirds of the states elected their supreme and superior court judges. *See* M. KELLER, AFFAIRS OF STATE 358 (Harvard Univ. Press 1977).

62. *See* Horwitz, *Republicanism and Liberalism in American Constitutional Thought,* 29 WM. & MARY L. REV. 57 (1987).

63. T. COOLEY, TREATISE ON THE LAW OF TAXATION 3–4 (Callaghan 1876).

64. *Id.* at 2.

65. F. HILLIARD, THE LAW OF TAXATION 290 (Little, Brown 1875). *See* Diamond, *The Death and Transfiguration of Benefit Taxation: Special Assessments in Nineteenth Century America,* 12 J. LEGAL STUD. 201 (1983); M. KELLER, *supra* note 61, at 323, 332.

66. 2 W. NEWHOUSE, CONSTITUTIONAL UNIFORMITY AND EQUALITY IN STATE TAXA-TION 1702–7 (2d. ed., William S. Hein 1984).

67. *Id.* at 1709–11.

68. T. COOLEY, *supra* note 63, at iv.

69. *Id.* at 125.

70. *Id.* at 127–28.

71. *Id.* at 128.

72. *Id.* at 2.

73. *Id.* at iv.

74. *Id.* at 20.

75. *Id.* at 178 (quoting Lexington v. McQuillan's Heirs, 39 Ky. (9 Dana) 513, 516 (1839)) (emphasis retained).

76. Corwin, *The Basic Doctrine of American Constitutional Law,* 12 MICH. L. REV. 247 (1914).

77. T. COOLEY, *supra* note 63, at 178 (quoting Lexington v. McQuillan's Heirs, 39 Ky. (9 Dana) at 517).

78. *Washington Avenue,* 69 Pa. 352, 363 (1871).

79. *Id.* at 364.

80. For an elaborate discussion of the municipal bond cases, see C. FAIRMAN, *supra* note 15.

81. *See* Loan Association v. Topeka, 87 U.S. (20 Wall.) 655 (1874) (Miller, J.); People v. Salem, 20 Mich. 452 (1870) (Cooley, J.). *See also* M. KELLER, *supra* note 61, at 329–30.

82. *See* M. HORWITZ, *supra* note 2, at 259–61.

83. 87 U.S. (20 Wall.) 655, 664 (1874).

84. *See* L. HARTZ, ECONOMIC POLICY AND DEMOCRATIC THOUGHT: PENNSYLVANIA, 1776–1860 (Harvard Univ. Press 1948); Jones, *Thomas M. Cooley and "Laissez-Faire Constitutionalism": A Reconsideration,* 53 J. AM. HIST. 751 (1967); McCurdy, *Justice Field and the Jurisprudence of Government-Business Relations: Some Parameters of Laissez-Faire Constitutionalism, 1863–1897,* 61 J. AM. HIST. 970 (1975).

85. 83 U.S. (16 Wall.) 36 (1873).

86. 198 U.S. 45 (1905).

87. 87 U.S. (20 Wall.) 655 (1874). A diversity case is one in which the plaintiff and defendant come from different states; it may be brought in federal court.

88. *Id.* at 664.

89. Davidson v. New Orleans, 96 U.S. 97 (1877).

90. Santa Clara v. Southern Pac. R.R. Co., 18 F. 385 (C.C.D. Cal. 1883), *aff'd.,*

118 U.S. 394 (1886); Railroad Tax Cases, 13 F. 722 (C.C.D. Cal. 1882), *writ dism'd sub nom.* San Mateo County v. Southern Pac. R.R. Co., 116 U.S. 138 (1885).

91. Railroad Tax Cases, 13 F. 722, 733 (C.C.D. Cal. 1882).

92. *Id.* at 734.

93. *See supra* note 90.

94. 157 U.S. 429 (1895).

95. *See infra* ch. 5.

96. *See, e.g.*, A. PAUL, CONSERVATIVE CRISIS AND THE RULE OF LAW: ATTITUDES OF BAR AND BENCH, 1887–1895, at 2, 219–20 (Cornell Univ. Press 1960); S. FINE, LAISSEZ FAIRE AND THE GENERAL-WELFARE STATE 126–64 (Univ. of Michigan Press 1956); C. JACOBS, LAW WRITERS AND THE COURTS 85–93 (Univ. of California Press 1954); B. TWISS, LAWYERS AND THE CONSTITUTION (Princeton Univ. Press 1942).

97. *Id.* at 166–70.

98. Dillon, *Property—Its Rights and Duties in Our Legal and Social Systems*, 29 AM. L. REV. 161, 162–63 (1895).

99. *Id.* at 172.

100. *Id.*

101. *Id.*

102. *Id.* at 172–73.

103. *Id.* at 173.

104. *Id.*

105. Pollock v. Farmers' Loan & Trust Co., 157 U.S. 429, 532 (1895).

106. *Id.* at 504 (emphasis retained).

107. *Id.* at 586–608 (Field J., concurring).

108. *See* J. SCHUMPETER, *The Decline of Liberalism*, in HISTORY OF ECONOMIC ANALYSIS 759–71 (Oxford Univ. Press 1954).

109. 61 Mass. (7 Cush.) 53 (1851). *See* L. LEVY, THE LAW OF THE COMMONWEALTH AND CHIEF JUSTICE SHAW 247-54 (Harvard Univ. Press 1957).

110. *See infra* ch. 3.

111. 3 W. BLACKSTONE, COMMENTARIES *219, *cited in* M. HORWITZ, *supra* note 2, at 76–77.

112. A striking exception is the "reasonable use" doctrine that had triumphed in water law by 1850. *See* M. HORWITZ, *supra* note 2, at 34–42.

113. *See* Bone, *Normative Theory and Legal Doctrine in American Nuisance Law: 1850 to 1920*, 59 S. CAL. L. REV. 1101 (1986).

114. *See* Bohlen, *The Rule in Rylands v. Fletcher*, 59 U. PA. L. REV. 298 (1911).

115. *See* Kurtz, *supra* note 53.

116. 94 U.S. 113 (1876).

117. *See* J. GUSFIELD, SYMBOLIC CRUSADE: STATUS POLITICS AND THE AMERICAN TEMPERANCE MOVEMENT (Univ. of Illinois Press 1963); I. TYRRELL, SOBERING UP: FROM TEMPERANCE TO PROHIBITION IN ANTEBELLUM AMERICA, 1800–1860 (Greenwood Press 1979).

118. *See* M. KELLER, *supra* note 61, at 412–13.

119. 123 U.S. 623 (1887).

120. The famous *Wynehamer* case in New York does not contradict this view. Wynehamer v. People, 13 N.Y. 378 (1856). There the court refused to uphold a criminal conviction under a state prohibition statute for a sale of liquor prior to the passage of the statute while it freely conceded that the statute would apply to a subsequent sale.

121. *See* Powell v. Pennsylvania, 127 U.S. 678 (1888).

122. 83 U.S. (16 Wall.) 36 (1873).

123. T. COOLEY, A TREATISE ON THE CONSTITUTIONAL LIMITATIONS WHICH REST UPON THE LEGISLATIVE POWER OF THE STATES OF THE AMERICAN UNION (Little, Brown 1868).

124. *Id.* at 577.

125. 198 U.S. 45 (1905).

126. *Id.* at 60.

127. *Id.* at 59.

Chapter 2

1. 198 U.S. 45 (1905).

2. *See* L. FRIEDMAN, CONTRACT LAW IN AMERICA 184–94 (Univ. of Wisconsin Press 1965).

3. Pound, *Liberty of Contract*, 18 YALE L.J. 454 (1909).

4. Actually, Pound begins with a statement by Justice Harlan in Adair v. United States, 208 U.S. 161, 174–75 (1908):

> The right of a person to sell his labor upon such terms as he deems proper is, in its essence, the same as the right of the purchaser of labor to prescribe the conditions upon which he will accept such labor from the person offering to sell it. So the right of the employee to quit the service of the employer, for whatever reason, is the same as the right of the employer, for whatever reason, to dispense with the service of such employee. . . . In all such particulars the employer and the employee have equality of right, and any legislation that disturbs that equality is an arbitrary interference with the liberty of contract, which no government can legally justify in a free land.

Quoted in Pound, *supra* note 3, at 454.

5. *Id.*

6. *Id.* at 455.

7. *Id.*

8. *Id.* at 454, 457.

9. *Id.* at 464.

10. *Id.* at 460–61.

11. *See* M. HORWITZ, THE TRANSFORMATION OF AMERICAN LAW, 1780–1860, at 197–201 (Harvard Univ. Press 1977).

12. Corbin, *Offer and Acceptance, and Some of the Resulting Legal Relations*, 26 YALE L.J. 169, 206 (1917).

13. *See* R. WIEBE, THE SEARCH FOR ORDER (Hill & Wang 1967).

14. *See infra* ch. 4.

15. Holmes, *Codes, and the Arrangement of the Law*, 5 AM. L. REV. 1, 11 (1870).

16. W. KEENER, A TREATISE ON THE LAW OF QUASI-CONTRACTS (Baker, Voorhis 1893).

17. *See id.* at 3–25.

18. *See* M. HORWITZ, *supra* note 11, at 184–85.

19. O. W. HOLMES, THE COMMON LAW (1st ed., Little, Brown 1881).

20. *Id.* at 302–3. This runs parallel to my assertion in chapter 4, *infra*, that objectiv-

ism in tort law was for a long time not regarded as in conflict with, but as a supplement to, the principle of negligence.

21. M. HOWE, JUSTICE OLIVER WENDELL HOLMES: THE PROVING YEARS, 1870–1882, at 241 (Harvard Univ. Press 1963).

22. *Id.* at 245.

23. *Id.* at 242.

24. *Id.* Another continuing source of ambiguity can be found in the frequent assertion of Holmes that only external behavior can provide evidence of internal mental states. It is thereby possible to reduce his claim to one about the "best evidence." For example, Professor Howe writes: "The second edition of Holland's influential *Elements of Jurisprudence*, published after its author had read *The Common Law*, repudiated the subjective or will theory of contract liability and urged that in the field of contracts, as elsewhere, the law looks, not at the will itself, but at the will as voluntarily manifested." *Id.* at 246. I do not regard this as a strong repudiation of the will theory. Compare Theophilus Parsons's stronger statement in his 1855 contracts treatise: "[T]he rules of law as well as the rules of language may interfere to prevent a construction in accordance with the intent of the parties." 2 T. PARSONS, THE LAW OF CONTRACTS 6–9 (1st ed., Little, Brown 1855).

25. O. W. HOLMES, *The Path of the Law*, in COLLECTED LEGAL PAPERS 181 (Harcourt, Brace & Howe 1920).

26. I am uncertain, after all, whether, as Professor Howe asserts, Holmes had already completely recognized this point in *The Common Law*. In terms of the reception of his ideas, however, I am convinced that the statement in "The Path of the Law" marks the moment at which objectivism is generally understood to be incompatible with a will theory of contract.

27. Ashley, *Mutual Assent in Contract*, 3 COLUM. L. REV. 71 (1903) [hereafter Ashley, *Mutual Assent*]; Ashley, *Should There Be Freedom of Contract?* 4 COLUM. L. REV. 423, 427 (1904) [hereafter Ashley, *Freedom of Contract*].

28. Ashley, *Freedom of Contract, supra* note 27, at 424.

29. *Id.*

30. Ashley, *Mutual Assent, supra* note 27, at 78.

31. Costigan, *Constructive Contracts*, 19 GREEN BAG 512, 513 (1907).

32. *Id.*

33. For another example, see *id.* at 512–13, criticizing confusion of categories in Cook, *Agency by Estoppel*, 5 COLUM. L. REV. 36 (1905).

34. J. STORY, COMMENTARIES ON THE LAW OF AGENCY (1st ed., Little & Brown 1839).

35. Indeed, Story used the terms interchangeably. The "principal" is liable for his "agent's" torts, Story wrote, "although the principal did not authorize, or justify, or participate in, or, indeed, know of such misconduct, or even if he forbade them, or disapproved of them." *Id.* § 452, at 465. The rule of *respondeat superior* "is founded upon public policy and convenience. . . . In every such case, the principal holds out his agent as competent, and fit to be trusted; and thereby, in effect, he warrants his fidelity and good conduct in all the matters of the agency." *Id.* § 452, at 465–66.

36. "The whole doctrine rests on the maxim . . . *qui facit per alium, facit per se*; and it is a plain and obvious dictate of natural justice, that he, who is to receive the benefit, shall bear the burden; and that he, who has acquired, through his agent, certain fixed rights and remedies upon the contract against the other contracting party, shall be placed in a position of entire reciprocity in regard to the latter." *Id.* § 442, at 450–51.

37. *See* Holmes, *Agency* (pts. 1 & 2), 4 HARV. L. REV. 345, 5 HARV. L. REV. 1 (1891).

38. J. STORY, *supra* note 34, § 126, at 115.

39. *Id.* § 131, at 121.

40. A. CHANDLER, THE VISIBLE HAND: THE MANAGERIAL REVOLUTION IN AMERICAN BUSINESS 15 (Harvard Univ. Press 1977).

41. *Id.* at 20.

42. J. STORY, *supra* note 34, § 127, at 117 n.1.

43. *Id.* § 443, at 451.

44. *Id.*

45. *Id.* § 133, at 123.

46. A. CHANDLER, *supra* note 40, at 14.

47. *Id.* at 15.

48. *See* Wigmore, *Responsibility for Tortious Acts: Its History* (pt. 2), 7 HARV. L. REV. 383 (1894).

49. *See* 1 W. CLARK & H. SKYLES, TREATISE ON THE LAW OF AGENCY 1085–89 (Keefe-Davidson 1905); F. MECHEM, TREATISE ON THE LAW OF AGENCY § 740, at 577 (Callaghan 1889). Of the American cases cited by Mechem and Clark & Skyles, two were decided in the 1850s, five in the 1860s, fifteen in the 1870s, eleven in the 1880s, and seven in the 1890s.

Perhaps, however, the formerly subjective command requirement had itself only been objectivized as courts created the new category of "independent contractor" whose torts did not result in vicarious liability for his employer. The judicial justification of the distinction between servants and independent contractors thus tended to replicate the older emphasis on the extent of the master's command and control. In any event, once one was found to be a servant, the question of command entirely dropped out.

50. Holmes, *supra* note 37.

51. F. WHARTON, COMMENTARY ON THE LAW OF AGENCY AND AGENTS (Kay & Brother 1876).

52. Mechanics' Bank v. New York & N.H.R.R., 13 N.Y. 599, 632 (1856) (Comstock, J.).

53. 1 T. PARSONS, THE LAW OF CONTRACTS 44 (5th ed., Little, Brown 1864).

54. Pole v. Leask, 33 L.J. 155, 162 (1863) Ch. (Lord Cranworth), *quoted in* F. WHARTON, *supra* note 51, § 459, at 299.

55. F. WHARTON, *supra* note 51, § 19, at 15–16.

56. W. ANSON, PRINCIPLES OF THE ENGLISH LAW OF CONTRACT vii (6th ed., Oxford Univ. Press 1891).

57. F. WHARTON, *supra* note 51, § 122, at 75, 77.

58. *See* Farmers & Mechanics' Bank v. Butchers & Drovers' Bank, 16 N.Y. 125 (1857); Griswold v. Haven, 25 N.Y. 595 (1862).

59. New York & N.H.R.R. v. Schuyler, 34 N.Y. 30, 69 (1865).

60. Griswold v. Haven, 25 N.Y. 595, 599 (1862).

61. Mechanics' Bank v. New York & N.H.R.R., 13 N.Y. 599, 634 (1856).

62. *Id.*

63. *See* 1 T. PARSONS, THE LAW OF CONTRACTS 43 (3d ed., Little, Brown 1857); 1 T. PARSONS, THE LAW OF CONTRACTS 46 (6th ed., Little, Brown 1873).

64. New York & N.H.R.R. v. Schuyler, 34 N.Y. 30, 70 (1865).

65. Griswold v. Haven, 25 N.Y. 599, 600 (1862).

66. Corbin, *Ratification in Agency Without Knowledge of Material Facts*, 15 YALE L.J. 331 (1906).

67. Ames, *Undisclosed Principal—His Rights and Liabilities*, YALE L.J. 443 (1906).

68. J. H. BEALE, A *Summary of the Conflict of Laws*, in 3 A SELECTION OF CASES ON THE CONFLICT OF LAWS § 92, at 542 (Harvard Law Review Publishing Association 1902).

69. *See* S. GREENLEAF, TREATISE ON THE LAW OF EVIDENCE (3 vols., Little & Brown 1842–1853); W. STORY, TREATISE ON THE LAW OF CONTRACTS NOT UNDER SEAL (Little & Brown 1844). As early as the 1840s, both W. W. Story in his treatise on contracts and Simon Greenleaf in his treatise on evidence had maintained that all implied contracts were actually proven on the basis of inferences from the parties' behavior. Thus, there were no implied-in-law contracts; all contractual obligation was derived from the parties' wills. But the elaborate development of implied-in-law contracts beginning in the 1850s eventually left no doubt that all implied contracts could not be grounded in the parties' wills. *See* M. HORWITZ, *supra* note 11, at 185.

70. Cook, *supra* note 33, at 38.

71. The major paths through which the doctrine of apparent authority developed were cases in which courts imputed authority from the course of business dealings. *See* Whitney, *Agency Imputed from "Course of Business,"* 3 COLUM. L. REV. 395 (1903). Whitney protested this development, which he traced back to a dictum in Martin v. Webb, 110 U.S. 7 (1884). "There is nothing contractual about it," he complained. Whitney, *supra*, at 400. The doctrine had originally developed in cases against banks that gave credit.

72. Cook, *supra* note 33, at 40.

73. *Id.*

74. Costigan, *supra* note 31, at 513–15.

75. *See* G. GILMORE, THE DEATH OF CONTRACT (Ohio State Univ. Press 1974); P. ATIYAH, THE RISE AND FALL OF FREEDOM OF CONTRACT (Oxford Univ. Press 1979).

76. Ames, *supra* note 67, at 443; Lewis, *The Liability of the Undisclosed Prinicpal in Contract,* 9 COLUM. L. REV. 116 (1909).

77. Lewis, *supra* note 76, at 135.

78. O. W. HOLMES, *supra* note 25, at 181.

79. Corbin's earliest writing was his alumni address at the University of Kansas, his alma mater, in 1906. "We should have no tendency to be overcome by the glamour of the Eastern universities or of the larger universities. A school is not to be judged by its size or by its age or by its money or by its geographical location or by its assumption of learning." Corbin, *The Almnus and the Law,* 32 U. KAN. L. REV. 763, 764 (1984). There was also an expression of the frontier's influence on the spirit of equality. "I am here to argue for democracy in education and for democracy in thought. Without blinding himself to the value of what he has, the alumnus must cease to be an intellectual aristocrat and become an intellectual democrat." *Id.* at 766. *See also* Jerry, *Arthur L. Corbin: His Kansas Connection,* 32 U. KAN. L. REV. 753 (1984); G. E. WHITE, EASTERN ESTABLISHMENT AND THE WESTERN EXPERIENCE (Yale Univ. Press 1968).

80. Dean Christopher Columbus Langdell of Harvard Law School was one of the most prominent examples in law of what Peter Novick has called the "conservative evolutionism" of late-nineteenth-century American thought. P. NOVICK, THAT NOBLE DREAM: THE "OBJECTIVITY QUESTION" AND THE AMERICAN HISTORICAL PROFESSION 80–81, 87 (Cambridge Univ. Press 1988). *See* Grey, *Langdell's Orthodoxy,* 45 U. PITT. L. REV. 1 (1983). On the relationship between Turner and Eastern conservatism, *see* R. HOFSTADTER, THE PROGRESSIVE HISTORIANS 65–70 (Knopf 1968) and Horwitz, *History and Theory,* 96 YALE L.J. 1825, 1826 (1987).

81. J. DEWEY, *The Influence of Darwinism on Philosophy*, in 4 THE MIDDLE WORKS, 1899–1924, at 14 (J. Boydston ed., Southern Illinois Univ. Press 1977), *cited in* J. KLOP-

PENBERG, UNCERTAIN VICTORY: SOCIAL DEMOCRACY AND PROGRESSIVISM IN EUROPEAN AND AMERICAN THOUGHT, 1870–1920, at 10 (Oxford Univ. Press 1986).

82. Corbin, *Quasi-Contractual Obligations*, 21 YALE L.J. 533, 543 (1912).

83. *Id.* at 552.

84. Corbin, *Discharge of Contracts*, 22 YALE L.J. 513, 515 (1913).

85. Corbin, *supra* note 12, at 206.

86. Corbin, *Contracts for the Benefit of Third Persons*, 27 YALE L.J. 1008 (1918). *See also* Corbin, *Does a Pre-Existing Duty Defeat Consideration?—Recent Noteworthy Decisions*, 27 YALE L.J. 362 (1918), in which he criticizes the consideration doctrines that supposedly followed from the will theory. He congratulated Judge Benjamin N. Cardozo for his recent decision in DeCicco v. Schweizer, 221 N.Y. 431, 117 N.E. 807 (1917), calling it "a righteous decision." Corbin, *Does a Pre-Existing Duty Defeat Consideration?*, *supra*, at 381.

87. Seavey, *The Rationale of Agency*, 29 YALE L.J. 859 (1920).

88. *Id.* at 868.

89. *Id.* at 878.

90. *Id.*

91. *Id.* at 868.

92. *Id.* at 884.

93. *See* Priest, *The Invention of Enterprise Liability: A Critical History of the Intellectual Foundations of Modern Tort Law*, 14 J. LEGAL STUD. 461 (1985).

94. *See* Laski, *The Basis of Vicarious Liability*, 26 YALE L.J. 105 (1916); Douglas, *Vicarious Liability and the Administration of Risk*, 38 YALE L.J. 584 (1928).

95. F. BACON, *Maxims of the Law*, in 7 WORKS 307, 327 (J. Spedding, R. Ellis & D. Heath eds., Longman 1879).

96. *See* M. HOWE, *supra* note 21, at 151.

97. [Green] *Proximate and Remote Cause*, 4 AM. L. REV. 201, 211 (1870), *reprinted in* N. GREEN, ESSAYS AND NOTES ON THE LAW OF TORT AND CRIMES (J. Frank ed., Banta 1933).

98. *Id.*

99. *See* P. WEINER, EVOLUTION AND THE FOUNDERS OF PRAGMATISM, 152–71 (Harvard Univ. Press 1949).

100. Green, *supra* note 97, at 213.

101. [Green], *Torts Under the French Law* (Book Review), 8 AM. L. REV. 508, 519 (1874), *reprinted in* N. GREEN, *supra* note 97.

102. Green, *supra* note 97, at 213.

103. *Id.* at 215.

104. M. HOWE, *supra* note 21, at 74–76; Fisch, *Justice Holmes, the Prediction Theory of Law and Pragmatism*, 39 J. PHIL. 85 (1942).

105. F. WHARTON, A SUGGESTION AS TO CAUSATION 3 (Riverside Press 1874). [hereafter F. WHARTON, SUGGESTION]. John Stuart Mill's challenge to orthodox ideas of causation was first presented in J. S. MILL, SYSTEM OF LOGIC (2 vols., John W. Parker 1843) and J. S. MILL, AN EXAMINATION OF SIR WILLIAM HAMILTON'S PHILOSOPHY (Longmans 1865). Mill's ideas on causation came to Wharton's attention through R. HAZARD, TWO LETTERS ON CAUSATION AND FREEDOM IN WILLING (Longmans 1869), which contests Mill's ideas. *See* F. WHARTON, A TREATISE ON THE LAW OF NEGLIGENCE § 155, at 137 n.1 (2d. ed., Kay 1878) [hereafter F. WHARTON, NEGLIGENCE]. The issue was apparently revived for Wharton by the posthumous publication of J. S. MILL, AUTOBIOGRAPHY (Longmans

1873). The significance of Mill's epistemology for American philosophy is discussed in B. KUKLICK, THE RISE OF AMERICAN PHILOSOPHY: CAMBRIDGE, MASSACHUSETTS, 1860–1930, at 20–21 (Yale Univ. Press 1977). Just as Wharton's treatise was about to be published, he wrote a separate pamphlet, *Suggestion*, which he intended as an appendix to his treatise. In addition to his treatise, his ideas on causation are elaborated in *Liability of Railroad Companies for Remote Fires*, 1 S.L. REV. (n.s.) 729 (1876) [hereafter Wharton, *Remote Fires*].

106. F. WHARTON, SUGGESTION, *supra* note 105, at 5, 10.

107. *Id.* at 8.

108. *Id.* at 10.

109. *Id.* at 11.

110. *Id.* at 10.

111. *Id.* at 10–11.

112. J. S. MILL, AUTOBIOGRAPHY, in 1 COLLECTED WORKS OF JOHN STUART MILL 232 (J. Robson & J. Stillinger eds., Univ. of Toronto Press 1981).

113. O. W. HOLMES, *supra* note 25, at 173.

114. *See* M. HOWE, *supra* note 21, at 74–76; B. KUKLICK, *supra* note 105, at 48–50; Fisch, *supra* note 104.

115. F. WHARTON, NEGLIGENCE, *supra* note 105, § 138, at 112.

116. *Id.* § 75, at 63.

117. Palsgraf v. Long Island R. Co., 248 N.Y. 339, 341, 162 N.E. 99, 99 (1928) ("Proof of negligence in the air, so to speak, will not do.") (quoting F. POLLOCK, THE LAW OF TORTS 455 (11th ed., Stevens 1920)).

118. 35 N.Y. 210 (1866).

119. *Id.* at 217.

120. T. COOLEY, A TREATISE ON THE LAW OF TORTS 76 (Callaghan 1879) (quoting Ryan v. New York Cent. R. R., 35 N.Y. at 216).

121. The decision was rejected in England and in most American states. *Id.* at 76–77. Only New York and Pennsylvania, in Pennsylvania R.R. v. Kerr, 62 Pa. 353 (1870), adopted the *Ryan* rule. Even in New York, the case was "much criticized, limited, distinguished, and to some extent, at least, overruled. . . ." 1 T. SHEARMAN & A. REDFIELD, A TREATISE ON THE LAW OF NEGLIGENCE 60 n.30 (6th ed., Baker, Voorhis 1913). "[T]he weight of this case as a precedent was somewhat diminished" by subsequent Pennsylvania decisions as well. T. COOLEY, *supra* note 120, at 76 n.3.

122. F. WHARTON, NEGLIGENCE, *supra* note 105, at 110.

123. *Id.* § 150, at 125.

124. *Id.* § 150, at 135. (quoting Hoyt v. Jeffers, 30 Mich. 181, 200 (1874) (Christiancy, J.)).

125. Wharton, *Remote Fires*, *supra* note 105, at 729.

126. *Id.* at 730.

127. *Id.* at 730–31.

128. F. WHARTON, NEGLIGENCE, *supra* note 105, § 139 at 114–15.

129. *Id.* § 75, at 63.

130. Green, *supra* note 97, at 215.

131. *See* THE PROBABILISTIC REVOLUTION (2 vols, L. Krüger ed., MIT Press 1987).

132. O. W. HOLMES, *supra* note 25, at 187.

133. O. W. HOLMES, *supra* note 19, at 96, 163.

134. O. W. HOLMES, *supra* note 25, at 182–83.

135. *See* Friedman & Ladinsky, *Social Change and the Law of Industrial Accidents,* 67 COLUM. L. REV. 50 (1967); J. WEINSTEIN, THE CORPORATE IDEAL IN THE LIBERAL STATE, 1900–1918, at 40–61 (Beacon Press 1968).

136. Beale, *The Proximate Consequences of an Act,* 33 HARV. L. REV. 633 (1920).

137. H. HART & A. HONORE, CAUSATION IN THE LAW 91–92 (Oxford Univ. Press 1959).

138. *See* Malone, *The Formative Era of Contributory Negligence,* 41 ILL. L. REV. 151 (1946); Green, *Illinois Negligence Law,* 39 ILL. L. REV. 36, 116, 197 (1944). The most prominent example of attacks on assumption of risk were those on the fellow-servant rule in worker injury cases. *See* Kales, *The Fellow Servant Doctrine in the United States Supreme Court,* 2 MICH. L. REV. 79 (1903); James, *Assumption of Risk,* 61 YALE L.J. 141 (1952).

139. "There is a decided tendency to leave every question [concerning proximate cause] to the bewildered jury, under some vague instruction which provides no effective guide." W. PROSSER & W. KEETON, PROSSER AND KEETON ON THE LAW OF TORTS 319 (5th ed., West 1984). This is a prominent area in which the Legal Realists' influence was in the direction of facilitating plaintiffs' efforts to get cases to the jury. *Cf.* L. KALMAN, LEGAL REALISM AT YALE, 1927–1960, at 21, 31 (Univ. of North Carolina Press, 1986).

140. Gregory, *Proximate Cause in Negligence—A Retreat from "Rationalization,"* 6 U. CHI. L. REV. 36, 41 (1938).

141. *Id.* at 58–59.

142. Edgerton, *Legal Cause* (pts. 1 & 2), 72 U. PA. L. REV. 211, 343 (1924).

143. L. GREEN, RATIONALE OF PROXIMATE CAUSE (Vernon 1927). *See also Festschrift for Leon Green,* 56 TEX. L. REV. 381 (1978); G. E. WHITE, TORT LAW IN AMERICA: AN INTELLECTUAL HISTORY 75–78, 82–83, 92–96 (Oxford Univ. Press 1980).

144. 248 N.Y. 339, 162 N.E. 99 (1928).

145. *Id.* at 351, 162 N.E. at 103.

146. *Id.* at 352, 354, 162 N.E. at 103, 104.

147. *Id.* at 346, 162 N.E. at 101.

148. *Id.* at 341, 162 N.E. at 99.

149. 217 N.Y. 382, 111 N.E. 1050 (1916).

150. Brett, M. R., afterwards Lord Esher, in Heaven v. Pender, L.R. 11 Q.B.D. 503 (1883). *See* Holmes, *The Theory of Torts,* 7 AM. L. REV. 652 (1873); G. E. WHITE, *supra* note 143.

151. "The conduct of the defendant's guard, if a wrong in its relation to the holder of the package, was not a wrong in its relation to the plaintiff, standing far away. Relatively to her it was not negligence at all." 248 N.Y. 339, 341, 162 N.E. 99 (1928).

152. *See* 2 W. WALLACE, CAUSALITY AND SCIENTIFIC EXPLANATION 163 (Univ. of Michigan Press 1974).

153. *See* T. HASKELL, THE EMERGENCE OF PROFESSIONAL SOCIAL SCIENCE (Univ. of Illinois Press 1977).

154. *Id.* at 13, 14–15.

155. *Id.* at 40.

Chapter 3

1. *See* D. ROSS, ORIGINS OF AMERICAN SOCIAL SCIENCE 53 (Cambridge Univ. Press 1990). For general works on the Gilded Age, see R. WIEBE, THE SEARCH FOR ORDER, 1877–1920 (Hill & Wang 1967); A. TRACHTENBERG, INCORPORATION OF AMERICA: CUL-

TURE AND SOCIETY IN THE GUILDED AGE (Hill & Wang 1982); M. DUBOFSKY, INDUSTRI-
ALISM AND THE AMERICAN WORKER (Crowell 1975); L. GOODWYN, DEMOCRATIC PROMISE:
THE POPULIST MOMENT IN AMERICA (Oxford Univ. Press 1976); H. F. MAY, THE END OF
AMERICAN INNOCENCE: A STUDY OF THE FIRST YEARS OF OUR OWN TIME, 1912–1917
(Knopf 1959). For the influence of the Paris Commune in America, see N. PAINTER,
STANDING AT ARMAGEDDON: THE UNITED STATES, 1877–1919, at 17–24 (Norton 1987).
See also Grob, *The Railroad Strikes of 1877*, 6 MIDWEST J. 16, 21–33 (1954–1955), *cited
in* P. FONER, THE GREAT LABOR UPRISING OF 1877, at 103 n.1 (Monad Press 1977); R.
BRUCE, 1877: YEAR OF VIOLENCE 225–29 (Bobbs-Merrill 1959). This idea was originally
suggested to me by Graham, *Justice Field and the Fourteenth Amendment*, 52 YALE L.J.
851, 857 (1943) [hereafter Graham, *Justice Field*].

2. 118 U.S. 394 (1886).

3. Lochner v. New York, 198 U.S. 45 (1905) (state regulations limiting the hours of
employment in bakeries violate the right to freedom of contract guaranteed by the Fourteenth Amendment of the U.S. Constitution).

4. *See* Graham, *Justice Field*, *supra* note 1, at 853; Graham, *The "Conspiracy Theory"
of the Fourteenth Amendment*, 47 YALE L.J. 371, 403 (1938). *See also* C. BEARD, CON-
TEMPORARY AMERICAN HISTORY, 1877–1913, at 208, 210–13 (Macmillan 1914).

5. 118 U.S. at 396.

6. Dartmouth College v. Woodward, 17 U.S. (4 Wheat.) 518 (1819).

7. *See* Graham, *Justice Field*, *supra* note 1, at 853. There can be no doubt that recent
cases like First National Bank v. Bellotti, 435 U.S. 765 (1978), which recognizes a constitutional right of corporations to spend money to influence elections, have contributed enormously to the political and economic power of big business.

8. Santa Clara v. Southern Pac. R.R., 18 F. 385, 402–05 (C.C.D. Cal. 1883); San
Mateo v. Southern Pac. R.R., 13 F. 722, 746–48 (C.C.D. Cal. 1882) (companion cases).

9. Dewey, *The Historical Background of Corporate Legal Personality*, 35 YALE L.J.
655 (1926).

10. *See* Fuller, *American Legal Realism*, 82 U. PA. L. REV. 429 (1934).

11. Dewey, *supra* note 9, at 669–70.

12. Cohen, *Transcendental Nonsense and the Functional Approach*, 35 COLUM. L.
REV. 509 (1935).

13. Lochner v. New York, 198 U.S. 45, 76 (1905).

14. *See* Cohen, *The Ethical Basis of Legal Criticism*, 11 YALE L.J. 201, 215–19 (1931);
Dewey, *Logical Method and Law*, 10 CORNELL L. REV. 17 (1924).

15. San Mateo v. Southern Pac. R.R., 13 F. 722 (C.C.D. Cal. 1882); Sacramento v.
Central Pac. R.R., 18 F. 385 (C.C.D. Cal. 1883); California v. Northern Ry., 18 F. 385
(C.C.D. Cal 1883); California v. Central Pac. R.R., 18 F. 385 (C.C.D. Cal 1883); Cali-
fornia v. Southern Pac. R.R., 18 F. 385 (C.C.D. Cal. 1883); Santa Clara v. Southern
Pac. R.R., 18 F. 385 (C.C.D. Cal. 1883).

16. The Slaughterhouse Cases, 83 U.S. (16 Wall.) 36 (1873).

17. *See id.* at 100–01.

18. *See id.* at 104–05.

19. Argument for Defendant at 12, San Mateo v. Southern Pac. R.R., 116 U.S. 138
(1885) (collected in Cases and Points (available in Harvard Law School Library)) (emphasis
in the original).

20. *Id.* at 10 (emphasis in the original).

21. San Mateo v. Southern Pac. R.R., 13 F. 722, 743–44 (C.C.D. Cal. 1882).

22. O. GIERKE, DIE STAATS- UND KORPORATIONSLEHRE DES ALTERTHUMS UND DES

MITTELALTERS UND IHRE AUFNAHME IN DEUTSCHLAND (Weidmann 1881). (vol. 3 of DAS DEUTSCHE GENOSSENSCHAFTSRECHT).

23. For a good bibliography, see 4 R. POUND, JURISPRUDENCE 200–01 (West 1959) (unnumbered note).

24. O. GIERKE, POLITICAL THEORIES OF THE MIDDLE AGE (F. Maitland trans. Cambridge Univ. Press 1900).

25. F. MAITLAND, *Moral Personality and Legal Personality*, in 3 COLLECTED PAPERS 304 (H. Fisher ed., Cambridge Univ. Press 1911).

26. E. FREUND, THE LEGAL NATURE OF CORPORATIONS (Univ. of Chicago Press 1897).

27. F. MAITLAND, *supra* note 25, at 317.

28. F. MAITLAND, *Trust and Corporation*, in *supra* note 25, at 321.

29. F. MAITLAND, *supra* note 25, at 317.

30, *See* 1 S. THOMPSON, COMMENTARIES ON THE LAW OF PRIVATE CORPORATIONS vi (1st ed., Bancroft-Whitney 1895).

31. *See* Frug, *The City as a Legal Concept*, 93 HARV. L. REV. 1057, 1083–90 (1980).

32. *See* Laski, *The Personality of Associations*, 29 HARV. L. REV. 404 (1916). *See generally* W. Y. ELLIOTT, THE PRAGMATIC REVOLT IN POLITICS (Macmillan 1928); Hager, *Bodies Politic: The Progressive History of Organizational "Real Entity" Theory*, 50 U. PITT. L. REV. 575 (1989).

33. *See* R. WIEBE, *supra* note 2; Galambos, *Technology, Political Economy, and Professionalization: Central Themes of the Organizational Synthesis*, 57 BUS. HIST. REV. 471 (1983); Galambos, *The Emerging Organizational Synthesis in Modern American History*, 44 BUS. HIST. REV. 279 (1970).

34. *See* 1 P. VINOGRADOFF, OUTLINES OF HISTORICAL JURISPRUDENCE 147–48 (Oxford Univ. Press 1920); White & Vann, *The Invention of English Individualism*, 8 SOC. HIST. 345, 352–54 (1983); Sugarman & Rubin, *Towards a New History of Law and Material Society in England, 1750–1914*, in LAW, ECONOMY AND SOCIETY, 1750–1914, at 28–30 (G. Rubin & D. Sugarman eds., Professional Books 1984).

35. F. MAITLAND, *supra* note 26, at 317.

36. *See* Dartmouth College v. Woodward, 17 U.S. (4 Wheat.) 518, 636 (1819), *quoted in* J. W. HURST, THE LEGITIMACY OF THE BUSINESS CORPORATION IN THE LAW OF THE UNITED STATES, 1780–1970, at 9 (Univ. Press of Virginia 1970).

37. *Id.*

38. *See infra* note 48 and accompanying text.

39. *See infra* notes 143–47 and accompanying text.

40. *See infra* notes 125–27 and accompanying text.

41. 201 U.S. 43 (1905). As late as 1904, the Supreme Court declared: "A corporation, while by fiction of law recognized for some purposes as a person, and for purposes of jurisdiction as a citizen, is not endowed with the inalienable rights of a natural person." Northern Sec. Co. v. United States, 193 U.S. 197, 362 (1904). And in 1906 it stated that "the liberty guaranteed by the fourteenth amendment against deprivation without due process of law is the liberty of natural, not artificial, persons." Western Turf Ass'n v. Greenberg, 204 U.S. 359, 363 (1906) (citing Northwestern Life Ins. Co. v. Riggs, 203 U.S. 243, 255 (1906)). This way of thinking began to crumble with *Hale* and was finally put to rest in 1910 in a series of "unconstitutional conditions" cases involving foreign corporations. *See infra* note 67, and G. HENDERSON, *infra* note 62, at 132–47.

42. *See* A. CHANDLER, THE VISIBLE HAND: THE MANAGERIAL REVOLUTION IN AMERICAN BUSINESS 161 (Harvard Univ. Press 1977).

43. *See infra* note 200 and accompanying text.

44. E. FREUND, *supra* note 26, at 10.

45. *Id.* at 48.

46. *See generally* C. HAINES, THE REVIVAL OF NATURAL LAW CONCEPTS (Harvard Univ. Press 1930).

47. The most dramatic, largely because it seems so out of place, is Chief Justice Marshall's effort, in Bank of United States v. Devereux, 9 U.S. (5 Cranch) 61 (1809), to base the diversity jurisdiction of corporations on the residence of their shareholders. By the 1840s this approach was abandoned, with the conclusive presumption that the shareholders were citizens of the state of incorporation. Louisville R.R. v. Letson, 43 U.S. (2 How.) 497 (1844). A more far-reaching act of disaggregation—which remained ambiguous and muted—was the implied distinction in the Dartmouth College Case between, on the one hand, the artificial and socially created corporation and, on the other hand, the vested rights of the shareholders. *See also* J. W. HURST, *supra* note 36, at 15–22.

48. Bank of Augusta v. Earle, 38 U.S. (13 Pet.) 519, 586 (1839).

49. State v. Standard Oil Co., 49 Ohio St. 137, 30 N.E. 279 (1892).

50. R. REESE, THE TRUE DOCTRINE OF ULTRA VIRES IN THE LAW OF CORPORATIONS 2 (T. H. Flood 1897).

51. *See* Colson, *The Doctrine of Ultra Vires in the United States Supreme Court Decisions* (pt. 1), 42 W. VA. L.Q. 179, 184–89 (1936).

52. *Id.*

53. *See infra* text accompanying notes 97–108.

54. 5 S. THOMPSON, *supra* note 30, at 4629.

55. 1 W. COOK, TREATISE ON STOCK AND STOCKHOLDERS, BONDS, MORTGAGES, AND GENERAL CORPORATION LAW 971–73 (3d ed., Callaghan 1894).

56. 5 S. THOMPSON, *supra* note 30, at 4664–78.

57. *Compare* National Bank v. Matthews, 96 U.S. 258 (1877) *and* San Antonio v. Mehaffy, 96 U.S. 312 (1877) *with* Thomas v. West Jersey R.R., 101 U.S. 71 (1879). *See also* Colson, *supra* note 51, at 207–9, 213.

58. *See* Colson, *The Doctrine of Ultra Vires in United States Supreme Court Decisions* (pt. 2), 42 W. VA. L.Q. 297, 330 (1936).

59. *See* Carpenter, *Should the Doctrine of Ultra Vires Be Discarded?*, 33 YALE L.J. 49 (1923).

60. 1 W. COOK, TREATISE ON THE LAW OF CORPORATIONS HAVING A CAPITAL STOCK, vii–viii (4th ed., Callaghan 1898). "In the federal courts . . . the old rule against ultra vires contracts is upheld in all its rigor and applied with all its severity. The tendency of modern jurisprudence to relax on that subject finds no favor in the federal courts." 2 *id.* at 1374.

61. *See* Colson, *supra* notes 51 and 58.

62. G. HENDERSON, THE POSITION OF FOREIGN CORPORATIONS IN AMERICAN CONSTITUTIONAL LAW 42 (Harvard Univ. Press 1918).

63. 38. U.S. (13 Pet.) 519, 587–88 (1839).

64. *Id.* at 588.

65. *See* Paul v. Virginia, 75 U.S. (8 Wall.) 168 (1868).

66. *See* Western Union Tel. Co. v. Kansas, 216 U.S. 1 (1910); Pullman Co. v. Kansas, 216 U.S. 56 (1910); Ludwig v. Western Union Tel. Co., 216 U.S. 146 (1910); Southern Ry. v. Greene, 216 U.S. 400 (1910).

67. *See* Horwitz, *Progressive Legal Historiography*, 63 OR. L. REV. 679 (1984).

68. *See* United States v. Trans-Missouri Freight Ass'n, 166 U.S. 290 (1897); United States v. Joint Traffic Ass'n, 171 U.S. 505 (1898); Hopkins v. United States, 171 U.S. 578 (1898); Anderson v. United States, 171 U.S. 604 (1898); Addyson Pipe Steel Co. v. United States, 175 U.S. 211 (1899). The clearest statement of this "literalist" interpretation was given by Justice Peckham in *Trans-Missouri:*

> When, therefore, the body of an act pronounces as illegal every contract or combination in restraint of trade or commerce among the several States, etc., the plain and ordinary meaning of such language is not limited to that kind of contract alone which is in unreasonable restraint of trade, but all contracts are included in such language, and no exception or limitation can be added without placing in the act that which has been omitted by Congress.

166 U.S. at 328.

69. Standard Oil Co. v. United States, 221 U.S. 1 (1911).

70. *See* J. M. Blum, The Republican Roosevelt 116–17 (Harvard Univ. Press 1954); R. Hofstadter, The Age of Reform 247–50 (Vintage 1955); *see also* Kales, *Good and Bad Trusts*, 30 Harv. L. Rev. 830 (1917).

71. 3 J. Dorfman, The Economic Mind in American Civilization 138 (Viking Press 1949).

72. *See, e.g.*, S. Dillaye, Monopolies, Their Origin, Growth and Development (R. H. Darby 1882).

73. Lloyd, *The Story of a Great Monopoly*, 47 Atlantic Monthly 317 (1881).

74. H. Thorelli, The Federal Antitrust Policy 134 (Johns Hopkins Univ. Press 1954) (citing Lloyd, *Lords of Industry*, 138 N. Am. Rev. 535–53 (1884)).

75. A. Chandler, *supra* note 42, at 323.

76. *See* Hovenkamp, *The Sherman Act and the Classical Theory of Competition*, 74 Iowa L. Rev. 1019 (1989); Hovenkamp, *The Antitrust Movement and the Rise of Industrial Organization*, 68 Tex. L. Rev. 105 (1989); Hovenkamp, *Antitrust Policy, Federalism, and the Theory of the Firm: An Historical Perspective*, 59 Antitrust L.J. 75 (1990); May, *Antitrust Practice and Procedure in the Formative Era: The Constitutional and Conceptual Reach of State Antitrust Law, 1880–1918*, 135 U. Pa. L. Rev. 495 (1987); May, *Antitrust in the Formative Era: Political and Economic Theory in Constitutional and Antitrust Analysis, 1880–1918*, 50 Ohio St. L.J. 257 (1989); May, *The Role of the States in the First Century of the Sherman Act and the Larger Picture of Antitrust History*, 59 antitrust L.J. 93 (1990); Millon, *The First Antitrust Statute*, 29 Washburn L.J. 141 (1990); Peritz, *A Counter-History of Antitrust Law*, 1990 Duke L.J. 263.

77. Dwight, *The Legality of Trusts*, 3 Pol. Sci. Q 592, 631 (1888).

78. Thompson, *The Power of the People Over Corporate and Individual Monopolies*, Proc. Ill. St. B. Ass'n 81, 84 (1891). Thompson concluded that "as a general rule, we may safely trust to the operation of natural laws and to the inherent weakness of every human combination for a sufficient remedy." *Id.* at 90.

79. A. Hadley, Railroad Transportation 69 (G. P. Putnam's Sons 1885) *quoted in* W. Cook, *supra* note 55, at 127.

80. *See* M. Furner, Advocacy and Objectivity: A Crisis in the Professionalization of American Social Science, 1865–1905, at 76 and *passim* (Univ. Press of Kentucky 1975). *Cf.* T. Haskell, The Emergence of Professional Social Science 177–89 (Univ. of Illinois Press 1977).

81. Adams, *The Relation of the State to Industrial Action*, 1 PUBLICATIONS AM. ECON. ASS'N 7, 61 (1887).

82. *Id.* at 64.

83. *Id.*

84. Andrews, *Trusts According to Official Investigations*, 3 Q.J. ECON. 117 (1889).

85. Andrews, *The Economic Law of Monopoly*, 26 J. SOC. SCI. 1 (1890).

86. E. BELLAMY, PLUTOCRACY OR NATIONALISM—WHICH? 2 (n.p. 1889).

87. *Id.* at 3.

88. *Id.* at 5.

89. *Id.* at 1, 5.

90. J. H. FLAGLER, TRUSTS: AN ADDRESS . . . BEFORE THE COMMERCIAL CLUB OF PROVIDENCE, RHODE ISLAND (DECEMBER 15, 1888) (n.p. n.d.) (copy at Univ. of Wisconsin Library).

91. *See* People v. Chicago Trust Co., 130 Ill. 268, 22 N.E. 789 (1887); People v. North River Sugar Ref. Co., 22 Abb. N. Cas. 164 (N.Y. Sup. Ct. 1889); State v. Nebraska Distilling Co., 29 Neb. 700, 46 N.W. 155 (1890). *See Louisiana v. American Cotton-oil Trust*, 1 RY. & CORP. L.J. 509 (1887); *California v. American Sugar Refining Co.*, 7 RY. & CORP. L.J. 83 (1890).

92. *See North River Sugar Ref. Co.*, 22 Abb. N. Cas. 164; State v. Standard Oil Co., 49 Ohio St. 137, 30 N.E. 279 (1892).

93. E. VON HALLE, TRUSTS OR INDUSTRIAL COMBINATIONS AND COALITIONS 94 (Macmillan 1895).

94. A. R. DEAN, A TRIBUTE TO WILLIAM NELSON CROMWELL 69 (n.p. 1955).

95. *Id.* at 70.

96. A. CHANDLER, *supra* note 42.

97. 1889 N.J. Laws ch. 269, § 4 at 414.

98. *See* A. R. DEAN, *supra* note 94, at 99.

99. United States v. E. C. Knight Co., 156 U.S. 1 (1895).

100. C. BOSTWICK, LEGISLATIVE COMPETITION FOR CORPORATE CAPITAL 22 (n.p. 1899).

101. W. COOK, *supra* note 55, at vi.

102. Steffens, *New Jersey: A Traitor State*, 25 McCLURE'S MAG. 41 (1905).

103. C. BOSTWICK, *supra* note 100, at 1.

104. *Id.* at 4.

105. *Id.* at 15.

106. *Id.* at 11.

107. *See* W. LETWIN, LAW AND ECONOMIC POLICY IN AMERICA 71–85 (Random House 1965).

108. W. COOK, THE CORPORATION PROBLEM 226 (G. P. Putnam's Sons 1891).

109. E. VON HALLE, *supra* note 93, at 113.

110. *See* 1 W. COOK, TREATISE ON THE LAW OF CORPORATIONS HAVING A CAPITAL STOCK vii (5th ed., Callaghan 1903).

111. 1 A. EDDY, THE LAW OF COMBINATIONS 665–66 (Callaghan 1901).

112. *Id.*

113. W. COOK, *supra* note 110, at vii.

114. E. VON HALLE, *supra* note 93, at 113.

115. *Compare* St. Louis, V. & T.H.R.R. v. Terre Haute & I.R.R., 145 U.S. 393 (1892) *with* Pullman's Palace Car Co. v. Central Transp. Co., 71 U.S. 138 (1898). *See* Harriman, *Ultra Vires Corporation Leases*, 14 HARV. L. REV. 332 (1900); W. C. NOYES,

Treatise on the Law of Intercorporate Relations 349–52 (1st ed., Little, Brown 1902).

116. See Camden & A.R.R. v. May's Landing & E.H.C.R.R., 48 N.J.L. 530, 7 A. 523 (1886).

117. Bath Gas Light Co. v. Claffy, 151 N.Y. 24, 34, 45 N.E. 390, 395 (1896).

118. W. Cook, supra note 55, at viii.

119. 7 S. Thompson, supra note 30, at 7032.

120. See H. Thorelli, supra note 74, at 73–76.

121. See supra note 97 and accompanying text.

122. Northern Sec. Co. v. United States, 193 U.S. 197 (1904).

123. 1 A. Eddy, supra note 111, at 601–02.

124. See Metcalf v. American School Furniture Co., 122 F. 115 (W.D.N.Y. 1903).

125. See, e.g., Mason v. Pewabic Mining Co. 133 U.S. 50 (1890); State ex rel. Brown v. Bailey, 16 Ind. 46 (1861); McCray v. Junction R.R., 9 Ind. 358 (1857); Stevens v. Rutland & B.R.R., 29 Vt. 545 (1851). See also Carney, Fundamental Corporate Changes, Minority Shareholders and Business Purposes, Am. B. Found. Res. J. 69, 88–89 (1980).

126. See J. Angell & S. Ames, Treatise on the Law of Private Corporations Aggregate 537, 569 (11th ed., Little, Brown 1882).

127. See 1 V. Morawetz, A Treatise on the Law of Private Corporations iii (2d ed., Little, Brown 1886). See also Carney, supra note 125, at 77–78.

128. W. Cook, Treatise on the Law of Stock and Stockholders 60 (1st ed., Baker, Voorhis 1887).

129. See statutes cited in W. C. Noyes, supra note 115, at 29 n.1.

130. W. C. Noyes, supra note 115, at 36 n.1, 84 n.2. These states were: Alabama (1896), Colorado (1891), Connecticut (1901), Delaware (1899), Illinois (1895), Kentucky (1894), Louisiana (1874), Maryland (1888), Missouri (1889), Nevada (1883), New Jersey (1896), New York (1890), Pennsylvania (1901), Utah (1898). Noyes's list of thirteen states does not include the Pennsylvania statute of 1901. Actual dates of enactment for Colorado (1877), Illinois (1872), Kentucky (1893), and Utah (1896) are found in the following compilations of state laws: 1 J. W. Mills, Mills' Annotated Statutes of the State of Colorado 688 (Mills 1891); 2 W. C. Jones & K. H. Addington, Annotated Statutes of the State of Illinois 1588–89 (Callaghan 1913); J. Barbour & J. Carroll, Kentucky Statutes 350 (3d ed., Courier-Journal 1903); R. W. Young, G. H. Smith, & W. A. Lee, Revised Statutes of the State of Utah 163 (State Journal 1897).

131. See Metcalf v. American School Furniture Co., 122 F. 115 (W.D.N.Y. 1903); Traer v. Lucas Prospecting Co., 124 Iowa 107, 99 N.W. 290 (1904); Tanner v. Lindell Ry., 180 Mo. 1, 79 S.W. 155 (1904); Beidenkopf v. Des Moines Life Ins. Co. & National Life Ins. Co., 160 Iowa 629, 142 N.W. 43 (1913); Lange v. Reservation Mining & Smelting Co. 48 Wash 167, 93 P. 208 (1908); Butler v. New Keystone Copper Co., 10 Del. Ch. 371, 93 A. 380 (1915).

132. W. C. Noyes, supra note 115, at 174–75.

133. Bowditch v. Jackson Co., 76 N.H. 351, 82 A. 1014, 1017 (1912).

134. Carney, supra note 125, at 88–89.

135. Id. at 90.

136. See In re Timmis, 200 N.Y. 177, 93 N.E. 522 (1910) for the New York statutory history. The leading case on shareholder unanimity is Abbott v. American Hard Rubber Co., 33 Barb. 578 (N.Y. App. Div. 1861).

137. The Delaware statute appears in W. C. Noyes, supra note 115, at 94 n.4. The

New Jersey statute, broadening an 1896 law, appears in W. C. NOYES, TREATISE ON THE LAW OF INTERCORPORATE RELATIONS 232 n.2 (2d ed., Little, Brown 1909). These appraisal statutes, Noyes wrote, "are probably broad enough to be available in aid of a reorganization through the transfer of corporate assets in exchange for stock." *Id.* at 232.

138. Weiner, *Payment of Dissenting Stockholders*, 27 COLUM. L. REV. 547 (1927).

139. J. ANGELL & S. AMES, TREATISE ON THE LAW OF PRIVATE CORPORATIONS AGGREGATE 166 (6th ed., Little, Brown 1858).

140. Mason v. Pewabic Mining Co., 133 U.S. 50, 59 (1890).

141. E. FREUND, *supra* note 26, at 10.

142. *Id.* at 48.

143. 1 V. MORAWETZ, *supra* note 127, at iii.

144. V. MORAWETZ, TREATISE ON THE LAW OF PRIVATE CORPORATIONS 24 (1st ed., Little, Brown 1882).

145. *Id.*

146. H. TAYLOR, A TREATISE ON THE LAW OF PRIVATE CORPORATIONS HAVING CAPITAL STOCK iv (Kay 1884).

147. Note, *The Legal Idea of a Corporation*, 19 AM. L. REV. 114, 115 (1885).

148. *See supra* note 48 and accompanying text.

149. H. TAYLOR, *supra* note 147, at 12.

150. Jones, *A Corporation as "A Distinct Entity,"* 2 COUNS. 78, 81 (1892) (emphasis added).

151. Dorfman, *Introduction* to H. C. ADAMS, RELATION OF THE STATE TO INDUSTRIAL ACTION AND ECONOMICS AND JURISPRUDENCE at 47–48 (J. Dorfman ed., Columbia Univ. Press 1954).

152. Adams, Suggestions for a System of Taxation, PUBLICATIONS MICH. POL. SCI. ASS'N 49, 60 (1894).

153. C. TIEDEMAN, TREATISE ON STATE AND FEDERAL CONTROL OF PERSONS AND PROPERTY IN THE UNITED STATES (F. H. Thomas 1900).

154. *Id.* at 382–83.

155. *Id.* at 609–10.

156. *See* Shiras, *Classification of Corporations*, 4 YALE L.J. 97, 99–100 (1895).

157. *See* Beardstown Pearl Button Co. v. Oswald, 130 Ill. App. 290, 294–95 (1906).

158. G. HENDERSON, *supra* note 62, at 169.

159. J. T. CARTER, THE NATURE OF THE CORPORATION AS A LEGAL ENTITY 160 (M. Curlander 1919).

160. 30 F. Cas. 435 (C.C.D. Me. 1824) (No. 17,944). The Supreme Court adopted the trust fund doctrine in Sawyer v. Hoag, 84 U.S. (17 Wall.) 610 (1873).

161. A second question was whether, in the absence of a national bankruptcy law, the trust fund doctrine prevented an insolvent corporation from exercising a preference about the order in which it paid its creditors, since it was concededly legal for an insolvent individual to exercise such discretion.

162. W. COOK, *supra* note 55, at vii.

163. Hawkins v. Glenn, 131 U.S. 319 (1889). *See also* Glenn v. Liggett, 135 U.S. 533 (1890); Pincoffs, *Corporations: Capital Stock A Trust Fund for Creditors*, 26 AM. L. REV. 100, 102 (1892).

164. W. COOK, *supra* note 55, at v.

165. The emphasis in histories of limited shareholder liability has been on identifying the periods in which shareholder liability to creditors of an insolvent corporation diverged

from unlimited partnership liability. From this perspective, *any* limitation on otherwise unlimited liability is significant. *See, e.g.*, Dodd, *The Evolution of Limited Liability in American Industry: Massachusetts*, 61 HARV. L. REV. 1351, 1379 (1948) (identifying when American common law diverged from English common law and assumed limited liability as the norm in the absence of a legislative provision for liability). As a result, scholars have tended to under-emphasize the fact that, in most jurisdictions throughout the nineteenth century, the usual statutory provision made the shareholder liable for much more than—normally twice—the value of his shares.

166. 1848 N.Y. Laws, ch. 40.

167. W. COOK, *supra* note 55, at 203–06.

168. *See* 3 S. THOMPSON, *supra* note 31, at chs. 46, 50.

169. Navin & Sears, *The Rise of a Market for Industrial Securities, 1887–1902*, 29 BUS. HIST. REV. 105, 106 (1955).

170. *Id.* at 109.

171. *Id.* at 109 n. 4.

172. *Id.* at 109.

173. *See id.* at 109–10.

174. *Id.* at 106.

175. *Id.* at 137.

176. *See* J. W. HURST, LAW AND THE CONDITIONS OF FREEDOM IN THE NINETEENTH-CENTURY UNITED STATES 72 (Univ. of Wisconsin Press 1956).

177. Friedrich, *Stocks and Stock Ownership*, 14 ENCYCLOPEDIA OF SOCIAL SCIENCES 403 (E. Seligman ed., Macmillan 1934).

178. S. THOMPSON, *supra* note 30, at vii.

179. *See* Christensen v. Eno, 106 N.Y. 97, 102, 12 N.E. 648 (1887); Southworth v. Morgan, 205 N.Y. 293, 93 N.E. 490 (1912); Jeffrey v. Selwyn, 220 N.Y. 77, 115 N.E. 275 (1917). *See generally* W. COOK, *supra* note 60.

180. Hospes v. Northwestern Mfg. Co., 48 Minn. 174, 50 N.W. 1117 (1892).

181. Ballantine, *Stockholders Liability in Minnesota*, 7 MINN. L. REV. 79, 88 (1923); Note, *The Nature of the Stockholder's Liability for Stock Issued at a Discount*, 29 HARV. L. REV. 854, 856 (1916).

182. 139 U.S. 417 (1891). *See also* Clark v. Bever, 139 U.S. 96 (1891); Fogg v. Blair, 139 U.S. 118 (1891).

183. 2 S. THOMPSON, *supra* note 30, at 1295.

184. *Id.* at 1296.

185. Pepper, *Recent Development of Corporation Law by the Supreme Court of the United States* (pt. 2), 34 AM. L. REG. (n.s.) 448, 457 n.2 (1895).

186. *Id.* at 456. *See also* Pepper, *The "Trust Fund Theory" of the Capital Stock of a Corporation*, 32 AM. L. REG. (n.s.) 175 (1893).

187. *See, e.g.*, Harriman, *Corporate Assets as a "Trust Fund for the Benefit of Creditors,"* 2 NW. L. REV. 115, 206 (1894); McMurtrie, *Is Unpaid Capital a Trust Fund in Any Proper Sense?*, 25 AM. L. REV. 749 (1891).

188. *Compare* Camden v. Stuart, 144 U.S. 104 (1892) *with* Hollins v. Brierfield Coal & Iron Co., 150 U.S. 371 (1893), *See* Pepper, *supra* note 185, at 450.

189. Note, *supra* note 181, at 856.

190. Steacy v. Little Rock R.R., 22 F. Cas. 1142, 1152 (C.C.E.D. Ark. 1879) (No. 13,329).

191. W. COOK, *supra* note 60, at 498 n.1. This idea first appeared in Cook's treatise,

§ 257 n.2, as early as 1889 (2d ed.), except that he predicted that "some time hereafter" the rule of full negotiability would be established. The statement in the text, from the third edition (1895), was the first to declare it as the "established rule." By the eighth edition in 1923, Cook had eliminated the statement that it had already become the established rule and simply cited cases for the proposition that it was "the better opinion, and the one most in accord with the usages and demands of trade." 2 W. COOK, TREATISE ON THE LAW OF CORPORATIONS HAVING A CAPITAL STOCK § 257 n.2, at 854 (8th ed., Baker, Voorhis 1923).

192. *See* Navin & Sears, *supra* note 170, at 137–38.

193. *See* 1 W. COOK, *supra* note 191, at 291 nn.4 & 5; Bonbright, *The Dangers of Shares without Par Value*, 24 COLUM. L. REV. 449, 458 (1924).

194. Bonbright, *supra* note 193, at 460.

195. *Id.* at 432.

196. Pepper, *Recent Development of Corporation Law by the Supreme Court of the United States* (pt. 1), 34 AM. L. REG. (n.s.) 296, 296 (1895).

197. Pepper, *supra* note 185, at 453.

198. Pepper, *A Brief Introduction to the Study of the Law of Association*, 40 AM. L. REG. (n.s.) 255, 267 (1901).

199. Hunt, *The Trust Fund Theory and Some Substitutes for It*, 12 YALE L.J. 63, 67 (1902).

200. H. SPELLMAN, A TREATISE ON THE PRINCIPLES OF LAW GOVERNING CORPORATE DIRECTORS 237 (Prentice-Hall 1931).

201. Union Pacific Ry. v. Chicago R.I. & P. Ry., 163 U.S. 564, 596 (1896).

202. Cass v. Manchester Iron & Steel Co., 9 F. 640, 642 (C.C.W.D. Pa. 1881).

203. *See* H. SPELLMAN, *supra* note 200, at 6 n.24.

204. 3 S. THOMPSON, *supra* note 30, at 2878.

205. *Id.* at 2878–79 (emphasis retained).

206. Bank of the U.S. v. Dandridge, 25 U.S. (12 Wheat.) 64, 76, 78, 114–15 (1827).

207. 3 S. THOMPSON, *supra* note 30, at 2881.

208. *Id.* at 2881–82.

209. J. ANGELL & S. AMES, TREATISE ON THE LAW OF PRIVATE CORPORATIONS AGGREGATE 257 (7th ed., Little, Brown 1861).

210. *Id. See also* 3 S. THOMPSON, *supra* note 30, at 2862–63.

211. G. FIELD, TREATISE ON THE LAW OF PRIVATE CORPORATIONS (J. D. Parsons, Jr. 1877).

212. E. FREUND, *supra* note 26, at 53.

213. *Id.* at 48.

214. Manson v. Curtis, 223 N.Y. 313, 322, 119 N.E. 558, 562 (1918). H. SPELLMAN, *supra* note 200, at 9–12. The leading case on the subject became Hoyt v. Thompson's Ex'r, 19 N.Y. 207 (1859), which was largely ignored by the New York courts until it later became a favorite "old" citation for recognizing plenary power in the board of directors. *See* Beveridge v. New York Elevated R.R., 112 N.Y. 1, 22–23, 19 N.E. 489, 494–95 (1889); People *ex rel.* Manice v. Powell, 201 N.Y. 194, 200, 94 N.E. 634, 637 (1911); *Manson*, 223 N.Y. at 322, 119 N.E. at 562. A second early favorite, frequently cited in the twentieth century, was an opinion by Chief Justice Shaw in Burrill v. Nahant Bank, 43 Mass. (2 Met.) 163 (1840). More typical cases reflecting the early view of directors as agents who could not delegate their powers are Mechanics Bank v. New York & N.H.R.R., 22 N.Y. 258, 295 (1860) (opinion of Selden, J.); Brokaw v. New Jersey R.R., 32 N.J.L. 328, 332 (1867).

215. H. Spellman, *supra* note 200, at 4–5.

216. E. Freund, *supra* note 26, at 58.

217. *Id.* at 60.

218. 1 A. Eddy, *supra* note 111, at 602.

219. People v. North River Sugar Ref. Co., 121 N.Y. 582, 625, 24 N.E. 834, 840–41 (1890).

220. *See, e.g.*, Brown, *The Personality of the Corporation and the State*, 21 L.Q.R. 365 (1905).

221. *See* Jones, *supra* note 150, at 80–81.

222. Davis, *The Nature of Corporations*, 12 Pol. Sci. Q. 273, 278 (1897).

223. E. Freund, *supra* note 26, at 13.

224. *Id.* at 11.

225. *Id.* at 48.

226. *Id.* at 51.

227. *Id.*

228. *Id.* at preface, 5.

229. *Id.* at 52.

230. *Id.* at 47.

231. *Id.* at 59–60.

232. Williams, *An Inquiry into the Nature and Law of Corporations*, 38 Am. L. Reg. (n.s.) 1, 3 (1899).

233. Brown, *supra* note 220, at 379.

234. *See* Raymond, *The Genesis of the Corporation*, 19 Harv. L. Rev. 350, 362 (1906).

235. Machen, *Corporate Personality*, 24 Harv. L. Rev. 253, 261–62 (1911).

236. *Id.*

237. G. Henderson, *supra* note 62, at 3.

238. *Id.* at 166.

239. *Id.* at 167.

240. *Id.* at 165–66.

241. *Id.* at 165.

242. *Id.* at 174.

243. *Id.*

244. *Id.* at 5, 8.

245. *Id.* at 169.

246. *Id.* at 3.

247. 201 U.S. 43 (1905). *See also* cases cited *supra* note 41.

248. Dartmouth College v. Woodward, 17 U.S. (4 Wheat.) 518 (1819).

Chapter 4

1. Holmes, *Codes, and the Arrangement of the Law*, 5 Am. L. Rev. 1 (1870), *reprinted in* 44 Harv. L. Rev. 725 (1931).

2. O. W. Holmes, The Common Law (1st ed., Little, Brown 1881).

3. Holmes wrote in 1930 that "if a man was to do anything he must do it before 40." Letter from O. W. Holmes to Mrs. Charles S. Hamlin (Oct. 12, 1930), *reprinted in*

M. Howe, Justice Oliver Wendell Holmes: The Proving Years, 1870–1882, at 8 n.18 (Harvard Univ. Press 1963).

4. O. W. Holmes, *The Path of the Law*, in Collected Legal Papers 167 (Harcourt, Brace & Howe 1920).

5. This was Holmes's "favorite phrase," according to Professor Paul Freund. *See* Freund, *Oliver Wendell Holmes*, in 3 The Justices of the United States Supreme Court, 1789–1969, at 1756 (L. Friedman & F. Israel eds., Chelsea House 1969). The "cosmos" was a frequent topic of discussion between Holmes and William James. *See, e.g.*, 1 R. Perry, The Thought and Character of William James 504–6 (Little, Brown 1935); Holmes used the phrase "twist the tail of the cosmos" late into his life. *See, e.g.*, Letter from O. W. Holmes to John Wu (May 14, 1923), *reprinted in* The Mind and Faith of Justice Holmes 420 (M. Lerner 1st ed., Little, Brown 1943).

6. Recent excellent articles on Holmes include White, *The Integrity of Holmes' Jurisprudence*, 10 Hofstra L. Rev. 633 (1982); Touster, *Holmes a Hundred Years Ago: The Common Law and Legal Theory*, 10 Hofstra L. Rev. 673 (1982); Gordon, *Holmes' Common Law as Legal and Social Science*, 10 Hofstra L. Rev. 719 (1982); Grey, *Holmes and Legal Pragmatism*, 41 Stan. L. Rev. 787 (1989).

7. O. W. Holmes, The Common Law 5 (M. Howe ed., Harvard Univ. Press 1963).

8. Lochner v. New York, 198 U.S. 45, 76 (1905) (Holmes, J., dissenting).

9. *See* White, *The Rise and Fall of Justice Holmes*, 39 U. Chi. L. Rev. 51, 61–65 (1971) (stating that, by 1941, "Holmes had emerged as a 'deity . . . an Olympian who in judgment could do no wrong. . . .' " (quoting Hamilton, *On Dating Justice Holmes*, 9 U. Chi. L. Rev. 206 (1957)).

10. O. W. Holmes, *supra* note 7, at 38.

11. *Id.* at 37.

12. *Id.* at 40.

13. *Id.* at 41.

14. *Id.* at 40.

15. *Id.* at 37.

16. *Id.*

17. *Id.* at 41.

18. *Id.* at 42.

19. *Id.*

20. *Id.* at 38.

21. *Id.* at 66.

22. *Id.* at 66–67.

23. *Id.* at 85.

24. *Id.* at 88.

25. *Id.*

26. *Id.*

27. M. Howe, *supra* note 3, at 151–53, 169–72, 202–4.

28. Chancellor Kent, in 1832, proposed the orthodox view that "the plain intent" of the parties to a contract should prevail even "over the strict letter of the Contract" and that "[t]o reach and carry . . . the mutual intention of the parties . . . into effect, the law, when it becomes necessary, will control even the literal terms of the contract, if they manifestly contravene the purpose." 2 J. Kent, Commentaries on American Law 554, 555 (2d ed., O. Halsted 1832). *See generally* M. Horwitz, The Transformation of

American Law, 1780–1860 ch. 6 (Harvard Univ. Press 1977). *See also* the discussion of objectivism *supra* ch. 2.

29. *See* Horwitz, *The Legacy of 1776 in Legal and Economic Thought*, 19 J.L. & ECON. 621 (1976).

30. 2 T. PARSONS, THE LAW OF CONTRACTS 3–4 (1st ed., Little, Brown 1855).

31. *See* M. HORWITZ, *supra* note 28, at 258.

32 *See, e.g.,* Proprietors of the Charles River Bridge v. Proprietors of the Warren Bridge, 36 U.S. (11 Pet.) 420 (1837) (property rights redefined in order to encourage economic development); Losee v. Buchanan 51 N.Y. 476 (1873) (holding the defendant not liable for a non-negligent boiler explosion: "We must have factories, machinery, dams, canals and railroads. They are demanded by the manifold wants of mankind, and they lay at the basis of all our civilization."). *See generally* Horwitz, *supra* note 29, at 624–627; M. HORWITZ, *supra* note 28, *passim*.

33. *See infra* text accompanying notes 140–49 and 97–102.

34. O. W. HOLMES, *supra* note 7, at 37.

35. *See id.* at 77–78 ("The undertaking to redistribute losses simply on the ground that they resulted from the defendant's act would not only be open to [the objection of being inefficient] but, . . . to the still graver [objection] of offending the sense of justice.").

36. *Id.* at 43.

37. *See infra* text accompanying notes 39–50.

38. S. GREENLEAF, TREATISE ON THE LAW OF EVIDENCE (1st ed., Little, Brown 1842).

39. T. SEDGWICK, A TREATISE ON THE MEASURE OF DAMAGES (1st ed., Baker, Voorhis 1847).

40. *See* M. HORWITZ, *supra* note 28, at 82–84.

41. F. HILLIARD, LAW OF REMEDIES FOR TORTS 600–601 (2d ed., Little, Brown 1873).

42. Eliot, *Exemplary Damages*, 20 AM. L. REG. 570, 573–74. (1881).

43. *Id.*

44. Maxwell, *Exemplary Damages*, 7 S.L. REV. 675, 681 (1881).

45. *Id.*

46. Letter to editor, 6 CENT. L.J. 74 (1878) (signed "G.K.").

47. *Id.* at 74–75.

48. Fay v. Parker, 53 N.H. 342, 382 (1873).

49. *Id.*

50. *Id.* at 397.

51. Murphy v. Hobbs, 7 Colo. 541, 551 (1884).

52. *Id.*

53. 1 T. SEDGWICK, A TREATISE ON THE MEASURE OF DAMAGES 515 (A. Sedgwick & J. Beale, 8th ed., Baker Voorhis 1891).

54. *See, e.g.,* 1 T. BEVEN, NEGLIGENCE IN LAW 20–50 (2d ed., Stevens & Haynes 1895) ("[t]here is no matter within the range of jurisprudence that had given rise to more controversy than that which is concerned with determining what degrees of negligence are recognized by law. . . ."); F. WHARTON, A TREATISE ON THE LAW OF NEGLIGENCE 21–58 (2d ed., Kay 1878); 1 S. THOMPSON, COMMENTARIES ON THE LAW OF NEGLIGENCE IN ALL RELATIONS 18–22 (Bowen-Merrill 1901); 1 T. SHEARMAN & A. REDFIELD, A TREATISE ON THE LAW OF NEGLIGENCE 48–57 (4th ed., Baker, Voorhis 1888).

55. Coggs v. Bernard, 2 Ld. Raym. 909, 92 Eng. Rep. 107 (Q.B. 1703).

56. F. WHARTON, *supra* note 54. *See also* 1 S. THOMPSON, *supra* note 54, at 18–22 (of Holt's three-part division of negligence, Thompson writes, "[i]t is plain that such re-

finements can have no place in the practical administration of justice." *Id.* at 18. Of the state of the law he writes, "[n]o effort can extract from the current American decisions the conclusion that there are three degrees of culpable negligence." *Id.* at 19). *But see* 1 T. SHEARMAN & A. REDFIELD, *supra* note 54, at 48–57 (arguing for "three degrees of negligence" and applying the standard of "great care" to passenger carriers).

57. *See e.g.*, T. SHEARMAN & A. REDFIELD, A TREATISE ON THE LAW OF NEGLIGENCE 21, 25–26 (2d ed., Baker, Voorhis 1870) (stating with regard to railroads, "from those whose business or occupation necessarily involves great risk of life, it demands a peculiar degree of vigilance, and sagacity, sometimes called the utmost care"). Francis Wharton, who sought to eliminate three degrees of negligence, feared the strict liability implications of "slight negligence." "[T]here exist . . . certain necessary though dangerous trades, of which we can say statistically that in them will be sacrificed prematurely the lives . . . of third persons. . . . Yet in such cases (*e.g.* gas-factories and railroads), we do not hold that liability for such injuries attaches to those who start the enterprise forseeing these consequences." F. WHARTON, A TREATISE ON THE LAW OF NEGLIGENCE 61–62 (1st ed., Kay 1874).

58. *See, e.g.*, sources cited *supra* note 54.

59. *See generally* R. WIEBE, THE SEARCH FOR ORDER, 1877–1920 (Hill & Wang 1967); G. FREDRICKSON, THE INNER CIVIL WAR: NORTHERN INTELLECTUALS AND THE CRISIS OF THE UNION 166–80 (Harper 1965).

60. *See, e.g.*, 2 T. PARSONS, *supra* note 30, at 3–4.

61. O. W. HOLMES, *supra* note 7, at 101.

62. G. FREDRICKSON, *supra* note 59, at 176–77. *See also* E. WILSON, *Justice Oliver Wendell Holmes*, in PATRIOTIC GORE: STUDIES IN THE LITERATURE OF THE AMERICAN CIVIL WAR 743 (Oxford Univ. Press 1962).

63. *See* Touster, *In Search of Holmes from Within*, 18 VAND. L. REV. 437, 449 (1965).

64. *See generally* C. COOK, THE AMERICAN CODIFICATION MOVEMENT 23–45 (Greenwood Press 1981); Gordon, *The American Codification Movement: A Study of Antebellum Legal Reform*, 36 VAND. L. REV. 431 (1983).

65. *See id.* at 46–66; L. LEVY, THE LAW OF THE COMMONWEALTH AND CHIEF JUSTICE SHAW 196–202 (Harvard Univ. Press 1957).

66. THE CIVIL CODE OF THE STATE OF NEW YORK, REPORTED COMPLETE BY THE COMMISSIONERS OF THE CODE iii (Weed Parsons 1865) (quoting the act of April 6, 1857 appointing the commissioners) [hereafter CIVIL CODE].

67. EIGHTH REPORT OF THE COMMISSIONERS OF THE CODE—PENAL CODE lxiv, 406, clxvii (Weed, Parsons 1865) (completed draft of the code); FOURTH REPORT OF THE COMMISSIONERS OF PRACTICE AND PLEADINGS—CODE OF CRIMINAL PROCEDURE lxxxi, 263 (Weed, Parsons 1848). The criminal code was enacted into law thirty-three years later, 1881 N.Y. Laws 442.

68. THIRD REPORT OF THE COMMISSIONERS OF THE CODE xlvii, 607 (Weed, Parsons 1860) (containing the text of the political code that was never adopted).

69. *See* CIVIL CODE, *supra* note 66.

70. *Id.* at xxxi.

71. *Id.*

72. On the creation and history of the California Civil Code, see Pomeroy, *The True Method of Interpreting the Civil Code*, 4 W. COAST REP. 145 (1884); Harrison, *The First Half Century of the California Civil Code*, 10 CALIF. L. REV. 185 (1922); Van Alstyne, *The California Civil Code*, in WEST'S ANNOTATED CALIFORNIA CODES: CIVIL CODE 1–43

(West 1954); England, *Li v. Yellow Cab Co.—A Belated and Inglorious Centennial of the California Civil Code*, 65 CALIF. L. REV. 4 (1977).

73. ASSOCIATION OF THE BAR OF THE CITY OF NEW YORK, FOURTH ANNUAL REPORT OF THE SPECIAL COMMITTEE TO URGE THE REJECTION OF THE PROPOSED CIVIL CODE app. (n.p. 1884). For a general discussion of the Bar Association's opposition to codification, *see* G. W. MARTIN, CAUSES AND CONFLICTS: THE CENTENNIAL HISTORY OF THE ASSOCIATION OF THE BAR OF THE CITY OF NEW YORK 143–157 (Houghton Mifflin 1970).

74. J. C. CARTER, THE IDEAL AND THE ACTUAL IN THE LAW 10 (Dando 1890).

75. *Id.*

76. J. C. CARTER, THE PROPOSED CODIFICATION OF OUR COMMON LAW 83–84 (Evening Post 1884).

77. *Id.* at 6.

78. *Id.*

79. *Id.* at 6–7 (emphasis in original).

80. J. C. CARTER, *supra* note 74, at 11.

81. *Id.* at 10 (emphasis in the original).

82. *Id.* (emphasis in the original).

83. J. C. CARTER, LAW: ITS ORIGIN, GROWTH AND FUNCTION 85 (G. P. Putnam's Sons 1907).

84. J. C. CARTER, *supra* note 74, at 18.

85. J. C. CARTER, *supra* note 76, at 40.

86. J. C. CARTER, *supra* note 74, at 28.

87. *Id.*

88. *Id.* at 22.

89. *Id.* at 21.

90. *Id.*

91. *Id.*

92. *Id.* at 22.

93. R. HOFSTADTER, SOCIAL DARWINISM IN AMERICAN THOUGHT 60 (rev. ed., Bacon Press 1955).

94. *Id.*

95. *Id.* at 60–61 (quoting W. SUMNER, *The Absurd Effort to Make the World Over*, in 1 ESSAYS OF WILLIAM GRAHAM SUMNER 105 (A. Keller & M Davie eds., Yale Univ. Press 1934)).

96. J. C. CARTER, *supra* note 83, at 141.

97. *See* M. CAPPELLETTI, JUDICIAL REVIEW IN THE CONTEMPORARY WORLD 32–43 (Bobbs-Merrill 1971).

98. *See* P. J. KING, UTILITARIAN JURISPRUDENCE IN AMERICA: THE INFLUENCE OF BENTHAM AND AUSTIN ON AMERICAN LEGAL THOUGHT IN THE NINETEENTH CENTURY ch. 5 (Garland 1986).

99. Maine, the founder of legal anthropology, wrote his *Ancient Law* out of an evolutionist perspective. *See* Elliot, *The Evolutionary Tradition in Jurisprudence*, 85 COLUM. L. REV. 38, 41–46 (1985). See also J. W. BURROW, EVOLUTION AND SOCIETY 137 (Cambridge Univ. Press 1970). For Maine's influence on Holmes, see M. HOWE, *supra* note 3, at 148–150.

100. J. C. CARTER, *supra* note 83, at 141–42.

101. *Id.* at 143.

102. *Id.*

103. J. C. CARTER, *supra* note 74, at 10.

104. M. HOWE, *supra* note 3, at 63. *See also* Holmes, *supra* note 1, at 4.

105. Holmes, *supra* note 1, at 1.

106. O. W. HOLMES, TOUCHED WITH FIRE: CIVIL WAR LETTERS AND DIARY 71 (M. Howe ed., Harvard Univ. Press 1946), *quoted in* G. FREDRICKSON, *supra* note 59, at 170.

107. L.R. 3 H.L. 330 (1868), *See generally* C. Dalton, Losing History: The Case of *Rylands v. Fletcher* (unpublished manuscript).

108. *See, e.g.*, Brown v. Collins, 53 N.H. 442 (1873); Losee v. Buchanan, 51 N.Y. 476, 484 (1873).

109. O. W. HOLMES, *supra* note 7, at 86.

110. *Id.* at 77.

111. *Id.*

112. *Id.* at 78.

113. *Id.*

114. *Id.* at 129.

115. *Id.* at 118.

116. *Id.* at 31.

117. *Id.* at 32.

118. *Id.*

119. *See* A. PAUL, CONSERVATIVE CRISIS AND THE RULE OF LAW: ATTITUDES OF BAR AND BENCH, 1887–1895 (Cornell Univ. Press 1960).

120. O. W. HOLMES, *supra* note 7, at 78.

121. O. W. HOLMES, *supra* note 4, at 182–83.

122. *See, e.g.*, J. SALMOND, THE LAW OF TORTS 20 (1st ed., Stevens & Haynes 1907) (arguing that the objective theory is based on "a defective analysis of the conception" of negligence. Negligence "cannot be ascertained save by looking into the mind of the defendant in order to see what his mental attitude was towards the act and its consequences."); J. SALMOND, ESSAYS IN JURISPRUDENCE AND LEGAL HISTORY 159 (Stevens & Haynes 1891) (stating that liability should be restricted "to the person actually in fault."); Bohlen, *The Rule in Rylands v. Fletcher* (pt. 1), 59 U. PA. L. REV. 298, 313 (1911) ("To be of any service as a test of liability, fault must be used in its actual, its subjective meaning of some conduct repugnant to accepted moral or ethical ideas. . . ."); M. BIGELOW, THE LAW OF TORTS 19 (8th ed., Little, Brown 1907) ("[N]egligence is a state of mind; a fact obscured by the circumstance that stated external standards are applied to the proof of it."). *But see* Isaacs, *Fault and Liability*, 31 HARV. L. REV. 954, 974 (1918) ("I find it impossible to fence off a field of law in which liability is based exclusively on fault. In the first place, even in those cases in which fault is admittedly the basis of liability, it is not the individual fault of the particular culprit, but rather a type of culpable conduct that must be considered. Take for example the case of negligence.").

123. Ames, *Law and Morals*, 22 HARV. L. REV. 97, 99 (1908–09).

124. *Id.* at 103.

125. *Id.* at 99.

126. *See supra* note 122.

127. Isaacs, *supra* note 122, at 974.

128. *Id.* at 975.

129. *Id.* at 976.

130. Seavey, *Negligence—Subjective or Objective*, 41 HARV. L. REV. 1, 27 (1927).

131. *Id.* at 27–28.

132. *Id.* at 28.

133. *Id.*

134. *Id.*

135. O. W. HOLMES, *supra* note 4, at 187.

136. *Id.* at 182.

137. *See* Rogat, *Mr. Justice Holmes: A Dissenting Opinion*, 15 STAN. L. REV. 254 (1962–1963).

138. O. W. HOLMES, *Privilege, Malice and Intent*, in COLLECTED LEGAL PAPERS, *supra* note 4, at 117 (reprinted from 8 HARV. L. REV. 1 (1894)).

139. *Id.* at 129–130.

140. O. W. HOLMES, *supra* note 7, at 167.

141. *Id.* at 163.

142. *Id.*

143. *Id.* at 167.

144. *Id.*

145. *Id.* at 167.

146. *Id.* at 173.

147. *Id.*

148. *Id.*

149. Hohfeld, *Fundamental Legal Conceptions as Applied in Judicial Reasoning*, 23 YALE L.J. 16 (1913). *See also* Singer, *The Legal Rights Debate in Analytical Jurisprudence from Bentham to Hohfeld*, 1982 WIS. L. REV. 975. *See also* the discussions of Hohfeld *supra* ch. 3 and *infra* ch. 6.

150. O. W. HOLMES, *supra* note 7, at 80.

151. *Id.* at 5.

152. Holmes, book review, 14 AM. L. REV. 233, 234 (1880).

153. Lochner v. New York, 198 U.S. 45, 76 (1905) (Holmes, J., dissenting).

154. *See infra* notes 215–221 and accompanying text.

155. O. W. HOLMES, *supra* note 4, at 183.

156. *Id.* at 182.

157. *Id.* at 181.

158. O. W. HOLMES, *supra* note 138.

159. *See* C. GREGORY & H. KATZ, LABOR AND THE LAW ch. 2 (3d ed., W. W. Norton 1979).

160. O. W. HOLMES, *supra* note 138, at 119.

161. O. W. HOLMES, *supra* note 7, at 115.

162. *Id.* at 128.

163. O. W. HOLMES, *supra* note 138, at 126.

164. *Id.*

165. *Id.* at 125.

166. For an overview of the development of the balancing test around the turn of the century, see Aleinikoff, *Constitutional Law in the Age of Balancing*, 96 YALE L.J. 943, 952–63 (1987).

167. *See, e.g.*, Schenck v. United States, 249 U.S. 47 (1919); Standard Oil v. United States, 221 U.S. 1 (1911); Terry, *Negligence*, 29 HARV. L. REV. 40 (1915) (which was reflected in Learned Hand's opinion in United States v. Carroll Towing, 159 F.2d 169 (2d Cir. 1947)); Pennsylvania Coal Co. v. Mahon, 260 U.S. 393 (1922). For an early influential jurisprudential justification of balancing tests, see Roscoe Pound, *A Theory of Social*

Interests, 15 PAPERS & PROC. AM. SOC. SOC'Y 16 (1921), published (with revisions) as *A Survey of Social Interests,* 57 HARV. L. REV. 1 (1943).

168. Temperton v. Russell, 1 Q.B. 715.

169. O. W. HOLMES, *supra* note 138, at 127.

170. Mogul Steamship Co. v. McGregor, 23 Q.B.D. 598 (1892).

171. O. W. HOLMES, *supra* note 138, at 128.

172. *Id.*

173. *Id.* at 129.

174. *Id.*

175. *See infra* text accompanying note 193.

176. O. W. HOLMES, *supra* note 138, at 129.

177. *Id.*

178. *Id.*

179. O. W. HOLMES, *supra* note 4, at 184.

180. O. W. HOLMES, *supra* note 138, at 130.

181. *Id.* at 124.

182. O. W. HOLMES, *supra* note 7, at 104. On Holmes's shift, see Lundquist, Comment, *Oliver Wendell Holmes and External Standards of Criminal and Tort Liability: Application of Theory on the Massachusetts Bench,* 28 BUFF. L. REV. 607 (1979).

183. *Id.* at 111.

184. *Id.* at 45.

185. *Id.* at 110.

186. *Id.* at 45.

187. 167 Mass. 92, 44 N.E. 1077 (1896).

188. *Id.* at 95.

189. *Id.*

190. *Id.*

191. *Id.*

192. *Id.* at 98, 44 N.E. at 1077.

193. *Id.* at 105–07, 44 N.E. at 1080–81 (Holmes, J., dissenting).

194. *Id.* at 108, 44 N.E. at 1081 (Holmes, J., dissenting).

195. Allen v. Flood, [1898] A.C. 1.

196. 167 Mass. at 103.

197. O. W. HOLMES, *Law in Science and Science in Law,* in COLLECTED LEGAL PAPERS, *supra* note 4, at 210.

198. *Id.* at 241.

199. *Id.*

200. *Id.*

201. *Id.*

202. *Id.*

203. O. W. HOLMES, *supra* note 138, at 126.

204. *Id.* at 128.

205. *Id.* at 129.

206. O. W. HOLMES, *supra* note 197, at 241.

207. *See* O. W. HOLMES, *supra* note 138, at 127.

208. *Id.* at 125.

209. *Id.* at 129.

210. *Id.* at 128.

211. O. W. HOLMES, *supra* note 7, at 80.

212. [1898] A.C. 1.

213. O. W. HOLMES, *supra* note 138, at 125.

214. The discussion of spite fences that follows is drawn from Alexandre Kedar, The History of Anglo-American Legal Discourses About Obstruction of Lights 107–175 (unpublished L.L.M. thesis, Harvard Law School 1989).

215. T. COOLEY, A TREATISE ON THE LAW OF TORTS 688 (1st ed., Callaghan 1879). Chapter XXII was entitled "The Place of Evil Motive in the Law of Torts." Cooley continued: "Any transaction which would be lawful and proper if the parties were friends, cannot be made the foundation of an action merely because they happened to be enemies. As long as a man keeps himself within the law by doing no *act* which violates it, we must leave his motives to HIM who searches the heart."

216. Kedar, *supra* note 214, at 116.

217. 148 Mass. 368 (1889). The case involved the constitutionality of a Massachusetts statute giving a right of action for spite fences, so Holmes's views on the common law were dicta. Moreover, despite the language in the text, Holmes managed to find a way to uphold the statute.

218. *Id.* at 372.

219. *See* M. HORWITZ, *supra* note 28, at 107.

220. *See* [Nockelby], *Tortious Interference with Contractual Relations in the Nineteenth Century: The Transformation of Property, Contract and Tort*, 93 HARV. L. REV. 1510, 1529–39 (1980).

221. Int'l News Serv. v. Associated Press, 248 U.S. 215, 246 (1918) (Holmes, J.).

222. O. W. HOLMES, *supra* note 4, at 241.

223. *See generally* Vandevelde, *The New Property of the Nineteenth Century: The Development of the Modern Concept of Property*, 29 BUFFALO L. REV. 325 (1980).

224. *See also* the evolution of the duty of lateral support of land. In 1850, the New York Supreme Court declared that such a duty "would often deprive men of the whole beneficial use of their property." Such a duty would leave the landowner with "but a nominal right to his property." Radcliff's Ex'rs v. Mayor of Brooklyn, 4 N.Y. 195, 203 (1850). The refusal to extend correlative rights to the law governing waters percolating in subterranean channels was also explained in the language of absolute property rights. In the Pennsylvania case of Wheatley v. Baugh, 25 Pa. 528 (1855), the court insisted that to apply the riparian doctrine of reciprocal rights to percolating streams "would amount to a total abrogation of the right to property." *Id.* at 532. The New York Supreme Court declined to apply reciprocal rights to sub-surface streams, in 1855 declaring "the rule that a man has a right to the free and absolute use of his property unless he caused direct injury." Ellis v. Duncan, 21 Barb. 230, 235 (N.Y. App. Div. 1855).

225. *See generally* [Nockelby], *supra* note 220, at 1510; Vandevelde, *supra* note 223; Cohen, *Property and Sovereignty*, 13 CORNELL L.Q. 8 (1927); Singer, *supra* note 149. See the discussion of rights in chapter 5, *infra* text accompanying notes 77–96.

226. O. W. HOLMES, *supra* note 4, at 173.

227. *Id.* at 172.

228. *Id.* at 173.

229. *Id.* at 180.

230. *Id.* at 181.

231. *See* G. GILMORE, THE DEATH OF CONTRACT 143, n.256 (Ohio State Univ. Press

1974); Horwitz, book review, 42 U. CHI. L. REV. 787, 796 (1975) (reviewing G. GILMORE, *supra*); Gordon, *supra* note 6, at 727.

232. O. W. HOLMES, *supra* note 4, at 194–95.

233. *Id.* at 195.

234. *Id.* at 186–87.

235. *Id.* at 182.

236. *Id.* at 195.

237. James, *Philosophical Conceptions and Practical Results*, U. CHRONICLE, September 1898 (a lecture delivered before the Philosophical Union at Berkeley, California, in 1898), *reprinted in* W. JAMES, COLLECTED ESSAYS AND REVIEWS 406 (R. Perry ed., Longmans, Green 1920).

238. *See* D. ROSS, THE ORIGINS OF AMERICAN SOCIAL SCIENCE 165 (Cambridge Univ. Press 1990). *See also* B. KUKLICK, CHURCHMEN AND PHILOSOPHERS: FROM JONATHAN EDWARDS TO JOHN DEWEY 241–49 (Yale Univ. Press 1985).

239. *See* M. WHITE, SOCIAL THOUGHT IN AMERICA: THE REVOLT AGAINST FORMALISM (rev. ed., Beacon Press 1957); R. SUMMERS, INSTRUMENTALISM AND AMERICAN LEGAL THEORY (Cornell Univ. Press 1982).

240. *See* B. KUKLICK, *supra* note 238, at 218–29.

241. 198 U.S. 45 (1905).

242. *See, e.g.*, A BENTLEY, THE PROCESS OF GOVERNMENT (1st ed., Principia Press 1908).

Chapter 5

1. *See* Vandevelde, *The New Property of the Nineteenth Century: The Development of the Modern Concept of Property*, 29 BUFFALO L. REV. 325 (1980).

2. 83 U.S. (16 Wall.) 36, 127 (1872).

3. J. COMMONS, LEGAL FOUNDATIONS OF CAPITALISM 14 (Macmillan 1924).

4. 94 U.S. 113 (1876).

5. *Id.* at 143.

6. Chicago, M. & St. P. Ry. v. Minnesota, 134 U.S. 418 (1890).

7. J. COMMONS, *supra* note 3, at 16 (emphasis retained).

8. *See* M. HORWITZ, THE TRANSFORMATION OF AMERICAN LAW, 1780–1860, at 71–74, 132 (Harvard Univ. Press 1977).

9. *See id.* at 74–80, 132.

10. J. LEWIS, A TREATISE ON THE LAW OF EMINENT DOMAIN IN THE UNITED STATES I (Collaghan 1888).

11. *Id.*

12. *Id.*

13. *Id.* at 41, 43.

14. Old Colony & F.R.R.R. v. County of Plymouth, 80 Mass. (14 Gray) 155, 161 (1859).

15. J. LEWIS, *supra* note 10, at 45.

16. *Id.*

17. T. SEDGWICK, A TREATISE ON THE RULES WHICH GOVERN THE INTERPRETATION

AND CONSTRUCTION OF STATUTORY AND CONSTITUTIONAL LAW 456–57 (2d ed., Baker, Voorhis 1874).

18. *Id.* at 462–63.

19. J. LEWIS, *supra* note 10, at 46.

20. 51 N.H. 504 (1872).

21. *Id.* at 511.

22. *Id.* (citations omitted).

23. Thompson v. Androscoggin River Improvement Co., 54 N.H. 545, 552 (1874).

24. *Id.*

25. 80 U.S. (13 Wall.) 166 (1871).

26. *Id.* at 177–78.

27. After *Pumpelly*, there were two lines of Supreme Court cases. Transportation Co. v. Chicago, 99 U.S. 635, 642 (1878) tried to limit *Pumpelly* by characterizing it as "the extremist qualification" of the traditional doctrine that consequential damages are noncompensable. *See also* Mugler v. Kansas, 123 U.S. 623, 667, 668 (1887). But *Pumpelly* is favorably cited in Louisiana *ex rel.* Folsom v. New Orleans, 109 U.S. 285, 295–96 (1883); Chicago v. Taylor, 125 U.S. 161, 162–63 (1888); Pennsylvania R.R. v. Miller, 132 U.S. 75, 81 (1889); United States v. Alexander, 148 U.S. 181, 191–92 (1893); Monongahela Navigation Co. v. U.S., 148 U.S. 312 (1893). For the significance of *Monongahela Navigation*, see Commons, *supra* note 3, at 182–86.

28. *See* J. LEWIS, *supra* note 10, at 46.

29. Siegel, *Understanding the Lochner Era: Lessons from the Controversy Over Railroad and Utility Rate Regulation*, 70 VA. L. REV. 187, 243–47 (1984).

30. 3 U.S. (3 Dall.) 386 (1798).

31. *Id.* at 400.

32. B. WRIGHT, THE CONTRACT CLAUSE OF THE CONSTITUTION 27–61 (Harvard Univ. Press 1938).

33. *See* T. COOLEY, A TREATISE ON THE CONSTITUTIONAL LIMITATIONS WHICH REST UPON THE LEGISLATIVE POWER OF THE STATES OF THE AMERICAN UNION 438–76 (5th ed., Little, Brown 1883).

34. 25 U.S. (12 Wheat.) 213 (1827).

35. *See* Sturges v. Crowninshield, 17 U.S. (4 Wheat.) 122 (1819).

36. 25 U.S. (12 Wheat.) at 344–45.

37. In Barron v. Mayor of Baltimore, 32 U.S. (7 Pet.) 243 (1833), the Supreme Court held that the Fifth Amendment's just compensation clause—and the Bill of Rights generally—did not serve as a limitation on the states. This changed after the enactment of the Fourteenth Amendment. Before the Civil War, therefore, the contracts clause often served as the closest functional equivalent to a takings clause.

38. *See* Grey, *The Disintegration of Property*, in PROPERTY: NOMOS XXII 69 (J. Pennock & J. Chapman eds., New York Univ. Press 1980).

39. Hohfeld, *Some Fundamental Legal Conceptions as Applied in Judicial Reasoning*, 23 YALE L.J. 16, 30 (1913).

40. Kennedy & Michelman, *Are Property and Contract Efficient?*, 8 HOFSTRA L. REV. 711, 751–52 (1980).

41. Hohfeld, *A Vital School of Jurisprudence and Law: Have American Universities Awakened to the Enlarged Opportunities and Responsibilities of the Present Day?* 1914 A. AM. L. SCH. PROC. 76.

42. *Id.* at 76, 79.

43. *Id.* at 96, 98.

44. *Id.* at 102.

45. *Id.* at 101.

46. *See* Singer, *The Legal Rights Debate in Analytical Jurisprudence from Bentham to Hohfeld,* 1982 WIS. L. REV. 975.

47. *See id.* at 1050 n.210.

48. J. AUSTIN, LECTURES ON JURISPRUDENCE (3 vols., J. Murray 1863).

49. Hart, *Introduction* to J. AUSTIN, THE PROVINCE OF JURISPRUDENCE at viii (H. L. A. Hart ed., Noonday Press 1954).

50. *Id.* at xvi.

51. 2 J. AUSTIN, *supra* note 48, at 61.

52. *Id.* at 66 (emphasis retained).

53. *See* J. BENTHAM, A COMMENT ON THE COMMENTARIES AND A FRAGMENT ON GOVERNMENT (J. Burns & H. Hart eds., Humanities Press 1977).

54. J. BENTHAM, *Anarchical Fallacies: Being in Examination of the Declarations of Rights Issued During the French Revolution,* in 2 WORKS 489 (J. Bowring ed., W. Tait 1843).

55. *See* E. HALEVY, THE GROWTH OF PHILOSOPHIC RADICALISM 76–81 (Macmillan 1928).

56. *See* J. BENTHAM, *supra* note 54.

57. *See* Touster, *In Search of Holmes from Within,* 18 VAND. L. REV. 437 (1965), and discussion *supra* ch. 4.

58. Holmes, *Codes, and the Arrangement of the Law,* 5 AM. L. REV. 1, 3 (1870).

59. *See supra* text accompanying notes 38–47.

60. *See* Vandevelde, *supra* note 1.

61. *See* Hurvitz, *American Labor Law and the Doctrine of Entrepreneurial Property Rights: Boycotts, Courts, and the Juridical Reorientation of 1886–1895,* 8 INDUS. REL. L.J. 307 (1986).

62. *See* Forbath, *The Ambiguities of Free Labor: Labor and the Law in the Gilded Age,* 1985 WIS. L. REV. 767; Hattam, *Workers as Conspirators: Judicial Regulation of Labor Under the Common Law Doctrine of Criminal Conspiracy,* in LABOR LAW IN AMERICA: HISTORICAL AND CRITICAL ESSAYS (C. Tomlins & A. J. King eds., Johns Hopkins Univ. Press forthcoming).

63. Boomer v. Atlantic Cement, 26 N.Y.2d 219, 257 N.E.2d 870, 309 N.Y.S.2d 312 (1970), gave courts discretion in granting injunctions against nuisances. It overruled Whalen v. Union Bag & Paper Co., 208 N.Y. 1, 101 N.E. 805 (1913), which held that such injunctions were not discretionary. The *Whalen* rule seems to have derived from the desire of the New York Court of Appeals to show that labor injunctions were not discretionary. Therefore, it created a general rule that if a nuisance were found, an injunction followed as a matter of course. *Cf.* Halper, *Nuisance, Courts and Market in the New York Court of Appeals, 1850–1915,* 54 ALB. L. REV. 301 (1990).

64. 167 Mass. 92, 44 N.E. 1077 (1896).

65. Holmes, *Privilege, Malice, and Intent,* 8 HARV. L. REV. 1 (1894).

66. *See supra* ch. 4.

67. *See id.*

68. Even Holmes was susceptible to such a view. In Davis v. Massachusetts, 162 Mass. 510, 511, 39 N.E. 113, 113 (1895), he upheld restrictions on an open air speaker as follows: "For the legislature absolutely or conditionally to forbid public speaking in a

highway or public park is no more an infringement of the rights of a member of the public than for the owner of a private house to forbid it in his house."

69. In JUSTICE ACCUSED: ANTISLAVERY AND THE JUDICIAL PROCESS (Yale Univ. Press 1975), Robert M. Cover showed how antebellum judges who believed slavery was contrary to natural right nevertheless did not go behind positive law to follow their beliefs. They preserved a distinction between positive law and political philosophy. Stanley N. Katz made a similar argument about a different property relation in *Republicanism and the Law of Inheritance in the Revolutionary Era*, 76 MICH. L. REV. 1, 6 (1977). He emphasized "the mainstream . . . tradition . . . clearly marked by the positivist spirit of Blackstone and the theorists of legislative sovereignty" which made Nunnemacher v. State, 129 Wis. 190, 202–03, 108 N.W. 627, 630 (1906), "an isolated moment in the history of American jurisprudence." In that case, the Wisconsin Supreme Court held that "the right to demand that property pass by inheritance or will is an inherent right subject only to reasonable regulation by the Legislature." See further discussion *infra* text accompanying note 92.

70. Kennedy & Michelman, *supra* note 40, at 752–53.

71. Hitchman Coal & Coke Co. v. Mitchall, 245 U.S. 229 (1917).

72. Cook, *Privileges of Labor Unions in the Struggle for Life*, 27 YALE L.J. 779 (1918).

73. *Id.* at 790.

74. *See* Vandevelde, *supra* note 1, at 359–62.

75. Corbin, *Taxation of Seats on the Stock Exchange*, 31 YALE L.J. 429, 429 (1922). *See also* Grey, *supra* note 38, at 79.

76. Vandevelde, *supra* note 1, at 361.

77. *See* C. HAINES, THE REVIVAL OF NATURAL LAW CONCEPTS (Harvard Univ. Press 1930); E. CORWIN, THE "HIGHER LAW" BACKGROUND OF AMERICAN CONSTITUTIONAL LAW (Great Seal Books 1955) (originally published in 42 HARV. L. REV. 149, 365 (1928–29)); B. WRIGHT, AMERICAN INTERPRETATIONS OF NATURAL LAW (Harvard Univ. Press 1931).

78. *See* S. FINE, LAISSEZ FAIRE AND THE GENERAL-WELFARE STATE 126–64 (Univ. of Michigan Press 1956); C. JACOBS, LAW WRITERS AND THE COURTS 85–93 (Univ. of California Press 1954); A. PAUL, CONSERVATIVE CRISIS AND THE RULE OF LAW: ATTITUDES OF BAR AND BENCH, 1887–1895, at 209–21 (Cornell Univ. Press 1960); B. TWISS, LAWYERS AND THE CONSTITUTION (Princeton Univ. Press 1942).

79. *See* C. BECKER, THE DECLARATION OF INDEPENDENCE 24–79 (Harcourt, Brace 1922).

80. *See* O. GIERKE, NATURAL LAW AND THE THEORY OF SOCIETY (2 vols., E. Barker trans., Cambridge Univ. Press 1934); A. P. D'ENTREVES, NATURAL LAW (Hutchinson's Univ. Library 1951).

81. *See* J. GOUGH, FUNDAMENTAL LAW IN ENGLISH CONSTITUTIONAL HISTORY (Clarendon Press 1955).

82. *See* I. SHAPIRO, THE EVOLUTION OF RIGHTS IN LIBERAL THEORY (Cambridge Univ. Press 1986); J. FINNIS, NATURAL LAW AND NATURAL RIGHTS (Oxford Univ. Press 1980); C. B. MACPHERSON, THE POLITICAL THEORY OF POSSESSIVE INDIVIDUALISM (Oxford Univ. Press 1962); M. KAMMEN, A MACHINE THAT WOULD GO OF ITSELF: THE CONSTITUTION IN AMERICAN CULTURE (Knopf 1986).

83. *See* B. BAILYN, IDEOLOGICAL ORIGINS OF THE AMERICAN REVOLUTION 175–98 (Harvard Univ. Press 1967).

84. *See* G. WILLS, INVENTING AMERICA 93–110 (Doubleday 1978).

85. 3 U.S. (3 Dall.) 386 (1798). *See* Grey, *Do We Have an Unwritten Constitution?* 27 STAN. L. REV. 703 (1975).

86. *See* Corwin, *The Basic Doctrine of American Constitutional Law*, 12 MICH. L. REV. 247 (1914).

87. *See supra* ch. 1.

88. 17 U.S. (4 Wheat.) 316 (1819).

89. *See supra* ch. 2.

90. *See infra* ch. 7.

91. R. COVER, *supra* note 69, at 120–21 (quoting State v. Hoppess, 2 W.L.J. 279, 285 (Ohio 1845), *reprinted in* 10 Ohio Dec. Reprint 105, 110–11 (1896)).

92. *Id.* at 34.

93. C. TIEDEMAN, A TREATISE ON THE LIMITATIONS OF THE POLICE POWER IN THE UNITED STATES (F. H. Thomas 1886). *See* sources cited *supra* note 78.

94. *Id.* at 7.

95. *Id.* at 10.

96. T. COOLEY, A TREATISE ON THE CONSTITUTIONAL LIMITATIONS WHICH REST UPON THE LEGISLATIVE POWER OF THE STATES OF THE AMERICAN UNION 232–33 (7th ed., Little, Brown 1903).

97. 169 U.S. 466 (1898).

98. Henderson, *Railway Valuation and the Courts*, 33 HARV. L. REV. 902, 913 (1920).

99. Siegel, *supra* note 29, at 227.

100. McCardle v. Indianapolis Water Co., 272 U.S. 400 (1926).

101. Siegel, *supra* note 29, at 233–34.

102. *See infra* text accompanying notes 106–127; Siegel, *supra* note 29, at 247–50; Peller, *The Metaphysics of American Law*, 73 CALIF. L. REV. 1151, 1227–39 (1985).

103. Henderson, *supra* note 98, at 906.

104. Ruggles v. Illinois, 108 U.S. 526 (1883).

105. Cotting v. Kansas City Stock Yards Co., 183 U.S. 79, 94 (1901).

106. Richberg, *Value—By Judicial Fiat*, 40 HARV. L. REV. 567 (1927).

107. *Id.* at 578.

108. *Id.* at 576.

109. *Id.* at 580.

110. Cohen, *Property and Sovereignty*, 13 CORNELL L.Q. 8 (1927).

111. Henderson, *supra* note 98.

112. *Id.* at 910.

113. *Id.* at 912.

114. *Id.* at 910.

115. J. COMMONS, *supra* note 3, at 25.

116. *Id.* at 196.

117. *Id.*

118. Henderson, *supra* note 98.

119. *Id.* at 917. Robert L. Hale should perhaps be given credit for first seeing the relationship between present value and future income. *The Supreme Court's Ambiguous Use of "Value" in Rate Cases*, 18 COLUM. L. REV. 208, 210–11 (1918). While his article is quite dense and does not highlight the circularity issue, I would suppose that Henderson was stimulated by it.

This point soon became a standard observation in the literature or rate making. "What . . . is meant by present value?" James C. Bonbright asked in 1927. "[I]f we measure . . . worth by [property's] market value as a going concern, we are involved in that hopeless vicious circle of basing rates on a value which in turn depends on the rates." *Depreciation and Valuation for Rate Control*, 27 COLUM. L. REV. 113, 122 (1927). Bonbright was to become the leading authority on rate setting.

120. Hale, *Rate Making and the Revision of the Property Concept*, 22 COLUM. L. REV. 209 (1922).

121. *Id.* at 212.

122. *Id.* at 213.

123. *Id.* at 214.

124. Cohen, *supra* note 110.

125. Hale, Coercion and Distribution in a Supposedly Non-Coercive State, 38 POL. SCI. REV. 470 (1923). *See* discussion *infra* ch. 7.

126. Hale, *supra* note 120, at 214.

127. *Id.* at 214–15.

128. Cohen, *supra* note 110.

129. *Id.* at 8.

130. *Id.* at 12.

131. *Id.* at 23–24.

132. *Id.* at 24.

133. *Id.* at 12.

134. R. ELY, STUDIES IN THE EVOLUTION OF INDUSTRIAL SOCIETY 405 (Macmillan 1903).

135. *Id.* at 406.

136. A BERLE AND G. MEANS, THE MODERN CORPORATION AND PRIVATE PROPERTY 333–39 (Commerce Clearing House, 1932).

137. *Id.* at 340.

Chapter 6

1. Lochner v. New York, 198 U.S. 45 (1905).

2. *See infra* ch. 8.

3. *See* Friedman & Ladinsky, *Social Change and the Law of Industrial Accidents*, 67 COLUM. L. REV. 50 (1967); J. WEINSTEIN, THE CORPORATE IDEAL IN THE LIBERAL STATE, 1900–1918, at 40–61 (Beacon Press 1968).

4. *See* J. KLOPPENBERG, UNCERTAIN VICTORY: SOCIAL DEMOCRACY AND PROGRESSIVISM IN EUROPEAN AND AMERICAN THOUGHT, 1870–1920 (Oxford Univ. Press 1986).

5. *See* E. PURCELL, THE CRISIS OF DEMOCRATIC THEORY: SCIENTIFIC NATURALISM AND THE PROBLEM OF VALUE 3–12 (Univ. Press of Kentucky 1973); H. MAY, *The Rebellion of the Intellectuals, 1912–1917*, in IDEAS, FAITHS, AND FEELINGS: ESSAYS ON AMERICAN INTELLECTUAL AND RELIGIOUS HISTORY, 1952–1982, at 3–19 (Oxford Univ. Press 1983).

6. Compare HERBERT CROLY'S THE PROMISE OF AMERICAN LIFE (Macmillan 1909) with WALTER LIPPMANN'S PUBLIC OPINION (Harcourt Brace 1922). *See* R. STEEL, WALTER LIPPMANN AND THE AMERICAN CENTURY 58–59, 180–85 (Little, Brown 1980).

7. The literature on Legal Realism has become quite extensive. The interpretation whose perspective I most share is Singer, *Legal Realism Now*, 76 CALIF. L. REV. 465 (1988) (reviewing L. KALMAN, LEGAL REALISM AT YALE, 1927–1960 (Univ. of North Carolina Press 1986)). Among the most useful additional sources are L. Kalman, *supra*; E. PURCELL, *supra* note 5; W. RUMBLE, AMERICAN LEGAL REALISM (Cornell Univ. Press 1968); W. TWINING, KARL LLEWELLYN AND THE REALIST MOVEMENT (2d ed., Univ of

Oklahoma Press 1985); Dawson, *Legal Realism and Legal Scholarship*, 33 J. LEGAL EDUC. 406 (1983); Gilmore, *Legal Realism: Its Cause and Cure*, 70 YALE L.J. 1037 (1961); Hull, *Some Realism about the Llewellyn-Pound Exchange over Realism: The Newly Uncovered Private Correspondence, 1927–1931*, 1987 WIS. L. REV. 921; Purcell, *American Jurisprudence between the Wars: Legal Realism and the Crisis of Democratic Theory*, 75 AM. HIST. REV. 424 (1969); Schlegel, *American Legal Realism and Empirical Social Science: From the Yale Experience*, 28 BUFFALO L. REV. 459 (1979) [hereafter Schlegel, *Yale Experience*]; Schlegel, *American Legal Realism and Empirical Social Science: The Singular Case of Underhill Moore*, 29 BUFFALO L. REV. 195 (1980) [hereafter Schlegel, *Underhill Moore*]; White, *The Evolution of Reasoned Elaboration: Jurisprudential Criticism and Social Change*, 59 VA. L. REV. 279 (1973); White, *From Sociological Jurisprudence to Realism: Jurisprudence and Social Change in Early Twentieth-Century America*, 58 VA. L. REV. 999 (1972).

8. Llewellyn, *A Realistic Jurisprudence—The Next Step*, 30 COLUM. L. REV. 431 (1930).

9. *See* Pound, *The Call for a Realist Jurisprudence*, 44 HARV. L. REV. 697 (1931).

10. *See* Llewellyn, *Some Realism About Realism—Responding to Dean Pound*, 44 HARV. L. REV. 1222 (1931).

11. *Id.* at 1226 n.18. The sample included Walter Bingham (Stanford), Charles Clark (Yale), Walter Wheeler Cook (Hopkins), Arthur L. Corbin (Yale), William O. Douglas (Yale), J. Francis (Oklahoma), Jerome Frank (attorney, New York), Leon Green (Northwestern), J. C. Hutcheson (judge, 5th Circuit), S. Klaus (attorney, New York), Karl Llewellyn (Columbia), E. G. Lorenzen (Yale), Underhill Moore (Yale), Herman Oliphant (Hopkins), Edwin W. Patterson (Columbia), T. R. Powell (Harvard), Max Radin (Berkeley), Wesley Sturges (Yale), L. A. Tulin (Columbia), and Hessel E. Yntema (Hopkins). The Legal Realists' institutional affiliations in 1930–31 are from W. TWINING, *supra* note 7, at 76.

12. *See* Hull, *supra* note 7.

13. *See, e.g.*, White, *From Sociological Jurisprudence to Realism*, *supra* note 7.

14. W. TWINING, *supra* note 7, at 104.

15. *Id.* at 105. We need to acknowledge at this point the recent publication in English of K. LLEWELLYN, THE CASE LAW SYSTEM IN AMERICA (P. Gewirtz ed., Univ. of Chicago Press 1989), a translation of a book published in German by Llewellyn in 1933. The book arose out of a course of lectures that Llewellyn gave in 1928–29. While the book is an early example of Llewellyn's sophisticated reflection upon the case law system and the theory of precedent, it is nevertheless a narrowly focused piece of work that offers very little indication of broad reflections about the character of legal thought.

16. W. TWINING, *supra* note 7, at 105.

17. *Id.*

18. *See id.* at 26–55. *See also* L. KALMAN, *supra* note 7, at 111–14.

19. For Llewellyn's interest in German free law jurisprudence, see K. LLEWELLYN, *supra* note 15, at 2–3, Whitman, Note, *Commercial Law and the American Volk: A Note on Llewellyn's German Sources for the Uniform Commercial Code*, 97 YALE L.J. 156, 166–70 (1987).

20. W. TWINING, *supra* note 7, at 71.

21. *See infra* ch. 8.

22. Pound, *supra* note 9, at 709.

23. W. TWINING, *supra* note 7, at 72.

24. *Id.*

25. *Id.*

26. *Id.* at 73 (quoting an unpublished memo of 1931 in the Karl Llewellyn Papers, Univ. of Chicago).

27. *See* Pound, *Law in Books and Law in Action*, 44 AM. L. REV. 12 (1910). *See also infra* text accompanying notes 145–46 and ch. 7, text accompanying note 8.

28. Llewellyn, *supra* note 8, at 434.

29. *Id.* at 435 n.3 (emphasis added).

30. *Id.*

31. *Id.*

32. *Id.*

33. *Id.*

34. *See* R. POUND, JURISPRUDENCE (5 vols., West 1959).

35. Llewellyn, *supra* note 8, at 434 (emphasis in the original).

36. *See* L. KALMAN, *supra* note 7, at 58–59.

37. *See* D. WIGDOR, ROSCOE POUND: PHILOSOPHER OF LAW 249–50 (Greenwood Press 1974).

38. *Id.* at 251.

39. *See* Hull, *Reconstructing the Origins of Realistic Jurisprudence: A Prequel to the Llewellyn-Pound Exchange Over Legal Realism*, 1989 DUKE L.J. 1302, 1324.

40. J. FRANK, LAW AND THE MODERN MIND (Brentano's 1930); *Law and the Modern Mind: A Symposium*, 31 COLUM. L. REV. 82 (1931).

41. *See* L. KALMAN, *supra* note 7, at 240 n.83; W. TWINING, *supra* note 7, at 77; Hull, *supra* note 7, at 956–57.

42. None of the publishers of the successive editions of *Law and the Modern Mind* can locate sales figures for the book.

43. Frank's marginal position meant, among other things, that his name encountered a good deal of resistance when it was mentioned for any academic appointment. Arthur Corbin, for example, was set against Frank's appointment at Yale. He felt that Frank's polemical book marked him as a "propagandist and an agitator rather than a teacher and investigator." Schlegel, *Underhill Moore*, *supra* note 7, at 314 n.720 and accompanying text (quoting a letter from Corbin to Members of the Governing Board of the School of Law (February 8, 1935) (Moore Papers, Yale Univ. Library)). According to Kalman, "Corbin, however, opposed a 1935 proposal to appoint Frank not only becauss he thought *Law and the Modern Mind* revealed Frank to be a 'propagandist and an agitator rather than a teacher and investigator' but also because Frank was an ardent New Dealer and a Jew." L. KALMAN, *supra* note 7, at 138.

44. In his book on the Second Circuit under Learned Hand's leadership, Marvin Schick comments that ". . . Frank was regarded as perhaps the most critical and abrasive of the legal realists who had vociferously attacked many of the foundations of American jurisprudence." M. SCHICK, LEARNED HAND'S COURT 10 (Johns Hopkins Univ. Press 1970).

45. R. GLENNON, THE ICONOCLAST AS REFORMER: JEROME FRANK'S IMPACT ON AMERICAN LAW 16 (Cornell Univ. Press 1985).

46. *Id.* at 17.

47. *Id.* at 20.

48. *Id.* at 21.

49. J. FRANK, *supra* note 40, at 14–23.

50. *Id.* at 19.

51. O. W. HOLMES, *The Path of the Law*, in COLLECTED LEGAL PAPERS 181 (Harcourt, Brace & Howe 1920).

52. J. FRANK, *supra* note 40, at 18.

53. *Id.* at 18–19.

54. *See* S. AHLSTROM, A RELIGIOUS HISTORY OF THE AMERICAN PEOPLE 767–72 (Yale Univ. Press 1972); J. ROBERTS, DARWINISM AND THE DIVINE IN AMERICA (Univ. of Wisconsin Press 1988).

55. *See* L. LEVINE, DEFENDER OF THE FAITH 324–57 (Oxford Univ. Press 1965). For a different view of Bryan, see G. WILLS, UNDER GOD: RELIGION AND AMERICAN POLITICS (Simon & Schuster 1990).

56. Thurman Wesley Arnold (1891–1969) practiced and taught law in his native Laramie, Wyoming, after graduating from Harvard Law School in 1914. He became dean of West Virginia University Law School in 1927 and joined the faculty of Yale Law School in 1930. While there, he wrote his two most famous works, T. ARNOLD, THE FOLKLORE OF CAPITALISM (Yale Univ. Press 1937) and T. ARNOLD, THE SYMBOLS OF GOVERNMENT (Yale Univ. Press 1935), which established his reputation as an irreverent critic of law, society, and economic thought. *See also* Arnold, *Professor Hart's Theology*, 73 HARV. L. REV. 1298 (1960); Griswold, *The Supreme Court, 1959 Term—Foreword: Of Time and Attitudes—Professor Hart and Judge Arnold*, 74 HARV. L. REV. 81 (1960). In 1938 Franklin Roosevelt appointed Arnold assistant attorney general in charge of the antitrust division of the Department of Justice, where he remained until his appointment in 1943 to the U.S. Court of Appeals for the District of Columbia Circuit. He left the bench in 1945 and, with Paul Porter and future Supreme Court Justice Abe Fortas, formed what today is the Washington, D.C., law firm of Arnold & Porter. *See generally* E. KEARNY, THURMAN ARNOLD, SOCIAL CRITIC (Univ. of New Mexico Press 1970).

57. *See* J. FRANK, *supra* note 40, at 53–61. "Bealism is stronger in our profession than Fundamentalism among the clergy," he proclaimed in an "addenda to the second printing." *Id.* at 397.

58. *Id.* at 3–13.

59. *Id.* at 10, 11.

60. *Id.* at 10.

61. *Id.* at 11.

62. *Id.* at 10, 19 (emphasis retained).

63. *Id.* at 219–55.

64. *Id.* at 228 n.8.

65. *Id.* at 230.

66. *Id.* at 252–255.

67. *Id.* at 253–54.

68. *Id.* at 255.

69. *Id.*

70. *Id.* at 270–77.

71. *Id.* at 270.

72. *Id.* at 276.

73. Ackerman, *Law and the Modern Mind*, 103 DAEDALUS 119, 125 (1974).

74. Schlegel, *Underhill Moore*, *supra* note 7, at 314 n.720 (quoting a letter from Corbin, *supra* note 43).

75. Llewellyn, *Legal Illusion*, 31 COLUM. L. REV. 82, 90 (1931).

76. Adler, *Legal Certainty*, 31 COLUM. L. REV. 91 (1931).

77. *Id.* at 107. Years later, Frank "regret[ted]" having used the label "realists." He wrote:

The label enabled some of their critics to bracket the realists as a homogeneous "school," in virtual accord with one another on all or most subjects. This misconception—not certainly the result of any careful reading of their works—led to the specious charge that the "realistic school" embraced fantastically inconsistent ideas. Actually no such "school" existed. In the article mentioned above, I referred to one critic's use of this lumping-together method as follows: "It may be roughly described thus: (1) Jones disagrees with Smith about the tariff. (2) Robinson disagrees with Smith about the virtues of sauerkraut juice. (3) Since both Jones and Robinson disagree with Smith about something, it follows that (a) each disagrees with Smith about everything, and that (b) Jones and Robinson agree with one another about the tariff, the virtues of sauerkraut juice, the League of Nations, the quantity theory of money, vitalism, Bernard Shaw, Proust, Lucky Strikes, Communism, Will Rogers—and everything else. Llewellyn, Green, Cook, Yntema, Oliphant, Hutcheson, Bingham, and Frank in their several ways have expressed disagreement with conventional legal theory. Dickinson therefore assumes (a) that they disagree with that theory for identical reasons; and (b) that they agree with one another on their proposed substitutes for that theory. It is as if he were to assume that all men leaving Chicago at a given instant were going north and were bound for the same town. Dickinson has produced a composite photograph of the writers he is discussing. One sees, so to speak, the hair of Green, the eyebrows of Yntema, the teeth of Cook, the neck of Oliphant, the lips of Llewellyn. . . . The picture is the image of an unreal imaginary creature, of a strange, mis-shapen, infertile, hybrid." J. FRANK, *supra* note 40, at ix–x. (Preface to sixth printing, 1948)

78. *Id.*

79. Hull, *supra* note 7, at 943 n.153 and accompanying text (quoting a letter from Pound to Llewellyn (March 21, 1931) (Llewellyn Papers)).

80. *Id.*

81. *Id.* at 944.

82. *Id.* (quoting a letter from Pound to Llewellyn (March 21, 1931) (Pound Papers, Harvard Law School Library).

83. *Id.* at 945.

84. *Id.* at 947 (quoting a letter from Frank to Mack (April 27, 1931) (Frank Papers, Yale Univ. Library)).

85. Kalman correctly identifies Cook, Oliphant, Yntema, and Moore as "the most scientific of the realists." *See* L. KALMAN, *supra* note 7, at 20. "Their strong ties to the social sciences or physical sciences," she writes, "probably accounted for their rigorous concept of scientific objectivity." *Id.* at 241 n.85. Purcell similarly describes Oliphant, Cook, and Yntema as among the most scientific realists when he mentions their joint founding of the Institute of Law at Johns Hopkins in 1929. *See* E. PURCELL, *supra* note 5, at 80.

Charles E. Clark began his teaching career at Yale in 1919 and followed Robert Maynard Hutchins as dean of the Yale Law School in 1929. As dean, Clark championed empirical social science. *See* Clark & Trubek, *The Creative Role of the Judge: Restraint and Freedom in the Common Law Tradition*, 71 YALE L.J. 255 (1961). Indeed, as John Schlegel points out, Clark in his dean's report for the 1929–30 academic year "divided all research into field research and library research, and then showed where his heart was with loving descriptions of the field research and perfunctory treatment of the library research." Schlegel, *Yale Experience*, *supra* note 7, at 495. Clark engaged in his own empirical studies on how courts worked, his research resulting in a number of articles and a book written with Harry Shulman, C. CLARK & H. SHULMAN, A STUDY OF LAW ADMINISTRATION IN CONNECTICUT (Yale Univ. Press 1937). Despite his empirical efforts, Clark's methodology has been described as backward when placed in the context of developments in the social sciences. *See* Schlegel, *Yale Experience, supra* note 7, at 497. Clark became an important force in the framing of the Federal Rules of Civil Procedure and was appointed by Roosevelt to the Second Circuit, but he retained an interest in empirical research, sitting as chairman of the Committee on Statistics of the Judicial Conference of the United States.

Underhill Moore (1879–1949) taught law at Wisconsin before he began teaching in 1916 at Columbia, where he remained until his move to Yale in 1929. Initially a scholar of negotiable instruments, Moore became one of the most ardent empiricists among the Legal Realists. He announced his conversion to social science, including a strong interest in psychology, with his essay, Moore, *The Rational Basis of Legal Institutions*, 23 COLUM. L. REV. 609 (1923), and in 1929 co-authored with Theodore Hope a heavily social-scientific study of commercial banking law, Moore & Hope, *An Institutional Approach to the Law of Commercial Banking*, 38 YALE L.J. 703 (1929). Stories abound about Moore's counting cars on the streets of New Haven, but whether or not those stories are apocryphal, as suggested in Schlegel, *Underhill Moore, supra* note 7, at 201 n.17, Moore was clearly an empirical enthusiast. And entering one of the subject areas of the Legal Realists, Moore, according to Purcell, "made the most elaborate attempt to work out a behavioral system for studying and predicting judicial decisions. . . ." E. PURCELL, *supra* note 5, at 87. For an excellent discussion of Moore's methodological development in the context of Columbia and Yale, see Schlegel, *Underhill Moore, supra* note 7.

Herman Oliphant, whose career as a legal scholar followed a career as a philologist, taught at the University of Chicago and in 1922 joined the faculty of Columbia Law School, where, among other things, he taught a seminar jointly with James Bonbright of Columbia's Business School. From Columbia he moved to the Johns Hopkins Institute of Law, along with Walter Wheeler Cook and Hessel Yntema. In 1934 he became General Counsel to the Treasury Department. *See, e.g.,* Oliphant & Bordwell, *Legal Research in Law Schools*, 5 AM. LAW SCH. REV. 293 (1924).

Hessel Yntema, who came to law after a career as a political scientist, obviously had a social science background. *See* L. KALMAN, *supra* note 7, at 241 n.85. In addition to attacking the restatement movement and the traditions of legal education, Yntema addressed himself to an analysis of legal research methodology. *See, e.g.,* Yntema, *Legal Science and Reform*, 34 COLUM L. REV. 207 (1934); Yntema, *The Purview of Research in the Administration of Justice*, 16 IOWA L. REV. 337 (1931).

William O. Douglas (1898–1980), best known for his strident liberalism on the Supreme Court, was an important figure in the Legal Realist circles of both Columbia, where he taught from 1925 to 1928 in close association with Underhill Moore, and Yale, where he taught from 1928 to 1934. Douglas's scholarly and pedagogical specialty was business law, and during the New Deal he was asked to work for the newly founded Securities and Exchange Commission, serving as its chairman from 1936 to 1939. *See* Clark, Douglas, & Thomas, *The Business Failures Project—A Problem in Methodology*, 39 YALE L.J. 1013 (1930); Douglas & Thomas, *The Business Failures Project—II. An Analysis of Methods of Investigation*, 40 YALE L.J. 1034 (1931).

Before turning to a career in law, Walter Wheeler Cook (1873–1943) pursued a career in mathematics and science. *See* L. KALMAN, *supra* note 7, at 241 n.85. Once within the legal profession, he began teaching at Columbia in 1901 and at four other law schools before arriving at Yale in 1916. After a brief stint at Columbia, he returned to Yale in 1922 and stayed there until his move in 1928 to John Hopkins, where he spearheaded the new Johns Hopkins Institute of Law, which he conceived as a pure research institute rather than a teaching faculty.

86. See L. KALMAN, supra note 7, at 97, 205, 212–15; Trubek, Where the Action Is: Critical Legal Studies and Empiricism, 36 STAN. L. REV. 575 (1984); A. GOULDNER, THE COMING CRISIS OF WESTERN SOCIOLOGY (Basic Books, 1970).

87. See W. TWINING, supra note 7, at 518–523 (quoting K. LLEWELLYN, THE COMMON LAW TRADITION 509–10 (Little Brown 1960)).

88. John Chipman Gray's name has been placed alongside Holmes's in the genealogy of legal realism. See W. FRIEDMANN, LEGAL THEORY 292–93 (5th ed., Columbia Univ. Press 1967); see also E. PURCELL, supra note 5, at 76. Best known for his articulation of the hyper-technical Rule against Perpetuities, Gray taught at Harvard Law School from 1869 to 1913 and concentrated his studies on the law of real property. His realism centered on a belief that the development of legal doctrine was affected by a large range of non-legal factors. See J. C. GRAY, THE NATURE AND SOURCES OF THE LAW (Columbia Univ. Press 1909).

89. Roscoe Pound, who taught as a professor of law at Harvard Law School from 1910 to 1936 and served as its dean from 1917 to 1936, espoused an explicitly sociological jurisprudence and in doing so provided an important precedent for Legal Realism. Of great significance to the development of American Legal Realism was his essay, Pound, The Scope and Purpose of Sociological Jurisprudence (pts. 1–3), 24 HARV. L. REV. 591 (1911), 25 HARV. L. REV. 140, 489 (1911–12). Pound's fondness for the social sciences is reflected by his appointment as legal editor of the ENCYCLOPAEDIA OF THE SOCIAL SCIENCES (15 vols., Macmillan 1930–35). On Pound, see D. WIGDOR, supra note 37. See also infra ch. 8.

90. Louis D. Brandeis (1856–1941) gained a reputation first in Boston and then nationally as the "people's lawyer" due to his work in areas like insurance law, utilities law, and labor law. In 1916 he was appointed Associate Justice of the Supreme Court by Woodrow Wilson and remained on the Court until 1939. Brandeis's real impact derived from his strong dissenting opinions on an essentially conservative Court, and it was his progressive voice in labor law and regulation cases that made him important to the Legal Realists. For a sense of his social and political orientation, see selected opinions in THE SOCIAL AND ECONOMIC VIEWS OF MR. JUSTICE BRANDEIS (A. Lief ed., Vanguard Press 1930); appropriately, the volume includes an introduction by Charles Beard. Of Brandeis's own publications, see L. BRANDEIS, BUSINESS—A PROFESSION (Small, Maynard 1914); L. BRANDEIS, OTHER PEOPLE'S MONEY (Frederick A. Stokes 1914). On Brandeis, see A. T. MASON, BRANDEIS: A FREE MAN'S LIFE (Viking 1946); P. STRUM, LOUIS D. BRANDEIS: JUSTICE FOR THE PEOPLE (Harvard Univ. Press 1984); R. BURT, TWO JEWISH JUSTICES: OUTCASTS IN THE PROMISED LAND (Univ. of Calif. Press 1988); M. UROFSKY, LOUIS D. BRANDEIS AND THE PROGRESSIVE TRADITION (Little, Brown 1981); Jaffe, Was Brandeis an Activist? The Search for Intermediate Premises, 80 HARV. L. REV. 986 (1967). See also the discussion of Brandeis supra ch. 5.

91. In his jurisprudence, Benjamin N. Cardozo (1870–1938) was openly sensitive to the transformation of American social and cultural norms. See G. E. WHITE, THE AMERICAN JUDICIAL TRADITION 259–60 (expanded ed., Oxford Univ. Press 1988). Much more than his tenure on the Supreme Court, his years on the New York Court of Appeals (1914–1932) and as its chief judge (1927–1932) allowed him to make an important impact on the development of private law doctrine. See G. E. WHITE, TORT LAW IN AMERICA: AN INTEL-

LECTUAL HISTORY 114–38 (Oxford Univ. Press 1980) [hereafter G. E. WHITE, TORT LAW]. His writings especially B. CARDOZO, THE NATURE OF THE JUDICIAL PROCESS (Yale Univ. Press 1921), establish his carefully balanced but ultimately sociological view of how judges should go about their business. *See* Kaufman, *Mr. Justice Cardozo*, in MR. JUSTICE 250 (A. Dunham & P. Kurland rev. ed., Univ. of Chicago Press 1964). See the discussion of Cardozo, *infra* text accompanying notes 151–177.

92. Wesley N. Hohfeld (1879–1918) taught at Stanford Law School from 1905 to 1914 and at Yale until his death in 1918. He is most important for his effort to set out the structural relationships and differences among rights, privileges, duties, powers, immunities, disabilities, no-rights, and liabilities. As formalistic and abstract as his analysis might seem, it helped cut through some of the legal mythologies of his contemporaries. See Hohfeld's posthumous collection of essays, W. HOHFELD, FUNDAMENTAL LEGAL CONCEPTIONS AS APPLIED IN JUDICIAL REASONING (W. Cook ed., Yale Univ. Press 1919). On Hohfeld, see Singer, *The Legal Rights Debate in Analytical Jurisprudence from Bentham to Hohfeld*, 1982 WIS. L. REV. 975. See also the discussion of Hohfeld *supra* ch. 4. and ch. 5 and *infra* ch. 7.

93. Learned Hand (1872–1961) sat on the Federal District Court for the Southern District of New York from 1909 to 1924, and thereafter until his death sat on the Second Circuit—the fabled court that under his guidance as chief judge (1939–51) was often compared favorably to the Supreme Court in intellectual power and legal sophistication. Along with Cardozo, Learned Hand was placed by Llewellyn in the "grand style" tradition of jurisprudence, that of Marshall, Kent, and Mansfield, which was more open to policy and purpose than was strict formalism. *See* W. TWINING, *supra* note 7, at 210 (citing K. LLEWELLYN, *supra* note 87). See the discussion of Hand *infra* ch. 9.

94. Harlan Fiske Stone served as dean of Columbia Law School from 1910 to 1923, U. S. Attorney General from 1924 to 1925, when he was appointed to the Supreme Court, and as chief justice from 1941 to 1946. Although Stone expressed initial opposition to the importation of social thought and engineering into law, by the 1920s he had become convinced not only of the evolutionary character of the judicial process but also of the importance of social values to it. In his essay "Some Aspects of the Problem of Law Simplification," Stone ventured, "Sociological jurisprudence, rightly understood, ought to give a new inspiration and a new trend to legal development. . . ." Stone, *Some Aspects of the Problem of Law Simplification*, 23. COLUM. L. REV. 319, 328 (1923).

95. This group of economists, who founded the American Economics Association (AEA) in 1885, attempted to revolutionize their discipline by replacing the reigning orthodoxy of their profession with a reform-oriented economic science. Richard Ely and the other economists at the first meeting of the AEA should be seen within the context of turn-of-the-century reform and progressivism. E. GOLDMAN, RENDEZVOUS WITH DESTINY 112–117 (Knopf 1952). On the development of professional social science in America, see D. ROSS, ORIGINS OF AMERICAN SOCIAL SCIENCE (Cambridge Univ. Press 1990); M. FURNER, ADVOCACY AND OBJECTIVITY: A CRISIS IN THE PROFESSIONALIZATION OF AMERICAN SOCIAL SCIENCE, 1865–1905 (Univ. Press of Kentucky 1975); T. HASKELL, THE EMERGENCE OF PROFESSIONAL SOCIAL SCIENCE (Univ. of Illinois Press 1977).

96. Richard T. Ely (1854–1943) and John R. Commons (1862–1945) were reform-oriented economists whose work focused largely on questions of law and public policy. Merle Curti mentions both Commons and Ely in his discussion of the "democratic conception of the scholar's role." M. CURTI, THE GROWTH OF AMERICAN THOUGHT 575–76 (3d ed., Harper & Row 1964). Richard T. Ely, who taught economics at Johns Hopkins, Wisconsin, and Northwestern, was instrumental in the founding of the AEA, which, as

mentioned above, began as a Young Turk attack on orthodox economics. Ely's criticism of classical economics and its political implications is embodied in his monograph, R. Ely, The Past and the Present of Political Economy (Johns Hopkins Univ. 1884). In the essay, Ely not only attacked the prevailing economic model for its conservatism but proposed a new model for economic thought. Ely's political perspective may be seen in his close ties to the late-nineteenth-century Christian Socialist movement and his concern for American labor and the American consumer. See J. Everett, Religion in Economics 75–98 (King's Crown Press 1946); R. Hofstader, Social Darwinism in American Thought 146–47; (rev. ed., Beacon Press 1955); B. Rader, The Academic Mind and Reform: The Influence of Richard T. Ely in American Life (Univ. of Kentucky Press 1966).

Like Ely, John R. Commons (1862–1945), who taught political economy at Wesleyan, Oberlin, Syracuse, Indiana, and Wisconsin, drew heavily from disciplines outside economics and addressed a number of practical social questions. Very much the reformer, Commons served as president of the National Consumer's League from 1923 to 1935. Among his most influential books are J. Commons, Legal Foundations of Capitalism (Macmillan 1924) and J. Commons, Institutional Economics (Macmillan 1934). The Legal Realist interest in Commons is evident, for example, in Llewellyn, The Effect of Legal Institutions upon Economics 15 Am. Econ. Rev. 665 (1925); there Llewellyn singled out Commons's Legal Foundations of Capitalism as a model of symbiosis between law and economics.

97. Gerard Henderson wrote The Position of Foreign Corporations in American Constitutional Law (Harvard Univ. Press 1918) while working as a lawyer for the federal government; on Robert Lee Hale see infra ch. 7 note 12. James Bonbright, professor at the Columbia Business School, co-taught a seminar with Oliphant, a course that was visited by both Moore and Hale. See Schlegel, Underhill Moore, supra note 7, at 208–09.

98. A. Berle & G. Means, The Modern Corporation and Private Property (Macmillan 1932). See J. Schwarz, Liberal: Adolf A. Berle and the Vision of an American Era 50–68 (Free Press 1987).

99. The editor-in-chief was Edwin R. A. Seligman, professor of political economy at Columbia. He was assisted by Alvin Johnson and Max Lerner of the New School for Social Research. Roscoe Pound, the legal editor of the Encyclopaedia of the Social Sciences, chose a number of Legal Realists to contribute articles, including Harold Laski, Karl Llewellyn, Walter Wheeler Cook, Harold Lasswell, Max Radin, and Walton H. Hamilton.

100. Llewellyn admired Dewey but saw that in the study of legal processes "his potential had not been exploited. Llewellyn's private ambition, as he once confessed in a lecture, was to perform the role of a Dewey in jurisprudence, trying to do for law what the great man had done for other subjects." W. Twining, supra note 7, at 422 n.130.

101. See D. Hollinger, The Problem of Pragmatism in American History, in In the American Province 23 (Indiana Univ. Press 1985); J. Kloppenberg, supra note 4; B. Kuklick, The Rise of American Philosophy: Cambridge, Massachusetts, 1860–1930 (Yale Univ. Press 1977); B. Kuklick, Churchmen and Philosophers: From Jonathan Edwards to John Dewey 241–53 (Yale Univ. Press 1985); C. West, The American Evasion of Philosophy (Univ. of Wisconsin Press 1989); M. White, Social Thought in America: The Revolt Against Formalism (Viking 1949); R. Rorty, Consequences of Pragmatism (Univ. of Minnesota Press 1982).

102. W. Twining, supra note 7, 521–22.

103. Bohlen appeared on the longer, subsequent list that Llewelyn sent to Pound. See Hull, supra note 7, at 967–69.

104. Leon Green, who taught at Texas and Yale before becoming the dean of North-western Law School in 1929, clearly deserved his place on Llewellyn's list. As G. Edward White writes, Green "produced the most original and revisionist torts scholarship of the Realist years," although White goes on to say with Charles Gregory that many of the Legal Realists did not appreciate him as much as they should have. G. E. WHITE, TORT LAW, *supra* note 91, at 76. If Green was not sympathetic to doctrinal distinctions within the law of torts, he did important revisionist work within specific doctrinal areas, such as his essay, Green, *The Duty Problem in Negligence Cases* (pts. 1 & 2), 28 COLUM. L. REV. 1014 (1928), 29 COLUM. L. REV. 255 (1929), and addressed broader issues such as in his discussion of the role of judges and juries in torts cases in L. GREEN, JUDGE AND JURY (Vernon 1930). In addition, Green produced what might be described as the first Realist casebook in torts, L. GREEN, THE JUDICIAL PROCESS IN TORT CASES (West 1931), and actively supported the New Deal. *See* Green, *Case for the Sit-Down Strike*, 90 NEW REPUBLIC 199 (Mar. 24, 1937); Green, *Unpacking the Court*, 90 NEW REPUBLIC 67 (Feb. 24, 1937). The *Texas Law Review* devoted the entire February 1978 issue to Green. For a careful analysis of Green's relationship to Legal Realism, see Robertson, *The Legal Philosophy of Leon Green*, 56 TEX. L. REV. 393 (1978). For a discussion of Green's major doctrinal contribution, his critique of objective causation, see *supra* ch. 2.

Francis Bohlen (1868–1947) taught at Harvard and the University of Pennsylvania, and served as reporter of the Restatement of Torts in 1923. Although Bohlen remained ambivalent about some aspects of Legal Realism, White correctly gives him an important place as a transitional figure in his narrative of the "impact of realism on tort law." *See* G. E. WHITE, TORT LAW, *supra* note 91, at 78–87. Still wedded to the doctrinal division of the law of torts, Bohlen's work in torts represented an important break from formalism and an understanding of the significance of social developments. His three-part essay on Rylands v. Fletcher, L.R. 3 H.L. 330 (1868), is an effort to offer an economic interpretation of the law of torts. Bohlen, *The Rule in Rylands v.Fletcher* (pts. 1–3), 59 U. PA. L. REV. 298, 373, 423 (1911). *See also* Pound, *The Economic Interpretation and the Law of Torts*, 53 HARV. L. REV. 365 (1940). In a 1935 essay, Bohlen addressed himself explicitly to the growing Legal Realist movement and asserts that "there is great gain in the fact that in many of our principal law schools the reality of what the courts are doing is being brought to the attention of students." He went on to venture that perhaps these students as future judges will "tell the real reasons for their decisions and not conceal them beneath legalistic and often meaningless phrases." Bohlen, *Old Phrases and New Facts*, 83 U. PA. L. REV. 305, 313 (1935). *See also* F. BOHLEN, CASES ON THE LAW OF TORTS (2 vols., Bobbs-Merrill 1915). On Bohlen, see Lewis, *Francis Hermann Bohlen*, 91 U. PA. L. REV. 377 (1943).

Jeremiah Smith, who in 1893 revised Ames's original torts casebook of 1874, was, for the most part, well within the Harvard formalist tradition established by Ames. In his torts scholarship, Smith emphasized the fault aspect of torts and agreed with the contemporary classification system of the law of tort. Smith's connection to the Legal Realists comes rather from his article on workers' compensation. *See* Smith, *Sequel to Workmen's Compensation Acts* (pts. 1 & 2), 27 HARV. L. REV. 235, 344 (1914). *See also* Smith, *Legal Cause in Actions of Tort* (pts. 1–3), 25 HARV. L. REV. 103, 223, 303 (1911–12); Smith, *Tort and Absolute Liability—Suggested Changes in Classification* (pts. 1–3), 30 HARV. L. REV. 241, 319, 409 (1917).

Although Fleming James came to Yale too late to be enrolled on Llewellyn's list, he became an important part of Legal Realism. In 1942 he collaborated with Harry Shulman on a casebook in torts that was unambiguously Legal Realist in conception. *See* H. SHUL-

MAN AND F. JAMES, CASES AND MATERIALS ON THE LAW OF TORTS (Foundation Press 1942). As White notes, their foreword declared that law was involved "not so much with rule or doctrine as with problems in human relations." *Id.* at vii-viii, *quoted in* G. E. WHITE, TORT LAW, *supra* note 91, at 89.

Nathan Isaacs (1886–1941) taught at Harvard, Columbia, and Yale. *See* Isaacs, *Fault and Liability*, 31 HARV. L. REV. 954 (1918); Isaacs, *"The Law" and the Law of Change* (pts. 1 & 2), 65 U. PA. L. REV. 665, 748 (1917); Isaacs, *The Standardizing of Contracts*, 27 YALE L.J. 34 (1917).

In the British context, Harold Laski (1893–1950) was one of the most important intellectual forces in the inter-war period, serving on the Executive Committee of the Fabian Society from 1921 to 1936 and then on the Executive Committee of the Labour Party from 1936 to 1949, as party chairman from 1945–46. In his position at the London School of Economics, Laski provided socialist critiques of liberalism. But Laski is important as well in the story of American Legal Realism due to his work while teaching at Harvard from 1916 to 1920 and his close association with Holmes and Brandeis. Among Laski's American law review essays, see Laski, *The Basis of Vicarious Liability*, 26 YALE L.J. 105 (1916); Laski, *Judicial Review of Social Policy in England*, 39 HARV. L. REV. 832 (1926); Laski, *The Theory of Popular Sovereignty*, 17 MICH. L. REV. 201 (1919).

105. *See* Cook, *Agency by Estoppel*, 5 COLUM. L. REV. 36 (1905); Seavey, *Negligence—Subjective or Objective?*, 41 HARV. L. REV. 1 (1927); Seavey, *The Rationale of Agency*, 29 YALE L.J. 859 (1920). Seavey ended his article on negligence with these thoughts:

> Liability for conduct follows, usually belatedly, popular conceptions of justice. In primitive law it was "just" that the burden of loss should be shifted only where the cause of the harm was a knave or a fool. With a mechanistic philosophy as to human motives and a socialistic viewpoint as to the function of the state, we may return to the original result of liability for all injurious conduct, or conceivably have an absence of liability for any conduct, with the burden of loss shifted either to groups of persons or to the entire community. The lawyer cannot determine that our rules of liability for negligence are either just or unjust, unless he has first discovered what the community desires (which determines justice for the time and place), and whether the rules are adapted to satisfying those desires (which I assume to be the end of law).

Seavey, *Negligence, supra*, at 28.

106. *See* Arnold, *The Restatement of the Law of Trusts*, 31 COLUM. L. REV. 800 (1931); Clark, *The Restatement of the Law of Contracts*, 42 YALE L. J. 643 (1933); Corbin, *The Restatement of the Common Law by the American Law Institute*, 15 IOWA L. REV. 19 (1929); Green, *The Torts Restatement*, 29 ILL. L. REV. 582 (1935); Lorenzen & Heilman, *The Restatement of the Conflict of Laws*, 83 U. PA. L. REV. 555 (1935); Vance, *The Restatement of the Law of Property*, 86 U. PA. L. REV. 173 (1937). *See generally* L. FRIEDMAN, A HISTORY OF AMERICAN LAW 582 (2d ed., Simon & Schuster 1985); Gilmore, *supra* note 7, at 1044–45. *Cf.* Crystal, *Codification and the Rise of the Restatement Movement*, 42 WASH. L. REV. 239 (1979); Hull, *Restatement and Reform: A New Perspective on the Origins of the American Law Institute*, 8 LAW & HIST. REV. 55 (1990).

107. *See* RESTATEMENT OF THE LAW OF AGENCY, (2 vols., American Law Institute 1933); RESTATEMENT OF THE LAW OF CONFLICT OF LAWS (American Law Institute 1934); RESTATEMENT OF THE LAW OF CONTRACTS (2 vols., American Law Institute 1932); RESTATEMENT OF THE LAW OF TORTS (4 vols., American Law Institute 1934–39).

108. *See* Dawson, *Economic Duress—An Essay in Perspective*, 45 MICH. L. REV. 253 (1947); Fuller & Perdue, *The Reliance Interest in Contract Damages* (pts. 1 & 2), 46 YALE L. J. 52, 373 (1936–37). *See also* G. GILMORE, THE DEATH OF CONTRACT (Ohio State Univ. Press 1974).

109. *See* Cavers, *A Critique of the Choice-of-Law Problem*, 47 HARV. L. REV. 173 (1933). Though the Restatement was published in 1934, Cavers knew of the ALI's work. *See id.* at 208. *Compare* Cook, *The Logical and Legal Bases of the Conflict of Laws*, 33 YALE L. J. 457 (1924).

110. Fuller & Perdue, *supra* note 108.

111. Norris-LaGuardia Act, ch. 90, 47 Stat. 70 (1932).

112. *See* F. FRANKFURTER & N. GREENE, THE LABOR INJUNCTION 205–220 (Macmillan 1930).

113. *See* W. HOHFELD, *supra* note 92; Cook, *The Privileges of Labor Unions in the Struggle for Life*, 27 YALE L. J. 779 (1918). See the discussion *supra* ch. 5. In Truax v. Corrigan, 257 U.S. 312 (1921), the Supreme Court struck down an Arizona anti-injunction law on equal protection, not due process, grounds, as had some previous state cases. See, *e.g.*, Bogni v. Perotti, 224 Mass. 152 (1916). Justice Brandeis's dissent in *Truax* is an important articulation of the rights-remedy position. In retreating to equal protection, even Chief Justice Taft's majority opinion concedes the power of the legislature to eliminate the injunctive remedy, if only it is extended equally to non-labor injunctions as well. The logical connection between rights and remedies was thus severed.

114. *See* Klare, *Contracts Jurisprudence and the First-Year Casebook* (book review), 54 N.Y.U. L. REV. 876, 882 (1979).

115. Llewellyn, *supra* note 10, at 1227 n.18.

116. W. TWINING, *supra* note 7, at 93 (quoting K. Llewellyn, Non-Conformist Puzzles over Education (1924) (unpublished manuscript in Llewellyn Papers)).

117. *Id.* at 88 (quoting K. Llewellyn, *supra* note 116).

118. *Id.*

119. *Id.* at 94 (quoting HISTORY OF THE [YALE] CLASS OF NINETEEN-FIFTEEN 246–47 (n.p. n.d.)).

120. *Id.* at 95.

121. *Id.*

122. *Id.* at 96.

123. *Id.*

124. *Id.*

125. *Id.* at 97. Twining mistakenly treats Hohfeld as a representative of Classical Legal Thought. *See id.* at 34–37.

126. *Id.*

127. *Id.* at 125.

128. *Id.* at 100.

129. *Id.*

130. *Id.* at 114.

131. *Id.*

132. *See id* at 102, 109–110, 112.

133. *Id.* at 90, 116 (quoting K. Llewellyn, Law in Our Society (unpublished course materials in Llewellyn Papers)).

134. *Id.* at 117 (emphasis retained).

135. *Id.* at 116 (quoting transcripts of Llewellyn's Jurisprudence Lectures of 1956, § I, at 5–7).

136. On Dewey, see works cited *supra* note 101. On Morris Cohen, see D. HOLLIN-
GER, MORRIS R. COHEN AND THE SCIENTIFIC IDEAL (MIT Press 1975). For Felix Cohen,
see *The Ethical Basis of Legal Criticism*, 41 YALE L. J. 201 (1931). *See generally* R. J.
BERNSTEIN, BEYOND OBJECTIVISM AND RELATIVISM (Univ. of Pennsylvania Press 1983).

137. *Id.* at 120.

138. *Id.* at 521 (quoting a letter from Llewellyn to G. B. J. Hughes (August 10, 1954)
(Llewellyn Papers)).

139. *Id.* at 518 (quoting K. LLEWELLYN, *supra* note 87).

140. *Id.* at 93 (quoting K. Llewellyn, *supra* note 116).

141. *Id.* at 423 n.133 (quoting K. Llewellyn, Position re Religion (1943) (Llewellyn
Papers)) (emphasis retained).

142. *Id.* at 100.

143. Llewellyn, *supra* note 10, at 1226 n.18.

144. Along with Frederick Jackson Turner and Charles Beard, the Progressive historiographical current as a whole should be mentioned in this context, for in their social critical
project, the Progressive historians provide an important parallel to the sociological and
critical side of American jurisprudence. Horwitz, *Progressive Legal Historiography*, 63 OR.
L. REV. 679 (1984). Among their important works, see C. BEARD, THE ECONOMIC BASIS
OF POLITICS (Knopf 1922); C. BEARD, AN ECONOMIC INTERPRETATION OF THE CONSTITU-
TION OF THE UNITED STATES (Macmillan 1913); C. BEARD & M. BEARD, THE RISE OF
AMERICAN CIVILIZATION (2 vols., Macmillan 1927); V. PARRINGTON, MAIN CURRENTS IN
AMERICAN THOUGHT (3 vols., Harcourt, Brace 1927–30); J. A. SMITH, THE SPIRIT OF
AMERICAN GOVERNMENT (Macmillan 1907); F. J. TURNER, THE FRONTIER IN AMERICAN
HISTORY (H. Holt 1920); F. J. TURNER, RISE OF THE NEW WEST (Harper 1906); F. J.
TURNER, THE SIGNIFICANCE OF SECTIONS IN AMERICAN HISTORY (H. Holt 1932); F. J.
TURNER, THE UNITED STATES, 1830–1850 (H. Holt 1935).

The central book on the Progressive historiographical tradition remains R. HOFSTAD-
TER, THE PROGRESSIVE HISTORIANS (Knopf 1968); *see also* R. A. BILLINGTON, FREDERICK
JACKSON TURNER (Oxford Univ. Press, 1973); E. GOLDMAN, *supra* note 95, at 149–55; H.
MAY, THE END OF AMERICAN INNOCENCE (Knopf 1959); P. NOVICK, THAT NOBLE DREAM:
THE "OBJECTIVITY QUESTION" AND THE AMERICAN HISTORICAL PROFESSION 86–108 (Cam-
bridge Univ. Press 1988); C. STROUT, THE PRAGMATIC REVOLT IN AMERICAN HISTORY:
CARL BECKER AND CHARLES BEARD (Yale Univ. Press 1958); Goldman, *The Origins of
Beard's Economic Interpetation of the Constitution*, 13 J. HIST. IDEAS 234 (1952); Hofstad-
ter, *Beard and the Constitution: The History of an Idea*, 2 AM. Q. 195 (1950).

145. *See, e.g.*, Pound, *The End of Law as Developed in Juristic Thought* (pts. 1 & 2),
27 HARV. L. REV. 605 (1914), 30 HARV. L. REV. 201 (1917); Pound, *The End of Law as
Developed in Legal Rules and Doctrines*, 27 HARV. L. REV. 195 (1914); Pound, *Justice
According to Law* (pts. 1–3), 13 COLUM. L. REV. 696 (1913), 14 COLUM. L. REV. 1, 103
(1914).

146. Pound, *Mechanical Jurisprudence*, 8 COLUM. L. REV. 605 (1908).

147. The term "revolt against formalism" comes from M. WHITE, *supra* note 101.
White places Holmes's legal revolt against formalism alongside discussions of John Dewey,
Thorstein Veblen, James Harvey Robinson, and Charles Beard. And Edward Purcell discusses the development of a "scientific naturalism" in E. PURCELL, *supra* note 5, at 3–12;
see also P. NOVICK, *supra* note 144, at 133–67.

148. See *infra* ch. 7, text accompanying notes 85–104.

149. *See* Grey, *Langdell's Orthodoxy*, 45 U. PITT. L. REV. 1. (1983).

150. *See* W. Hohfeld, *supra* note 92.

151. For a discussion of both Cardozo's and Traynor's significance in the development of private-law doctrine, especially the expansion of the realm of strict liability, see G. E. White, Tort Law, *supra* note 91, at 114–38, 180–210.

152. B. Cardozo, *supra* note 91, at 65–66. *The Nature of the Judicial Process* sold 24,795 copies in hard cover and 147,000 paperback copies through 1989. *See* Letter from John Covell, Yale University Press, to Morton J. Horwitz (January 5, 1990) (in the possession of the recipient).

153. B. Cardozo, *supra* note 91, at 115. *See also* Cohen, *The Process of Judicial Legislation*, 48 Am. L. Rev. 161 (1914), *reprinted in* M. Cohen, Law and the Social Order 112 (Harcourt, Brace 1933).

154. B. Cardozo, *supra* note 91, at 119.

155. *Id.* at 161.

156. *Id.* at 66.

157. *Id.* at 67.

158. *Id.* at 73, 77–78, 98–141.

159. *Id.* at 66; *see also id.* at 98–141.

160. *Id.* at 103.

161. *Id.* at 102.

162. *Id.*

163. *Id.* at 133–34.

164. H. May, *supra* note 5, at 18.

165. Cohen, *The Ethical Basis of Legal Criticism*, 41 Yale L. J. 201 (1931).

166. B. Cardozo, *supra* note 91, at 28.

167. *Id.* at 34.

168. *Id.* at at 114–115, 137.

169. *Id.* at 173.

170. *Id.*

171. *Id.* at 115.

172. *Id.* at 116.

173. *Id.* at 10.

174. *Id.*

175. *Id.* at 14.

176. *Id.* at 162.

177. *Id.* at 136.

Chapter 7

1. S. Levinson, *The Constitution as American Civil Religion*, in Constitutional Faith 9 (Princeton Univ. Press 1988).

2. On the desire to produce an autonomous legal realm separate from politics, see M. Horwitz, The Transformation of American Law, 1780–1860, at 253–66 (Harvard Univ. Press 1977).

3. *See* Hovenkamp, *Evolutionary Models in Jurisprudence*, 64 Tex. L. Rev. 645 (1985) [hereafter Hovenkamp, *Evolutionary Models*]; Hovenkamp, *The Political Economy of Substantive Due Process*, 40 Stan. L. Rev. 379 (1988); Kennedy, *Toward an Historical Understanding of Legal Consciousness: The Case of Classical Legal Thought in America, 1850–*

1940, 3 RES. L. & SOC. 2 (1980); Siegel, *Understanding the Lochner Era: Lessons from the Controversy Over Railroad and Utility Rate Regulation*, 70 VA. L. REV. 187 (1984); Singer, *Legal Realism Now*, 76 CALIF. L. REV. 465, 475–82 (1988); Singer, *The Legal Rights Debate in Analytical Jurisprudence from Bentham to Hohfeld*, 1982 WIS. L. REV. 975 [hereafter singer, *Legal Rights Debate*]; Sunstein, *Lochner's Legacy*, 87 COLUM. L. REV. 873 (1987).

4. *See* Horwitz, *The Legacy of 1776 in Legal and Economic Thought*, 19 J. L. & ECON. 621. (1976).

5. 236 U.S. 1, 17 (1915).

6. *See supra* ch. 2.

7. *See* C. PEIRCE, *The Metaphysical Club and the Birth of Pragmatism*, in 3 WRITINGS OF CHARLES S. PEIRCE xxix (C. Kloesel & M. Fisch eds., Indiana Univ. Press 1986). Any effort to assess the basic thrust of pragmatist thought should begin with William James's classic statement, W. JAMES, PRAGMATISM (Longmans, Green 1907). The literature on pragmatism is immense, but among the works most useful for understanding those aspects of pragmatism finding resonances in Legal Realism, see R. HOFSTADTER, SOCIAL DARWINISM IN AMERICAN THOUGHT (rev. ed., Beacon Press 1955); J. KLOPPENBERG, UNCERTAIN VICTORY: SOCIAL DEMOCRACY AND PROGRESSIVISM IN EUROPEAN AND AMERICAN THOUGHT, 1870–1920 (Oxford Univ. Press 1986); B. KUKLICK, THE RISE OF AMERICAN PHILOSOPHY: CAMBRIDGE, MASSACHUSETTS, 1860–1930 (Yale Univ. Press 1977); H. SCHNEIDER, A HISTORY OF AMERICAN PHILOSOPHY (2d ed., Columbia Univ. Press 1963); M. WHITE, SOCIAL THOUGHT IN AMERICA: THE REVOLT AGAINST FORMALISM (Viking 1949); R. RORTY, PHILOSOPHY AND THE MIRROR OF NATURE (Princeton Univ. Press 1979).

8. *See* Pound, *Law in Books and Law in Action*, 44 AM. L. REV. 12 (1910).

9. *See* D. ROSS, ORIGINS OF AMERICAN SOCIAL SCIENCE 174, 419–20 (Cambridge Univ. Press 1990); A. SCHLESINGER JR., THE AGE OF ROOSEVELT: THE CRISIS OF THE OLD ORDER, 1919–1933 (Houghton Mifflin 1957).

10. The thought and political orientation of the Progressive economic tradition in America, as well as its successes and influence, have been well documented. *See* J. DORFMAN, THE ECONOMIC MIND IN AMERICAN CIVILIZATION (5 vols., Viking Press 1946–1959); J. DORFMAN, INSTITUTIONAL ECONOMICS: VEBLEN, COMMONS AND MITCHELL RECONSIDERED (Univ. of Calif. Press 1963); J. DORFMAN, THORSTEIN VEBLEN AND HIS AMERICA (Viking Press 1934); D. RIESMAN, THORSTEIN VEBLEN: A CRITICAL INTERPRETATION (Scribner's 1953); B. SELIGMAN, MAIN CURRENTS IN MODERN ECONOMICS (2 vols., Free Press, 1962). For a more recent treatment contrasting the political orientation of Progressive economists in the United States to those in Britain, see Ross, *Socialism and American Liberalism: Academic Social Thought in the 1880's*, 11 PERSP AM. HIST. 7 (1977–78).

11. *See* Kennedy, *The Role of Law in Economic Thought: Essays on the Fetishism of Commodities*, 34 AM. U. L. REV. 939 (1985).

12. Robert Hale (1884–1969), who brought much of the Progressive economic framework into the field of law, began his career as a professional economist working on rate regulation. He was teaching economics at Columbia when Harlan Fiske Stone, then dean of the Columbia Law School, asked him to teach in the law school in 1922. As Warren Samuels has told us, Hale not only contributed a great deal to the developing law of public utilities, but he also produced a sophisticated economic analysis of legal relationships. *See* Samuels, *The Economy as a System of Power and Its Legal Bases: The Legal Economics of Robert Lee Hale*, 27 U. MIAMI L. REV. 261 (1973). For a comparison of Hale's theory of compulsion with themes in Legal Realism and critical legal studies, see N. Duxbury, Robert Hale and the Economy of Legal Force (1989) (unpublished manuscript).

13. Hale, *Coercion and Distribution in a Supposedly Non-Coercive State*, 38 POL. SCI. Q. 470 (1923).

14. *Id.* at 474 (emphasis retained).

15. *Id.* Note the similarity to Chief Justice White's opinion in Standard Oil Co. v. United States, 221 U.S. 1 (1911), in which he established the balancing test in antitrust doctrine under the rule of reason. Undermining the populist-literalist reading of "all contracts in restraint of trade" in the Sherman Act, he showed instead that since *all* contracts are in restraint of trade, we must distinguish between reasonable and unreasonable restraints. White's underlying point was that all contracts are inherently coercive.

16. Hale, *supra* note 13, at 474–75.

17. *See* Dawson, *Economic Duress—An Essay in Perspective*, 45 MICH. L. REV. 253 (1947).

18. *Id.* at 266.

19. *Id.*

20. Hale, *supra* note 13, at 474.

21. Lochner v. New York, 198 U.S. 45, 75 (1905) (Holmes, J., dissenting) ("This case is decided upon an economic theory which a large part of the country does not entertain. . . . The Fourteenth Amendment does not enact Mr. Herbert Spencer's Social Statics.").

22. The question of whether news could be considered property arose in International News Service v. Associated Press, 248 U.S. 215 (1918), which specifically answered the question of whether the news published by the Associated Press on the East coast could be protected from its use by the International News Service on the West coast. See discussion *supra* ch. 5 and *infra* text accompanying notes 54–61. The debate over whether certain economic combinations were to be considered basically unfair or, alternatively, legitimate forms of competition emerged in an important trilogy of British cases: Mogul Steamship Co. v. McGregor, Gow & Co., 23 Q.B.D. 598 (1889), *aff'd.*, [1892] A.C. 25; Allen v. Flood, [1898] A. C. 1; and Quinn v. Leathem, [1901] A.C. 495. Charles Gregory has analyzed these three cases in LABOR AND LAW (3d ed., W. W. Norton 1979). Holmes set up a framework to discuss this issue, anticipating the three British cases, in Holmes, *Privilege, Malice, and Intent*, 8 HARV. L. REV. 1 (1894). See discussion of Holmes and competition *supra* ch. 4. Basically, Holmes argued that the harm caused by economic combination must find its justification in policy. In his passionate dissent in Vegelahn v. Guntner, 167 Mass. 92, 44 N.E. 1077 (1896), Holmes expressed little doubt as to the policy justification for competition:

> One of the eternal conflicts out of which life is made up is that between the effort of every man to get the most he can for his services, and that of society, disguised under the name of capital, to get his services for the least possible return. Combination on the one side is patent and powerful. Combination on the other side is the necessary and desirable counterpart, if the battle is to be carried on in a fair and equal way.

Id. at 108, 44 N. E. at 1081 (Holmes, J., dissenting).

23. *See* W. HOHFELD, FUNDAMENTAL LEGAL CONCEPTIONS AS APPLIED IN JUDICIAL REASONING (W. Cook ed., Yale Univ Press 1919); Cook, *The Privileges of Labor Unions in the Struggle for Life*, 27 YALE L. J. 779 (1918); Grey, *The Disintegration of Property*, in PROPERTY: NOMOS XXII 69 (J. Pennock & J. Chapman eds., New York Univ. Press 1980).

24. "Property, a creation of law, does not arise from value, although exchangeable—a matter of fact." International News Service v. Associated Press, 248 U.S. 215 246 (1918) (Holmes, J., concurring).

25. In his opinion for the court in Pennsylvania Coal v. Mahon, 260 U.S. 393, 415 (1922), Holmes insisted that although "property may be regulated to a certain extent, if regulation goes too far it will be recognized as a taking." In his dissent, Brandeis recognized the Pennsylvania law at issue as an exercise of the police power. In that case, restrictions on property were justified: "The restriction upon the use of this property can not, of course, be lawfully imposed, unless its purpose is to protect the public." *Id.* at 417 (Brandeis, J., dissenting).

26. See the discussion of rate making *supra* ch. 5.

27. *See* Siegel, *supra* note 3, at 243–47.

28. *See* J. LOCKE, *An Essay Concerning the True Original, Extent, and End of Civil Government,* in TWO TREATISES OF GOVERNMENT 283 (P. Laslett ed., Cambridge Univ. Press 1960) (1st ed. 1690); C. B. MACPHERSON, THE POLITICAL THEORY OF POSSESSIVE INDIVIDUALISM (Oxford Univ. Press 1962); R. NOZICK, ANARCHY, STATE, AND UTOPIA (Basic Books 1974); W. SCOTT, IN PURSUIT OF HAPPINESS: AMERICAN CONCEPTIONS OF PROPERTY FROM THE SEVENTEENTH TO THE TWENTIETH CENTURY (Indiana Univ. Press 1977); I. SHAPIRO, THE EVOLUTION OF RIGHTS IN LIBERAL THEORY 80–148 (Cambridge Univ. Press 1986); Katz, *Thomas Jefferson and the Right to Property in Revolutionary America,* 19 J. L. & ECON. 467 (1976).

29. *See supra* ch. 3.

30. Hale himself later challenged the act-omission distinction in *Prima Facie Torts, Combination and Non-Feasance,* 46 COLUM. L. REV. 196 (1946). *See also* Weinrib, *The Case for a Duty to Rescue,* 90 YALE L. J. 247 (1980).

31. *See* Holmes, *supra* note 22 at 7.

32. *See* Katz, *Studies in Boundary Theory: Three Essays in Adjudication and Politics,* 28 BUFFALO L. REV. 383 (1979). Duncan Kennedy has coined the term "power absolute within its sphere." Kennedy, *supra* note 3, at 8–9.

33. See discussion *supra* ch. 1.

34. *See* W. B. MICHAELS, THE GOLD STANDARD AND THE LOGIC OF NATURALISM: AMERICAN LITERATURE AT THE TURN OF THE CENTURY (Univ. of Calif. Press 1987).

35. *See* G. HIMMELFARB, VICTORIAN MINDS (Knopf 1968); Ross, *Historical Consciousnesss in Nineteenth-Century America,* 89 AM. HIST. REV. 909 (1984).

36. The attacks on essentialism and formalism in law never really adopted the historicist mode that was so powerful an influence in turning the social sciences toward relational thinking. *See* Ross, *supra* note 35. The closest approximation in law was the anthropological mode of Sir Henry Maine, which Holmes finally rejected in "The Path of the Law." *See supra* ch. 4.

37. *See* P. NOVICK, THAT NOBLE DREAM: THE "OBJECTIVITY QUESTION" AND THE AMERICAN HISTORICAL PROFESSION 157, 282 (Cambridge Univ./ Press 1988), on "cognitive relativism" and "value relativism."

38. Lochner v. New York, 198 U.S. 45, 76 (1905) (Holmes, J., dissenting).

39. *See* Cohen, *The Ethical Basis of Legal Criticism,* 41 YALE L. J. 201 (1931); Dewey, *Logical Method and Law,* 10 CORNELL L. Q. 17 (1924).

40. Cohen, *Transcendental Nonsense and the Functional Approach,* 35 COLUM, L. REV. 809 (1935); Cohen's reference is to VON JEHRING, IM JURISTISCHEN BERGRIFFSHIMMEL, IN SCHERZ UND ERNST IN DER JURISPRUDENZ 245 (11th ed. 1912).

41. On scientific jurisprudence and the Benthamite and Austinian legal traditions, see E. HALEVY, THE GROWTH OF PHILOSOPHIC RADICALISM (MacMillan 1928). *See also* H. L. A. HART, ESSAYS ON BENTHAM (Oxford Univ. Press 1982); W. TWINING, THEORIES OF

EVIDENCE: BENTHAM AND WIGMORE (Stanford Univ. Press 1985); Gordon, *Holmes' Common Law as Legal and Social Science*, 10 HOFSTRA L. REV. 719 (1982); Pound, *The Progress of the Law: Analytical Jurisprudence, 1914–1927*, 41 HARV. L. REV. 174 (1927); Singer, *Legal Rights Debate*, *supra* note 3.

42. See discussion of Hohfeld, *supra* ch. 5.

43. *See* Hohfeld, *Some Fundamental Legal Conceptions as Applied in Judicial Reasoning*, 23 YALE L. J. 16 (1913); *Fundamental Legal Conceptions as Applied in Judicial Reasoning*, 26 YALE L. J. 710 (1917).

44. *See* Cook, *Introduction* to W. HOHFELD, *supra* note 23; Corbin, *Legal Analysis and Terminology*, 29 YALE L. J. 163 (1919).

45. Kennedy & Michelman, *Are Property and Contract Efficient?*, 8 HOFSTRA L. REV. 711, 751 (1980).

46. Gabel, *Reification in Legal Reasoning*, 3 RES. L. & SOC. 25 (1980); Peller, *The Metaphysics of American Law*, 73 CALIF. L. REV. 1151, 1157–58 (1985).

47. Cohen, *Justice Holmes and the Nature of Law*, 31 COLUM. L. REV. 352, 363 (1931) (emphasis retained).

48. Jerome Frank is responsible for the distinction between "rule-skepticism" and "fact-skepticism." *See* J. FRANK, LAW AND THE MODERN MIND x-xi (Brentano's 1930).

49. *See* Note, *The First Amendment Overbreadth Doctrine*, 83 HARV. L. REV. 844 (1970) (written by Lewis D. Sargentich).

50. Fuller, *American Legal Realism*, 82 U. PA. L. REV. 429, 443 (1934).

51. *See* Horwitz, book review, 27 BUFFALO L. REV. 47 (1978) (reviewing G. GILMORE, THE AGES OF AMERICAN LAW (Yale Univ. Press 1977).

52. *See* Cohen, *supra* note 39 at 215–16; Cohen, *supra* note 40; Oliphant, *A Return to Stare Decisis* (pts. 1 & 2), 14 A.B.A. J. 71, 159 (1928); Radin, *Case Law and Stare Decisis: Concerning Präjudizienrecht in Amerika*, 33 COLUM. L. REV. 199 (1933).

53. R. Rantoul, *Oration at Scituate*, in MEMOIRS, SPEECHES AND WRITINGS OF ROBERT RANTOUL, JR. 278 (L. Hamilton ed., J. P. Jewett 1854).

54. *See* Story, *Law, Legislation, and Codes*, in J. MCCLELLAN, JOSEPH STORY AND THE AMERICAN CONSTITUTION 350 (Univ. of Oklahoma Press 1971).

55. *See supra* ch. 5.

56. International News Service v. Associated Press, 248 U.S. 215 (1918).

57. *Id.* at 246 (Holmes, J., concurring).

58. *Id.* at 250, 262–63, 267 (Brandeis, J., dissenting).

59. The concept of the bipolar lawsuit comes from Chayes, *Public Law Litigation and the Burger Court*, 96 HARV. L. REV. 4 (1982).

60. 248 U.S. at 248 (Holmes, J., concurring).

61. Warren & Brandeis, *The Right to Privacy*, 4 HARV. L. REV. 193 (1890).

62. *See* Horwitz, *supra* note 51.

63. *See generally The Public/Private Distinction*, 130 U. PA. L. REV. 1289 (1982).

64. Dartmouth College v. Woodward, 17 U.S. (4 Wheat.) 518, 666 (1819) Story J., concurring).

65. *See* M. HORWITZ, *supra* note 2, at 259–61.

66. *See* The Civil Rights cases, 109 U.S. 3 (1883).

67. See *supra* ch. 1.

68. See *supra* ch. 4.

69. Munn v. Illinois, 94 U.S. 113 (1877). *See* Scheiber, *The Road to Munn: Eminent*

Domain and the Concept of Public Purpose in the State Courts, 5 PERSP. AM. HIST. 329 (1971).

70. *See* N. COTT, THE BONDS OF WOMANHOOD: "WOMAN'S SPHERE" IN NEW ENGLAND, 1780–1835, at 61–62, 199 (Yale Univ. Press 1977).

71. *See* C. LASCH, HAVEN IN A HEARTLESS WORLD: THE FAMILY BESIEGED (Basic Books 1977); E. ZARETSKY, CAPITALISM, THE FAMILY & PERSONAL LIFE (Harper & Row 1976).

72. *See* B. BLEDSTEIN, THE CULTURE OF PROFESSIONALISM (W. W. Norton 1976).

73. *See supra* ch. 3.

74. Cohen, *The Basis of Contract*, 46 Harv. L. Rev. 553 (1933).

75. 334 U.S. 1 (1948).

76. *See* Henkin, *Shelley v. Kraemer: Notes for a Revised Opinion*, 110 U. PA. L. REV. 473 (1962).

77. *See* R. HIMMELBERG, THE ORIGINS OF THE NATIONAL RECOVERY ADMINISTRATION: BUSINESS, GOVERNMENT, AND THE TRADE ASSOCIATION ISSUE, 1921–1933 (Fordham Univ. Press 1976); Galambos, *The Emerging Organizational Synthesis in Modern American History*, 44 BUS. HIST. REV. 279 (1970); Galambos, *Technology, Political Economy, and Professionalization: Central Themes of the Organizational Synthesis*, 57 BUS. HIST. REV. 471. (1983); Hawley, *Herbert Hoover, the Commerce Secretariat, and the Vision of an 'Associative State,' 1921–1928*, 61 J. AM. HIST. 116 (1974); Hawley, *Three Facets of Hooverian Associationalism: Lumber, Aviation, and Movies, 1921–1930*, in REGULATION IN PERSPECTIVE 95 (T. McCraw ed., Harvard Univ. Press 1981).

78. *See* Frug, *The City as a Legal Concept*, 93 HARV. L. REV. 1057, 1075–76 (1980).

79. *See supra* ch. 3.

80. *See* E. HAWLEY, THE NEW DEAL AND THE PROBLEM OF MONOPOLY (Princeton Univ. Press 1966). D. BRAND, CORPORATISM AND THE RULE OF LAW: A STUDY OF THE NATIONAL RECOVERY ADMINISTRATION 25–27, 63–68, 143, 157–58 (Cornell Univ. Press 1988), revises Hawley's interpretation.

81. Carter v. Carter Coal Co., 298 U.S. 238 (1936).

82. Jaffe, *Law Making by Private Groups*, 51 HARV. L. REV. 201 (1937).

83. Schechter Poultry Corp. v. United States, 295 U.S. 495 (1935).

84. *See supra* note 80.

85. 208 U.S. 412 (1908).

86. There were, in addition, fifteen pages of excerpts from state and foreign laws limiting women's hours. *See* P. STRUM, LOUIS D. BRANDEIS: JUSTICE FOR THE PEOPLE 121 (Harvard Univ. Press 1984).

87. On the alliance between the social sciences and the legal reform movement, see L. KALMAN, LEGAL REALISM AT YALE, 1927–1960 (Univ. of North Carolina Press 1986); Ross, *The Development of the Social Sciences*, in THE ORGANIZATION OF KNOWLEDGE IN MODERN AMERICA, 1860–1920, at 107 (A. Oleson & J. Voss eds., Johns Hopkins Univ. Press 1979); E. FITZPATRICK, ENDLESS CRUSADE: WOMEN SOCIAL SCIENTISTS AND PROGRESSIVE REFORM (Oxford Univ. Press 1990); Schlegel, *American Legal Realism and Empirical Social Science: From the Yale Experience*, 28 BUFFALO L. REV. 459 (1979); Schlegel, *American Legal Realism and Empirical Social Science: The Singular Case of Underhill Moore*, 29 BUFFALO L. REV. 195 (1980) [hereafter Schlegel, *Underhill Moore.*]

88. The critical group includes Robert Hale, Roscoe Pound, John Dewey, and both Felix and Morris Cohen, while what might be described as the constructive group includes figures like Charles Clark, Underhill Moore, and Hessel Yntema. *See* L. KALMAN, *supra* note 87, at 20.

89. *See* P. NOVICK, *supra* note 37, at 133–54.

90. This is particularly true of Oliphant and Yntema. *See* L. KALMAN, *supra* note 87, at 20–21, 32–33, 241 n. 85.

91. Llewellyn, *Some Realism About Realism—Responding to Dean Pound*, 44 HARV. L. REV. 1222, 1236 (1931) (emphasis retained).

92. *See infra* ch. 8.

93. Max Weber in 1918 made the classical statement on the ideology of professional expertise and the distancing of social science from the ethical. *See* M. WEBER, *Science as a Solution*, in FROM MAX WEBER (H. Gerth & C. W. Mills eds., Oxford Univ. Press 1946); *see also* M. WEBER, THE METHODOLOGY OF THE SOCIAL SCIENCES (E. Shils & H. Finch eds., Free Press 1949). [hereafter M. WEBER, METHODOLOGY]. On the development of a similar ideology in the United States, See B. BLEDSTEIN, *supra* note 72; M. BULMER, THE CHICAGO SCHOOL OF SOCIOLOGY (Univ. of Chicago Press 1984); R. FRIEDRICHS, A SOCIOLOGY OF SOCIOLOGY (Free Press 1970); M. FURNER, ADVOCACY AND OBJECTIVITY: A CRISIS IN THE PROFESSIONALIZATION OF AMERICAN SOCIAL SCIENCE, 1865–1905 (Univ. Press of Kentucky 1975); T. HASKELL, THE EMERGENCE OF PROFESSIONAL SOCIAL SCIENCE (Univ. of Illinois Press 1977); B. KUKLICK, *supra* note 7; F. MATTHEWS, QUEST FOR AN AMERICAN SOCIOLOGY: ROBERT E. PARK AND THE CHICAGO SCHOOL (McGill-Queens Univ. Press 1977); E. PURCELL, THE CRISIS OF DEMOCRATIC THEORY: SCIENTIFIC NATURALISM AND THE PROBLEM OF VALUE (Univ. Press of Kentucky 1973); Ross, *supra* note 87.

94. *See* L. KALMAN, *supra* note 87, at 30–35. Llewellyn himself said, "I read all the results, but I never dug out what most of the counting was for." *Quoted in id.* at 33.

95. *See* Schlegel, *Underhill Moore*, *supra* note 87; L. KALMAN, *supra* note 87, at 97 205, 212–15; Clark & Trubek, *The Creative Role of the Judge: Restraint and Freedom in the Common Law Tradition*, 71 YALE L. J. 255 (1961); Trubek, *Where the Action Is: Critical Legal Studies and Empiricism*, 36 STAN. L. REV. 575, 595–609. (1984).

96. On logical positivism see A. JANIK & S. TOULMIN, WITTGENSTEIN'S VIENNA (Simon & Schuster 1973); LOGICAL POSITIVISM (A. J. Ayer ed., Free Press 1959). On ethical positivism, see M. WEBER, METHODOLOGY, *supra* note 93, and his famous lecture, M. WEBER, *Science as a Vocation*, in FROM MAX WEBER, *supra* note 93, at 129. On legal positivism, see O. W. HOLMES, *The Path of the Law*, in COLLECTED LEGAL PAPERS 167 (Harcourt, Brace & Howe 1920); Howe, *The Positivism of Mr. Justice Holmes*, 64 HARV. L. REV. 529 (1951); H. KELSEN, PURE THEORY OF LAW (M. Knight trans., Univ of Chicago Press 1967). Perhaps a more comprehensive distinction than that among logical, ethical, and legal positivism is Novick's distinction between "cognitive" and "value" skepticism. *See* P. NOVICK, *supra* note 37, at 157, 282.

97. *See supra* ch. 4.

98. On the concern about justifying values either by science or by religion, see H. HOVENKAMP, SCIENCE AND RELIGION IN AMERICA, 1800–1860 (Univ. of Pennsylvania Press 1978); H. MAY, THE END OF AMERICAN INNOCENCE (Knopf 1959); E. PURCELL, *supra* note 93; Hovenkamp, *Evolutionary Models*, *supra* note 3.

99. *See* O. W. HOLMES, *supra* note 96, at 187.

100. Fuller, *supra* note 50, at 461.

101. *Id.*

102. *Id.*

103. *Id.* at 451. Perhaps Morris Cohen needs to be credited with making Fuller's point three years earlier.

It is the essence of positivism to view the law exclusively as uniformities of existing behavior, in total disregard of any ideals as to what should be. This, however, cannot but result in an unavowed natural law in which habit and inertia become the absolute norm or rule. Behavioristic theories are thus bound, if consistently carried out, to end where our old conservative natural-law theories did.

Cohen, *supra* note 47, at 360.

104. *See, e.g.*, Danzig, *A Comment on the Jurisprudence of the Uniform Commercial Code*, 27 STAN. L. REV. 621 (1975); *but see* Wiseman, *The Limits of Vision: Karl Llewellyn and the Merchant Rules*, 100 HARV. L. REV. 465 (1987).

Chapter 8

1. Jones v. Securities & Exch. Comm'n, 298 U.S. 1, 28 (1936).
2. *Id.* at 23.
3. J. LANDIS, THE ADMINISTRATIVE PROCESS 139 (Yale Univ. Press 1938).
4. 298 U.S. at 23.
5. *Id.* at 23–24.
6. J. LANDIS, *supra* note 3, at 139.
7. *Id.* at 140.
8. *Id.* at 142.
9. *Id.*
10. Schechter Poultry Corp. v. United States, 245 U.S. 495 (1935). *See* E. HAWLEY, THE NEW DEAL AND THE PROBLEM OF MONOPOLY (Princeton Univ. Press 1966).; A. SCHLESINGER JR., THE AGE OF ROOSEVELT: THE NEW DEAL IN ACTION, 1933–1937 (Macmillan 1958).
11. J. LANDIS, *supra* note 3, at 140.
12. *Id.* at 141.
13. *Id.*
14. *Id.*
15. *Id.* at 4–5.
16. *Id.* at 30.
17. *Id.* at 31.
18. *Id.*
19. *Id.*
20. *Id.* at 32–33
21. *Id.* at 33–34.
22. *Id.* at 34.
23. *Id.* at 36.
24. *Id.*
25. *Id.* at 35.
26. *Id.* at 41.
27. *Id.* at 33.
28. *Id.*
29. *Id.* at 23.

30. *Id.* at 24.

31. *See* Stewart, *The Reformation of American Administrative Law*, 88 HARV. L. REV. 1667 (1975); T. LOWI, THE END OF LIBERALISM (W. W. Norton 1969).

32. *See* F. GOODNOW, THE PRINCIPLES OF THE ADMINISTRATIVE LAW OF THE UNITED STATES 1–7, 66–68, (G. P. Putnam's Sons 1905); Weber, *The Presuppositions and Causes of Bureaucracy*, in READER IN BUREAUCRACY (R. Merton ed., Free Press 1952).

33. J. LANDIS, *supra* note 3, at 68–69.

34. *Id.* at 69 (emphasis supplied).

35. *Id.* at 12.

36. *Id.* at 72.

37. *Id.* at 75.

38. *Id.*

39. *Id.* at 69.

40. Pound, *The Causes of Popular Dissatisfaction with the Administration of Justice*, 40 AM. L. REV. 729 (1906).

41. Pound, *Mechanical Jurisprudence*, 8 COLUM. L. REV. 605 (1908).

42. Pound, *Justice According to Law*, 14 COLUM. L. REV. 1, 25 (1914).

43. Pound, *The Growth of Administrative Justice*, 2 WIS. L. REV. 321 (1924).

44. *Id.* at 330–31.

45. *Id.* at 331.

46. *Id.* at 329.

47. *Id.* at 331–32.

48. *Id.* at 331.

49. *Id.* at 332.

50. *Id.*

51. *Id.* at 336.

52. *Id.* at 333.

53. *Id.*

54. *Id.* at 339.

55. *Id.* at 330.

56. *Id.* at 334.

57. *Id.*

58. J. LANDIS, *supra* note 3, at 141.

59. Pound, *Report of the Special Committee on Administrative Law*, 63 REP. AM. B. ASS'N (1938) [hereafter *Pound Committee Report*].

60. J. FRANK, IF MEN WERE ANGELS 338 (1st ed., Harper 1942).

61. *Pound Committee Report*, *supra* note 59, at 339.

62. *Id.* at 343.

63. *Id.* at 340.

64. Cohen, *Transcendental Nonsense and the Functional Approach*, 35 COLUM. L. REV. 809, 833 (1935).

65. *Pound Committee Report*, *supra* note 59, at 340.

66. *Id.* at 343.

67. *Id.* (citing Landis, *Business Policy and the Courts*, 27 YALE. REV. 235, 237 (1938)).

68. *Pound Committee Report*, *supra* note 59, at 343.

69. *Id.* at 344.

70. Pound, *Do We Need a Philosophy of Law?*, 5 COLUM. L. REV. 339, 352 (1905).

71. Pound, *supra* note 42, at 13.

72. D. Wigdor, Roscoe Pound: Philosopher of Law 270 (Greenwood Press 1974).

73. *Id.* at 271.

74. *Id.* at 263.

75. *Id.*

76. *See* C. Goetsch, *Simeon E. Baldwin's 1910 Controversy With Theodore Roosevelt Over the Federal Employer's Liability Act*, in Essays on Simeon E. Baldwin 82–185 (Univ. of Connecticut School of Law Press 1981). *See also* J. Weinstein, *Leadership in Social Reform: Workmen's Compensation*, in The Corporate Ideal in the Liberal State, 1900–1918, at 40–61 (Beacon Press 1968).

77. S. Skowronek, Building A New American State: The Expansion of National Administrative Capacities, 1877–1920, at 6 (Cambridge Univ. Press 1982).

78. *Id.* at 8.

79. *Id.* at 27.

80. *Id.* at 28.

81. *Id.* at 13.

82. *See* T. McCraw, Prophets of Regulation (Harvard Univ. Press 1984); W. Chase, The American Law School and the Rise of Administrative Government (Univ. of Wisconsin Press 1982).

83. *See* J. Mashaw, Bureaucratic Justice: Managing Social Security Disability Claims (Yale Univ. Press 1983).

84. *See* M. Sklar, The Corporate Reconstruction of American Capitalism. 1890–1916 (Cambridge Univ. Press. 1988).

85. 245 U.S. 495 (1935). *But see* Industrial Union Dep't, AFL-CIO v. American Petroleum Inst., 448 U.S. 607, 671–88 (1980) (Rehnquist, J., concurring). All the justices agreed that at some point a delegation would become invalid.

86. J. Dickinson, Administrative Justice and the Supremacy of Law in the United States 215 (Harvard Univ. Press 1927).

87. *Id.* at 216.

88. *See* C. Edley, Administrative Law: Rethinking Judicial Control of Bureaucracy 14, 67–68 (Yale Univ. Press 1990). *See generally* Frug, *The Ideology of Bureaucracy in American Law*, 97 Harv. L. Rev. 1277, 1286–92, 1318–34 (1984).

89. F. Goodnow, *supra*, note 32, at 8.

90. *Id.* at 68. *See generally* W. Nelson, *The Quest for a Scientific Morality*, in The Roots of American Bureaucracy, 1830–1900, at 82–112 (Harvard Univ. Press 1982).

91. *See* W. Nelson, *supra* note 90, at 119–33; L. White, Republican Era, 1869–1901: A Study in Administrative History (Macmillan 1958); on Goodnow see Konefsky, *Men of Great and Little Faith: Generations of Constitutional Scholars*, 30 Buff. L. Rev. 365 (1981).

92. *See* A. M. Edwards, Comparative Occupation Statistics for the United States, 1870–1940, at 111 (G.P.O. 1943).

93. *See* E. Durkheim, Professional Ethics and Civic Morals (C. Brookfield trans. Free Press 1958). The translation derives from "the sole text of a final draft" of Durkheim's lectures delivered between 1898 and 1900. *Id.* at x.

94. *See* Grey, *Langdell's Orthodoxy*, 45 U. Pitt. L. Rev. 1 (1983); P. Novick, That Noble Dream: The "Objectivity Question" and the American Historical Profession 47–60 (Cambridge Univ. Press 1988); Chase, *The Birth of the Modern Law School*, 23 Am. J. Legal Hist. 329 (1979).

95. *See* E. Purcell, The Crisis of Democratic Theory: Scientific Naturalism

AND THE PROBLEM OF VALUE (Univ. Press of Kentucky 1973); D. ROSS, ORIGINS OF AMER-
ICAN SOCIAL SCIENCE (Cambridge Univ. Press 1990).

96. A. V. DICEY, LECTURES INTRODUCTORY TO THE STUDY OF THE LAW OF THE CON-
STITUTION (1st ed., Macmillan 1885).

97. *Id.* at 215.

98. *Id.* at 187.

99. *Id.* at 192.

100. *Id.* at 215.

101. R. COSGROVE, THE RULE OF LAW: ALBERT VENN DICEY, VICTORIAN JURIST 94
(Univ. of North Carolina Press 1980). Sugarman, Book review, 46 MODERN L. REV. 102
(1983).

102. H. W. R. WADE, ADMINISTRATIVE LAW 7 (3d ed, Clarendon Press 1971).

103. S. A. DeSMITH, JUDICIAL REVIEW OF ADMINISTRATIVE ACTION 5 (2d ed., Stevens
1968).

104. A. V. DICEY, LECTURES ON THE RELATION BETWEEN LAW AND PUBLIC OPINION
IN ENGLAND DURING THE NINETEENTH CENTURY (Macmillan 1905).

105. *See* L. T. HOBHOUSE, LIBERALISM (H. Holt 1911); G. RUGGIERO, THE HISTORY
OF EUROPEAN LIBERALISM (R. Collingwood trans., Oxford Univ. Press 1927); T. H. GREEN,
Lecture on Liberal Legislation and Freedom of Contract, in 3 WORKS 365 (R. Nettleship
3d ed., Longmans, Green 1900).

106. COSGROVE, *supra* note 101, at 193.

107. *Id.*

108. G. HEWART, THE NEW DESPOTISM 8 (E. Benn 1929).

109. *Id.* at 35.

110. *Id.* at 30.

111. *Id.* at 39.

112. *Id.* at 43.

113. *Id.* at 44.

114. *Id.* at 45.

115. *Id.* at 21–22.

116. Pound, *Individualization of Justice,* 7 FORDHAM L. REV. 153 (1938).

117. *Id.* at 161.

118. F. HAYEK, THE ROAD TO SERFDOM 2–4 (Univ. of Chicago Press 1944).

119. *Id.*

120. *Id.* at 41–42.

121. *Id.* at 72–87.

122. *Id.*

123. *Id.* at 72.

124. *Id.* at 73

125. *Id.*

126. *Id.* at 73–74.

127. *Id.* at 78.

128. *Id.* at 79.

129. *Id.* at 74.

130. *Id.* at 78.

131. *See id.* at 82.

132. *Id.* at 78.

133. 5 U.S.C. §§551 *et seq.*

134. Universal Camera Corp. v. NLRB, 340 U.S. 474, 482 (1951).

135. Verkuil, *The Emerging Concept of Administrative Procedure*, 78 COLUM. L. REV. 258, 272 (1978), (quoting the President's veto message, 86 CONG. REC. 13,943 (1940) [hereafter Veto Message], which in turn quoted from ASSOCIATION OF THE BAR OF THE CITY OF NEW YORK, REPORT OF THE COMMITTEES ON ADMINISTRATIVE LAW AND FEDERAL LEGISLATION).

136. *Id.* at 271.

137. *Id.* at 273 (quoting Veto Message, *supra* note 135, at 13,942–43).

138. *Id.* (quoting Veto Message, *supra* note 135, at 13,943).

139. *Id.* at 274.

140. *Id.* at 275 (quoting THE PUBLIC PAPERS AND ADDRESSES OF FRANKLIN DELANO ROOSEVELT—1940, at 622 (S. Rosenman ed., Macmillan 1941).

141. *Id.* at 277.

142. *Id.* at 276.

143. *Id.* at 277.

144. *Id.* at 277 n. 97.

145. *See* E. RYERSON, THE BEST-LAID PLANS: AMERICA'S JUVENILE COURT EXPERIMENT (Hill & Wang 1978). As Ellen Fitzpatrick points out in ENDLESS CRUSADE: WOMEN SOCIAL SCIENTISTS AND PROGRESSIVE REFORM 97–101 (Oxford Univ. Press 1990), crime was attributed to an array of evils in the social environment. Sophonisba Breckinridge and Edith Abbott, in their study of delinquent children handled by Chicago's juvenile court, hoped to enhance the courts' understanding of children and provide them with more knowledge about children under stress by conducting exhaustive social scientific research. *Id.* at 183–87.

146. "It is to a study of the underlying causes of juvenile delinquency and to a realization of these preventive and positive measures that the trained professional men of the United States, following the splendid lead of many of their European brethren, should give some thought and some care." Mack, *The Juvenile Court*, 23 HARV. L. REV. 104, 122 (1909). Juvenile offenders were to be dealt with "as a wise and merciful father" dealt with his own children. *Id.* at 107. Such an approach was only "just and proper," *id.*, "when we neglect to destroy the evils that are leading them into careers of delinquency, when we fail not merely to uproot the wrong, but to implant in place of it the positive good. . . ." *Id.* at 122.

147. *In re* Gault, 387 U.S. 1, 15 (1967).

148. *Id.*

149. *See id.* at 15 n.14.

150. *See id.* at 21.

151. *Id.* (quoting Foster, *Social Work, the Law and Social Action*, in 45 SOC. CASEWORK 386 (1964)).

152. 214 F.2d 862 (D.C. Cir 1954).

153. *Id.* at 871.

154. *Id.* at 874. *See generally id.* at 870–76 for the core of Bazelon's discussion of scientific expertise.

155. *See id.* at 869; *see also* L. WEINREB, CRIMINAL LAW: CASES, COMMENTS, QUESTIONS 559 n. 26 (4th ed., Foundation Press 1986).

156. 214 F.2d at 875.

157. *Id.* at 872. Judge Bazelon's opinion did emphasize that the question of insanity would need to be determined by "juries [that] will continue to make moral judgments"

about responsibility. It added, however, that "in making such judgments, they will be guided by wider horizons of knowledge concerning mental life." *Id.* at 876.

158. United States v. Brawner, 471 F.2d 969 (D. C. Cir. 1972). For Judge Bazelon's account of the history of the insanity defense from *Durham* to *Brawner*, see D. L. BAZELON, QUESTIONING AUTHORITY 24–70 (Knopf 1988).

159. *Id.* at 981.

160. *Id.* at 977–79.

161. *Id.* at 982.

162. *Id.* at 977.

163. *Id.* at 1010–11 (Bazelon, C. J., concurring in part, dissenting in part).

164. *Id.* at 1011.

165. Universal Camera v. NLRB, 340 U.S. 474 (1951).

166. *See* C. TOMLINS, THE STATE AND THE UNIONS: LABOR RELATIONS, LAW, AND THE ORGANIZED LABOR MOVEMENT IN AMERICA 1880–1960, at 276–77, 285–87 (Cambridge Univ. Press 1985).

167. 179 F.2d 749, 751–52 (2nd Cir. 1950).

168. 340 U.S. at 487.

169. *Id.* at 485.

170. *Id.* at 478.

171. *Id.*

172. *Id.* at 479 n.8 (citing NLRB v. Standard Oil Co., 138 F.2d 885, 887 (L. Hand, J.)).

173. *Id.* at 482.

174. *Id.* at 480 n.12 (quoting FINAL REPORT OF ATTORNEY GENERAL'S COMMITTEE at 92).

175. *Id.* at 483.

176. 5 U.S.C. § 706 (2) (E) (1946).

177. Frankfurter, *The Task of Administrative Law*, 75 U. PA. L. REV. 614, 621 (1927).

178. *Id.* at 618.

179. For an oversimplified account of the development of academic administrative law, see W. CHASE, *supra* note 82.

180. 1 M. PARRISH, FELIX FRANKFURTER AND HIS TIMES 200 (Free Press 1982).

181. *Id.* at 200–01 (citing F. FRANKFURTER, THE PUBLIC AND ITS GOVERNMENT 151–55 (Yale Univ. Press 1930)).

182. *Id.* at 201 (citing F. FRANKFURTER, *supra* note 181, at 159–60).

183. M. PARRISH, *supra* note 180, at 201.

184. *See id.* at 81–117; C. TOMLINS, *supra* note 166.

185. Jaffe, *The Judicial Universe of Mr. Justice Frankfurter*, 62 HARV. L. REV. 357, 376 (1949).

186. *Id.*

187. Jaffe, *The Report of the Attorney General's Committee on Administrative Procedure*, 8 U. CHI. L. REV. 401, 401, (1941).

188. Jaffe, *Invective and Investigation in Administrative Law*, 52 HARV. L. REV. 1201, 1245 (1939).

189. *Id.* at 1236.

190. *Id.* at 1232.

191. *Id.* at 1239.

192. *Id.* at 1242.

193. Jaffe, *supra* note 187, at 440.

194. *Id.* at 405.

195. *Id.* at 401.

196. *Id.*

197. *Id.*

198. *Id.* at 440.

199. Jaffe, book review, 42 COL. L. REV. 1382, 1383 (1942) (reviewing R. POUND, ADMINISTRATIVE LAW: ITS GROWTH, PROCEDURE AND SIGNIFICANCE (Univ. of Pittsburgh Press 1942)).

200. *Id.* at 1382.

201. *Id.* at 1382–83.

202. *Id.* at 1385.

203. *Id.* at 1383.

204. Jaffe, *Administrative Procedure Re-examined: The Benjamin Report*, 56 HARV. L. REV. 704, 705 (1943).

205. Jaffe, *supra* note 185, at 410.

206. *Id.* at 410–11.

207. *Id.*

208. Jaffe, *The Effective Limits of the Administrative Process*, 67 HARV. L. REV. 1105 (1954).

209. *Id.* at 1106.

210. *Id.* at 1109.

211. Jaffe, *supra* note 185, at 373–74.

212. *See* Jaffe, *supra* note 208, at 1129–30.

213. *Id.* at 1113.

214. Jaffe, *James Landis and the Administrative Process*, 78 HARV. L. REV. 319, 322–23 (1964).

215. *Id.* at 322.

216. *Id.* at 322–23.

217. Jaffe, *The Illusion of the Ideal Administration*, 86 Harv. L. Rev. 1183, 1187 (1973).

218. Jaffe, *Judicial Review: Question of Law*, 69 HARV. L. REV. 239, 271 (1955); *see generally* Jaffe, *supra* note 214; Jaffe, *supra* note 217.

219. W. GELLHORN, INDIVIDUAL FREEDOM AND GOVERNMENTAL RESTRAINTS 15–16 (Louisiana State Univ. Press 1956).

220. *Id.* at 8.

221. *Id.* at 19.

222. *Id.* at 22.

223. J. LANDIS, REPORT ON REGULATORY AGENCIES TO THE PRESIDENT-ELECT 70 (G.P.O. 1960).

224. *Id.* at 71.

225. *Id.* at 58.

226. *See, e.g.*, R. FELLMETH, THE INTERSTATE COMMERCE COMMISSION (Grossman Publishers 1970) Fellmeth, *The Regulatory-Industrial Complex*, in WITH JUSTICE FOR SOME 244. (B. Wasserstein & M. Green eds., Beacon Press 1970); Green & Nader, *Economic Regulation vs. Competition: Uncle Sam the Monopoly Man*, 82 YALE L. J 871 (1973) Lazarus & Onek, *The Regulators and the People*, 57 VA. L. REV. 1069 (1971); G. KOLKO,

RAILROADS AND REGULATION, 1877–1916 (Princeton Univ. Press 1965); T. LOWI, *supra* note 31, at 85–93; Stewart, *supra* note 31, at 1684–87, and sources cited therein.

227. *See* P. NOVICK, *supra* note 94, at 518.

228. Leventhal, *Environmental Decisionmaking and the role of the Courts,* 122 PA. L. REV. 509, 523–24 (1974).

229. *Id.* at 512.

230. *Id.* (citing Environmental Defense Fund v. Ruckelshaus, 439 F.2d 584, 597 (D.C. Cir. 1971).

231. *Id.* at 512.

232. Sive, *Forward: Roles and Rules in Environmental Decisionmaking,* 62 IOWA L. REV. 637 638 (1977).

233. *Id.*

234. *Id.*

235. *Id.* at 639.

236. 439 U.S. 961 (1978).

237. Scalia, *Vermont Yankee: The APA, the D. C. Circuit, and the Supreme Court,* 1978 SUP. CT. REV. 345, 395.

238. *Id.* at 359.

239. *Id.* at 346.

240. *Id.* at 401.

241. *Id.* at 402.

242. *Id.* at 401.

243. *Id.* at 402.

244. *Id.*

245. *Id.*

246. *Id.* at 404 (quoting his *Forward* to the 1973–74 ANNUAL REPORT OF THE ADMINISTRATIVE CONFERENCE OF THE UNITED STATES 2 (1974)).

247. *Id.* at 404–05.

248. *Id.* at 405.

249. *Id.*

250. J. Landis, Address Before the Administrative Law Section, American Bar Association in St. Louis 5–6 (Aug. 7, 1961) (typescript in Harvard Law School Library).

251. *Id.* at 6.

252. *Id.*

253. *Id.* at 7.

254. *Id.*

255. *Id.*

256. *Id.*

257. *Id.* at 8.

258. *See e.g.,* E. JOHNSON, JUSTICE AND REFORM: THE FORMATIVE YEARS OF THE OEO LEGAL SERVICES PROGRAM (Russell Sage Foundation 1974).

259. Reich, *The New Property,* 73 YALE L. J. 733 (1964).

260. *Id.* at 733.

261. *Id.*

262. *Id.* at 786.

263. *Id.* at 768.

264. *Id.*

265. *Id.* at 774.

266. *Id.* at 778.

267. *Id.* at 771–72.

268. *See id.* at 747–49, 756–58, 762 n.149, 763–64, 767–69, 775–77.

269. 363 U.S. 603 (1960).

270. Goldberg v. Kelly, 397 U.S. 254, 262 n.8, 265 (1970). By 1965, Reich had explicitly applied his idea to welfare rights in Reich, *Individual Rights and Social Welfare: The Emerging Legal Issues*, 74 YALE L. J. 1245 (1965).

Chapter 9

1. Brown v. Board of Educ., 347 U.S. 483 (1954).

2. E. PURCELL, THE CRISIS OF DEMOCRATIC THEORY: SCIENTIFIC NATURALISM AND THE PROBLEM OF VALUE 219 (Univ. Press of Kentucky 1973).

3. *Id.* at 176.

4. *Id.* at 218.

5. *Id.* at 176–77.

6. K. LLEWELLYN, THE BRAMBLE BUSH 8 (Oceana 1951).

7. *Id.*

8. *Id.* at 9.

9. *Id.*

10. See discussion of Llewellyn, *supra* ch. 6.

11. Llewellyn, *On Reading and Using the Newer Jurisprudence*, 40 COLUM. L. REV. 581, 603 (1940).

12. W. LIPPMANN, THE PUBLIC PHILOSOPHY 174–75 (Little, Brown 1955).

13. *Id.* at 172.

14. K. LLEWELLYN, *supra* note 6, at 10.

15. *See* M. BELKNAP, COLD WAR POLITICAL JUSTICE (Greenwood 1977); T. REEVES, THE LIFE AND TIMES OF JOE MCCARTHY (Stein & Day 1982); D. CAUTE, THE GREAT FEAR: THE ANTI-COMMUNIST PURGE UNDER TRUMAN AND EISENHOWER (Simon & Schuster 1978); S. KUTLER, THE AMERICAN INQUISITION (Hill & Wang 1982); E. SCHRECKER, NO IVORY TOWER: MCCARTHYISM AND THE UNIVERSITIES (Oxford Univ. Press 1986).

16. K. LLEWELLYN, *supra* note 6, 153.

17. *Id.* at 154.

18. K. LLEWELLYN, THE COMMON LAW TRADITION (Little, Brown 1960).

19. K. LLEWELLYN, *supra* note 6, at 10.

20. K LLEWELLYN, *supra* note 18, at 3–4.

21. *Id.* at 4.

22. *See* E. PURCELL, *supra* note 2, "Relativist Democratic Theory and Postwar America" at 235–266.

23. *See* E. HOFFER, THE TRUE BELIEVER (Harper & Row 1951); T. W. ADORNO et al., THE AUTHORITARIAN PERSONALITY (Harper 1950).

24. *See* D. BELL, THE END OF IDEOLOGY (Free Press 1960); D. BOORSTIN, THE GENIUS OF AMERICAN POLITICS (Univ. of Chicago Press 1953); H. BRICK, DANIEL BELL AND THE DECLINE OF INTELLECTUAL RADICALISM (Univ. of Wisconsin Press 1986).

25. *See* M. WEBER, THE METHODOLOGY OF THE SOCIAL SCIENCES (Free Press 1949); M. WEBER, *Science as a Vocation*, in FROM MAX WEBER (H. Gerth & C. W. Mills eds.,

Free Press 1949); A. KRONMAN, MAX WEBER (Stanford Univ. Press 1983); A. BRECHT, POLITICAL THEORY: THE FOUNDATIONS OF TWENTIETH-CENTURY POLITICAL THOUGHT (Princeton Univ. Press 1959).

26. Max Lerner uses these words in his collection, THE MIND AND FAITH OF JUSTICE HOLMES 5 (Little, Brown 1943).

27. See LOGICAL POSITIVISM (A. J. Ayer ed., Free Press 1959); A. JANIK & S. TOULMIN, WITTGENSTEIN'S VIENNA (Simon & Schuster 1973).

28. See Howe, The Positivism of Mr. Justice Holmes, 64 HARV. L. REV. 529 (1951); H. KELSEN, PURE THEORY OF LAW (Univ. of Cal. Press 1967); Hart, Positivism and the Separation of Law and Morals, 71 HARV. L. REV. 593 (1958); Fuller, Positivism and Fidelity to Law—A Reply to Professor Hart, 71 HARV. L. REV. 630 (1958).

29. See L. Fuller, The Problem of the Grudge Informer, published as the Appendix to THE MORALITY OF LAW (Yale Univ. Press 1964). Fuller called the piece "something that I wrote long before I undertook" the lectures on which the book was based.

30. "If there was, as John Higham maintained at the time, a veritable 'cult' of consensus in American historiography in the 1950s, and if counterprogressive themes were overwhelmingly dominant, they never, as we have seen, went completely unchallenged." P. NOVICK, THAT NOBLE DREAM: THE "OBJECTIVITY QUESTION" AND THE AMERICAN HISTORICAL PROFESSION 345 (Cambridge Univ. Press 1988). For example, "[w]hen the first volume of Boorstin's The Americans appeared, Bernard Bailyn termed it an 'apologia for his disillusioned conservatism.' " Id. at 334. See also Higham, The Cult of the "American Consensus", 27 COMMENTARY 93 (1959); R. HOFSTADTER, THE PROGRESSIVE HISTORIANS 437–66 (Knopf 1968).

31. See supra ch. 4.

32. See supra ch. 6; Llewellyn, James Coolidge Carter, 3 ENCYCLOPEDIA OF SOCIAL SCIENCE 243 (Macmillan 1937).

33. See Palko v. Connecticut, 302 U.S. 319 (1937), where Cardozo discusses the "principle of justice so rooted in the traditions and conscience of our people as to be ranked as fundamental" (302 U.S. at 325) and "those fundamental principles of liberty and justice which lie at the base of all of our civil and political institutions" (302 U.S. at 328). Justice Frankfurter expressed a similar view in Rochin v. California, 342 U.S. 165, 167 (1952), regarding "those canons of decency and fairness which express notions of justice of English-speaking people. . . ."

34. See R. HOFSTADTER, SOCIAL DARWINISM IN AMERICAN THOUGHT (rev. ed., Beacon Press 1955).

35. See L. HARTZ, THE LIBERAL TRADITION IN AMERICA 306–9 (Harcourt, Brace 1955).

36. See L. FULLER, THE MORALITY OF LAW, supra note 29. Fuller states:

[W]e may speak of a procedural, as distinguished from a substantive natural law. What I have called the internal morality of law is in this sense a procedural version of natural law, though to avoid misunderstanding the word "procedural" should be assigned a special and expanded sense so that it would include, for example, a substantive accord between official action and enacted law. The term "procedural" is, however, broadly appropriate as indicating that we are concerned, not with the substantive aims of legal rules, but with the ways in which a system of rules for governing human conduct must be constructed and administered if it is to be efficacious and at the same time remain what it purports to be.

Id. at 96–97.

37. *See* H. PRITCHETT, THE ROOSEVELT COURT (Macmillan 1948); S. KONEFSKY, CHIEF JUSTICE STONE AND THE SUPREME COURT (Macmillan 1945); A. MASON, HARLAN FISKE STONE: PILLAR OF THE LAW (Viking 1956).

38. United States v. Carolene Prods. Co., 304 U.S. 144, 152 n.4 (1938);

It is unnecessary to consider now whether legislation which restricts those political processes which can ordinarily be expected to bring about repeal of undesirable legislation, is to be subjected to more exacting judicial scrutiny under the general prohibitions of the Fourteenth Amendment than are most other types of legislation . . . [n]or need we enquire whether similar considerations enter into the review of statutes directed at particular religious, . . . or national, . . . or racial minorities . . . whether prejudice against discrete and insular minorities may be a special condition, which tends seriously to curtail the operation of those political processes ordinarily to be relied upon to protect minorities, and which may call for a correspondingly more searching judicial inquiry.

39. West Virginia State Bd. of Educ. v. Barnette, 319 U.S. 624 (1943), *overruling* Minersville School Dist. v. Gobitis, 310 U.S. 586 (1940).

40. *See* Danzig, *Justice Frankfurter's Opinions in the Flag Salute Cases*, 36 STAN. L. REV. 675 (1984).

41. *See* Horwitz, *The Jurisprudence of Brown and the Dilemmas of Liberalism*, 14 HARV. C.R.-C.L. L. REV. 599 (1979); R. KLUGER, SIMPLE JUSTICE (Vintage Books 1977).

42. Mapp v. Ohio, 367 U.S. 643 (1961).

43. This view, termed the "counter-majoritarian difficulty" by Alexander Bickel, THE LEAST DANGEROUS BRANCH 16–23 (Bobbs-Merrill 1962), has been criticized. *See* Wright, *Professor Bickel, the Scholarly Tradition and the Supreme Court*, 84 HARV. L. REV. 769 (1971); Purcell, *Alexander M. Bickel and the Post-Realist Constitution*, 11 HARV. C.R.-C.L. L. REV. 521 (1976); Parker, *The Past of Constitutional Theory—And Its Future*, 42 OHIO ST. L.J. 223 (1981); Eule, *Judicial Review of Direct Democracy*, 99 YALE L.J. 1503, 1531–33 (1990); Ackerman, *Constitutional Politics/Constitutional Law*, 99 YALE L.J. 453, 472–478.

44. *See* A. GOULDNER, THE COMING CRISIS OF WESTERN SOCIOLOGY (Basic Books 1970).

45. *See* T. EAGLETON, LITERARY THEORY: AN INTRODUCTION (Univ. of Minnesota Press 1983).

46. C. SCHORSKE, FIN-DE-SIECLE VIENNA xx (Knopf 1980).

47. H. HART & A. SACKS, THE LEGAL PROCESS (tent. ed., Harvard Univ. 1958); White, *The Evolution of Reasoned Elaboration: Jurisprudential Criticism and Social Change*, 59 VA. L. REV. 279 (1973); Peller, *In Defense of Federal Habeas Corpus Relitigation*, 16 HARV. C.R.-C.L. L. REV. 579, 669–690 & n.431 (1982); Peller, *The Metaphysics of American Law*, 73 CALIF. L. REV. 1152, 1182–87 (1985); Peller, *Neutral Principles in the 1950's*, 21 U. MICH. J. L. REF. 561 (1988); Parker, *supra* note 43; Kennedy, *Form and Substance in Private Law Adjudication*, 89 HARV. L. REV. 1685, 1753–66 (1976); Tushnet, *Truth, Justice, and the American Way: An Interpretation of Public Law Scholarship in the Seventies*, 57 TEX. L. REV. 1307 (1979).

48. H. HART & A. SACKS, *supra* note 47, at iii.

49. *Id.* at 1–3.

50. *Id.* at 3–4.

51. "Against totalitarian certitude, free society can only offer modern man devoured

by alienation and fallibility. The great issue of this century is who is right. Is man a creature of doubt and ambiguity. . . . Or has he mastered the secrets of history and nature sufficiently to become ruthless, monolithic and infallible, to know whom to spare and whom to kill?" A. SCHLESINGER, THE VITAL CENTER 59 (Houghton Mifflin 1949). "[T]he Brandeises and the Parringtons were caught off guard . . . nothing in their system prepared them for totalitarianism. . . ." Id. at 163. "Some perceive dangers in [the] new directions of liberalism. It is argued that the abandonment of the old faith in the full rationality of man leaves no foothold short of authoritarianism. Yet is it not rather the belief in the perfectibility of man which encourages the belief that a small group of men are already perfect and hence may exercise total power without taint or corruption?" Id. at 169. This form of discourse led even liberals to speak of "social engineering" as if it led to the gulag or the concentration camp. See Keeton, Conditional Fault in the Law of Torts, 72 HARV. L. REV. 401, 408 (1959).

52. H. HART & A. SACKS, supra note 47, at 3.

53. J. SCHUMPETER, CAPITALISM, SOCIALISM, AND DEMOCRACY (Harper 1942).

54. Id. at 269.

55. Id. at 273.

56. H. MAYO, AN INTRODUCTION TO DEMOCRATIC THEORY 227 (1960).

57. Id. at 240.

58. J. R. PENNOCK, LIBERAL DEMOCRACY: ITS MERITS AND PROSPECTS 309 (Rinehart 1950). Pennock added that "It is only natural that [the working classes] should tend to minimize the value of liberty." Id. at 310.

59. R. DAHL, A PREFACE TO DEMOCRATIC THEORY (Univ. of Chicago Press 1956).

60. "No interpretive tendency of the 1950s was more typical of the general movement of intellectual opinion, or reverberated more widely throughout the culture, than the sharp downward turn in the historical reputation of the Populists. . . . Rather than a democratic movement against exploitation, whose program prefigured subsequent reforms, the Populists came to be portrayed as a backward-looking band of nativist book burners obsessed with imaginary grievances. . . . [T]he assault on Populism spread throughout the social sciences and the intellectual world at large. . . . The immediate context of the reevaluation of the Populists was the early 1950s phenomenon of McCarthyism, which a number of analysts quickly connected with agrarian radicalism, LaFollette Progressivism, and in particular, Populism. In this view McCarthy's crusade, like that of the Populists, was a democratic and anti-intellectual revolt of dispossessed groups against educated elites. . . . The approach which Hofstadter took to the Populists was the first important example of what became a common feature of cold war historical scholarship, the social-psychologizing of dissidence and insurgency. . . . The most controversial of Hofstadter's assertions about the Populists . . . was the charge that anti-Semitism was central to their world view. . . . Privately, Hofstadter acknowledged that he had exaggerated. . . ." P. NOVICK, supra note 30, at 337–38. Novick is referring to R. HOFSTADTER, THE AGE OF REFORM 80 (Knopf 1955) and R. HOFSTADTER, ANTI-INTELLECTUALISM IN AMERICAN LIFE (Knopf 1963).

61. R. DAHL, supra note 59, at 132.

62. H. LASSWELL, POLITICS: WHO GETS WHAT, WHEN, HOW (McGraw-Hill 1936). See D. BELL, supra note 24.

63. R. DAHL, supra note 59, at 132–133.

64. Id. at 134.

65. Id. at 137.

66. Id. at 138.

67. *See, e.g.*, R. HOFSTADTER, *supra* note 30, at 460–61; Higham, *supra* note 30, at 95.

68. *See* R. DAHL, *supra* note 59.

69. *See* M. HARRINGTON, THE OTHER AMERICA: POVERTY IN THE UNITED STATES (Macmillan 1962).

70. *See* T. BRANCH, PARTING THE WATERS: AMERICA IN THE KING YEARS, 1954–63, at 881–883 (Simon & Schuster 1988).

71. One is surprised to learn how late it was that legal academics actually sought to defend the *Brown* decision. *See, e.g.*, Pollak, *Racial Discrimination and Judicial Integrity: A Reply to Professor Wechsler*, 108 U. PA. L. REV. 1 (1959); Black, *The Lawfulness of the Segregation Decisions*, 69 YALE L.J. 421 (1960).

72. *See* L. HAND, THE BILL OF RIGHTS (Harvard Univ. Press 1958).

73. *Id.* at 1.

74. *Id.* at 10.

75. *Id.* at 50.

76. *Id.*

77. *Id.* at 54.

78. 163 U.S. 537 (1896).

79. *Id.* at 54–55.

80. *Id.* at 55.

81. *Id.*

82. Letter from Felix Frankfurter to Learned Hand (June 25, 1954) (Folder #20, Hand Papers, Harvard Law School Library). I am grateful to the Harvard Law School for permission to quote from the manuscript. Special thanks to Sanford Levinson for calling these Frankfurter-Hand letters to my attention.

83. Letter from Frankfurter to Hand (February 13, 1958). Frankfurter continued: "In short, I deemed it on the whole a misfortune that the Due Process Clause (more than the Equal Protection Clause) had not been regarded like unto some other provisions of the Constitution as raising 'political questions' and therefore unfitted for the adjudicatory process." Just at the moment when it appeared that the statement quoted in the text referred only to the due process clause, not to the equal protection clause, under which the major state cases like *Brown* were decided, Frankfurter continued: "One reason why you ought to find a source of relief in not having been on this Court is that you would have had one helluva time whenever you would have been called upon to act in these due process cases. Thus, I doubt very much whether in the end you would have held out against the decision in the *Segregation Cases*." Frankfurter thus slipped right back to treating the whole of the Fourteenth Amendment as one undifferentiated "misfortune."

84. L. HAND, *supra* note 72, at 54. *See* Cooper v. Aaron, 358 U.S. 1 (1958).

85. *See* Pennsylvania v. Nelson, 350 U.S. 497 (1956) (reversing the conviction of a Communist under Pennsylvania's sedition law); Konigsberg v. State Bar, 353 U.S. 252 (1957) (reversing the refusal of bar examiners to admit a former Communist to the California bar); Jencks v. United States, 353 U.S. 657 (1957) (reversing the conviction of a union official accused of falsely stating that he was not a member of the Communist Party); Watkins v. United States, 354 U.S. 178 (1957) (reversing a conviction for refusal to answer questions before the House Committee on Un-American Activities); Sweezy v. N.H., 354 U.S. 234 (1957) (reversing a conviction for refusal to answer questions about Communist associations put by the state attorney general); Service v. Dulles, 354 U.S. 363 (1957) (invalidating a discharge of a Foreign Service officer by the Loyalty Security Board); Yates

v. United States, 354 U.S. 298 (1957) (reversing a conviction of "second string" Communist leaders under the Smith Act); Kent v. Dulles, 357 U.S. 116 (1958) (the Secretary of State had no power to deny a passport to a citizen because of alleged Communist associations).

86. 354 U.S. 298 (1957).

87. L. HAND, *supra* note 72, at 61.

88. *See* M. SHAPIRO, FREEDOM OF SPEECH: THE SUPREME COURT AND JUDICIAL REVIEW 46–72 (Prentice Hall 1966).

89. L. HAND, *supra* note 72, at 59. Hand continued, "and I cannot help thinking that for once Homer nodded . . .," which Professor Gerald Gunther interprets as a critical reference to Holmes's decision in the case of Schenck v. United States, 249 U.S. 47 (1919). G. GUNTHER, CONSTITUTIONAL LAW 1097 (Foundation Press 1975).

90. 183 F.2d 201 (1950).

91. Dennis v. United States, 341 U.S. 494, 510 (1951). Chief Justice Vinson quoted Hand's rule as "[I]n each case we must ask whether the gravity of the 'evil,' discounted by its improbability, justifies such invasion of free speech as is necessary to avoid the danger."

92. M. SHAPIRO, *supra* note 88. I do not mean to suggest that Judge Hand in any way approved of McCarthyism. His opinion in United States v. Coplon, 185 F.2d 629 (1950), in which he reversed a conviction of conspiracy to deliver national defense information, on the grounds of illegal arrest and illegal wiretapping, demonstrates his commitment to constitutional procedure even in the face of evidence that "made out a case which must have satisfied any fair minded jury that she was engaged in the conspiracy. . . ." Perhaps his concurrence in the opinion of Swan, C.J., in United States v. Remington, 191 F.2d 246 (1951), is a better example of resistance to political persecution. There the court reversed, for lack of evidence, the perjury conviction of a person who had denied earlier Communist Party membership before a witch-hunting grand jury.

93. Masses Publishing Co. v. Patten, 244 F. 535 (1917).

94. Professor Gunther has suggested that there was consistency between Hand's opinion in *Masses* and the views he expressed against the "clear and present danger" standard in *The Bill of Rights*, *supra* note 72. Hand, Gunther says, thought the clear and present danger test was "too dangerous to free expression." *See* Gunther, *Learned Hand and the Origins of Modern First Amendment Doctrine: Some Fragments of History*, 27 STAN. L. REV. 719 (1975). I am not persuaded. There is now a consensus among constitutional historians that during the summer of 1919 Zechariah Chafee, Jr., and Learned Hand pushed Holmes toward a more libertarian position on freedom of speech than he held when he wrote his opinion in Schenck v. United States, 249 U.S. 47 (1919). *See* RABBAN, THE EMERGENCE OF MODERN FIRST AMENDMENT DOCTRINE, 50 U. CHI. L. REV. 1205 (1983); Ragan, *Justice Oliver Wendell Holmes, Jr., Zechariah Chafee, Jr., and the Clear and Present Danger Test for Free Speech: The First Year, 1919*, 58 J. AM. HIST. 24 (1971); Gunther, *supra* at 720.

95. *See* Horwitz, *History and Theory*, 96 YALE L.J. 1825 (1987); Ackerman, *supra* note 43, at 462–465.

96. *See* L. HAND, *Chief Justice Stone's Concept of the Judicial Function*, in THE SPIRIT OF LIBERTY 201–208 (Knopf 1952).

97. *Id.* at 202–203.

98. *Id.* at 203. Hand is referring to James B. Thayer's *The Origin and Scope of the American Doctrine of Constitutional Law*, 7 HARV. L. REV. 129 (1893).

99. L. HAND, *supra* note 96, at 203.

100. *Id.* at 203–204.
101. *Id.* at 204.
102. *Id.*
103. *Id.* at 204–205.
104. *Id.* at 205.
105. *Id.*
106. *Id.*
107. *Id.* at 203.
108. *Id.* at 204.
109. *Id.* at 205–206.
110. *Id.* at 206.
111. *Id.*
112. *Id.*
113. *Id.* at 207.
114. L. HAND, *supra* note 72, at 60.
115. *Id.* at 60–61.
116. *Id.* at 54.
117. *Id.* at 34.
118. *Id.* at 61.
119. *Id.* at 60.
120. *Id.* at 71.
121. Wechsler, *Toward Neutral Principles of Constitutional Law,* 73 HARV. L. REV. 1 (1959).
122. *See* Shapiro, *The Most-Cited Law Review Articles,* 73 CALIF. L. REV. 1540 (1985).
123. Wechsler, *supra* note 121, at 20.
124. *Id.* at 25.
125. *Id.* at 19.
126. *Id.* at 12.
127. *Id.*
128. *Id.* at 14.
129. *Id.* at 26.
130. *Id.* at 27.
131. *Id.* at 31.
132. *Id.*
133. *Id.* at 33–34.
134. *Id.* at 34.
135. *Id.*
136. *Id.*
137. Another representative sample of post-war legal culture can be found in the annual Forewords to the Supreme Court issue of the *Harvard Law Review,* which began in 1951. Not until Archibald Cox's Foreword in 1966, *Constitutional Adjudication and the Promotion of Human Rights,* 80 HARV. L. REV. 91 (1966), did a defense of the Warren Court appear in its pages. It was frequently attacked, often by disciples of Felix Frankfurter. *See e.g.,* Brown, *Process of Law,* 72 HARV. L. REV. 77 (1958); Hart, *The Time Chart of the Justices,* 73 HARV. L. REV. 84 (1959); Bickel, *The Passive Virtues,* 75 HARV. L. REV. 40 (1961); Kurland, *Equal in Origin and Equal in Title to the Legislative and Executive Branches of the Government,* 78 HARV. L. REV. 143 (1964).

NAME INDEX

CASE INDEX

SUBJECT INDEX